M000087355

THE NATURAL GARDEN BOOK

A holistic approach to gardening

PETER HARPER
with Chris Madsen and Jeremy Light
FOREWORD BY JOHN JEAVONS

A GAIA ORIGINAL

A FIRESIDE BOOK
Published by Simon & Schuster Inc.
New York London Toronto Sydney Tokyo Singapore

SIMON & SCHUSTER/FIRESIDE

Simon & Schuster Building
Rockefeller Center
1230 Avenue of the Americas
New York, New York 10020

First published in the United Kingdom
in 1994 by Gaia Books Ltd.

A GAIA ORIGINAL

Conceived by Joss Pearson

Editorial
Michele Staple
Pip Morgan

Design
Bridget Morley

Illustration
Bridget Morley
Dave Sumner
Ann Savage
William Donohoe

Picture Research
Elly Beintema

Direction
Joss Pearson
Patrick Nugent

Printed and bound in Hong Kong

10 9 8 7 6 5 4 3 2 1 HC ISBN 0-671-74487-9
10 9 8 7 6 5 4 3 2 1 pbk ISBN 0-671-74323-6

Library of Congress Cataloging-in-publication Data

Harper, Peter, 1945-
The natural garden book / by Peter Harper and Jeremy Light.
p. cm.
"A Gaia original."
"A Fireside book."
ISBN 0-671-74487-9 : $32.95. – ISBN 0-671-74323-6 (pbk.) : $25.00
1. Organic gardening. 2. Gardening–Environmental aspects.
3. Garden ecology. 4. Gardening–Therapeutic use. I. Light,
Jeremy. II. Title.
SB453.5.H367 1993
635'.0484–dc20 93-19439
CIP

Foreword

In a world of shrinking resources, increasing deserts and pollution, and a desire for good fresh food and a healthy environment, each of us often wonders how we can bring more vitality and beauty into our lives. The Natural Garden Book charts such a path. It takes us back to our roots on the Earth, beginning with "primal ooze", and traces life on this planet through single-celled life forms and the development of plants and animal ecosystems to give us the context in which to breathe life back into our soils and planet – and in so doing into ourselves. Only when we can understand the intricate weaving of the biosphere's fabric is it possible to fully re-create in creation.

Once the ancient relationships between plants, animals, and micro-organisms are disrupted by the removal of one or more species, the fabric begins to be disrupted in a way that is not easy to reweave or replace. The challenge will be to live in a smaller area, so more of the world can be left in its untouched natural form. The Natural Garden Book demonstrates many ways to begin. It describes the importance of the garden each of us grows as providing for us the sense of place which we all need and which allows us to thrive. At its core it reveals the garden to be a celebration of the interaction of nature and human culture!

The book leads us to a change of attitude – "the need for all of us to take part in a renaissance of the mind and a partnership with nature based on a sustainability that heals rather than harms the environment". This partnership blends traditional wisdom and practices with the present, where the gardener is further taught by the garden and nature, and is offered an endless number of ever-changing combinations to explore and experience. I know you will enjoy using this book, with its hundreds of techniques, ideas for integrated gardens, enticing photographs, and its references for going more deeply into areas of special interest as you delight in the joys of creation!

John Jeavons

JOHN JEAVONS

Contents

Introduction . . . *8*

PART ONE
GARDENING FOR THE PLANET
CHAPTER ONE: *A Little Piece of Gaia . . . 12*
CHAPTER TWO: *A Partnership with Nature . . . 44*

PART TWO
PLANNING YOUR GARDEN
Introduction: Making Choices . . . *62*
CHAPTER THREE: *The Useful Garden . . . 66*
The Resourceful Garden, The Water-efficient Garden, The Productive Garden
CHAPTER FOUR: *The Wildlife Garden . . . 110*
CHAPTER FIVE: *The Healing Garden . . . 124*

PART THREE
THE GAIAN GARDEN
Introduction: Planning an Integrated Garden . . . *142*
CHAPTER SIX: *Habitat Gardens . . . 148*
The Urban Garden, The Mountain Garden, The Coastal Garden, The Woodland Garden, The Wetland Garden
CHAPTER SEVEN: *Climate Gardens . . . 180*
The Cool Temperate Garden, The Arid Garden

PART FOUR
NATURAL GARDENING TECHNIQUES
Introduction: Finding out about Your Garden . . . *194*
CHAPTER EIGHT: *Shaping the Land . . . 200*
CHAPTER NINE: *Recycling . . . 208*
CHAPTER TEN: *Improving Your Soil . . . 219*
CHAPTER ELEVEN: *Permanent Planting . . . 226*
CHAPTER TWELVE: *Vegetables and Herbs . . . 234*
CHAPTER THIRTEEN: *Fine Tuning . . . 245*
CHAPTER FOURTEEN: *Water Conservation . . . 256*
CHAPTER FIFTEEN: *Creating Microclimates . . . 260*

APPENDIX
Tools and Structures . . . *266* Plant Lists . . . *268*
Further Reading, Useful Organizations, and Suppliers . . . *276*
INDEX and ACKNOWLEDGEMENTS . . . *282*

Introduction

Your garden is unique, yet universal. Like one piece of an enormous jigsaw puzzle, it is different from all other pieces, yet plays its part in a larger whole. Imagine that, on closer inspection, each jigsaw piece was made of thousands of tinier pieces; and that, stepping back, the whole puzzle is revealed as yet one piece in an even greater whole. This is how the biosphere is structured: in billions of parts-within-parts, each with its own distinctive structure and together making up a coherent whole.

Your garden is one of these parts: an assemblage of diverse ecosystems, fitting with its neighbors into even larger systems, breathing the planetary air, drinking its waters, and transmuting the light of the sun. So your garden brings to a singular point the very latest results of three billion years of evolution and geological change, thousands of years of human habitation, hundreds of years of plant breeding, dozens of years of planners, architects, and builders; and finally your own unique contribution.

A Reflection of Society

The development of gardens themselves mirrors the evolution of society, from the aristocracies of the pre-democratic era to libertarian cultures of the present day. The landed classes, whether they lived in China, Persia, or England, created gardens to reflect their own world view and the "god-given" order of the society they ruled.

In this society, the rich pursued cultural and recreational goals while a class of artisans and peasants performed the useful, physical work. Everyone had a rank and a clear-cut role defined by their trade or position, where they stayed for life. Below the artisans stood the mob, to be kept at bay, out of sight, and out of mind at all costs.

The unmistakable influence of a classic garden tradition permeates the world. Its origins lie in the great country estates where it faithfully reflected the values and tastes of the landowning classes. Gradually, the bougeoisie reproduced the tradition in miniature, followed on an even humbler scale by the common folk. As a consequence, gardening became fixed and neatly defined. Its essence was control and its aim was to embody and display a genteel sense of order. Everything had its proper place and each element its due function.

As a practical result of these ideals, virtually every aspect of the garden was planned and managed.

The garden was both literally and metaphorically cultivated, with pride of place going to exotic and well-bred ornamental varieties, while merely useful plants were kept out of sight. All the plants were artificial to some degree – the so-called garden varieties – while the "wild" natives were banished, their mere presence suggesting that control was less than perfect.

In an almost mathematical way, the various functions of the garden were carefully allocated to separate areas, each element dedicated to one purpose: the garden boundary, herbaceous border, lawn, summer bedding, shrubbery, ornamental trees, patio, and paths. Even the area given over to food growing was deliberately partitioned: vegetable plots, fruit bushes, greenhouse, potting shed, compost pile, and chicken run.

To a large extent, gardening remains in the grip of this tradition, with its arbitrary rules and unhealthy dominance. An artificial creature, kept in being only by technological interventions whose full costs have never been assessed, it contributes to the steady deterioration of the wider environment. Wasteful of resources, it undermines local authenticity and true diversity; disguised by gaudy pseudo-variety, it has homogenized the very concept of gardening.

Gaian Gardening

The Gaian approach frees the gardener from the rigid hierarchy in which display and recreation dominates utility, and utility comes before nature.

Instead, we advocate giving equal space to each or even reversing the order. Far from putting "everything in its proper place" we physically mix the elements and combine their functions. And we allow the native species to take part on an equal basis, not just in "reservations". Such an approach reflects an entirely different vision of society, one that is much more relaxed, egalitarian, and natural.

Consequently, you will find that this is no ordinary garden book. It is all about how to see gardening in a different light as much as how to do gardening in a different way. Since the book starts out with the premise that your garden is "a little piece of Gaia", it is entirely appropriate for you to ask what or who Gaia really is.

The living part of the Earth, which we call the biosphere, is a spherical shell around the planet, about 1600km (100mi) deep. At school, most people learned that the physical features of this shell – the atmosphere, oceans, continents, and landforms – were the outcome of ancient physical and chemical processes which formed, by happy chance, a zone fit for life. In this view, life took the world as it found it, evolved, adapted, and flourished. The biosphere was simply the part where life survived.

Such a passive view of life convinces fewer and fewer people. The "fit" between the living and the non-living parts of the biosphere has been far too neat for far too long to be attributable to mere good fortune. And it is becoming increasingly clear that the physical environment is not at all what it "ought" to be, if it were simply the result of interacting physical and chemical processes. Some other factor is affecting and influencing it, and the only possible candidate is life itself.

Once you accept this premise, you discover that life does more than merely affect the environment: life creates, modifies, and maintains it. Suddenly, it is hard to see where life begins and ends. Even the "dead" parts of the Earth are conditioned by life, as are the shells and bones of animals or the woody hearts of trees. What's more, the living parts of planet Earth seem to resemble the cells that make up a huge body, coherently maintaining a system of staggering complexity with no single entity in charge. The biosphere does not just contain life; it is itself alive, by the same criteria that we attribute life to termites, trees, or tigers.

This is the nub of the Gaia hypothesis, proposed by James Lovelock and Lynn Margulis in the 1970s: that the biosphere is a complex system so closely analogous to a living organism that we might as well regard it as one. Gaia is the ancient Greek goddess of the Earth – her name has been assigned not only to the Gaia hypothesis, but more whimsically to the self-regulating organism itself. Here are some biographical details about Gaia:

- Gaia is three billion years old; more or less immortal, she does not need to reproduce;
- She is self-regulating just like any living thing; she keeps her temperature, atmospheric gas mixture, and fluid chemistry fairly constant;
- She is self-repairing, recovering rapidly even from very severe damage;
- She evolves, learns, and recycles her wastes;
- She is powered by the Sun and profoundly influenced by the Moon;
- She is the only one of her kind in the solar system and, as far as we know, in the Milky Way.

A Book in Four Parts

Part One of The Gaia Natural Garden Book looks at the biological, ecological, and historical background to gardening and ends with a review of the ideals and sources of natural gardening. Part Two is all about planning: surveying your land, finding out what's possible given the constraints of time, space, and conditions, and making choices about the design and content of your garden. Several areas are looked at in detail – energy and water efficiency, productivity, wildlife, restoration, and healing.

Part Three compares the language of traditional gardening with that of the integrated Gaian approach. In this context, and with the guidelines and themes of Part One and Part Two in mind, one chapter looks at the special situations of five habitat gardens (urban, mountain, coastal, woodland, and wetland) and another examines two climate gardens (cool temperate and arid).

Part Four details all the techniques and practical know-how needed to put the ideas and philosophy that have been discussed, mentioned, or outlined into practice. The Appendix gives a brief survey of garden tools and the kind of structures you can build from recycled materials, and then goes on to list recommended plants for a number of different garden situations and suggested resources and further reading.

PART I

GARDENING FOR THE PLANET

A LITTLE PIECE OF GAIA

Sitting quietly in the garden on a summer's evening is one of life's great delights. This is a unique moment: the garden has never been quite like this, nor will be again. It is also a unique place: there is nowhere else in the universe quite like it. As the birds sing, the flowers smile, and scents hang in the air, the experience deepens. The longer you sit, the more you notice.

Yet what you can directly perceive in the garden is only a small part of what is really going on. Some tiny creature might crawl across your hand, so small you can hardly see it. Have a closer look. You are peeping over the horizon of the microworld that lies behind the visible garden. Such a creature is a giant in the microworld, which goes on down through finer and finer scales, and ever greater numbers and diversity: mites, fungi, protozoa, bacteria, viruses, all organized in their own complex communities.

To these creatures the garden is unimaginably vast. Yet the garden is itself only a tiny part of the ecological region which surrounds it, and that in turn is part of a continental and, ultimately, a global ecological system – the biosphere. One of the great insights of recent biology is that the whole living world, from the smallest microorganisms to the entire planet, is part of a single system. It is all one, and it has evolved as one. Your garden happens to be right in the middle of the scale, between the very small and the very large, and from it you are able to gaze at least a little way in both directions.

One of the many names for the global ecosystem is Gaia – the living Earth. Your garden is a little piece of Gaia; but each piece of Gaia is a microcosm of the whole: a little Gaia in itself. Though Gaia is very old, and has been through many changes, the history of life on Earth is still with us, written in the marrow of everything that lives. Look again at the hundreds of plants in your garden. Where do you think they have come from? How did they get here?

Inventions from the Past

The history of life on Earth is rather more than we have been led to believe. Trilobites, dinosaurs, mammoths, sabre-toothed tigers, and cave people all existed, but as recent arrivals on the Gaian stage their role in shaping and maintaining the biosphere has been marginal. Most of the really fundamental innovations of evolution, such as DNA, complex nucleated cells, and photosynthesis, belong to bacteria and blue-green algae. Many of these microorganisms, known as prokaryotes, still exist.

In the beginning, some 4.5 billion years ago, the Earth was intensely hot and suffered volcanic eruptions, meteoric impacts, and general mayhem. After a billion years or so, things had settled down a bit. The Earth's surface was still hot, but there were oceans and an atmosphere of carbon dioxide, methane, and a little nitrogen. Simple life forms emerged, gathering energy from the organic "soup" around them.

When and how the DNA system of inheritance evolved remains a mystery. But it obviously swept the board, because all living organisms, from the humblest of bacteria to the birds and bees, the slug on your lettuce, the lettuce itself – and you, all share the same genetic code for translating genes into the stuff of life. So everything alive today has a common ancestry, starting with that incredible breakthrough. With DNA in place, evolution proceeded faster, although life was still single-celled, confined to the sea, and unable to obtain enough high-energy compounds.

At this point, all living things were what we would now call bacteria. But among these single-celled creatures was a distinction that has remained fundamental ever since. Some (biologists like to call them "autotrophs") had the ability to convert simple, naturally occurring chemicals into food for themselves; others ("heterotrophs") lived off the autotrophs or their products. These two classes are the primeval equivalent of plants and animals.

The next breakthrough saw the evolution of photosynthesis. Organisms discovered how to harness solar energy and eventually to use it to bind carbon dioxide and water into organic compounds. When broken down inside a cell, the compounds supplied energy – not only to the photosynthesizers but also to other organisms. The latter ate the photosynthesizers or mopped up any compounds that leaked out.

Photosynthesis produced oxygen, a gas that was very scarce in the atmosphere and a deadly poison to

The eukaryotic revolution
Complex multicellular organisms almost certainly evolved from specialized prokaryotes, such as bacteria. The diagram (right) shows a prokaryotic cell acting as a precursor to three specialized cells – a bacterium that respires aerobically, a unicellular organism with DNA confined to a nucleus, and a cyanobacterium (blue-green alga) that can photosynthesize. When the nucleated cell engulfed the other two – a process known as endosymbiosis – the result was a complex eukaryotic cell in which the bacterium became a mitochondrion and the cyanobacterium became a chloroplast. An aggregation of many such cells could then have developed into multicellular plants.

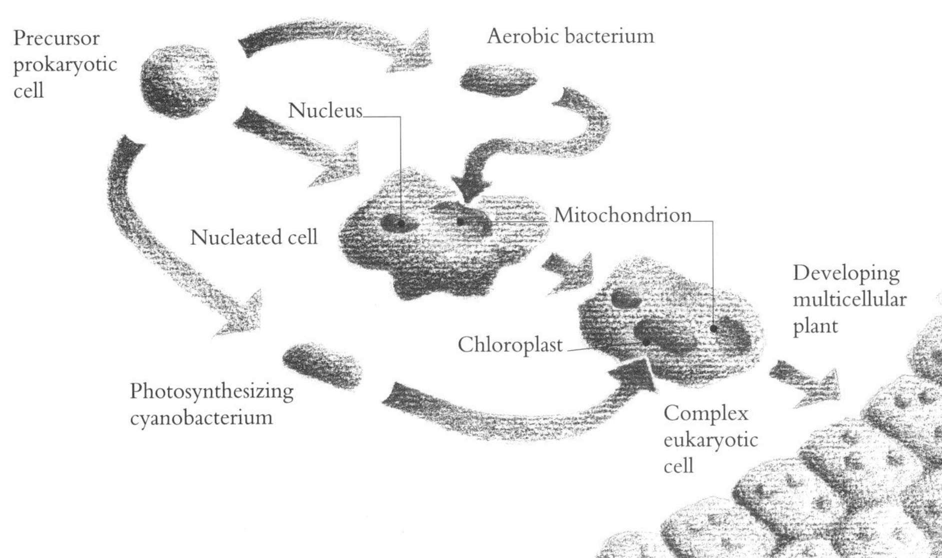

all the living things that were what we now call anaerobic. Their descendants are still with us, at the bottoms of swamps or in poorly made compost heaps. The anaerobes obtained their energy from organic compounds by rather inefficient fermentation processes. However, as oxygen gradually built up in the atmosphere, the way was open for an innovation of astonishing elegance – respiration. Organisms started to use oxygen to improve the efficiency of energy release from organic compounds. As water and carbon dioxide were generated, so photosynthesis and respiration came to complement each other perfectly by recycling each other's by-products.

The stage was set for advances in cellular organization. Bacteria are rather disorganized internally. Their functional parts, including a single strand of DNA, are jumbled together inside a cell membrane: they are prokaryotes, which means they do not have a nucleus. When ancient marine prokaryotes, many of them able to perform specialized functions such as photosynthesis, started combining with each other they formed complex cells (see above). These are called eukaryotes, which is another way of saying the cells possess a nucleus.

Spurred on by this eukaryotic revolution, the variety of living things started to unfold. At first single-celled eukaryotes – algae, fungi, and protozoa – evolved. Their functional parts, under the guidance of paired chromosomes in the nucleus, became organized into specialized structures called organelles: the two most important are chloroplasts (the site of photosynthesis in plants) and mitochondria (the seat of respiration in plants and animals).

Before the eukaryotes arrived on the scene, evolution had been a blurred, collective affair. Early bacteria were hardly distinct organisms because they were always dividing, merging, and swapping genetic material. The "organism" was really the local population; "individuals" were irrelevant. But eukaryotes, equipped with paired chromosomes that combined maternal and paternal characteristics, brought inheritance under control. Individual organisms belonging to distinct species emerged in their own right. And these individuals started to follow a life cycle that had definite stages of birth, growth, maturity, reproduction, and death.

Around 1.2 billion years ago, most of the major changes in evolution had already taken place. The regulation systems of Gaia were fully formed and were maintained almost entirely by microorganisms, as they still are today. The larger eukaryotes that consumed bacteria and small eukaryotes were the first animals.

The Fabric of the Biosphere

Your garden, wherever it is, plays a part in the great cycles of the biosphere. Basically, green plants are the builders and the producers: using the energy of the sun they combine inorganic raw materials – water, carbon dioxide, and smaller amounts of nitrogen, phosphorous, potash, and other minerals – and build them into highly complex, energy-rich organic molecules.

If this manufacturing and production process went on by itself indefinitely, the raw materials would eventually become locked into organic compounds and the system would grind to a halt. It would break one of the most fundamental laws of the biosphere: everything must be recycled. The recycling role is taken by animals, fungi, and bacteria. They are the breakers and the processors: taking the plant material living or dead, they break up the complex organic molecules, release the energy, and return every chemical eventually to its inorganic state.

The universal elements for life are the classical ones: earth, air, water and, if not exactly fire, the light and warmth of the sun. This applies right from the garden to the planetary scale, where the material elements are represented by three great domains: the Earth's crust, atmosphere, and oceans. These domains are clearly distinct, but not static. The elements of each interact with one another, aided and abetted by the organisms of the biosphere which play a leading role in the flow of energy and materials through and between the domains.

Life flourishes most vigorously where the domains meet: continental shelves, seashores, estuaries, river banks, hedgerows, surfaces of water, edges of woodland and forest. On a smaller scale, living things will thrive where the elements interpenetrate each other. In other words, where air has permeated water as dissolved gases or soil as soil gases and fixed nitrogen; where water has entered air as vapor or the earth as soil- and ground-water; or where earth enters water as silt and dissolved nutrients. If you want to produce the best from your natural garden remember that living things thrive best where unlike elements meet.

The Four Elements

Earth, air, water, and the light and heat of the sun are essential for life on our planet.

- Earth is the medium in which most plants grow. As soil, it provides minerals, houses most of the processors that recycle nutrients, and harbors the organisms that bring nitrogen out of the air.
- Air distributes heat and water, and provides three of the most important elements in a plant's structure: carbon, oxygen, and nitrogen.
- Water typically makes up 90% of a plant's tissue. It is the medium for nutrient transport and metabolism, as well as being a source of hydrogen.
- Light from the sun drives the biosphere, and in its daughter form of heat, keeps everything at the right temperature. Life itself controls the thermostat.

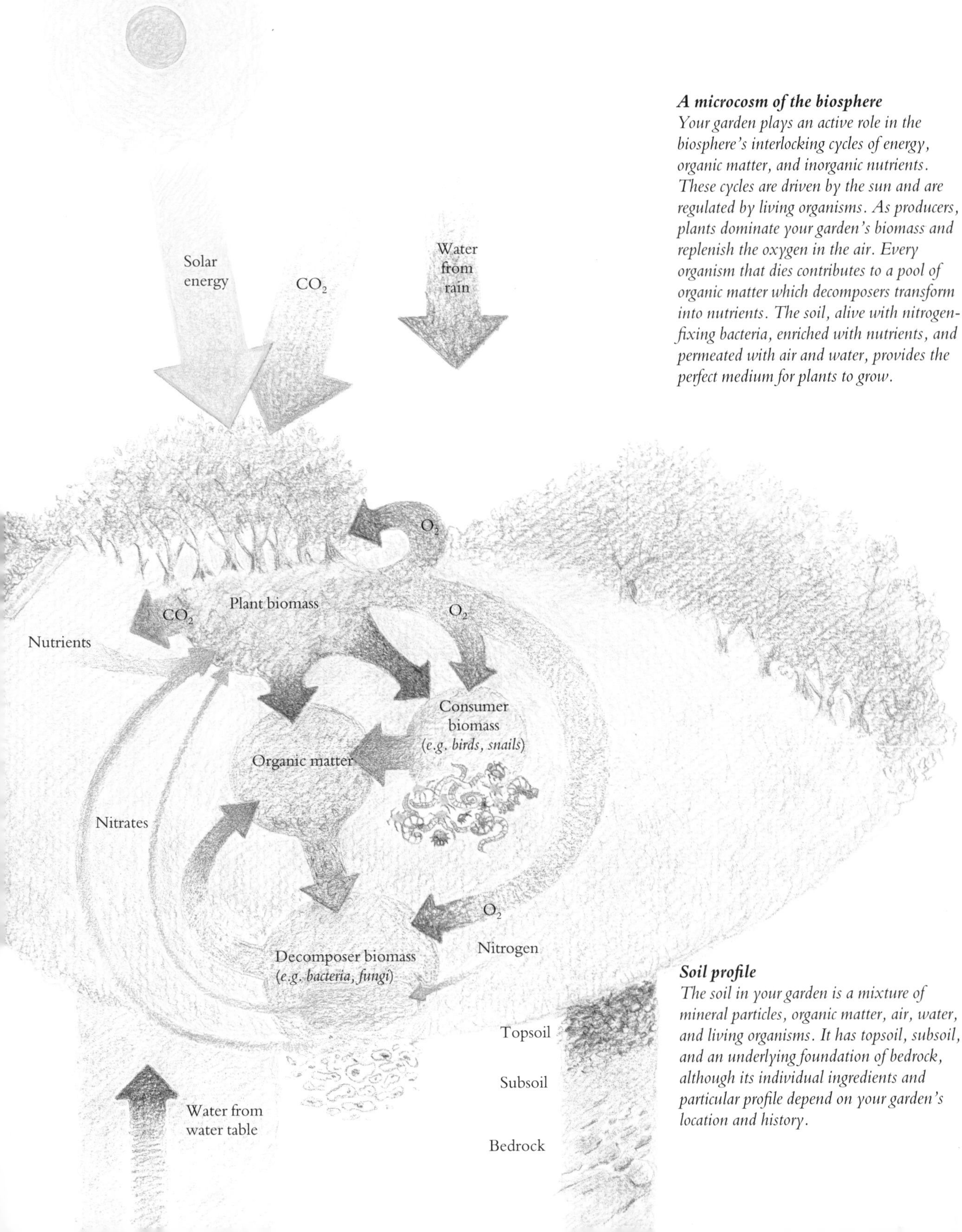

A microcosm of the biosphere

Your garden plays an active role in the biosphere's interlocking cycles of energy, organic matter, and inorganic nutrients. These cycles are driven by the sun and are regulated by living organisms. As producers, plants dominate your garden's biomass and replenish the oxygen in the air. Every organism that dies contributes to a pool of organic matter which decomposers transform into nutrients. The soil, alive with nitrogen-fixing bacteria, enriched with nutrients, and permeated with air and water, provides the perfect medium for plants to grow.

Soil profile

The soil in your garden is a mixture of mineral particles, organic matter, air, water, and living organisms. It has topsoil, subsoil, and an underlying foundation of bedrock, although its individual ingredients and particular profile depend on your garden's location and history.

Plants dominate the fabric of the biosphere, both in terms of biomass (see chart) and total metabolic activity. They consume most of what they produce, and far more plant material simply dies than gets eaten fresh by the primary consumers – the herbivores. And of these herbivores, insects eat more than all the vertebrates combined. Greater still is the part played by the decomposers, which are mostly bacteria and fungi but are also consumers such as woodlice.

Succession and Climax

All the organisms in your garden make up a kind of community. Communities can exist on all scales, from the microflora and fauna around a soil particle, to a rotting log, a lake, or a forest. Larger-scale communities tend to be named after dominant species or vegetation types: oak-juniper woodland, Sphagnum bog, or tall-grass prairie.

Communities do not appear overnight, fully formed. Rather, they unfold according to a process called succession (see illustration). A "new" habitat, such as the bare earth exposed by a landslide, is soon colonized by opportunist annual plants, many of them "weeds", followed by increasing numbers of perennials and trees. These plants are supported by the flora and fauna already present in the soil. Over the years, the perennials shade out the annuals, then the trees shade out the perennials. Early, quick-growing "pioneer" trees are eventually replaced by larger trees. At this point the rate of change slows down, and the community achieves a stable state, called a climax.

Any ground left to its own devices, if not already in the climax state, will tend to change toward it over the years. In many climates, if there is enough water, the climax will be a kind of forest. Most gardens are artificially held back from proceeding along their successional paths, but if you have a blank piece of ground and a few years to spare, natural succession is a fine thing to behold.

The succession of plants on disturbed ground in temperate climates illustrates the concept of contrary strategies. The seeds of annual "weeds", such as scarlet pimpernel and shepherd's purse, are programed to germinate when they are exposed to light after the ground is disturbed. Theirs is a short-term strategy: they grow rapidly, set lots of small seed, scatter it, then die. With any luck the seeds will germinate and give a second generation the same year.

Plants such as oak trees employ the opposite, long-term strategy. They make lots of vegetative growth in order to shade out other plants, establish a strong root system, and ultimately set larger seeds with a greater probability of survival. In successions we find

Biomass in Pounds per Acre of Land in USA

	(approximate figures)
Humans	16
Birds	27
Wild mammals	27
Livestock	55
Protozoa	130
Algae	130
Insects	890
Earthworms, etc.	890
Bacteria	1900
Fungi	2200
Plants	49,000

Colonizing a forest clearing
The first plants to colonize a clearing in a temperate forest are usually annuals that grow vigorously, produce huge numbers of seeds, and incidentally prevent soil erosion. Perennial grasses and shrubs succeed the annuals but are then dwarfed by pioneer trees, such as birch or acacias. Long-term plant strategists, such as oak or eucalyptus, slowly crowd out the pioneers and culminate, after many years, in a climax of mature trees with a shade-tolerant understory.

whole series of plants with longer and longer time perspectives and greater competitive ambitions. The climax is an assembly of mature trees that have spent years investing in vegetative growth before they start to reproduce and set seed.

The Cost of Living

For all its formidable achievements, natural selection cannot produce super-organisms able to do anything, survive anywhere, outcompete anybody, grow and reproduce anytime. Every species has a finite number of adaptations and abilities, as well as a narrow range of conditions within which it can operate. The floating leaves of water lilies, the thorns of roses, the tendrils of passionflowers, the fetid smell of the arum – all are clearly useful, but not universally so. It would not help a passionflower to have floating leaves, nor a rose to smell rotten. Surely, you may say, all plants could benefit from thorns to keep herbivores away; and tendrils could be handy to reach the sunlight.

But everything a plant does has a cost – in resources and metabolic energy. A plant cannot do everything; in a sense it has a tight budget and must make very careful choices. The metabolic cost of laying on special structures "just in case" would be enormous. To help them choose between reasonable probabilities plants rely on inherited information.

Every plant appears to have a general "strategy", in which it deploys resources in anticipation of the most likely circumstances it will encounter. Temperate plant species, for example, "know" for sure that winter is coming and choose standard responses that fit the rest of their life pattern: evergreens tough it out, deciduous trees shed leaves, perennials retreat to their roots, and annuals overwinter as dormant seed.

Such general strategies are complemented by "tactics" for dealing with uncertain circumstances. Plants aim to produce the maximum amount of seed, but have to guess whether to produce a little early or take the chance on a lot more later from a bigger plant. Given ideal conditions, most plants will put on a lot of leaf on the assumption that the good times will continue, but if conditions take a turn for the worse they go to seed quickly because it may be their last chance. Gardeners know this very well: overfed ornamentals may actually bloom poorly because they are too busy growing leaves, while a dry spell will make all the lettuces and spinach bolt.

Long-term strategists

Mature forest

Fallen tree creates new clearing and cycle begins again

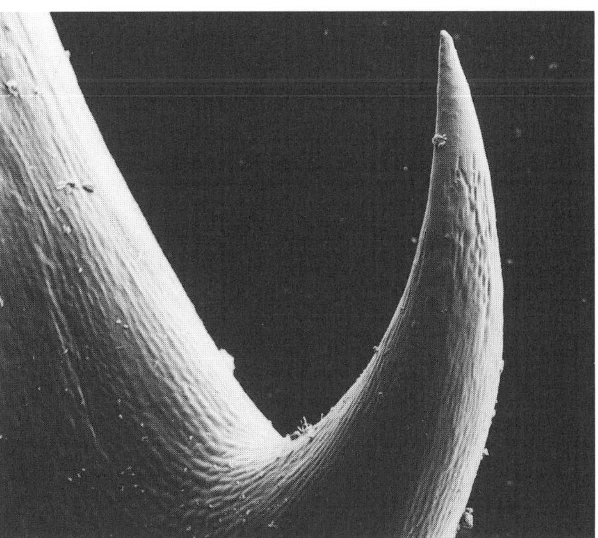

Thorns that deter herbivores form a large part of a rose's metabolic cost of living.

Plants: the Producers

As a tiny corner of the biosphere your garden features a diversity of plants, many of them able to flower. If you look closely you will probably discover a whole variety of non-flowering species – algae, lichens, mosses, and ferns. The ancestors of flowering and non-flowering plants can be traced back to the single-celled bacteria which inhabited the sea. These bacteria made most of the really important innovations (see pp. 12–17), such as DNA, RNA, photosynthesis, and respiration, that fostered the great diversity of living things. But do not be fooled into thinking that these ancient inventors have disappeared. They are with us still, performing the same essential planetary maintenance as they have always done. In fact, they do far more work than we usually give them credit for. Furthermore, they are doing it in your garden.

The Diversity of Plants

Your garden almost certainly contains representatives of every major group, from algae to angiosperms, in the astonishingly diverse plant kingdom (see below).

Fungi

As early colonizers of land, fungi pioneered a unique system of growth: they grow bigger by dividing their nuclei but not their cells and resemble very large, branched amoebae. Fungi do not photosynthesize but are vital processors in the nutrient cycle and have linked up with algae to create lichens.

Ferns

Ferns flourish typically in the filtered green light of shady habitats. Their main stem, or rhizome, supports an array of fronds beneath which few plants can survive. Like mosses they depend on watery conditions for the sexual phase of their reproductive cycle but are generally less bound to wet situations. One successful member of the group (which includes clubmosses and horsetails) is the bracken fern, Pteridium aquilinum. *Found all over the world, this fern forms virtual monocultures on the grazed uplands of some temperate regions.*

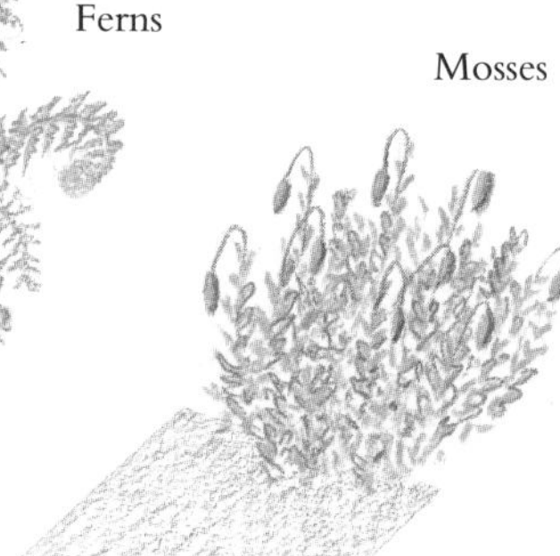

Algae

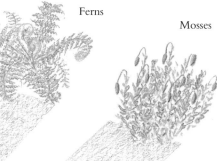

Colonies of algae grow wherever there is water or moist conditions: on the sides of trees, on paths, on the surface of soil, in puddles, in snow, and encrusting the panes of a greenhouse. The group contains green, red, and brown algae, dinoflagellates, diatoms, and euglenoid protozoa. Algae have no true stems, leaves, or roots; they all use chlorophyll as their photosynthetic pigment. Algae are crucial players in the cycles of the biosphere: they are primary producers in the food chain and are a key source of oxygen for aquatic organisms.

Lichens

Look at a "stain" on a rock, wall, or roof and you will probably find a lichen. Each lichen is a partnership between an alga, which produces food, and a fungus, which dissolves rock and soil minerals to provide nutrients. The variety of lichens in your garden will depend very much on the cleanliness of the air: their slow rate of growth means they can easily accumulate fatal levels of pollutants. Pollution apart, lichens are some of the toughest creatures alive, able to tolerate adversity and survive in almost any habitat with harsh conditions: deserts, tundra, or mountain tops.

Mosses

In the evolution of life on land, mosses and their associated processors are thought to have had a big impact on preparing soils for the later development of higher plants, such as gymnosperms. Like algae, mosses have no true roots, stems, or leaves; and most have no internal means of transporting nutrients, which they absorb from the rain or dust. Mosses may seem primitive, but they cover almost every surface in moist temperate conditions, especially in woodlands.

Some of the earliest complex organisms to emerge from the eukaryotic revolution (see p. 13) belong to the true algae, such as red and green algae. These photosynthesizers are mostly aquatic and exist either as individual cells or as assemblies of cells. Green algae are thought to be the ancestors of all other plants, largely because chlorophyll is their photosynthetic pigment and starch is their long-term energy store.

True algae were probably the first to colonize the land. We can imagine them coming up the rivers and establishing themselves in swamps and damp habitats, no doubt with bacteria and fungi in attendance. Enormous mats of algae almost certainly covered the wet parts of the land for a billion years prior to the evolution of fully fledged terrestrial plants. Algae remain successful – in the air, in the soil, and wherever there is water.

As terrestrial creatures it is hard for us to appreciate the enormous leap aquatic organisms made when they colonized the land. In the water, organisms are bathed in a solution of nutrients, oxygen, and carbon dioxide. They have no need of support, are in no danger of drying out, and to reproduce they release mobile sex cells into the surrounding water. The offspring resulting from the fusion of male and female sex cells are simply carried away on the tide. But once on land such organisms flop, dry out, and have to rely on rock weathering for minerals. One by one, these difficulties were overcome by plants.

The problem of dispersal on land was solved by mosses and liverworts. They produced tiny, single-celled units called spores that were resistant to desiccation and light enough to be scattered by the wind. Unlike sex cells, the spores were able to grow into a complete new plant. Look at a clump of moss and you should be able to see the spore capsules. The spores are ubiquitous in the air, ever ready to germinate and start a new plant if the conditions are right. Spores remained the method of choice for all plants to distribute themselves until seeds evolved.

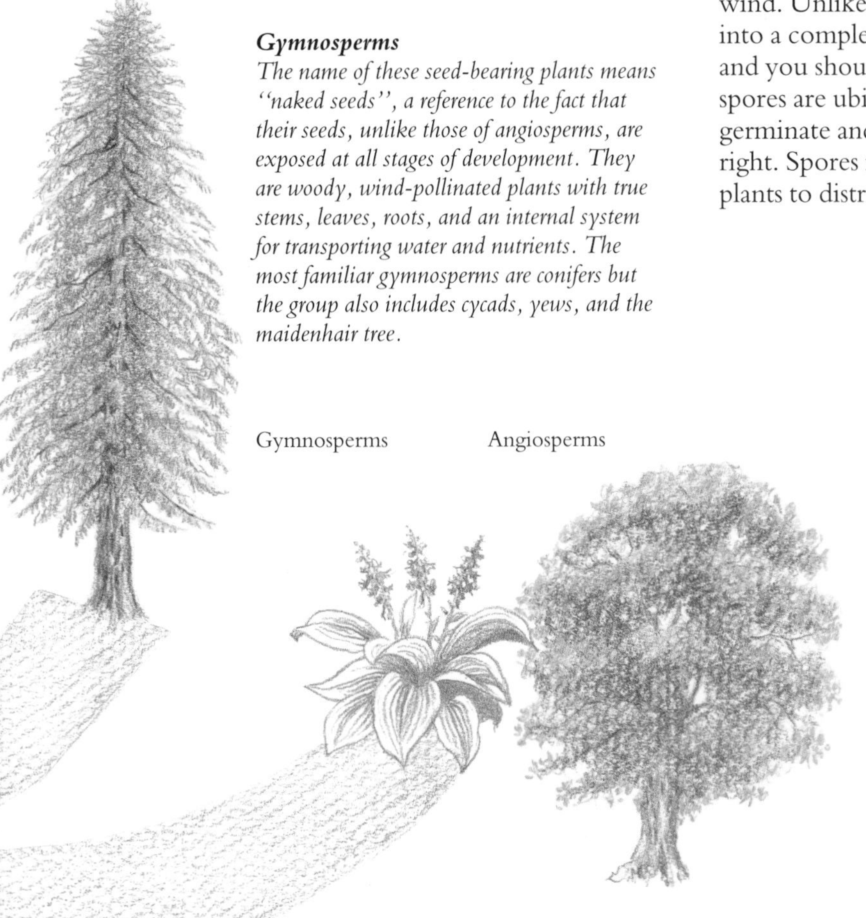

Gymnosperms
The name of these seed-bearing plants means "naked seeds", a reference to the fact that their seeds, unlike those of angiosperms, are exposed at all stages of development. They are woody, wind-pollinated plants with true stems, leaves, roots, and an internal system for transporting water and nutrients. The most familiar gymnosperms are conifers but the group also includes cycads, yews, and the maidenhair tree.

Gymnosperms Angiosperms

Angiosperms
More than 80% of all green plants are angiosperms, or plants with flowers. Their name refers to the fact that the seeds, or ovules, are enclosed in an ovary. These seeds either have one or two cotyledons (see p. 24). All agricultural crops, all garden flowers, and almost all broad-leaved trees, shrubs, and garden weeds are angiosperms. They can be divided into three groups according to the length of their life cycle: annuals (no more than a year); biennials (two years); and perennials (three or more years).

The Arrival of Tall Plants

The earliest plants for which any fossils survive were found in Scotland. Estimated to be around 400 million years old, these plants (which have the curious botanical name of *Rhyania gwynne-vaughani*) consisted of a creeping rhizome with stems that had branches bearing reproductive structures. The stems were photosynthetic and the rhizome developed associations with fungi in the soil to provide mineral nutrients. These fungi, known as mycorrhizae, play an essential role in most groups of modern plants.

The competition for light drove ancient pteridophytes (ancestors to the ferns) to develop leaves and stems. This pairing was a potential winner – so long as the stem was short. The pteridophytes were able to grow taller when they developed a two-way transport system bringing water and minerals from the soil, and sending sugars from their leaves to their roots.

The evolution of leaves and an internal network for transporting water and chemicals opened the way for the development of tall plants and eventually trees (see p. 21). The first plants to adopt the tree form were horsetails. Around 350 million years ago, woody horsetails formed dense forests in much of the northern hemisphere.

The credit for the next great innovation – the seed (see p. 24) – is usually given to the gymnosperms, which dominated the world's flora in the Jurassic Period about 200 million years ago. In fact, evidence suggests that the first seeds were probably produced by relatives of the ferns which subsequently became extinct, leaving the field wide open for the gymnosperms. This group is often associated with the conifers, although not all gymnosperms bear cones. The very earliest gymnosperms continued, as other plant groups did, to rely on water to achieve fertilization, and some, such as the tropical cycads and the Ginkgo tree, are still with us.

Conifers invented pollen, which finally overcame the problem of sex cells needing a liquid medium to come together and opened the way for the evolution of flowering plants. Conifers pack all the sperm cells into tiny but tough capsules called pollen grains which the wind blows on to the ovules of female cones on other trees. Although a hit-and-miss affair, this pollination can be carried out on a huge scale without needing a rainy day.

Flowering plants provided the final refinement – the flower. They may have evolved about 140 million years ago in the rift valley that now lies buried beneath the Atlantic Ocean between Africa and South America. The earliest flowering plant, or angiosperm, probably resembled a magnolia tree. A reproductive structure composed of modified leaves, the flower became conspicuous by a unique and spectacular alliance with insects (see p. 23). Despite many important exceptions, flowers are designed to attract insects as a means of ensuring that the plants to which they belong are efficiently cross-fertilized. So successful are the angiosperms that the sea is the only major ecosystem in which they – and coincidentally the insects – have made little or no progress.

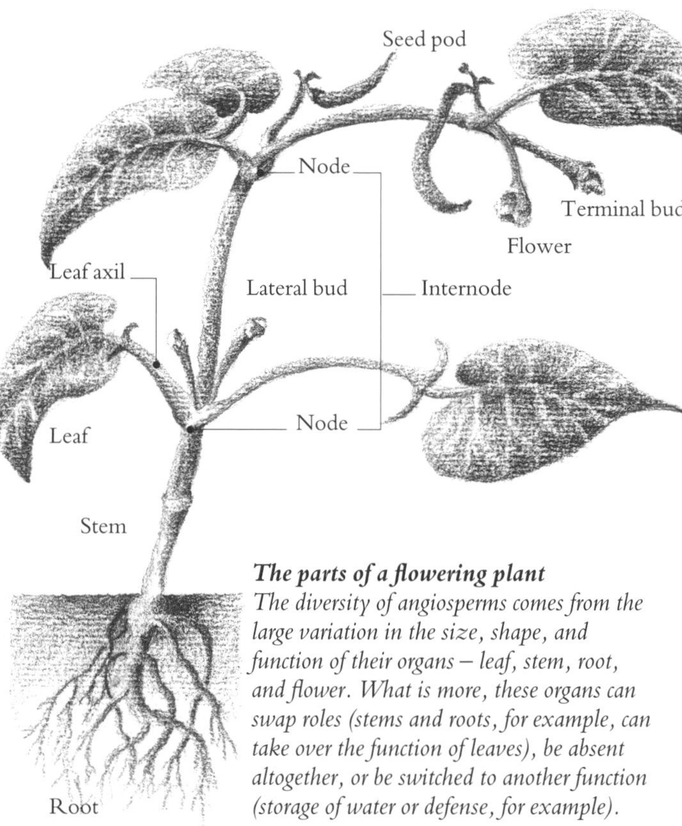

The parts of a flowering plant
The diversity of angiosperms comes from the large variation in the size, shape, and function of their organs – leaf, stem, root, and flower. What is more, these organs can swap roles (stems and roots, for example, can take over the function of leaves), be absent altogether, or be switched to another function (storage of water or defense, for example).

The Growth of Plants

We often take it for granted that plants grow but gardeners need to know how and where growth takes place. Plants are sensitive and can respond to stimuli, such as light and gravity, but also to touch, chemicals, the moon, other plants, and the treatment they receive from people. Light and gravity cause plant movements, or tropisms: shoots and stems move away from gravity and toward light, while roots grow toward gravity and water but away from light.

Plants grow only in particular regions called meristems where cells divide. Most plants have a main growing tip, or apical meristem, inside the terminal bud of the stem and at the tip of a root. Lateral meristems are located in the lateral buds where branches leave the stem and in leaf axils. These meristems are usually inhibited by hormones from the apical meristem. If you remove the latter the lateral buds will grow – pinching out the "leader" makes a plant bush out and shearing a hedge thickens it up. Sometimes you want to do the opposite: pinching out the side-shoots of a tomato plant, for example, makes it grow taller before diverting its energies into fruit-making.

In grasses the main vegetative meristem lies at the base of the plant. When herbivores graze the tips of the leaves they temporarily reduce the photosynthetic area but do not damage the growing point. This is why grass can tolerate grazing and mowing. Non-grass herbs suffer more from close-cropping: they lose their leaves and will die unless they can quickly replace them and re-establish photosynthesis.

Cambium

The transport system of all dicot plants (see p. 24) contains a meristem called cambium. As the plant grows the cambium divides and makes the stem thicker and better able to support new branches and leaves. This cell division produces phloem tubes for carrying sugars on the outside, and xylem vessels for carrying water on the inside. In woody plants the new cells assume the transport functions, while older cells form layers of secondary tissue – phloem becomes cork and bark, xylem turns into wood. As the stem thickens, the pith fills with resins and forms heartwood. More than 90% of a mature tree is made up of decommissioned xylem and phloem cells.

Cross-section through a Woody Stem

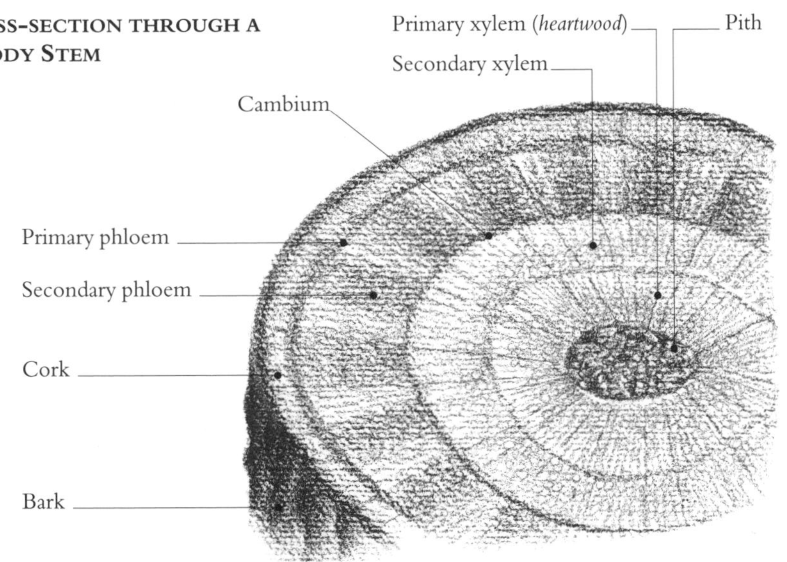

Trees

A tree is a woody plant. Inside the stem, dead cells, hardened with compounds such as lignin, build up as wood; the same material forms bark on the outside of the stem (see cambium, left). The living part of the tree is actually a thin-walled cylinder between the wood and the bark, extending into the branches, leaves, and roots. The ever-widening heartwood of a tree provides support for a high and wide leaf canopy. Most trees are programed to stop growing in unfavorable seasons and start again when conditions permit.

In general, trees are either coniferous or broad-leaved. Conifers are gymnosperms with scaly or needle-shaped leaves. They have the more ancient provenance and include the largest (sequoias) and among the oldest (bristlecone pines) living things. All conifers except larches and metasequoias are evergreen. Broad-leaved trees are woody flowering plants. Some are evergreen, while others are deciduous and drop their leaves in anticipation of unfavorable seasons.

Leaves: the Production of Carbohydrates

The evolution of leaves increased the photosynthetic area of plants and hence the energy available for growth. Leaves also brought the extra advantage of shading out rival plants in the competition for light. But leaves only worked efficiently when plants developed a two-way transport network, or vascular system. This was composed of xylem tubes that conducted water and nutrients up from the ground, and phloem tubes that carried sugars and other materials from the leaves to the rest of the plant.

In general, the characteristic look of a species is generated by the size and shape of its leaves combined with the way the leaves are arranged on a stem and the angle at which they are held. Leaves are usually held in one of three ways: opposite each other in pairs; in whorls; or alternately in a spiral fashion. The latter, which abides by a mathematical pattern known as the Fibonacci series, minimizes the chances of a leaf preventing sunlight from reaching the one below it.

A leaf often has a flat design since it needs to have a large surface area relative to its volume to absorb the diffuse resources of sunlight and carbon dioxide. Photosynthesis takes place in chloroplasts, where the pigment chlorophyll is concentrated. Plants can be divided into two groups – the so-called C4 plants, which increase their ability to photosynthesize no matter how bright the light and the C3 plants, which cannot improve their rate of photosynthesis beyond a specific light intensity (see illustration, right).

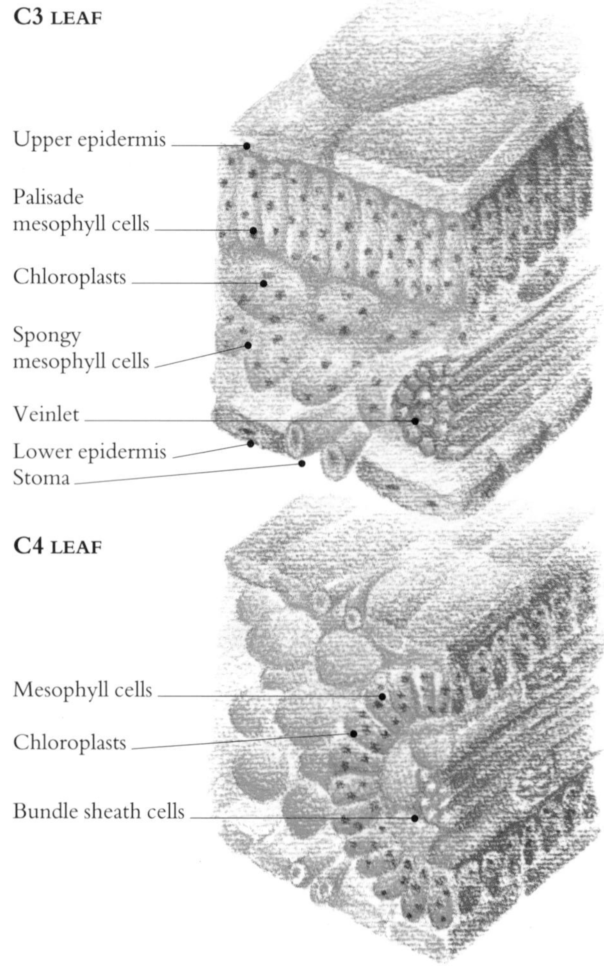

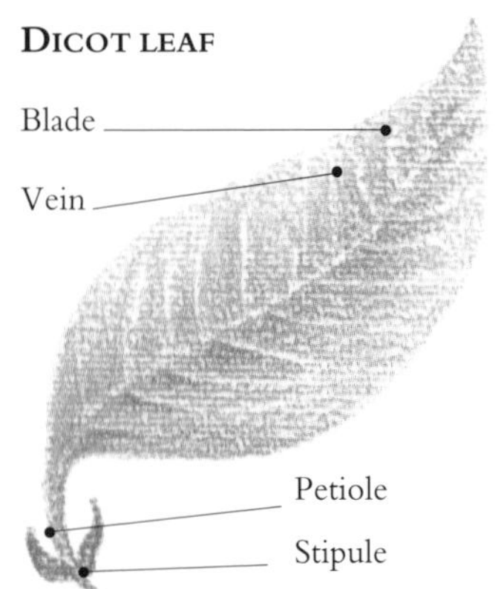

C3 and C4 leaves
Some plants, such as maize, have evolved a variation on normal photosynthesis which makes them far more efficient in bright sunlight. They are known as C4 plants because the reactions involve an intermediate compound containing four carbon atoms. Normal C3 photosynthesis involves an intermediate containing three carbon atoms. Since C4 plants use carbon dioxide more effectively, Gaia theory proposes that they evolved in response to low levels of carbon dioxide in the air. Most of the chloroplasts in a C3 dicot leaf are located on its upper side (top), close to the light and protected by a waxy cuticle. Carbon dioxide is absorbed through special pores, or stomata, on the underside of the leaf. A series of veins (left) from the vascular system brings water and minerals, and takes away carbohydrates. Chloroplasts in C4 monocots are clustered around the vascular tissue in the veins of the leaves (above).

The parts of a flower
Fundamentally, a flower is a set of four concentric whorls of modified leaves. In the center lies the female section, or pistil, encircled by the male organs, or stamens. Petals surround the stamens while sepals surround the petals. Variations on this basic pattern include: leaving parts out; one part pretending to be another; having male and female parts on different flowers or different plants; fusing elements together; expanding some parts; having lots of tiny flowers that together resemble a large one. In addition, flowers may have extra organs, such as nectaries or scent glands.

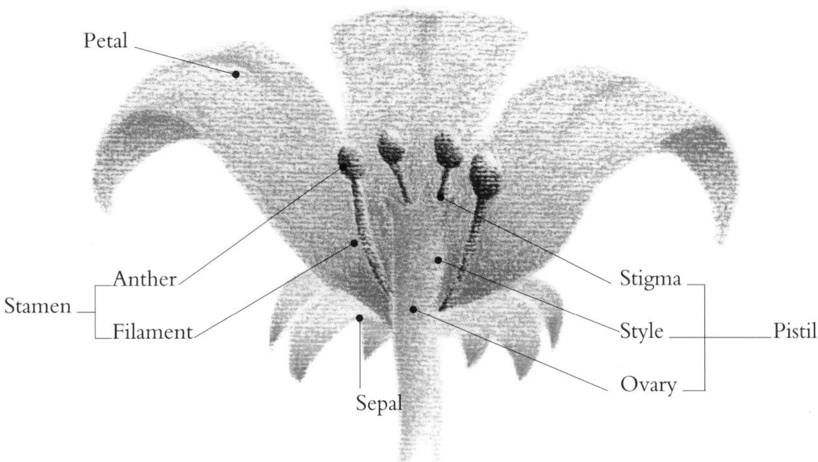

A leaf's main dilemma is how to get enough sunlight and carbon dioxide without drying out. Dry air causes a plant to transpire so that water evaporates through the pores, or stomata, of its leaves. So when conditions are dry, the stomata close. But when conditions are both sunny and dry, the leaf needs to open its stomata to let carbon dioxide in for photosynthesis. Leaves are designed, therefore, to balance the need to make sugars against the dangers of losing too much water.

Lack of moisture has a profound effect on plant growth and distribution. Plants in tropical rain forests are not exposed to the danger of drying out and consequently are very productive: the relative humidity of the air is so high they can proceed with photosynthesis at any time of year without risking desiccation. Plants adapted to dry conditions, however, tend to reduce evaporation by having rounded, folded, fleshy, or needle-like leaves, usually with a thick waxy layer or a hairy surface. Other plants drop their leaves in the dry season or, like cacti, do away with them altogether.

Within the plant kingdom, there are many other adaptations of leaves to their environment. These include a needle-like form, or a deciduous habit to avoid the rigours of seasonal cold; a water-repellent cuticle to prevent damage by excess moisture; a leathery texture, spines, stinging hairs, chemical defences, or mimicry to ward off the attentions of herbivores.

Flowers: the Organs of Reproduction

Every flower, no matter what its shape or form, shares the same sexual end: to introduce male pollen grains from the stamens of another flower on to the receptive stigma of its female pistil (see illustration above). The stigma contains special secretions which prevent the germination of pollen from other species. The pollen grain germinates and sends a tube into the stigma, down the style, and eventually to the ovary. Here, two male cells from the pollen fertilize three female cells, producing an embryo and the food store, or endosperm, of the seed (see p. 24). This numerical idiosyncrasy is shared by every one of the 350,000 species of flowering plant.

Except for wind-pollinated angiosperms, such as many trees and grasses, most of the variations in flower shape and form are driven by the need to give visiting insects (occasionally birds and bats) a good dusting of pollen and to force them into contact with the female part of the flower. To lure an insect to its heart a flower may use colors, scents, a profusion of pollen, shapes, lines, or nectar. The success of such strategies has led to many elaborate and sophisticated coevolutionary links between particular species of plant and insect. Furthermore, this coevolution has meant that flowering plants and insects dominate almost every region of the biosphere (and our gardens are a testament to this fact).

SEEDS: THE DISPERSAL OF THE SPECIES

After pollination and the fertilization of sex cells, a flower produces seeds – ready-to-go miniatures of the parent plant, packed up in a resistant shell with a food supply to get them started. A seed is usually dormant, but primed to wake up when external conditions become favorable. A plant's challenge is to ensure that at least some of its seeds reach fertile ground, where they can germinate, and become reproducers in their own right.

Since many plants have chosen the wind as a means of dispersal, their seeds have to be light and small. Although small seeds, such as the "dust" seeds of orchids, have less chance of germinating successfully than large seeds, they can be produced in great numbers at the same metabolic cost. Other strategies include wings and parachutes (see illustation, right). The most popular strategy, however, is to have no strategy at all, other than letting the seeds fall off the plant and hoping for the best. It seems unenterprising, but it works. These "drop-off" seeds can, of course, be bigger than windblown seeds, and

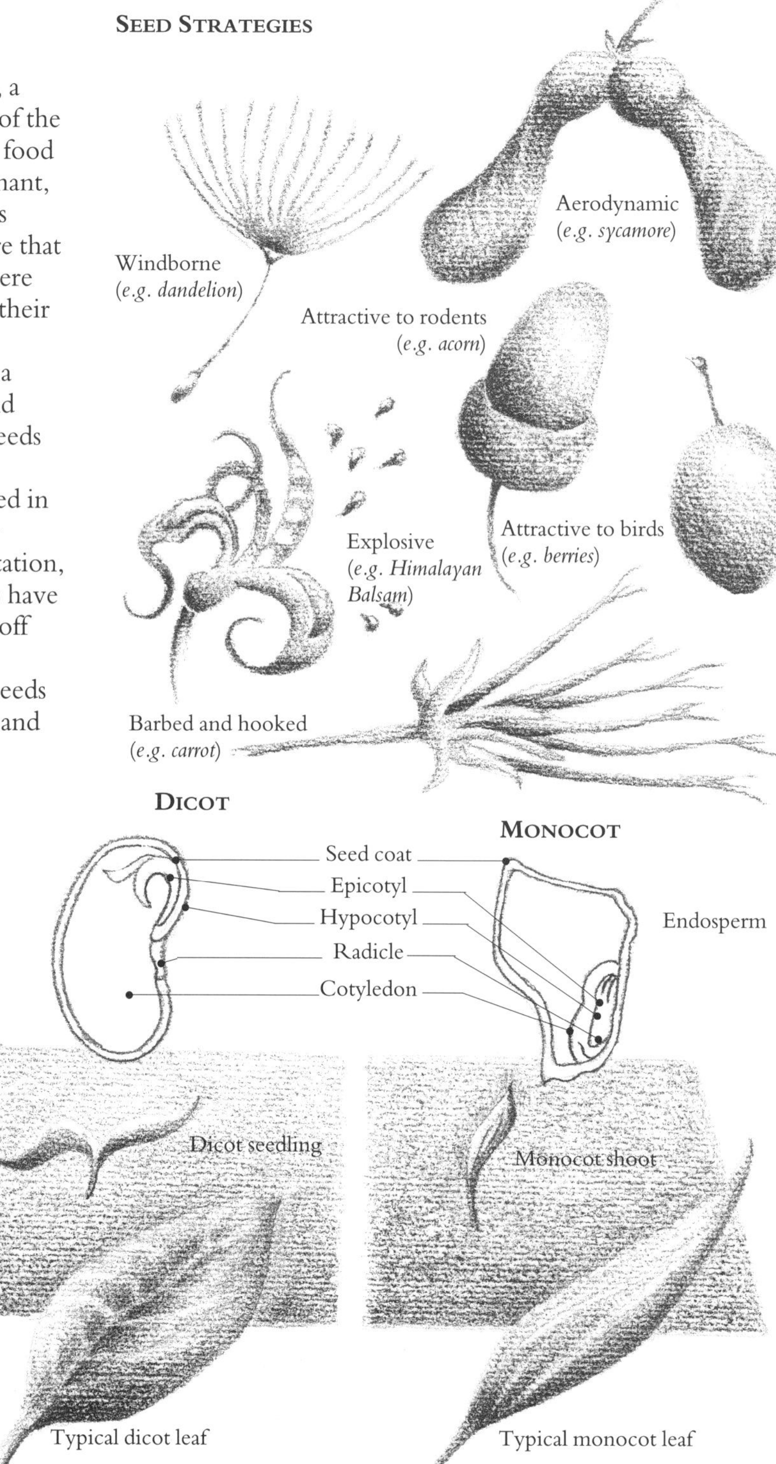

Dicots and monocots

Early in their evolution flowering plants divided into two groups that are easy to tell apart once you know what to look for. The difference is immediately obvious when a seed germinates. Either one or two "seed leaves", or cotyledons, will appear and will start photosynthesizing immediately. Most seedlings have a pair of cotyledons, but grasses, for example, have only one. The former plants are called dicotyledons, the latter monocotyledons – dicots and monocots, for short.

The leaves of monocots, such as grasses, irises, lilies, arums, palms, sedges, bromeliads, and orchids, have parallel veins which often give them a statuesque quality. The parts of monocot flowers, such as petals, tend to come in multiples of three. By contrast, dicots have leaf-veins that form a network and their floral parts are organized into groups of four or five.

so have a better chance of germinating into a successful seedling.

For us, the most interesting seeds are the ones we eat, such as grains, maize, peas, sunflower, beans, and sesame. We are also attracted by the fruits and nuts that plants produce for animals to eat. Edible fruits are a brilliant evolutionary strategy: as an animal eats the flesh of the fruit the seeds within pass through its gut and are deposited far and wide with a ready-made dressing of fertilizer. Sometimes the seeds lie dormant until triggered by this rather drastic experience. For example, the Calvaria tree from Mauritius depended entirely on the dodo to eat its seeds, but the extinction of the bird meant that no seeds were able to germinate. Luckily, an astute biologist worked out the problem and fed some seeds to turkeys, with the result that, for the first time in 200 years, new Calvaria trees are growing.

Roots: Providing Water and Nutrients

The underground root system of a plant usually occupies as great a volume as the stems, leaves, and flowers do above the ground. Roots have two principal functions: to anchor a plant in the soil and to extract water and nutrients from the soil. The roots of perennial plants may have a third function: to store nutrients and chemicals. Since nutrients are usually located near the soil surface while water is found at greater depths, plants often produce two different kinds of root – feeding roots to extract nutrients, water roots to provide water.

Roots are extremely opportunistic foragers but they have to direct their resources according to the most likely chances of success. They often take a cue from an early experience that turns out to be a wrong direction. For example, when there is plenty of surface water, a plant may invest its energy into superficial water roots, then suffer as the water withdraws into the ground later in the season. Gardeners know well that to "water rarely and copiously, not little and often" encourages plants to put down water roots deep into the soil.

Similar principles apply to feeding roots. Long branch roots grow until they find a nutrient-rich zone in the soil. Side-shoots and side-side-shoots subsequently proliferate until the resources are exhausted. Some plants, such as members of the cabbage family, have roots that absorb nutrients by themselves, but most plants use fungi called mycorrhizae to extract and transfer nutrients to their root cells. The plants, in return, exude sugars from the root tips which feed not only the mycorrhizae but many other organisms. This creates a special ecosystem known as a rhizosphere around the roots.

From a gardener's point of view, the most important distinctions between root systems are concerned with transplanting. Some plants, such as leeks and cabbages, transplant with astonishing ease – and thrive because of it. Others, such as peonies and members of the carrot family, refuse to co-operate. As a rule of thumb, those with fleshy roots and taproots do not like it, while those with fibrous roots do. Plants, such as potatoes, onions, and daffodils, which have underground storage organs that are not roots, transplant easily.

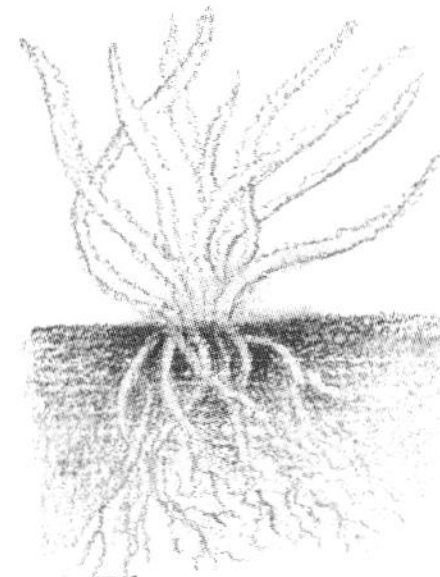

Root structure
Two common root systems are taproots and fibrous roots. The former possess a large central root with many branches, whereas the latter have a mass of roots of roughly equal size. Behind the cap of a root tip an apical meristem continually produces new cells in a growing zone. As the cells mature they sprout short-lived root hairs that increase the surface area for absorbing nutrients.

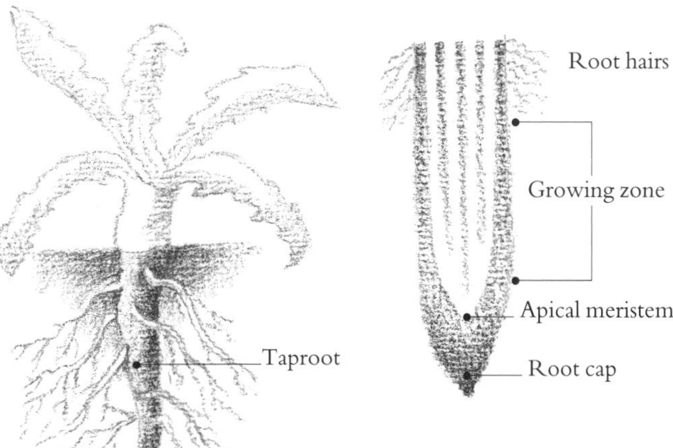

Processors: Recycling Essential Nutrients

It is one of Gaia's most fundamental principles that everything must be recycled. From simple raw materials the autotrophs build up energy-rich organic compounds; the heterotrophs break them down again and the cycle begins anew (see p.12). Plants can transform minerals, gases, and water into all the marvellous intricacies of the vegetable world. Then they die or get eaten, and the myriad processors complete the cycle.

The most obvious processors are the consumers like ourselves who either eat fresh plant material or other animals that eat it, or both. While consumers play an important role in the overall economy of the whole biosphere, most of the recycling work is performed by decomposers, which convert all the dead matter and waste products of animals and plants right back to the raw materials of plant growth.

Although decomposers are a vital part of this system, discussing them brings out our cultural prejudices, for theirs is a dark land of death, decay, germs, corpses, mold, dung, and all that is rotten. They are scavengers, undertakers, coprophages, and bodysnatchers. Clearing up creation's mess has no status in the sunlit world above, only in the biosphere's unconscious. Yet the biosphere will not work without them.

The principal decomposers are bacteria and fungi, which break down and mineralize organic matter, either by directly consuming available substances or by digesting them with secreted enzymes. Most of their animal colleagues in the soil (see soil fauna, right) also break down dead matter or, with plant roots, alter the structure of soil. Of these, microbivores "graze" on bacteria and fungi, and micro-carnivores eat other animals in the system. Kept in balance by forces of competition and mutual benefit, these organisms act together in a variety of complementary ways.

The Living Soil

Most soils are absolutely teeming with life. A single gram of the soil in your garden may contain as many as 2.5 billion bacteria and miles of fungal filaments. A few shovelfuls may harbor 1000 different "species", most of which live in the particles of topsoil. Of all the decomposers, bacteria generally outweigh everything else by a factor of ten, although fungi may predominate in some circumstances. Through sheer biochemical ingenuity bacteria have played a greater part in the evolution of our planet than any other group of organisms. One of the most important roles they play from the gardener's point of view is to make the nutrients exposed by worm casts available to the root hairs of plants.

Soil fungi are not far behind bacteria in the entrepreneurial stakes. Ranging from unicellular yeasts to multicellular toadstools, fungi usually break down and digest dead plant tissue. Some decompose dead animal tissue and a few, such as potato blight, are parasitic on live plants. Others prey on nematodes, catching them on sticky pads or strangling them with nooses made of fungal threads, or hyphae. Still others, called mycorrhizal fungi, develop a symbiotic relationship with live plant roots. They may, for example, grow into the cells of the roots where they improve the plant's supply of phosphorous.

Complete decomposer ecosystems, with their own complex successions, can vary from one locality to another and from one season to another. In "new" ground in temperate areas, arthropods usually dominate the soil fauna at first, later giving way to worms; in dry climates worms are replaced by ants and termites. Generally speaking, bacteria, fungi, and yeasts (which turn sugars to alcohol) are present almost everywhere and are often first on the scene when a dead leaf, shed skin, or fecal pellet appears. You can see them on moldy bread and processed food as they quickly consume the most available substances – sugars and starch.

Plant material presents a major biochemical challenge to decomposers, largely because of the cellulose, a polysaccharide common to the cells of all higher plants. This can be broken down by bacteria, fungi, and a very few animals such as slugs, snails, and the larvae of the deathwatch beetle. Termites, despite their reputation for digesting plant material, harbor bacteria in their intestines to do the job for them. In fact, bacteria are responsible for the decomposition of nearly all plant material.

Soil fauna

The enormous numbers of soil organisms are usually classified by size. Microfauna (protozoa and nematodes) live in the water films around soil particles and feed on bacteria, small pieces of detritus, and each other. Mesofauna (mites, springtails, and other small arthropods) live – often knee deep in water – in the spaces between particles and feed on fungi, nematodes, and each other. Macrofauna (earthworms – see Lumbricus terrestris, *above – and larger arthropods) heave soil particles aside, creating tunnels and burrows. Megafauna (small mammals and reptiles) create much larger holes and burrows.*

In terms of biomass (right), microfauna are most plentiful in the terrestrial systems of high latitudes, mesofauna in mid-latitudes, and macrofauna in tropical regions. The breakdown rate of litter is highest in tropical forests and lowest in the tundra. As a result, the accumulation of organic matter in the soil is greatest in the tundra and lowest in the tropical forest.

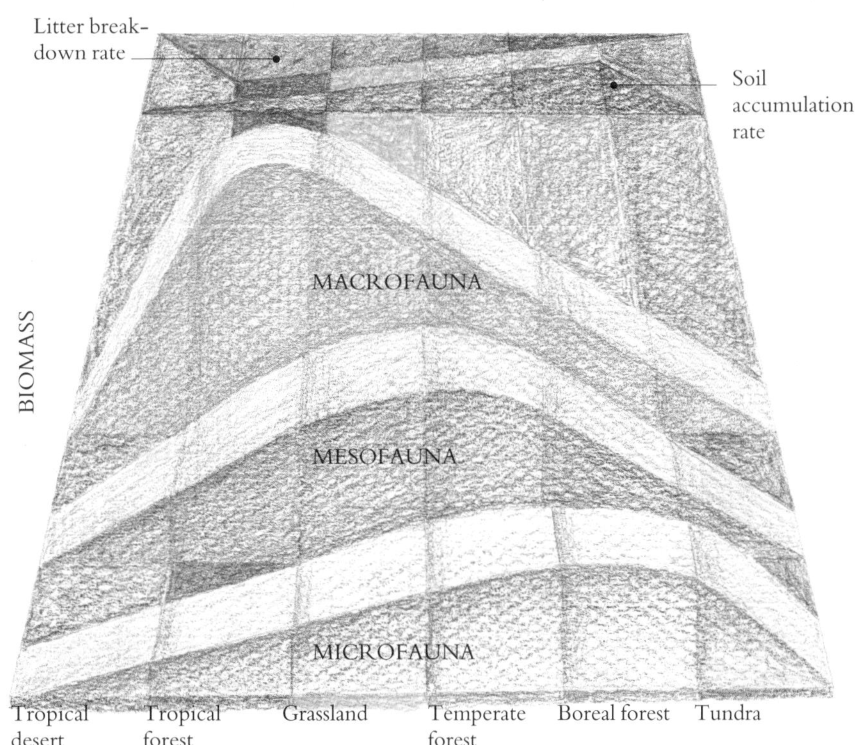

Hard as cellulose is to digest, the lignins and cork-like materials of woody plants present an even greater challenge. Fungi known as "white rots" have found a way to dismantle the lignin, leaving the white fibres of cellulose to be digested by fungi called "brown rots". No decomposer, however, seems able to break down the tannin accumulated in the heartwood of certain trees, such as the oak (see p. 32) and larch.

In the garden, the deathwatch beetle and other insects break down wood into substances that a wide range of bacteria, fungi, and small arthropods can digest. Animal bodies and feces are, on the whole, much easier for processors to deal with than raw plants. Bacteria and other microbes prefer material that has been chewed, shredded, or disturbed in a way that increases its surface area. Most detritivores prefer material that has been softened up by microbial attack. In every decomposition there is tremendous specialization and a multitude of biochemical pathways: the decay of pine needles, for example, involves an orderly succession of more than ten types of fungi, each of which attacks a different component of the needles.

The Formation of Soil

The Earth's crust, or lithosphere, is not a static, lifeless domain. It moves and changes slowly, sometimes spectacularly. Molten rock emerges from the crust, creating fresh landscapes; volcanoes and glaciers both deliver huge quantities of pulverized rock and create new soils.

The physical, non-living component of soil comes from the weathering of solid rock or from the accumulation of sediments. To a large extent, soils are determined by temperature and rainfall. The continual action of wind, rain, frost, and sun, forever breaks up rock into smaller and smaller particles over the land surface of our planet. Rocks, such as basalt and carbonates, will slowly dissolve in rainwater saturated with carbon dioxide. But living things, particularly plant roots and fauna, play a great but largely hidden role in creating soil. Roots, for instance, penetrate cracks in the bedrock or mineral fragments around them, secreting acids to break down soil into nutrients they can absorb. Animals play their part too. Snails, for example, accelerate weathering as they scour rock surfaces for algae and lichens.

Classes of soil
The soil triangle (right) helps you to find out the class of your soil, if you know the relative proportions of two of the three kinds of component particle – clay, silt, and sand. Suppose your soil contains 20% clay and 40% silt. Find 20% on the clay axis and follow the line parallel to the sand axis; then find 40% on the silt axis and follow the line parallel to the clay axis. Where the two lines meet – loam – tells you the class of your soil.

The following outlines the qualities of each soil particle:

- *Sandy soils drain freely, are well aerated, and easy to work. They dry out quickly, are often acidic, and tend to be low in available nutrients.*
- *Clay soils are rich in nutrients and hold water well. They drain poorly and are hard to work.*
- *Silt soils are easier to work than clay soils but they hold fewer nutrients. Like clay their drainage is poor but they hold less water.*

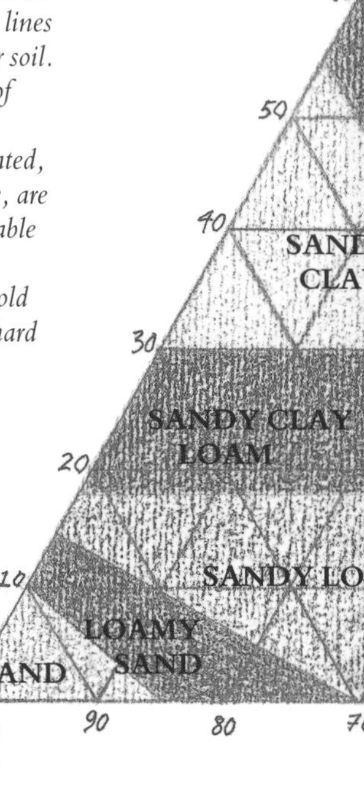

Weathering of rock creates new soil at a typical rate of a fifth of a ton per acre per year. At the same time, the land is constantly eroded, offloading soil into lowland plains and the sea. Erosion is a natural and necessary process that takes place all the time – and takes your garden soil, too. In natural habitats, where the soil is well stabilized by permanent vegetation, erosion losses are small. But tilled soils lose material at a fast rate – most farms, for instance, lose at least 12 tons per acre per year, and a few may even lose as much as 100.

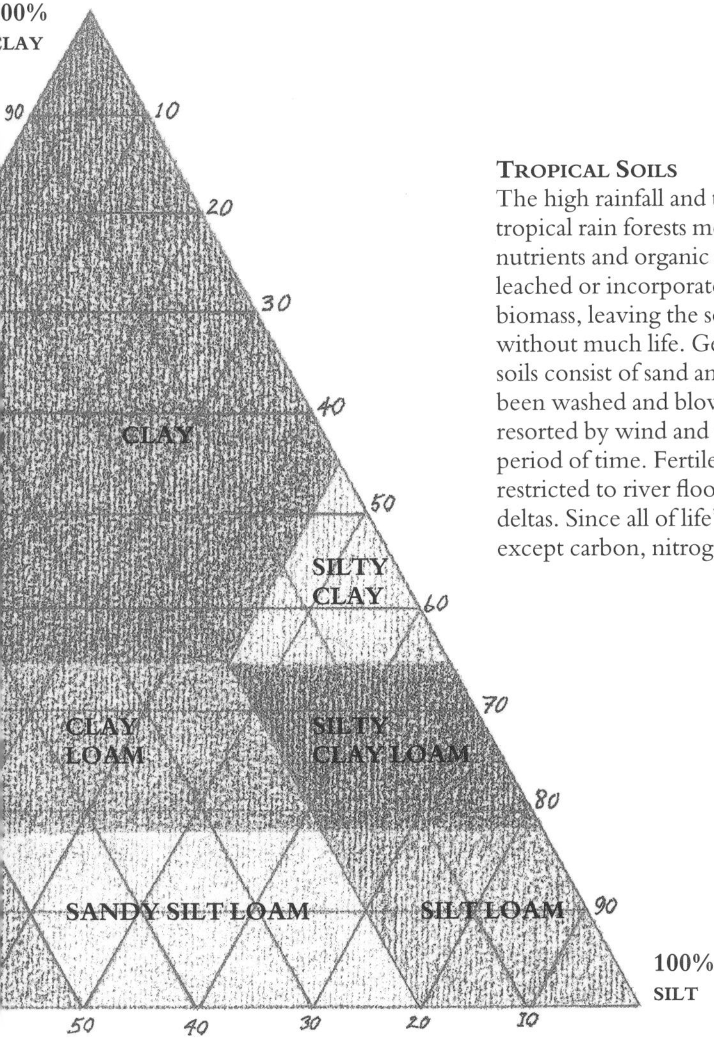

Tropical Soils

The high rainfall and temperatures in tropical rain forests mean that nearly all nutrients and organic matter are either leached or incorporated into the biomass, leaving the soils very poor and without much life. Generally, tropical soils consist of sand and clay that have been washed and blown, sorted and resorted by wind and water over a long period of time. Fertile soils are often restricted to river flood plains and deltas. Since all of life's elements, except carbon, nitrogen, oxygen, and hydrogen come ultimately from rock, the absence of glaciation (see below) in most parts of the tropics is a severe limitation on fertility. Furthermore, during the dry season, organic matter is oxidized by the heat, if not actually burned in fires. The soil is then easily blown away by the wind or washed away by the subsequent torrential rains. Useful tropical soils must be protected by trees, ground cover plants, and deep layers of mulch.

In the temperate and colder regions of the planet, glaciation has played a major part in the creation of soil and may even hold the key to long-term planetary soil fertility. Glaciation produces large amounts of silt as well as clay, sand, and gravel (see above). Temperate soils are frequently characterized by a large proportion of silt. Usually thick and full of various minerals in differently sized particles, they are influenced by the constant input of organic matter from both leaf fall or the die-back of grasses. They support a thriving network of living things which circulate the nutrients and create a fertile medium for plant growth. Such soils make excellent farmlands, to the extent that in many areas the original vegetation type has been almost entirely replaced by a cultivated but radically different ecosystem.

Organic matter, which breaks down more slowly in temperate soils than in the tropics, helps to protect against soil erosion, either as a surface cover or as part of the humus. It does not form part of the mineral element of the soil, but reacts intimately with sand, silt, and clay, and plays a key role in ameliorating their least beneficial properties by improving water retention, drainage, aeration, and nutrient capacity.

The soil in your garden will probably consist of about 50 percent solid material (particles of clay, silt, and sand, and organic matter) and 50 percent space. When the soil is wet but fully drained, the space is half-filled with water, which covers the particles in a thin film. The other half of the space is filled with air, which plant roots need for respiration. Poorly drained soils can be fatal to many plants because their air spaces become waterlogged and lacking in oxygen.

Soil is far more than a random collection of mineral and organic particles separated by air spaces and coated with water. The way the particles are arranged greatly increases the potential for organic activity in the soil. In moist temperate climates, plant roots and earthworms interact intimately to produce crumbs of a critical size. These crumbs are derived from worm casts, which are 0.16in (2mm) in diameter – just twice the length of the plant root hairs responsible for the uptake of nutrients.

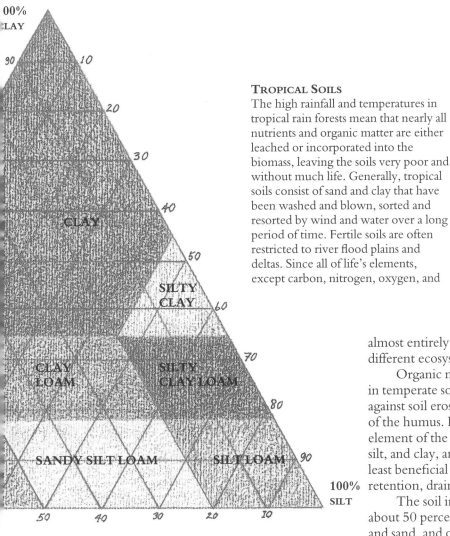

Large spaces, or "macropores", between the crumbs ventilate the soil and enable water to drain freely and quickly. A fertile garden soil has a good ability to drain; and soils with earthworms drain between four and ten times faster than soils without them. Tiny "micropore" spaces within each crumb can hold enough water for root hairs to draw on between successive showers of rain.

Undisturbed soil naturally forms layers, except for soils that have been worked by earthworms. A network of interdependent relationships between different processors characterizes each layer. Plowing and turning the soil upside down disrupts this network because it buries most of the soil fauna living in the top 1–2in (2.5–5.0cm).

A good topsoil is essential for healthy crop plants. Profiles of topsoils vary but in general a surface covering of coarse organic matter protects the richest, finest, and most active layer, where a large majority of soil organisms live. Often shallow and occasionally absent, this covering merges into the true soil below and needs a constant supply of decomposing organic matter from above. The bulk of the topsoil, which is usually between 4 and 12in (10 and 30cm) thick, should be well aerated by earthworms, and full of soil bacteria and small invertebrates. In addition, it should be well drained, easy to work, and dark in color owing to a high organic content. With all these ingredients in place, the topsoil becomes more and more fertile and, consequently, the place where most plants gain their nutrition.

The subsoil usually consists of the same mineral material as the topsoil above but there will be less air, less nutrients, and less soil life. Bedrock or clay will increase its density, thereby preventing adequate drainage from the topsoil. Coarse sand or gravel will increase its porosity, thereby causing the topsoil to suffer heavily in times of drought.

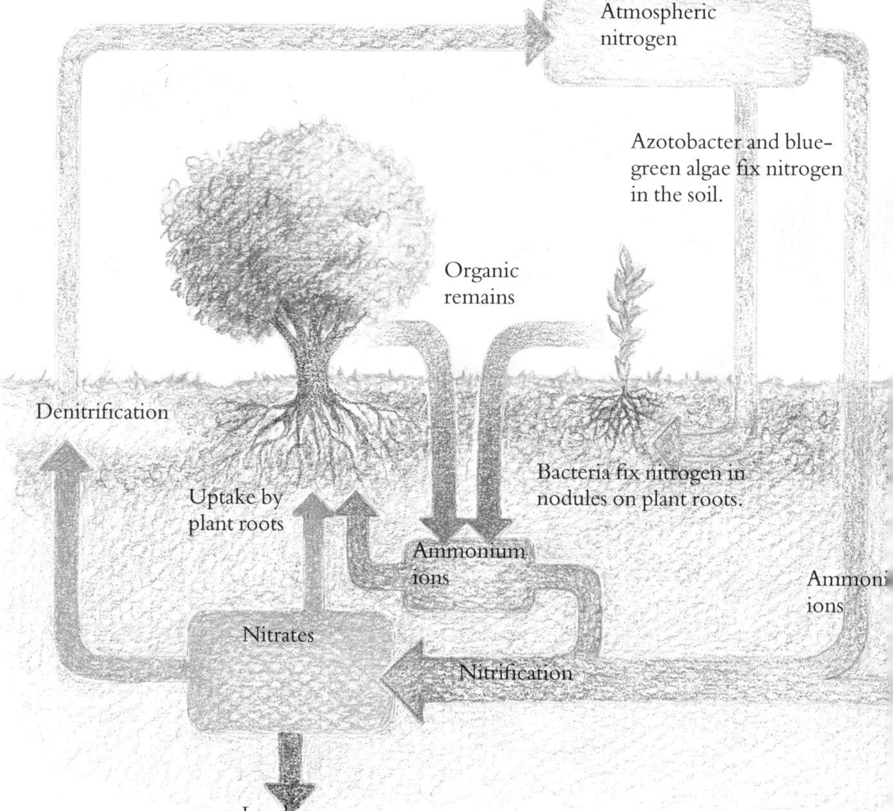

The nitrogen cycle
A few soil organisms "fix" nitrogen from the air and, in the process, ensure that the entire biosphere is able to function. Nitrogen is needed by every living thing because it is a vital ingredient of proteins and nucleic acids. A number of other organisms make sure that the nitrogen does not accumulate either as organic remains or as a pool of unused inorganic nutrients. As a result, the nitrogen circulates throughout the biosphere.

Bacteria, such as Azotobacter, *and blue-green algae turn nitrogen from the air into ammonium ions in the soil. Bacteria in root nodules make nitrogen directly available to their host plant (*Rhizobium *is associated with legumes, for example). Bacilli, Enterobacteria, and other microbes turn the nitrogen-containing compounds in animal feces and other organic remains into ammonium ions. In acidic soils, these ions are absorbed by plants; in aerated and not particularly acidic soils, nitrifying bacteria convert the ions into nitrates. Nitrates are taken up by roots, lost through leaching in the soil, or denitrified by bacteria and returned to the air.*

Nutrients for Plants

The huge range of soil processors supply plants with all the fertility they need by making nutrients available from mineral particles. If you remove plants from the soil you remove nutrients, too. They must be replaced with organic matter so that the processors are well nourished and can carry out their role. Hence, the maxim: feed the soil, not the plant (see p. 104).

Of all the mineral elements necessary for plant growth, carbon and oxygen come directly from the air. Nitrogen comes from the air via the soil and hydrogen comes from water, while all other nutrients, such as potash, phosphorous, magnesium, sulfur, calcium, manganese, iron, copper, zinc, and molybdenum are provided by the soil itself.

The character of soil life is conditioned by many factors, not least the availability of nutrients, which is affected by the acid-alkaline balance of the soil (see below and p. 105). Of these the most important is usually nitrogen, which is needed for proteins and nucleic acids. When the nitrogen level of the soil is low, nitrogen-fixing bacteria (see p.30) are stimulated, while at high levels these bacteria are inhibited.

The deficiency of any mineral element can affect plant growth, and the relative amounts in a soil can determine which kinds of plant will grow. One reason for this is that, because minerals diffuse through the soil at different rates, one type of root system may not be as good as another at exploiting a given situation. Nitrate ions, for example, diffuse quickly so a plant needs only a loose but extensive root system to colonize a large volume of soil. Phosphate ions, on the other hand, diffuse 10,000 times more slowly so that local supplies are quickly absorbed and exhausted. As a result, plants that tolerate low-phosphate soils develop a dense network of roots and mycorrhizae that "search" for phosphates.

Bacteria in animal faeces

Ammonium ions

Acid-alkaline balance

Plants have trouble absorbing enough nutrients unless the soil has the right acid-alkaline balance, or pH. The best pH for garden plants in temperate soils is 6.5, although 5.5 to 7.5 is adequate for most. The pH will vary considerably throughout a soil. Surface mulch, for example, tends to be more acid (i.e. has a lower pH) than the rest of the soil.

Rainfall and mineral composition largely determine the pH of a soil. Higher rainfall increases leaching, which normally makes a soil more acid. Pure rain does not alter soil pH, but acid rain will reduce it to 4 or even 3. This dissolves aluminum from rock and poisons the ecosystems concerned. Vegetation can also affect soil pH – conifers, for example, are noted for their tendency to increase the effects of acid rain.

Minerals may be bound up either as insoluble compounds or too closely to soil particles to be extracted. A change in soil pH can alter this situation. The chart shows the influence of pH on the availability of elements in organic soils (the widest part of each band indicates the greatest availability).

The optimum pH in which the elements (except manganese) become more soluble – and therefore more available – is 6.

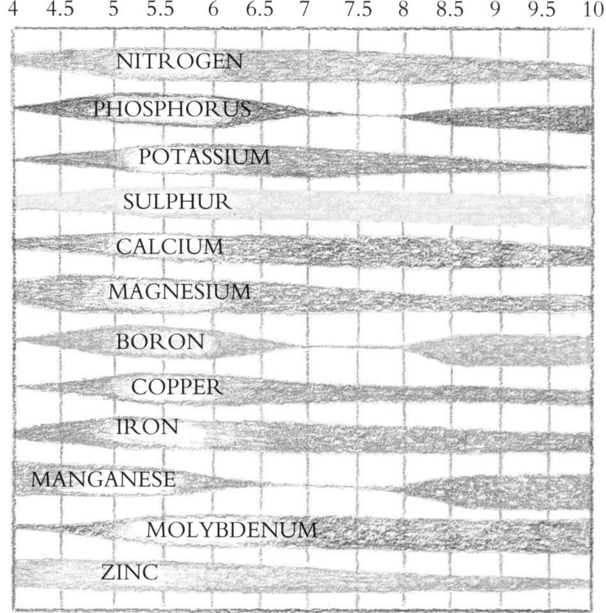

The Role of Consumers

Although consumers actually play a marginal role in the economics of terrestrial life – and hence your garden – they do have a use. They bite off chunks of food (plant or animal), chew it, partially digest it, and produce feces that are perfect for most of the microbial decomposers. This is why organic farmers prefer mixed arable and stock – herbivores process plant material to a form that microbes can readily turn back into plant food. In its lifetime, a herbivore produces an enormous mass of feces – far more than its individual biomass (see diagram). Herbivores, therefore, help the plant-decomposer system function more efficiently; and carnivores keep herbivore populations down, so preventing them from overgrazing the vegetation – while in the process providing further feces for the decomposers.

Herbivores have, during the course of evolution, overcome the immense difficulties in extracting nutrients from plants. Each herbivore species has worked on its own method and has become intensely specialized. Herbivores, then, tend to be far more fussy about their food sources than carnivores. Very often a herbivore will feed only on one species of plant and then on one part of the plant, whereas carnivores can eat almost any meat that comes along. Generally speaking, carnivores are predators – they kill their prey completely before eating it. Herbivores are grazers – they remove tissue but they do not actually kill the plant.

Balance of Nature

In the battle between predator and prey, or plant and herbivore, evolution often reaches a kind of balance. European oaks, for example, are notoriously rich in tannins and seem reluctant to give anything away. As a result, their leaves take a long time to decompose, so making leafmold with oak leaves a slow business. The heartwood also resists decay, which is why oak has always been in such demand for building houses and ships, and is now favored for fenceposts. And yet hundreds of insect species have specialized in oak, each with its own particular slot in the tree's vast anatomy. Oaks have become entire ecosystems in their own right.

The balance between plant and herbivore may sometimes be tipped in favor of the herbivore. We can think of locust plagues, overgrazed pasture, the failure of deforested areas to regenerate because of sheep or rabbits, and cabbages reduced to lace by an attack of caterpillars. But these are exceptional cases. The world is still, for the most part, green. Natural vegetation seems to stay well ahead of the grazers.

In fact, plants respond actively to being grazed. They redistribute their resources, they mobilize their reserves. They are able to increase the rate of photosynthesis in the undamaged leaves; they can produce defensive chemicals on the spot, quite apart from the ones they have all the time. They can increase the size of remaining seeds when some are lost. Some research has reported higher yields of cabbages after a modest attack by caterpillars. Plants have been around a long time. They are well prepared for herbivores.

But what about pests? Garden pests are bound to be herbivores of one kind or another, which means the carnivores that eat herbivores should be a gardener's allies. We ourselves are top-of-the-market omnivores. We insist on only the finest, starch-rich, proteinaceous, succulent produce – big fat seeds and fruits, huge storage organs .... We have bred plants to provide all this, taking care to breed out many of the qualities (spines, coarse skins, bitter tastes) that make plants unattractive to grazers. This is just asking for trouble! If we find it easy to digest this stuff, so will any passing herbivore, and many an omnivore, too.

Farmers and gardeners, it seems, have made it too easy for herbivores. But there is little prospect that the human race will pick a particularly unappetizing species that no other creature wants to eat, and then develop special enzymes to digest it. Our only option – and the insidious treadmill of chemical pesticides is not an option – is to understand the ecology of our pests and their predators, and work with them toward a balanced system. Then, we can use our knowledge of animal feeding strategies to get the carnivores on our side: our interests are different, but at least we can make them complementary.

Fungal-feeding Mites

For at least 400 million years, mites have been farming fungi in the soil. In so doing, they aid the breakdown of plant leaves by a succession of fungal species. Each fungus, however, produces antibiotics that can prevent the growth of the next species and, in effect, slow down the decomposition of the leaves. The mites disperse the fungi before this happens.

Each species of mite specializes on a particular species of fungus. The mites graze on fungal filaments and excrete the spores in their feces. The spores germinate in a ready-made pile of fertilizer and establish new fungal colonies in new locations. The ingenious element in this strategy is that the mites package their feces in gut lining impregnated with chemicals. These chemicals prevent the germination of the spores from other species of fungus and thereby ensure the mites' own fungus is propagated.

A sexton beetle (above) can bury dead animals in the ground as a food source for its developing larvae.

A resupinate fungus (below) actively decomposes the tissues of an elm tree and recycles essential nutrients.

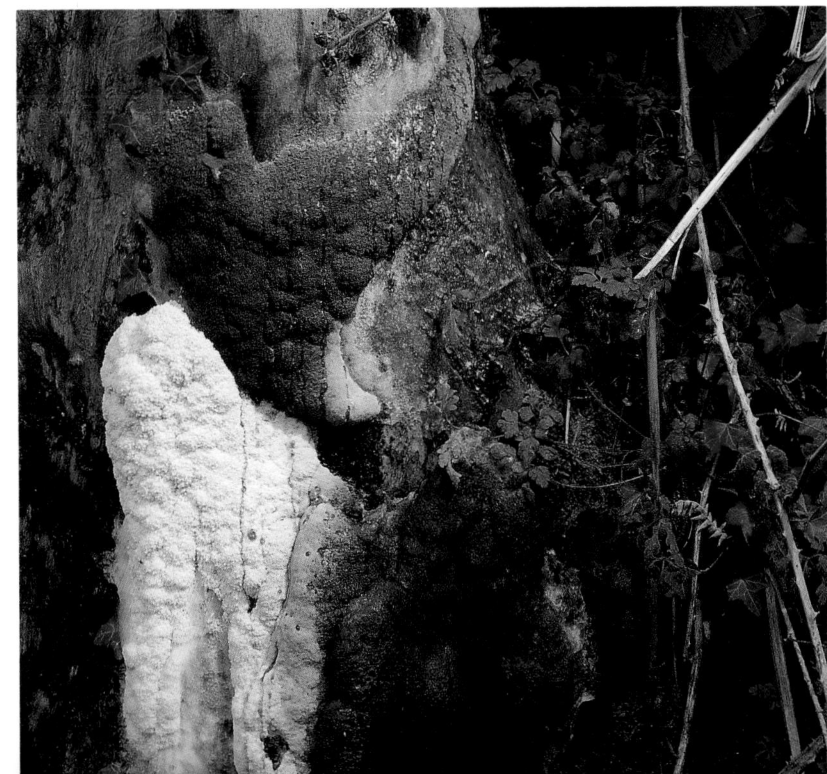

Climate: a Source of Variations

Your garden is powered by sunlight, largely through the photosynthetic agency of plants. Nearly all the sun's energy that reaches the Earth does so as visible light, and nearly all of this is converted ultimately into heat. We would therefore expect sunlight and temperature to correspond closely and it probably would if the planet was flat and featureless. But the Earth is spherical and covered in diverse terrain; it also rotates once a day on an axis that tilts away from the planet's plane of orbit around the Sun. As a result, latitude is the most important single factor in determining how much light and heat your garden receives through the year. Latitude sets a baseline for climate, too, by shaping patterns of rainfall and temperature. Since heat and water largely determine plant growth, the way these two factors interact profoundly influences the nature of vegetation at different latitudes.

For the gardener, the cycle of the seasons is both delightful and problematic. The typical snapshot of a vegetation type tends to show it "in its prime". But this is only half the story. The cycle of favorable and unfavorable seasons produces great changes, and each change is characteristic of that vegetation system. Broadly speaking, seasonal changes in the tropics revolve around periods of wetness and dryness which plants use to synchronize the phases of their life cycle: when to put out or drop leaves, or when to start flowering. As a rule, tropical plants enter a dormant state during dry periods.

In temperate latitudes, the seasons are marked by hot and cold periods, and by changes in the length of

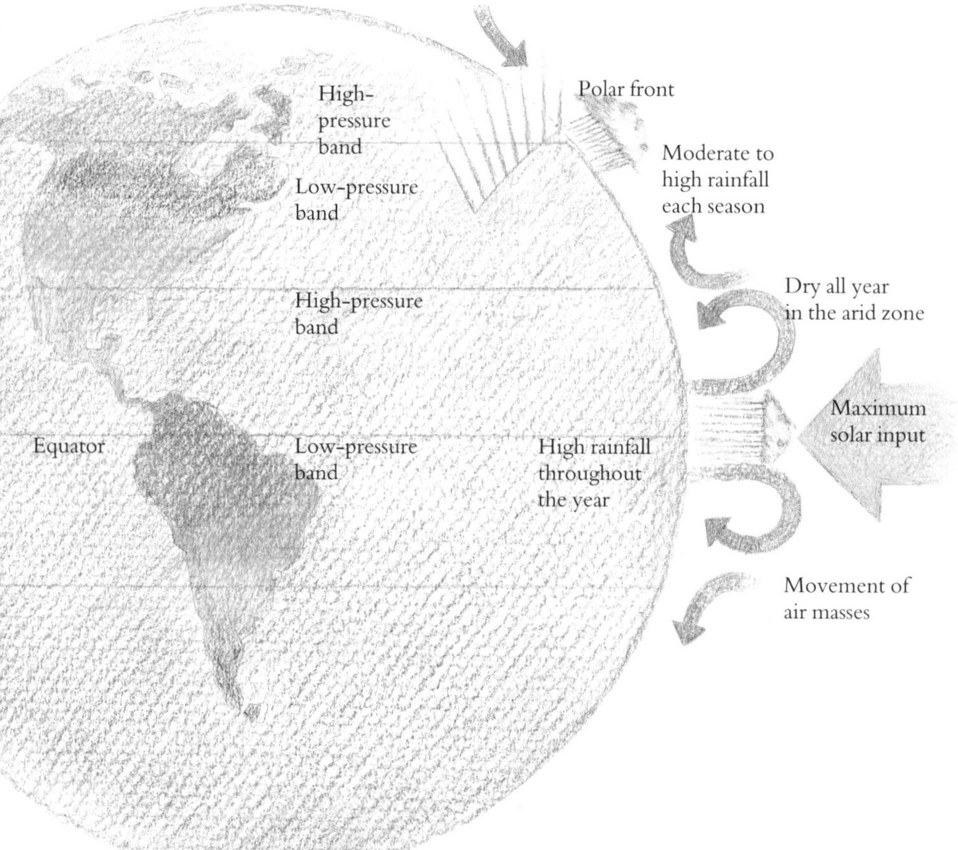

Bands of pressure
The daily rotation of our planet about its axis, coupled with the input of energy from the sun, sets up alternating bands of pressure in the atmosphere. These bands affect the movements of enormous masses of air and provide us with a baseline weather picture for the planet (right). A low-pressure band at the equator, where solar input is greatest, gives a high level of rainfall throughout the year. A high-pressure band at about 30 degrees latitude generates an arid zone between the seasonal tropics and warm temperate regions. A low-pressure band around 60 degrees latitude is accompanied by moderate to high rainfall throughout the year. A high-pressure zone over cold polar regions, where solar input is lowest, keeps precipitation to a minimum year-round.

day. As a result, plants tend to use temperature and changing day-length to synchronize their activities. Increasing day-length, for instance, tells them that spring is on the way and they had better get on with growing and flowering. By contrast, decreasing day-length warns them winter is approaching and that now is the time to store those hard-earned nutrients and become dormant.

The melting pot of the Earth's climate provides a complex and never-ending source of variations that the plant kingdom has learned to exploit. The daily and annual behavior of our planet generates fluctuations in both the atmosphere and oceans that set the pattern for winds, temperatures, water currents, air pressures (see illustration, left), and rainfall. This pattern establishes a number of climate types, including tropical rainy, dry, and cold humid climates. Mountains and other topographical features, combined with winds (see below), seasonal variations, and the proximity of land to seas, lakes, and oceans contribute to regional climates and help to establish the various biomes of the Earth (see pp. 40–1).

Topography provides one of the most important influences on the distribution of plant types. Topographical features, such as mountains, affect the climate of a region by altering the patterns of temperature and rainfall. This is due to the impact of altitude – the higher you go the colder it becomes – and the changes in the flow of air carrying heat (or cold) and moisture (or dryness).

The Power of Wind

Wind interacts strongly with topography and has a great effect on climate. Wind may bring moisture, dryness, searing heat, pleasant warmth, bitter cold, or any mixture of these in the course of the seasons. A plant's basic adaptation to harsh wind conditions, such as those on mountains and cliffs, and in deserts and the tundra, is to be short, thereby experiencing only the low windspeeds near the ground. In extreme cases trees, such as the southern beech in Tierra del Fuego (right), may become deformed or grow almost horizontally in the lee of a natural windbreak.

Apart from increasing evaporation and wind chill, winds can have other damaging effects. The very strong winds of tropical hurricanes, for example, can destroy plants by uprooting, mechanical damage, and sandblast. They can also erode soil. Near sea coasts wind can cause leaf scorching and the deposition of salt.

The direct effect of elevations in the land's surface is to mimic higher latitudes. Air temperature falls by approximately one degree Celsius for every rise of 600ft (200m), so going a few thousand feet up a mountain in the tropics is a bit like going on a journey of thousands of miles toward the nearest pole. You would pass successively from tropical forest through temperate-type broadleaf woodland, pine forests, a tundra-like zone of mosses and lichens, and finally arrive at an equivalent of a polar ice cap. Although the plant communities colonizing a mountain have adapted to the cooler climate, they are nevertheless drawn from the local stock.

Mountain environments are so complex that they are usually given a whole biome of their own; and they do have their own special flora, which gardeners know as alpine plants. But the plant communities on a mountain can usually be related to lowland "equivalents", and the montane zones can broadly be equated with lowland climatic zones.

Currents in the oceans and atmosphere are the circulation systems of the planet. They transfer heat from one part of the globe to another, creating and modifying regional climates. When different temperatures in the atmosphere cause areas of high and low pressure to form, winds are generated and water vapor gathers and then falls as precipitation, usually rain. But rainfall is not the only factor that determines how dry a place is; the other is evaporation (see right), which has a lot to do with temperature. Precipitation and evaporation interact to give a pattern of humid and arid zones from the equator to the poles (see illustration, p. 34). These two factors largely determine the climate and natural vegetation in each region of a continent.

The hot, wet equatorial zone, for example, has an uninterrupted supply of warmth and moisture, making it virtually perfect for plant growth. Other climates cannot live up to this largesse: they fall short, either of warmth or of moisture, or of both. Extreme situations occur in the polar regions, which are permanently too cold for almost anything to live, and in deserts, which are permanently too dry. All other regions are favorable to plant growth for at least some of the time.

A tropical thunderhead cloud over the sea (above) illustrates the large-scale convection currents at work in the atmosphere. Such currents broadly determine the amount of rainfall at various latitudes. The sculpted rock at Bourke's Luck potholes beside the Blyde River in South Africa (top right) demonstrates the power of water to erode the land. Below-zero temperatures fashion a frozen landscape of ice, snow, and running water in a cool temperate realm (bottom right).

WATER SOURCES

Fresh water makes up just 3% of the Earth's total water volume – the rest is salty. About 75% of fresh water is held as ice in glaciers, permafrost, and ice caps; 14% is groundwater, and only 1% is surface water in lakes and rivers. The actual soil water available to plants makes up a mere 0.06% of the total fresh water. But tiny proportions do not signify lack of importance. Water vapor, for example, represents only 0.001% of the total volume of the atmosphere, but without it there would be no rain, rivers, or lakes, and the land would be a howling desert. Likewise carbon dioxide makes up a mere 0.035% of the total volume of the atmosphere, yet it is one of Gaia's key metabolic gases. Water reaches the soil as precipitation from the atmosphere – as rain, snow, fog, or dew. Water in the air over land arises mostly from evapotranspiration. This is the combined loss of water through evaporation from the soil surface and transpiration from the leaves of plants. If precipitation exceeds evapo-transpiration, plants will receive plenty of water; but if the opposite is the case, the soil will gradually lose water until plants must take countermeasures or risk desiccation and death.

THE BIOMES OF THE EARTH

We can divide our planet into a dozen or so biomes – climatic regions with characteristic communities of plants and animals. Each biome has a certain "look". If you visit another outcrop of your own local biome in another part of the world, you may be surprised how familiar the terrain looks. Stepping closer, the plants have familiar forms and distribution. But when you move really close and try to identify the plants you may be surprised to find they are completely alien to you. This is because the plants in different parts of the world have different evolutionary histories. They may be doing the same jobs, be adapted to the same conditions, play the same role in their community, as the plants in your biome back home, but they are likely to have quite a different pedigree.

As gardeners will appreciate, no plant can do anything and grow anywhere. No plant can put up with drought and flood, salt and frost, and still hold its own with other plants that specialize in those conditions. In many ways it is not easy being a plant and there is strong pressure for each species to have its own strategy and its own special adaptations. The net result is that each habitat, each climatic zone, each biome of the Earth, has its own special set of plants.

Anyone living in a climate that is hot and wet throughout the year will know what an enormous variety of plants takes advantage of the conditions. Together, the plants and the climate create tropical rain forests throughout the equatorial zone: dense evergreen canopy, tall trees, many climbers and epiphytes, a very large variety of plant and animal species. But from a gardener's point of view the soils are very poor and fragile.

If you live at higher latitudes, your garden will experience the effects of seasons. Periods of wetness and dryness give rise to a different kind of forest, usually deciduous and with a more open canopy. Such tropical seasonal forest is found in South America either side of the rainforest belt, in East Africa, India, IndoChina, and northeastern Australia. Some regions have long dry periods that give rise to savanna, characterized by a mixture of grassland and drought-adapted trees, such as acacias, and home to large herds of grazing mammals. Savannas are found most notably in Africa, but also in Australia and Brazil.

Beyond the savanna, usually between latitudes 20 and 30 degrees, the climate becomes really dry because the atmospheric circulation produces a belt of high pressure with no source of moisture. The rain is occasional but unpredictable; and because the temperature is high, evapotranspiration easily outstrips precipitation. The result is desert, fringed with a semi-arid, seasonal grassland. This is a difficult environment for plants, although they have come up with many remarkable solutions to the problem. Characteristic desert flora are succulent, deep-rooted plants. As seeds, many annual opportunists wait their chance, often for years, for a suitable moment to burst forth, flower, set seed, then retreat again into dormancy. Farther to the poles, the deserts are colder, and plants have to cope with frost as well as a lack of moisture. Desert soils are usually poor in nutrients, and may be salty and alkaline.

If you live in a temperate grassland biome – prairie, veld, pampas, or steppe – the balance between precipitation and evaporation will be improved. Your garden will experience a large daily and seasonal temperature range, and summers will usually be dry. As with savannas, no-one is sure whether these grasslands are really natural. They may be the product of centuries of grazing and fire.

Gardens at still higher latitudes not only have to put up with wetter conditions (as precipitation outstrips evaporation) but also an increasingly cold climate. Coniferous trees, such as spruce, fir, pine, and larch, have become adapted to the cold conditions and form large forests known as taiga, or boreal forest. Little grows under the trees except a specialized community of lichens, mosses, and woody perennials. Boreal forest exists only in the northern hemisphere in an almost unbroken strip across Alaska, Canada, Scandinavia, and northern Russia.

At the highest latitudes on the edge of the polar regions, the climate is too harsh for trees: temperatures remain low all year and water is frozen except for a brief thaw in the summer when all plant growth must take place. This is the tundra. Plants adopt a low-growing habit to keep out of the wind. They grow

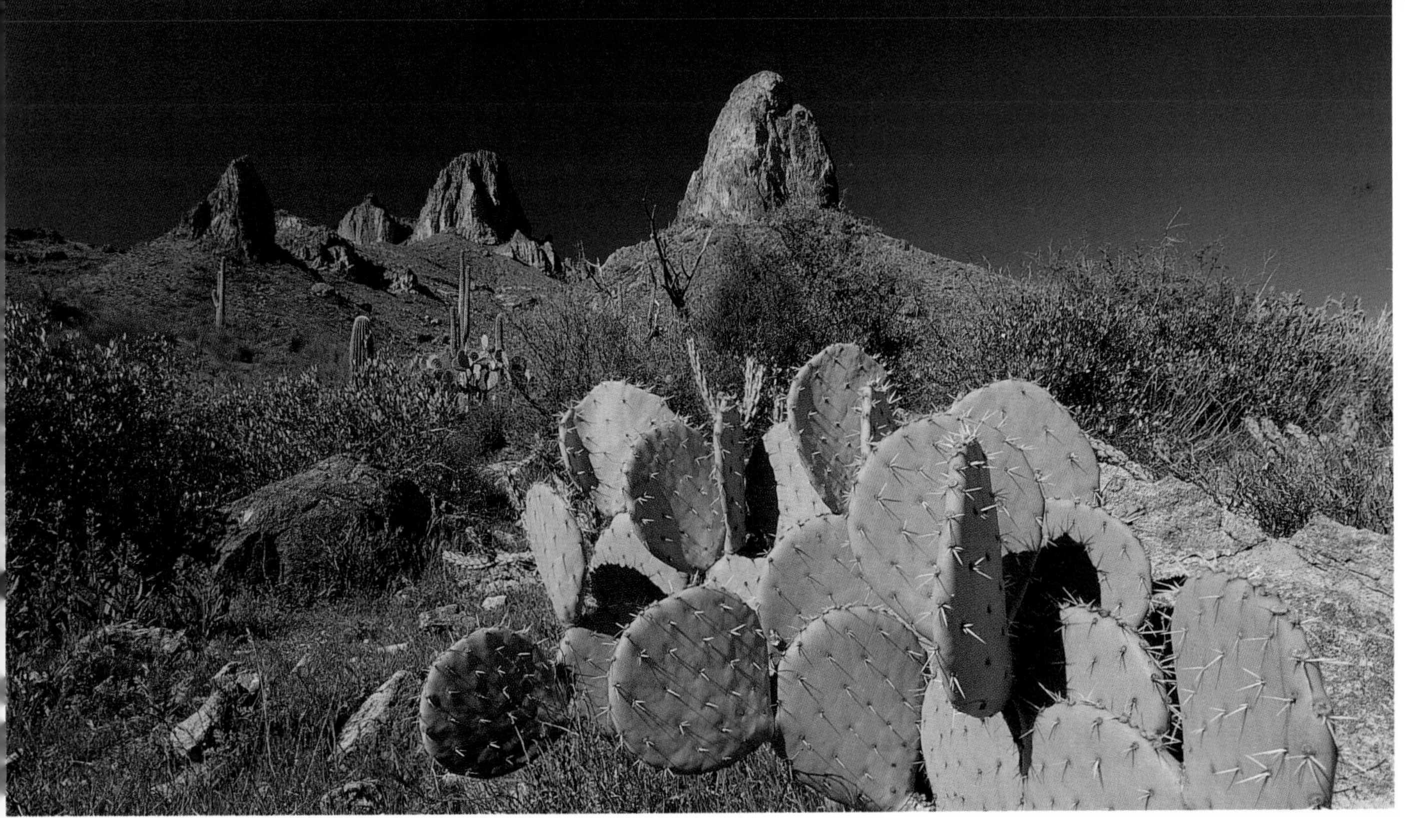

The arid conditions of the desert/semi-desert biome provoke drought adaptations from plants. Like many cacti, the prickly pear (above) has no leaves and its stem not only stores water but is covered in a thick cuticle to prevent evaporation.

slowly and are almost invariably perennials, since the growing season is not long enough for annuals to complete a seeding cycle. Non-flowering plants, particularly mosses and lichens, form a greater proportion of the flora than in any other zone. Beyond the tundra lies the polar desert, which is both too cold and too dry for life. In 400 million years of evolution on the land, only lichens seem to have cracked this problem.

If you live on the western or eastern seaboard of a large continent, you will know how much the oceans change the story. In the warm temperate zone between latitudes 30 and 45 degrees, the climate is less dry than in the interior – the west coast has a dry summer, the east coast a dry winter. From a plant's perspective, dry summers are harder to cope with because evaporation is much higher when the weather is hot. This leads, in western areas, to a zone of evergreen, drought-adapted plants also able to cope with occasional frosts. In this "Mediterranean" type of climate, plants tend to be shrubby and thick-leaved, and give rise to a particular kind of terrain known as chaparral. Apart from the Mediterranean area itself, this vegetation type is found in coastal California, central Chile, the Cape area of South Africa, and southwestern Australia.

The equivalent band of latitudes on the eastern margin of a continent has moist summers and temperate rain forests, deciduous forests, or evergreen mixed forests. Such vegetation is found in the southeastern United States, eastern China, eastern Australia, southeastern Brazil, and eastern South Africa.

The western seaboard of a continent in the cool temperate zone has an "oceanic" climate dominated by unpredictable polar weather fronts and the perpetual struggle between ocean and continental weather systems. Here, people joke "we don't have any climate here, just weather". Rainfall is plentiful throughout the year, the winters are mild, yet frost is almost inevitable. Summers may be cool, weather erratic, and skies cloudy. The vegetation is deciduous, or mixed evergreen and deciduous, temperate forest and is found in northwest United States, northwest Europe, and the west coasts of Tasmania and the South Island of New Zealand. The vegetation is similar on the eastern margin of a continent which generally has hot summers and severe winters.

Biomes of the world

Wherever you are in the world an underlying climate pattern determines the type of plants that will flourish not only in your garden but in the whole region around you. A regional climate type with distinctive flora and fauna is called a biome. The biomes in this may are organized into nearly 200 biogeographical provinces, and distributed throughout the world's eight biogeographical realms (Nearctic, Palaearctic, etc.).

Biomes are not homogeneous. They contain a range of local habitats – rivers, wetlands, woods, meadows, hilltops, and so on – which together create the region's biodiversity. The concept of the biome can be deepened further into a bioregion when the human cultural dimension is considered at the same time as the biological features.

Tropical rain forest
Temperatures between 20 and 28°C; rainfall always above 60in (1500mm); soil poor.

Subtropical/temperate rain forest and woodland
Higher than average rainfall promotes luxuriant forests.

Tropical dry forest
Warm year-round; dry season causes many trees to lose their leaves.

Boreal forest (taiga)
Hot summers and very cold winters; low rainfall; lots of snow; poor acidic soil.

Temperate broad-leaved forest
Steady rainfall throughout the year; winter frosts; trees deciduous; soil good.

Mediterranean
Winters cool and moist, summers hot and dry; alluvial soils rich, scrubland poor.

Warm deserts/semi-deserts
Little annual rain; hot year-round; nutrients almost completely absent from soil.

Cold winter deserts
Little annual rain; hot summers, cold winters; few nutrients in soil.

Tundra
Winters very cold, summers have a short dry season; peat and humus accumulate in soil.

Tropical grassland/savanna
Wet and dry seasons; warm throughout the year; soil poor in nutrients.

Temperate grassland
Cold, frosty winters and hot, dry summers; good soil with rapid recyling of nutrients.

Mixed mountain systems
As altitude rises so biomes change almost in parallel with increases in latitude.

Mixed island systems
Varied vegetation and climate but prominent as reservoirs of a unique biodiversity.

Lake systems
Freshwater biomes shaped by the inflow of sediment and dissolved minerals.

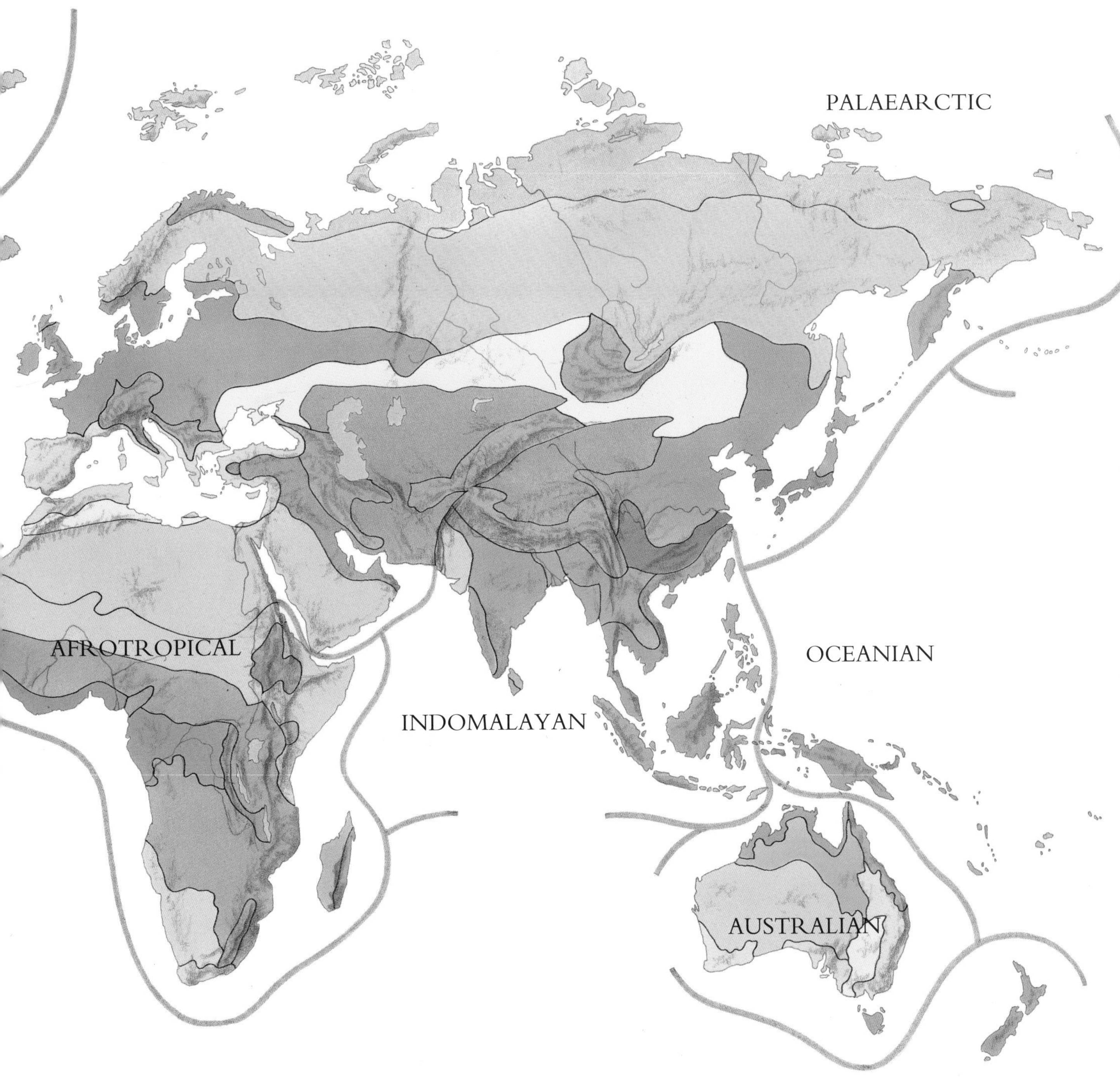
PALAEARCTIC
AFROTROPICAL
INDOMALAYAN
OCEANIAN
AUSTRALIAN

ANTARCTIC

Variations in Microclimate

The climate of your garden is unique. No other location integrates the same environmental factors of latitude, altitude, aspect, orientation to the sun, rainfall, distance from the sea, exposure to the wind, and so on. If you ask yourself a whole series of questions about your garden (see Questionnaire p. 43) the answers you give will provide you with a profile of its bioregional qualities.

If you look at your garden you will immediately see the existence of a number of microclimates: slight variations in the conditions, such as brightness and shade, exposure to and protection from the wind, have resulted in different plants thriving in different places – often in the space of a few feet or even inches. At almost any scale there are local differences in the daily and seasonal patterns of essential resources, such as light, warmth, moisture, oxygen, and nutrients; or of noxious factors, such as acidity, salt concentrations, frost, and toxic compounds. Even the pattern of decomposers and consumers will vary. So at each scale the diversity of these factors produces yet another landscape and another community of organisms.

Let us take a habitat type, such as deciduous woodland, and focus even closer. Imagine a strip of woodland 300ft (100m) wide, and a few hundred yards long, stretching from a stream bed up the side of a valley to a ridge. As in any habitat, variations in the conditions will be both systematic and random. Systematic variations include the gradual rise in altitude, from the cool shade on the valley bottom to the exposed, light but windy conditions on the ridge. The habitat is moister beside the stream, drier near the ridge. More random differences include rocky outcrops and abrupt changes of slope which affect the depth of soil and local soil moisture content. There may be frost-free hollows where leafmold and a richer soil accumulate. Where trees cannot grow an opening in the canopy will allow sunlight to reach the understorey and the ground. The orientation of the valley to the sun and its relation to the prevailing wind direction will determine on which side of trees and rocks certain mosses, lichens, and epiphytes will grow. Tree species will be a major influence on the

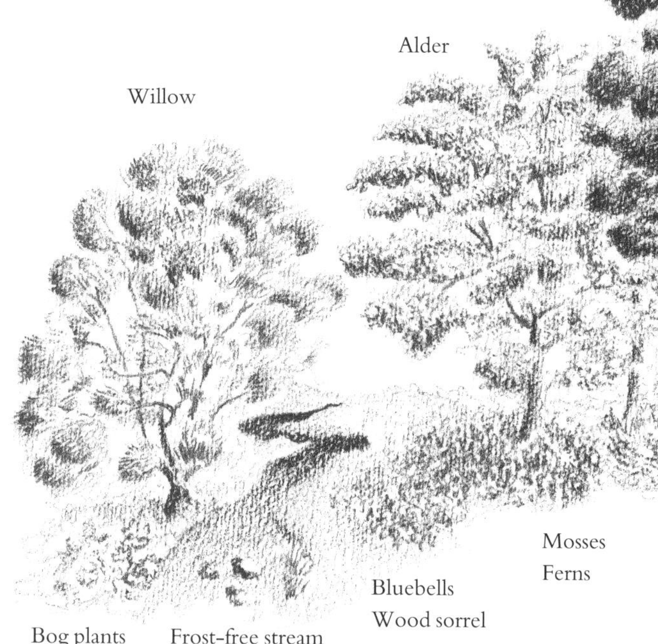

community of associated invertebrates, as well as the acidity and nutrient status of the soil. Fallen trees will attract particular groups of decomposer organisms. Floods may bring gully erosion, exposing fresh soil for colonization by fast-growing species, creating a new microhabitat.

Now shrink yourself to the size of a mouse and you will enter another "forest", the herbaceous jungle. Like the woodland habitat as a whole, this has its own set of microclimates and is far busier in terms of the diversity of animal life. The "ground" is less distinct; it is rougher, going through layers of litter until it becomes soil. Even here, nooks, galleries, caves, rocky walks, and purpose-made tunnels fashion a mini-landscape. The fauna graze on swards of moss and lichen, forage for seeds and spores, and feast on carrion and dead plant matter. Flowering plants are giants, growing in relatively shady conditions and casting yet more shade. Where conditions are just too shady and uncomfortable for flowering plants, the mosses, ferns, lichens, and liverworts take over. These plant groups like the damp, and need it to reproduce: after more than 300 million years on the land, they still rely on water to bring their sperm and eggs together.

A strip of woodland
The profile of a temperate deciduous woodland strip, some 300ft (100m) wide and a few hundred yards long, reveals the kind of variations that generate microclimates. Rocky outcrops, for instance, prevent trees from growing and create frost-free hollows, while the stream attracts water-loving plants, such as willow and alder.

When you shrink yourself even more to the size of an ant or a mite, the mosses themselves become trees. A huge variety of living things becomes visible. The distinction between on-the-ground and in-the-ground is just one of degree. The temperature and humidity are more reliable deep down – it's air conditioned. There's plenty to eat, and plenty of creatures to eat you! The main snackbars are the "rhizospheres" around the roots of plants: sugars and proteins ooze out of root tips, vast networks of fungal filaments stretch off into the soil and into the roots, and beasts of all kinds graze on the filaments and feed on each other. The main microclimates here – and we're getting very micro – center around the distribution of water. The air spaces between soil particles are generally very humid, but surrounding each particle is a thin film of water. Some of the soil creatures are so large in comparison with soil particles that they are oblivious to all this – they just shoulder the stuff aside. Smaller creatures are essentially sloshing about knee-deep in the surface films, and yet smaller ones are swimming about. At this scale, the ubiquitous presence of fungi and bacteria is overwhelming. Chemistry comes into its own and is all important. The smell must be awful. Small variations in pH or osmotic balance can make a lot of difference to which animals thrive and which struggle to survive. Torrential rain and flooding up above could waterlog the soil and cut off air supplies: as oxygen in the air spaces is used up, aerobic organisms would suffocate.

Questionnaire

Ask yourself detailed questions about your garden and the region where you live. Try to build up a profile of your local climate and habitat: itemize any special or general features, and any links to other parts of the Earth. Remember, your garden is a little piece of Gaia and everything in it is interconnected and part of the whole biosphere. The following questions will start you off:

- How high is your garden above sea level?
- What is its average annual rainfall?
- What is its minimum winter temperature and its maximum summer temperature?
- What biogeographical realm do you inhabit?
- What sort of biome do you live in?
- What other biomes are similar to yours?
- Which wild plant species have recently become extinct in your area? Are any endangered?
- What plant species are, or have been, traditionally cultivated in your area?
- What are the native tree species in your area?
- What geological processes produced your scenery?
- What was the land like one million years ago? 5000 years ago? 100 years ago?
- Was your garden covered by an ice-sheet 15,000 years ago?
- How old is the rock under your garden?
- What sort of rock is it? How hard is it?
- What is the pH of your soil? Are there pH variations in your garden?
- What is the chemical composition of your soil? Are any nutrients lacking?
- Where does your tap water come from?
- Where does your waste water go to?

A PARTNERSHIP WITH NATURE

People are as much a part of Gaia as the birds, bees, whales, and trees – and just as entitled to be so. Yet there is a problem. Despite our relatively recent arrival on the scene, we are already shifting the balance of the Gaian control systems that have evolved over billions of years. To us, nature has always been dangerous and unpredictable. Humans have never really felt secure, in spite of all our efforts. Safety, comfort, status, and pleasure were embraced only in an artificial realm where nature had been tamed. This chapter explores the balancing act between the human and the natural order, of which the garden is the clearest model.

The earliest humans were hunter-gatherers who, as they spread out over the Earth, developed many patterns of basic subsistence. Except possibly in grassland habitats (see below), these patterns scarcely impinged upon the environment let alone upset the balance of an ecosystem. In climates where plants grew abundantly throughout the year, people were mainly gatherers with largely vegetarian diets. In harsher climates, where plants grew slowly and were sparse or inedible, early people would have lived at least partly off the wild animals that had done the hard work of collecting and converting the plants. In extreme cases, such as deserts, humans would have lived almost entirely on a carnivorous diet.

The Neolithic Revolution

Regardless of its subsistence pattern, every culture must have noticed how food plants germinated from seeds in middens, either from rejected meals or excreted from the human gut. Nomads with a regular migration cycle almost certainly found some of their favorite food plants flourishing at a former settlement. A little enterprise and experiment would have enabled early people to cultivate plants on purpose.

At first, this cultivation would have been on a small scale, of little economic importance, and probably carried out by women. It was, perhaps, the earliest human activity we could call gardening. As yields increased, cultivation became a viable alternative to hunting and gathering, and this early gardening turned into farming. It required that people stay in fixed settlements. It also allowed an increase in population, but this meant that there was no going back to the old ways, which could only support small numbers. Some historians have argued that agriculture was a kind of trap into which Paleolithic societies stumbled without realizing the implications until it was too late.

Crop yields improved first by inadvertent, then intentional, selection of the best seed strains. Since the crops were in a fixed spot and needed looking after, territoriality and competition over land became an issue. Furthermore, the cultivators started to change the environment to meet their needs (see Giraffe and Beaver analogy, right).

Growth in populations brought food raids and, consequently, a warrior caste to defend the crops – this caste often became a powerful elite. At the same time, increased productivity allowed more social specialization, with the formation of an administration centre (often run by priests) to distribute food. Settlements eventually became villages, towns, cities....civilization.

This is a highly partial sketch of one of the great turning points in history, otherwise known as the Neolithic Revolution. From subsistence, no-growth, egalitarian, matriarchal, Earth-centered, goddess-worshipping, cyclical, mobile societies dominated by their environments, humanity moved largely to progressive, growth-oriented, hierarchical, patriarchal, sun-god-worshipping, territorial patterns; eventually bringing forth cities, written language, standing armies, division of labor, sophisticated technology; and totally dominating its environment. It is a curious thought that, in a certain sense, all this came from the deliberate act of cultivating of plants, from gardening.

The Rise of the Garden

Gardening remained inseparable from farming until people created a plot of land, often bounded by a wall or a fence, close to their dwellings. The garden became part of the domestic system, an enclosure with practical and symbolic functions. It would mark territory and conserve privacy; its management and size would have social significance; it would grow edible crops protected from weather, stray animals, or thieves; it would be the most intense, manicured part of a holding, a human statement of control over fickle nature. Desert cultures illustrate this point very clearly: life flourishes intensely in tiny pockets wherever there is water; high walls mark a dramatic contrast between the wild desert scrub on the outside and the lavish care given to plants within the walls. Such gardens were both useful and recreational.

The first gardeners, who hailed from Egypt and Mesopotamia, were deliberate in their actions: they placed a tree, such as a seedling fig or grapevine, so that it cast shade beside a house; they tended and nurtured plants not only to eat as food but to flavor meat. Medicinal herbs to remedy ailments and cure disease were raised in special gardens, particularly in China. Soon, gardens became leisure areas or playgrounds for the rich: the Egyptians, at least by 1500 BC, grew plants for their flowers alone in decoratively designed gardens; the Assyrians and Babylonians cultivated large parks for pleasure and hunting – a theme the Persians adopted in their "paradise" gardens.

The Greeks adapted the Persian influence and created inner courtyards decorated with a few trees, plants in containers, and several statues. From the 1st century BC, the Romans elaborated upon the Greek courtyard, developed the farmhouse, or villa rustica, and firmly established the garden as an integral part of the home.

In pre-Columbian America, the Incas cultivated fruits, vegetables, and plants that produced poisons, dyes, and contraceptives. The Aztecs of Mexico, who flourished some 700 years ago, had a passion for

The Giraffe and the Beaver

To clarify the two basic attitudes to the environment, let us put forward two symbolic creatures, the giraffe and the beaver. At some stage in their evolution they both encountered problems with trees – they were either the wrong size or shape, or in the wrong place. The giraffe changed itself, developing a long neck that enabled it to browse on the leaves at the tops of trees. By contrast, the beaver learned how to change its environment, cutting down and rearranging trees to construct dams and lodges in which to live.

In the course of history, we can see how we have steadily shifted from being hunter-gatherer giraffe-people to farming, gardening beaver-people – and beyond. Early humans adapted their behavior to their environment; later development of efficient tools, language, and the power to pass on knowledge to future generations meant that we could change and influence our environment.

Most unmodified environments present extreme difficulties to survival – not just for humans but for any organism. So it is not surprising that we used the power of cumulative knowledge and technology to change the world to suit ourselves. As we became beaver-people, we bent the energies of the biosphere in our direction. Populations grew and we bent the biosphere a little more. Without anyone noticing we went beyond the point where we could become giraffe-people again.

Modern food systems are the climax of millennia of compulsive beavering – indeed, of going beyond beavering to the point where we are not simply altering our environment, we are devastating it. Many people recognize the process must stop and there is a growing movement toward a hybrid tribe of giraffe-beaver people, who aim to live in a way that is both sustainable and forward-looking.

decorative flowers and developed elaborate terraced and floating gardens. Elsewhere in America, native societies developed sophisticated horticultural and agricultural techniques, and Europeans brought their own when they colonized the territory.

By the 18th century, landscaped gardens, as epitomized by the work of Capability Brown in England, and the grand designs beloved by the French, were leaving an indelible impact on Europe. But the interest in plants for their own sake or particular use, as opposed to building blocks in garden design, had already become established. The medieval herb gardens of European monasteries had evolved into physic gardens, such as the Chelsea Physic Garden that opened in London in 1673.

From Renaissance times onward, expeditions sent by European powers to colonize the world often brought back plants, such as tobacco. Many other exotic plant species found their way into botanical gardens where they were admired and grown either for their decorative qualities or for their curiosity value. And from the orangery, which was designed specifically to acclimatize citrus fruit trees, came the greenhouse and the sunroom.

The Mughal emperors of India, renowned for their great love of nature, created many beautiful gardens. The Mughal painting (left) depicts artisans at work in a four-square garden – the squares are divided and irrigated by a channel of flowing water.

The Japanese karesansui, or dry landscape garden lacks water and relies on rocks and raked sand for its beauty. Raking the lines, as at the Nanzenji Temple, Kyoto (below), opens up an infinity of parallel lines that are ideal for meditation and contemplation.

The gardens of Alcazar in Seville, Spain (top right), and the ordered box parterres at the Château of Villandry near Tours, France (bottom right), demonstrate the aristocratic desire for formality and display that has dominated the Western garden tradition for centuries.

Bending the Biosphere

Today, a few human groups, such as the Inuit, are still able to live successfully in their unaltered natural environment. As giraffe-people (see p. 45), they are immensely skilled, but knowledge and understanding are more important: we might say that they live more by science than technology. The rest of humanity has chosen, or been obliged, to exploit the immense powers that distinguish us from other animals. With the technology that these powers created, we daily bend the biosphere in order to feed ourselves. The question is – and one repeated throughout this book – how much, and in what way, can we bend the biosphere without breaking it?

The least harmful, and probably the most natural, way of bending the biosphere is shifting cultivation with small populations. The slash-and-burn techniques used by such rainforest peoples as the Yekuana of Venezuela (see illustration) epitomize the temporary replacement of the natural ecosystem with gardens and fields. When the nutrients in the soil are exhausted, the cultivators move on, clearing a fresh piece of ground and allowing the natural climax ecosystem to re-establish itself on the "used" land.

From a human point of view this system is arguably the most ecologically sound way of improving productivity. Provided the ratio of people to land is small enough, the system can be sustained indefinitely and its impact on the environment is small and readily absorbed. In ergonomic terms, too, the system is highly efficient – the crops yield far more energy than the people use to grow them. Shifting cultivation need not be limited to rain forests. Any genuinely wild habitat, whether in a forest, grassland, desert, mountain, swamp, or coast, is capable of supporting small populations of shifting cultivators.

Shifting cultivation is usually practiced on soils that are too poor to support a permanent agricultural system. They need time to regenerate, to recover from their brief period of cultivation. Where soils and climate permit, however, permanent replacement systems have been developed, allowing the growth of ever-larger human populations. Many traditional polyculture systems, such as the gum arabic cycle (see

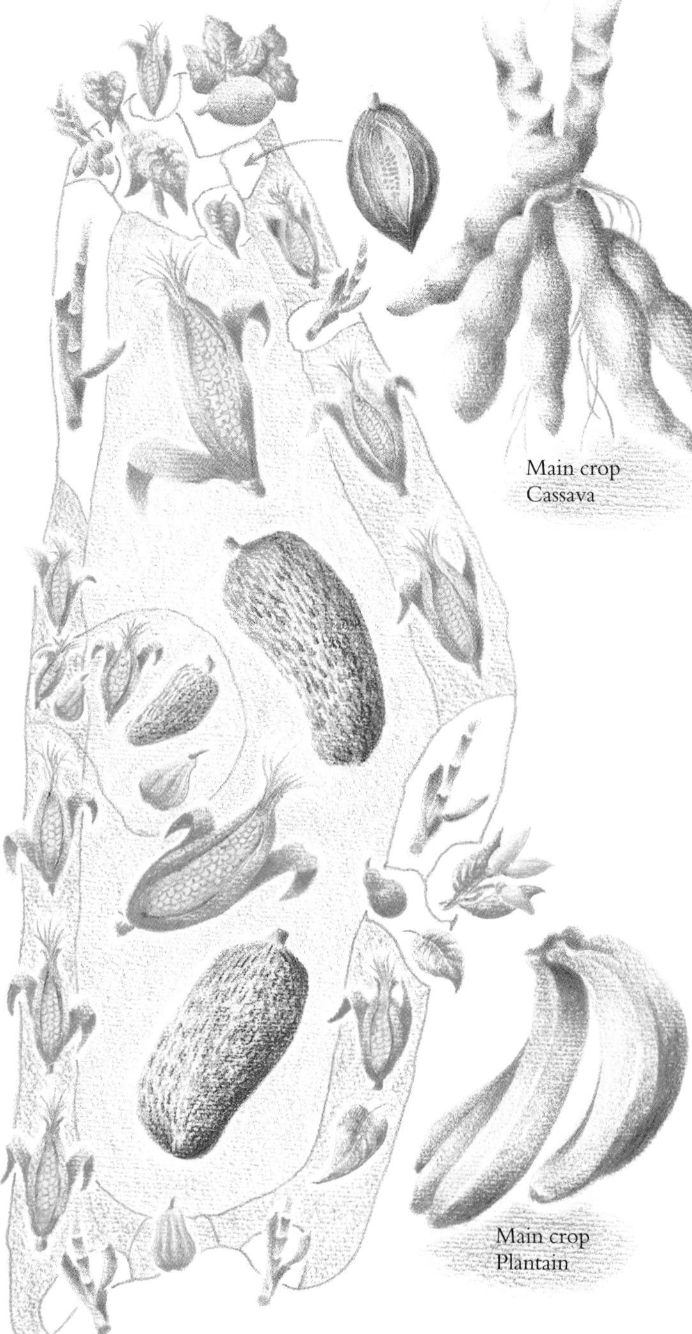

Yekuana Indian forest garden
In the rainforest of southern Venezuela the Yekuana Indians rely on shifting cultivation to provide their diet. First, they make a clearing by felling and burning most of the trees, and then plant selected food plants – either on their own or in mixed stands in the ash-fertilized soil. The garden is tended and harvested regularly for a few years, until the nutrients in the soil are exhausted and the plot is abandoned. In addition to cultivating crops in their forest gardens (see above), the Yekuana use more than 60 food plants.

Slash-and-Burn Energy Ratio

When anthropologist Roy Rappaport analysed the energy inputs and outputs of a slash-and-burn system in New Guinea, he found that the energy ratio was about 10:1. In other words, ten units of energy were derived from the food for every unit put into growing it. Furthermore, each unit put in was entirely human labor and therefore "renewable". Compared with various industrial food production systems, which may have a ratio of 1:20, slash-and-burn is far more efficient.

Bananas and yams are grown side by side in a garden in Papua New Guinea's tropical rain forest (above). Such intercropping of two productive plants is a fundamental feature of agroforestry, in which food and other crops are planted among naturally growing tree species to satisfy local needs.

Gum Arabic Cycle

Traditionally exploited in the semi-arid climate of Sudan, the gum arabic cycle links shifting and permanent cultivation. A small area of the scrub of a leguminous tree, *Acacia senegal*, is burned and planted with high-calorie crops, such as sorghum, for about four years. The trees are left to regrow for about eight years and are then tapped for gum arabic for five to ten years. They also supply forage for animals; seeds for food; root fibers for rope and nets; wood for poles, implements, charcoal, and firewood. When the trees die, the cycle begins anew. Staggering several plots gives a continuous supply of all the tree's products.

p. 49) practiced in Sudan and the home gardens of Java, provide attractive models for low-input, sustainable food production. In some cases, they blend so well with the local ecosystems that they may be difficult to distinguish from the natural environment. This quasi-natural structure of polycultures is almost a guarantee of stability and sustainability, and is the basis of many permaculture designs (see p.56).

The alternative to polyculture is monoculture, which offers a potential gain in productivity at the risk of over-exploiting what the environment can sustainably provide. For instance, attempts by the citizens of ancient Mesopotamia to "double crop" their hinterlands ended in failure because such intensive cultivation overworked the soil and consequently was unsustainable. As a result their empire crumbled.

But there can be sustainable monoculture systems, as four thousand years of Chinese agriculture amply demonstrates. In Britain, too, when the rulers encouraged the almost total deforestation of the country in the early Middle Ages, the farmers were fortunate that the climate was temperate and the soils were glacially enriched. These two factors allowed a transition to a stable kind of farming, the kind which has led, step by step, to many of the farming and gardening methods we practice in the West today.

The Influence of People on the Landscape

Although plants clearly dominate the landscape – they account for over 90 percent of living tissue on Earth – they are easily influenced by humans and animals. Grasslands, for example, would probably be forests were it not for huge herds of grazing herbivores. Increasing numbers of ecologists and paleo-anthropologists are coming to the conclusion that the world's major grasslands are not natural ecosystems, but have been modified by prehistoric peoples, mainly by using fire, to maintain a landscape suitable for easily hunted game.

More recently, we have taken this heroic landscape management a step further by converting many of the former grasslands to extensive arable croplands. The Great Plains of North America, for example, were probably once covered in forests until early people gradually transformed them into prairie between 20 and 30,000 years ago. The original fauna gave way to large ungulates (mostly bison) which were semi-domesticated. Europeans eliminated the bison and transformed the prairie into cropland, which was very productive for people, less so for wildlife. Recent evidence, however, suggests this pattern is already in the process of reversal – people are moving off the land and wildlife is returning.

Around one-quarter of the Earth's plant productivity is now "managed", but only a fraction of this is directly useful to people. In many areas this management has changed the flora, fauna, and soils to such an extent that the original habitat cannot be identified. Some managed habitat types are agreeable and diverse; others, such as the garrigue of the Mediterranean or the scrubby areas of cleared rain forest in the tropics, are unstable and tend to degenerate into eroded and unproductive land.

Human activity has now reached the stage where we have bent the biosphere almost to breaking point: we are threatening the world's natural vegetation. In the name of farming we are decimating forests (see p. 51); polluting the biosphere with fertilizers, pesticides, and insecticides; congregating vast herds of grazing herbivores that desertify the soil and prevent the resurrection of indigenous plant species; growing monocultures of such crops as wheat that, because of their genetic homogeneity, are vulnerable to disease and environmental changes; abandoning the primitive cultivars, or land races, of traditional crop plants; and forcing into extinction wild varieties of useful crops, thereby forsaking a crucial and irreplaceable storehouse of genetic diversity.

Perhaps most disastrous of all is the loss of soil and fertile ground. Human activity is now speeding up soil erosion so much through poor agricultural practice and deforestation that it is causing huge changes on a global scale. Overall soil erosion outstrips soil creation by a factor of two. Shortage of land for growing food (some estimates put the global loss of such land at about seven percent every decade) may curb the expanding human population sometime next century, causing social and political upheavals.

People versus Trees

For hundreds of millions of years, most of the Earth's land has been covered by trees – it has always been the fate of most bare ground ultimately to become dominated by forest. Around 20 to 30 million years ago, when the world was much warmer than it is today and ice caps were absent, forests took a hold even on Antarctica and beech trees grew in Greenland, Siberia, and Spitsbergen. The British Isles played host to sequoias, figs, palms, magnolias, cinnamon, and many genera, such as *Araucaria* (the monkey-puzzle tree), now associated with the southern hemisphere. Subsequent cooling of the globe brought enormous sheets of ice from the poles and forced trees to grow in lower latitudes of the Earth. This pattern continued despite cyclical periods of warmth called interglacials. To cut a long story short, trees occupied much of the land that would later be inhabited by people. In the last 2000 years, as human populations increased in size, they started to replace the forests.

At present, there are still more trees than people, but the balance is tipping. The global human population is expected to double, or even treble, before it starts to level off. And people need land, timber, and fuel. It is inevitable that many of the remaining forests will also disappear in their natural state. Yet we know that the cost of this process is high: carbon dioxide is released as the trees are felled and the forests burned; erosion increases on high ground while flooding and siltation devastates the valleys and floodplains; local weather changes – usually for the worse; unique ecosystems collapse as species lose their habitats, causing an overall reduction in biodiversity; and forest cultures die out and with them irreplaceable ingenuity and botanical wisdom.

Throughout the million years or so of humanity's existence, the environment has seemed incomparably larger than us and all our works. Until the last hundred years, it has been inconceivable that we could actually make a serious difference. But the world has changed. We have cleared forests, ploughed up virgin lands, built huge irrigation schemes, and drained wetlands. Our numbers have increased to unprecedented levels. We have brought to a rousing climax the Neolithic project of gaining control over the environment, and now we are beginning to ask whether we might have overdone it. Certainly nobody is afraid of the environment any more; instead, we fear *for* the environment.

The tree of life universally represents the powerful link between heaven and earth. In an engraving dated 1640, two priests nourish the tree of life at Zeus' sanctuary of Dodona at Epirus, Greece. According to Homer, this tree had the power of oracles and could communicate its message by rustling its leaves.

It is also increasingly clear that the various changes we have wrought in the environment for the benefit of humans are not necessarily for the best in the long run. We need to understand the whole system of Gaia and to apply intelligent regulation to allow sustainable enjoyment of her resources. And yet such essential regulation and restraint is at odds with the short-sighted and exploitative temper of modern industrialism.

A virtual monoculture of deep blue lavender graces a multitude of acres in Provence, France. The plant's aromatic oil is an essential ingredient of fine perfumes and cosmetics. One native and revered variety, known as "Super bleue", grows only above 2500ft (800m) and needs arid conditions during the spring. But, since the 1980s, a mystery disease has accompanied a change to rainy spring weather and threatens to decimate the crop.

In a scene unchanged for thousands of years, majestic coastal redwoods allow sunlight to penetrate the forest's canopy and illuminate the misty realm below. These coniferous evergreens, which belong to the cypress family and are the world's tallest trees, thrive in the fog that periodically blankets the coast from southwest Oregon to central California. Their remarkable fibrous bark, which may reach a thickness of 12in (30cm), can resist insects and fungi as well as fire.

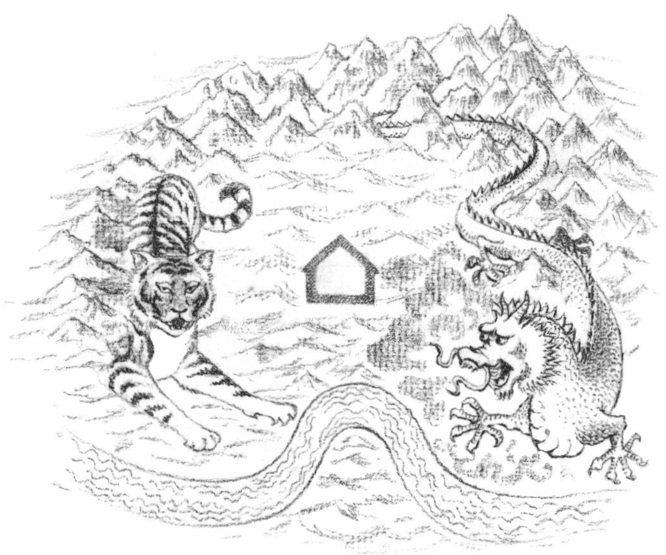

According to the ancient Chinese art of feng-shui, the ideal site for a house and garden is halfway up a mountain with a commanding view and with water nearby. Yin and yang, the two opposite but complementary forces of the world, are strongly featured. In the drawing, yin is represented to the west by a "white tiger" hill and yang to the east by a slightly higher "protective dragon" hill. The mountain stream in the foreground channels ch'i, the life-giving dragon's breath, through the site.

A Sense of Place

Practical and concerned people face a dilemma. We know that the Earth can get by quite well without us and we realize we are not contributing much to the wellbeing of Gaia. Just by being here we seem to be something of a problem. But we are not going to go away. Nor are we going back to the Middle Ages, much less the Stone Age. Somehow we have to find modes of life that are both sustainable and acceptable to the reasonable aspirations of humans everywhere. One part of this exploration must be a recognition of the importance – sanctity is not too strong a word – of non-human life that does not discriminate against genuine human interests.

There happens to be a useful model for this balancing act between the human and the non-human. It is the garden. A garden, by definition, is an artificial construction. Yet, also by definition, it has natural elements. We can imagine a continuum from the almost entirely "created" garden to that which bears only the lightest imprint of human interference. The natural garden is a celebration of the myriad ways in which nature interacts with culture between these two extremes.

A positive yet subtle impact that humanity has had on the land comes from the cultural history of the people who have settled it. Each human group has its own diet, crops, stock, traditions, and settlement pattern. Cultural sentiment creates a kind of second skin for natives in their homeland and is often reinforced by some physical feature which is woven into the folklore and imagination of all who live near it: Mount Fuji, Lake Baikal, the Grand Canyon.

On a smaller scale a "sense of place" can gather around a local feature: a rocky outcrop, a grove of ancient trees, a bend in a river, a waterfall, a distinctive hill, a gorge, or a viewpoint. Even without such obvious markers, each place – and this includes your garden – may be far more distinct than we think. Studies of birdsong and other sounds in remote areas of the United States revealed that places as little as 300ft (90m) apart had distinctive acoustic properties. In Britain, an instrument-maker took an aeolian harp (a harp played entirely by the rising and falling of the wind) to a number of places and found that each place produced a special quality of melody which he could not attribute merely to the strength of the wind. In Australia, the aboriginals undertake long journeys over unfamiliar territory, guided by "songs" that correspond exactly to the terrain. These songs are not word-pictures, but are echoes of an ancestral dream-time that somehow reflect the distinctive sound quality of a place. An innate empathy with plants and landscapes cannot be claimed as the inheritance of any one people or culture. Just as the Celts possessed a tree cult, which often manifested itself in a sacred grove around a spring, so the Chinese evolved the art of feng shui, which enabled them to shape the landscape according to its inherent earth energies.

So to resolve the dilemma we should be looking for sustainable approaches to building, agriculture, and horticulture that grow out of each region's distinctive climate, materials, and human culture. We should try to make each place different, not the same, and to rediscover our roots. And if the original roots have withered into oblivion, we must develop new ones. This is the basis of bioregionalism – achieving a living link with a particular place, using its resources respectfully and sustainably, and complementing its natural uniqueness.

Natural Gardening

To a large extent, gardening and farming share the same theories and practices – they also share the same pathologies. Like farmers, gardeners often use artificial fertilizers to bolster productivity, treat weeds and pests as enemies to be eradicated with poisons, view nature as a number of different parts instead of a whole, underestimate the vitality of soil, and so on.

Far from being a brand new approach to horticulture, natural gardening relies on integrating the ideals of sanctity of place, self-healing, collaboration with nature, and good, old-fashioned productivity. In practice, it draws its inspiration from a rich array of sources: ancient farming and gardening practices, tribal and cultural understanding of the environment, a compendium of gardeners' folklore and common knowledge, soil science, biological science, permaculture, biodynamics, and the various strands and approaches of organic gardening.

The following review of some of the major modern gardening movements gives some idea of the background to natural gardening.

Orthodox Organic Gardening

In less than a generation, organic gardening and farming have emerged from obscurity and derision to acceptance and respect. The absence of hard-and-fast rules has led to a rich variety of approaches, many of them complementary and differing only in personal interpretations. In general, they can be categorized according to one important distinction: that is, whether their adherents practice either "negative" or "positive" organics.

Negative organics involves no substantial change from traditional gardening methods, except to abstain from chemical inputs or to replace chemical inputs one-for-one with an organic substitute. Positive, or "deep", organics focusses on the health of the whole system, fostered by careful management, composting, the maintainence of healthy soils, and the use of physical, biological, and organizational, rather than chemical, control of pests and weeds. Perhaps the most familiar slogan of organic gardeners and farmers is: feed the soil, not the plant. In the case of farming, the positive organic approach also embraces the humane treatment of livestock, sound labor relations, local marketing, and minimization of energy inputs.

Organic gardeners who are not economically dependent on their produce often allow their garden system to move and develop in a more naturalistic, less controlled direction. The results of this so-called ultra-organics are often at the expense of yields, but the system explores the limits of the standard organic techniques and creates a richer and more varied habitat. Ultra-organic gardeners tolerate weeds, use no chemicals whatever, and are generous with patches of wild habitat in between cultivated plots.

No-dig Gardening

Digging, the gardener's answer to plowing, may be unnecessary and even harmful. Digging is not a feature of nature. The contents of the soil are moved around by worms, ants, and burrowing mammals, but are rarely turned over en masse. Critics of digging point out that bringing fresh soil to the surface allows long-dormant seeds to germinate, oxidizes nutrients, and damages soil structure and drainage. Consequently, no-diggers lay down plastic sheets or thick organic mulches to suppress the growth of weeds, then sow seeds or plant directly into the ground. The repertoire of most no-dig practitioners (but not Masanobu Fukuoka, see below) also includes nylon carpets to suppress weeds, the foliar feeding of plants, and even the use of herbicides. Apart from the absence of digging, the system is not particularly natural, but it works well enough.

Natural Farming

The uncompromising Japanese farmer, Masanobu Fukuoka, says of his natural farming methods: "I have sought to demonstrate the validity of five major principles: no tillage, no fertilizer, no pesticides, no weeding, and no pruning." The philosophical tenor of his approach can be judged from the opening sentence of one of his books: "Natural farming is based on a nature free of human meddling and intervention. It strives to restore nature from the destruction wrought by human knowledge and action, and to resurrect a humanity divorced from God". The results appear to be remarkable. Although Fukuoka's system produces a variety of crops in abundance, its primary purpose is sacramental – "the purpose of life is to know the purpose of life" – and its overall objective is based on the belief that the process of growing plants is an end in itself.

Permaculture

Pioneered in 1974 by two Australians, Bill Mollison and David Holmgren, permaculture (from *perma*nent agri*culture*) had as its goal the design of "an integrated, evolving system of perennial or self-perpetuating plant and animal species useful to man". Exasperated by the blindness and greed of the energy-expensive, mechanistic, and soil destructive actions of Western agribusiness, Mollison and his colleagues designed a complete, sustainable, low-energy, high-yield, agricultural system that could be adapted to suit any climate.

Permaculture has developed into a worldwide movement and a broad-based approach that goes well beyond gardening and farming to designing systems for communities of housing and trade. It has a strong and explicit ethical basis, and adherents of permaculture are adamant that people must make fundamental changes in their perceptions of how to conduct their lives. Moreover, these changes must incorporate the need for a positive, active contribution to the wellbeing of the world. How do you start to make this change? Bill Mollison, in the 1992 publication *Permaculture – A Global Perspective*, advises "...start with your nose, then your hands, your back door, your doorstep. If you get all that right, then everything is right. If all that is wrong, nothing can ever be right". Permaculture draws on old and new knowledge, and is widely used to refer to any agrosystem, such as the Guatemalan tropical garden/orchard system, that shows evidence of intelligent integrated design. The term "permaculture" would embrace most of the content and examples discussed in this book and has been linked with 'Edible Landscape', which was developed in the United States.

Biodynamics

Rudolf Steiner, a German mystic and founder of anthroposophy, believed that a deeper reality lies behind the world of everyday appearance. His perception of this inner world prompted Steiner to elaborate the ways in which it affects and influences the ordinary world in such spheres as art, architecture, and education.

Following a series of lectures on agriculture which he delivered in 1914,

Permaculture pioneer, Bill Mollison, sits on a footpath bridge that spans a swale (left). The swale is a means of capturing excess winter rain.

A vortex with a deep crater (right) is essential when stirring the ingredients of a biodynamic preparation. One such preparation, BD 500, should be briskly stirred – alternating quickly from one direction to another – for an hour. The overall aim, as biodynamic founder Rudolf Steiner (inset) intended, is to draw in supersensible forces from the cosmos and the centre of the Earth.

Steiner and his disciples developed biodynamics. Today, this movement flourishes in many parts of the world, particularly in Australia, where more than a million acres are farmed biodynamically.

Most biodynamic gardening and farming comes down to good husbandry and is, superficially, indistinguishable from organic methods. However, concepts of early chemistry, astrology, homeopathy, and so on give it a "magical" rather than a scientific quality. The importance of such influences is illustrated by the "biodynamic preparations", the most common of which is known as BD 500. This preparation is sprayed on to land to improve soil structure and plant growth (see pp. 254–5).

Skeptics will be surprised to discover that the effects are remarkable: in one year, BD 500 can alter soil structure in a way that would take nature a very long time, or the constant addition of organic manures between five and ten years. It is important to stress that these effects are not directly caused by the biodynamic preparations as such – like homeopathic remedies, there is far too little of them for that. The preparations are designed to stimulate the emergence of other forces – cosmic, telluric, bacteriological, fungal, etc. – that bring about the observed changes.

Bio-intensive Gardening

Developed in the US by Alan Chadwick, a disciple of Rudolf Steiner, bio-intensive gardening combines numerous ideas from biodynamics and the intensive market-garden systems found around Paris at the turn of the 20th century. The result was the raised-bed system, in which plants are grown very close together in loose, richly composted soil. It is not a no-dig system: in fact, the beds are double-dug annually, although the work gets easier year after year as the soil structure improves. A crucial aspect is richly aerated soil, said to mimic that of landslides; treading on the soil would destroy this structure, and for this reason beds are made narrow for easy access once they have been dug.

Chadwick built a model garden in California and named his system the biodynamic/French intensive method. After he died, his system was developed by John Jeavons. Despite its origins, bio-intensive gardening (as it came to be called) now bears few distinctively biodynamic features – even the lunar aspects are different.

Restoration

Conservation of wild habitats and endangered species has become a cornerstone of environmental activity. A complementary approach in recent years has been the restoration of degraded or altered land to its natural state – i.e. to what it would have been like, as near as we can guess, had it never been affected by the activities of humans. This is a hard task to achieve on the scale of a small urban garden; and, indeed, it has often proved puzzlingly difficult on larger scales.

The reason for this lies in the fact that natural communities of plants, animals, and microorganisms are held together by immensely complicated interactions that may have taken thousands, perhaps millions, of years to develop. Once disturbed, the pieces – even if we could find them all and bring them all together – do not just fall back into the same place they were before. And, in any case, natural systems are always changing and evolving: every place is unique. So the search for "authenticity" in reconstructing a native community of plants and animals usually turns into a quest for something that may not really exist. But what the attempted restoration of habitats can do is transform the seekers, giving them a profound understanding of natural systems – and their relationship to nature – that nothing else can match.

Restoration ecology (see p. 119) is closely connected with the concept of bioregion – that area defined by a distinctive combination of climate, physiography, and living communities, both human and otherwise (see p. 110).

Wildlife Gardening

Creating a space for the benefit of wildlife involves unlearning many old patterns, a relaxation of control, and finding out what can be persuaded to live in your garden. There is an art in creating a wildlife garden (see pp. 110–23); mere neglect does not always do the trick.

A flourishing wildlife community can bring people and nature into intimate contact, and provide hours of entertainment. The kitchen window is, in effect, an exceptionally well-appointed blind. From nature's point of view, wildlife gardening provides genuinely needed habitats in cities, establishes part of a corridor between larger areas of suitable habitat for various species; and offers a richer variety of habitat types than would naturally exist.

Conservation

Not every plant or variety is equipped to survive and succeed in your neighborhood or even your bioregion. The many that can – the native species and locally adapted varieties – offer you a rich and diverse choice of food plants, herbs, or flowers for cultivation. These varieties represent the botanical heritage of your area: they are not only repositories of irreplaceable genes and characteristics but are an essential part of local distinctiveness and history.

Of the 350,000 species of flowering plant, only a few hundred are grown for food, and of these only a few dozen are in common use. Most are not grown in their wild state but are elaborately bred to improve yield, palatability, and other qualities. These cultivars have spread far from their centers of origin, which in many cases are hard to identify. But when a cultivar is grown in a particular region for a long time, and the best seeds and cuttings taken, a strain, or "land race", tends to evolve that is suited to the region. The diversity of these land races constitutes a tremendous genetic resources, which is now threatened by commercialization and ill-considered legislation.

Unlike gardeners, commercial growers are primarily concerned with uniformity, the rate of growth, and the travelling quality of their crops. Flavour, disease resistance, and suitability to a particular region have only secondary importance. The economics of seed production mean that standard commercial varieties are easily and cheaply available, gradually replacing local "heritage" varieties. Even worse, legislation in some parts of the world forbids the sale of seeds that are non-standard and do not appear on government-approved lists, so leading to a tragic loss of diversity, both cultural and genetic.

Consequently, it is vital that local species and varieties are identified, conserved, cultivated, bred, and propagated for as many areas and bioregions as possible. To this end, networks of conservationists and bioregionalists within and between many countries are compiling essential information about these native plants. Moreover, the cultivation and legal exchange of heritage seeds has become an integral part of the natural garden movement and echoes the more general urge to restore the intimacy between environment and culture.

Pulling the Partnership Together

The modern approaches to natural gardening outlined in these pages are generally compatible with one another, and elements from one can be combined with elements from another. Permaculture is a good example of an approach which is really a hybrid from earlier ones. Occasional differences arise and are enlightening. Most approaches, for instance, strive for tight local cycling of nutrients. Biodynamics, however, forbids the recycling of human nutrients for use on food crops on the grounds that nutrients are not just chemicals, but acquire in their journeys through the biosphere a vital quality which is lost in the human digestive system.

Most approaches use annual crops and practice strict rotation to keep ahead of pests and diseases, and to make use of different components of the soil. But some systems emphasize the use of permanent crops, such as perennials and trees, which cannot be rotated. Some approaches permit or even insist on tilling, while others view it with distaste. Some methods discourage composting, preferring to put fresh material straight on to the ground where it provides food for worms and other soil organisms. Biodynamics, by contrast, insists that making a pile has a far wider significance than just recycling nutrients: it is essential for collecting certain important cosmic influences.

Natural gardening requires a change of attitude. This book promotes the urgent need for us all to take part in a renaissance of the mind and a partnership with nature based on a sustainability that heals rather than harms the environment. The idea is not to be self-sufficient but part of a growing, evolving community where you can renew yourself and others through reconciliation with Gaia. By preserving the fabric of the biosphere, restoring the appropriate ecosystem in your garden, and working with its natural relationships rather than imposing your will upon them, you can grow fresher, healthier food, fashion a leisure space that is a living extension of your home, and contribute to the essential work of conservation by cultivating rare local varieties.

PART II

PLANNING YOUR NATURAL GARDEN

Introduction: Making Choices

For nearly all of us who have gardens, there is no single overwhelming answer to the question: what is your garden for? Probably it just came with the house and so we accept the obligations it places on us. Most societies have a prevailing "garden culture" that gardeners slip into without perhaps examining their reasons. In Europe, for example, there's a traditional mix of lawn, flowers, shrubs, a tree or two, a patio, a slide for the kids, a shed for tools, and a vegetable plot. The garden is for recreation, something to look at, display, an extension of the house; the fact that it's there makes you do something to it. For many gardeners its purpose is precisely to *be gardened*.

It would be a pity if a new approach to gardening lost sight of this mixed and variable tradition. In this book we propose that another dimension be added: that your garden make a positive contribution to the health of the planet. In the words of the modern aphorism: it should be part of the solution, not part of the problem.

We would like to suggest three broad avenues of approach, which can be taken as they are, or mixed and matched in any way that takes your fancy.

- FIRST, think of the impact you make on the biosphere simply by being alive, living the way you do. It may not seem much, but when five billion of us are doing something similar, it adds up. How can your garden help you to "live more lightly on the Earth"? Can it reduce your energy consumption? Can it alter your demands on the food system? Can it reduce your consumption of natural resources, and your output of harmful waste products?
- SECOND, think of the natural habitats and wildlife displaced by the necessities of modern living – houses, roads, factories, air-bases, farms; or destroyed by the activities of people – logging, waste-dumping, driving, drainage, agriculture, industry. Can your garden make good some of these losses? Can it provide a direct home for creatures who soon may have nowhere else to go? Or a stopover for those with homes elsewhere?
- THIRD, think of the intensity and pace of life; its detachment from quiet and ancient satisfactions and from the Earth itself; the hunger it generates: its urge to consume, move about, be comfortable without regard to environmental cost, to find security in total control of natural forces. Can your garden help you find a way back to a nobler relationship with yourself and with your planet? Can it cut through the restless search for "a change of scenery", "where the action is", "what's next"? Can it help heal you, and those around you?

We shall walk down these three avenues in turn, and ask when and where each is appropriate, and how they might be combined. In some respects they appear to contradict one another: a wildlife garden is not very productive in material terms, and might not be as friendly to people as to plants and animals; the most productive gardens are ruthlessly managed for efficiency, not for cheerful prospects or the feeding of birds; sanctuaries may not lend themselves to the disciplines of productivity or the waywardness of the wild. Yes, choices must be made, but in all the thousands of possibilities, we will look for those which best harmonize the useful, the natural, and the spiritual qualities.

Faced with such a maze, many gardeners are reluctant to spend time in what might seem idle reflection. The garden will not wait; the urge to "get on with it" can be overwhelming. But hold on a minute. The garden may have been there before you were born, and will almost certainly outlast you. Its land, in fact, is probably centuries old, perhaps millennia; it's worth some reflection. A cornerstone of natural gardening, however you interpret it, is to s l o w d o w n.

A Year of Initiation

We would like to make the serious suggestion that you take a whole year to observe, tune in, and reflect before making any fundamental changes. The overall aim of this year, which we shall call the year of initiation, is to help you decide the best purposes for your garden. Basically, this involves collecting the necessary information for a sound, long-term strategy, observing a complete seasonal cycle, and tuning into the garden in an intimate way (see pp.194–5). It will also stop you doing anything hasty before you know what the implications are.

A whole year may sound rather daunting but need not be. Of course, it is not absolutely essential – you can get a rough picture from past experience, extrapolation, and shrewd guesswork. But if you approach the year of initiation as a prelude to your perennial enjoyment of the garden, it can be an enthralling process in itself.

There are two phases to the year. The first is measurement and logging of all the permanent features of the site. It is generally best to do most of this in a fairly intensive way at the beginning, but some can be added in the course of the year. The second phase – to observe and record the elements that change in the course of the seasons – will necessarily spread itself across the year.

Analyzing the Site

Make a checklist of all the elements in your garden, such as:

- General climate
- Topography and slope of the ground
- Orientation to sun and winds
- Relationship of your house to your garden
- The shape and size of your garden's boundaries
- Position of surrounding buildings and large, fixed structures, including trees
- The nature of the soil
- Changes of level (banks, walls, steps, etc.)
- Identity of mature trees, small trees and shrubs, established plantings, ponds, other water features
- The routes in and out of the garden, paths, and the main patterns of movement (the "desire lines")
- The whereabouts of the garbage, compost, shed, outhouse, garage/carport.

Quite apart from what you yourself observe, find out about the wider background in your bioregion. For details of your area, you can use maps, libraries, the local meteorological station and agricultural advisory service, and neighbors who have lived in the area a long time. No garden book can give you the detailed lowdown on a particular locality.

An essential part of your analysis is the map or plan of the garden; this will need to be a series of plans to cope with all the information. The best way to approach this is to measure the garden as accurately as possible with a long tape measure and make your own basic plan (see pp.64–5). Plot on it as many fixed features as you can manage, then make a series of photocopies of the basic plan, as large as possible, plus one extra-large copy to hang on the wall. This will be your master plan. Choose a scale that has a simple relation to the actual garden – for example, 10ft (3m) in a large garden represented by 1in (2·5cm) on the map. This makes it much easier to add details later.

Logging the permanent features calls for accuracy and clarity. But really getting to know your site needs an alchemical fusion of opposites: yin and yang, left brain and right brain. It demands the hardheaded, quantitative, and analytical as well the intuitive, sensual, and emotional. One of the best things to do is just spend time in the garden. If you sit quite still, you will notice all sorts of things: and don't forget the nighttime....

The Seasonally Changing Elements

Using the techniques listed on p.194–9, go out and observe, measure, and record the following as they change through the seasons:

- The path of the sun
- Patterns of light and shade
- Maximum and minimum temperatures
- Directions and effects of the wind
- Depth of the water table
- Patterns of drainage
- Patterns of rainfall
- Life cycles of major plants, both cultivated and "wild", and as many animals as you can monitor.

As you go through this process, the richness of detail will astonish you. At times you will find the possible combinations of different elements a bit overwhelming. But at the same time patterns will start to emerge; for example, maximum and minimum temperatures will be closer on cloudy than on clear days. Certain qualities will clump together – light/warm/dry, for example, and shady/cool/damp – but not always. Log the microclimates and any special parts of the garden with a distinct character, even on the tiniest scale. This is raw material to help you make your choices. As the year goes on, pencil in hypotheses about which areas might suit which purposes.

Planning Changes

At the end of your year of initiation, you will be ready to plan substantial changes. Of course, you have probably been unable to resist the temptation of making all manner of small tweaks and adjustments on the way; and your inclinations as to what you want from your garden, and what your garden can offer, will already be forming. The year will have helped you decide what is the best mix of uses for your own purposes, and which of these the garden can embrace with the least effort. In other words, you have a good idea what comes most "naturally" to both your garden and yourself.

Before you begin, there are several fundamental factors that will affect your strategy. Now is the time to examine them one at a time. Think about each at least once and consider how it applies to your garden. Firstly, your partner, children, other members of the household may have different values/tastes and want different things from the garden. You have to decide what the priorities are and then balance them so everyone is satisfied.

Secondly, whether you are renting a house with a garden, taking early retirement, or buying a house, you should proceed as if you will be there a long time. Remember that your garden is as much a process as a thing or a place. It changes and evolves; you cannot keep it exactly as you found it even if you wished to. The same is true of you and your family: your views, needs, and feelings will change over the years, and the mix of lobbies wanting this amenity or that facility will also change.

If your garden is small you can lavish a great deal of care per square inch; rejoice in having a small garden and refine your focus. Your choices are stark and your designs must be clever: you design to save space. Larger gardens bring opportunities and headaches in equal measure. Of course, the fact that you can do more may absolve you from making certain choices. But this very freedom can make you slapdash. And the very big garden needs a lot of looking after; many a large garden has turned into a life sentence with hard labor. In large gardens you design to save time.

Surveying your garden
The plan sketches (below) show a simple way to survey your garden. Make your measurements between various fixed points, assisted by sightings along the straight walls of the house. You can transfer the data to squared paper to create a master plan, which you can photocopy – and then use each copy to detail a particular aspect of your garden. The illustration (right) indicates the sort of places where measurements, such as temperature, light, soil pH, water, and wind speed, would be helpful. In general, look for broad zones of one quality or another, and places where factors change abruptly. But don't follow the illustration literally – use your common sense. The most obvious features of this site are: a low point in which water is likely to collect; a level, open area; tallish trees on the windward side. In a cool, humid climate the open area looks best for productive crops – you can confirm this by checking light patterns, soil, and drainage. In a hot, arid climate the low spot may be more suitable for edible crops because it is more moist and more sheltered.

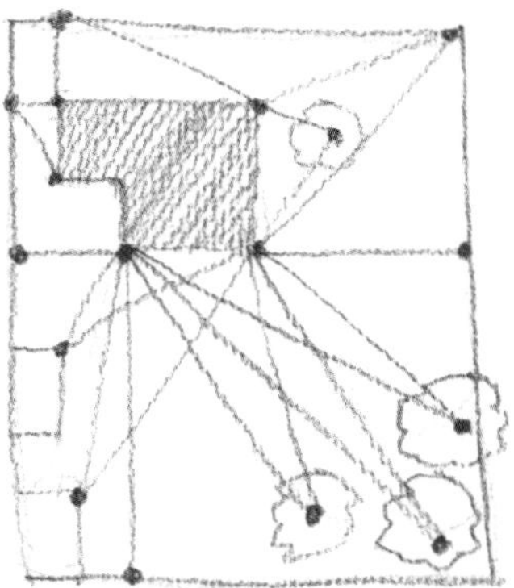

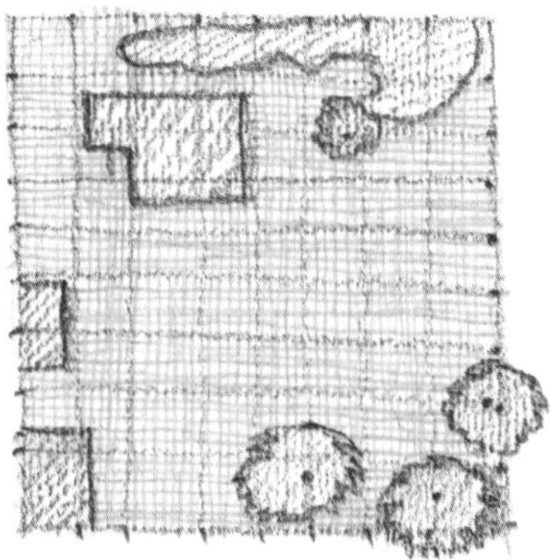

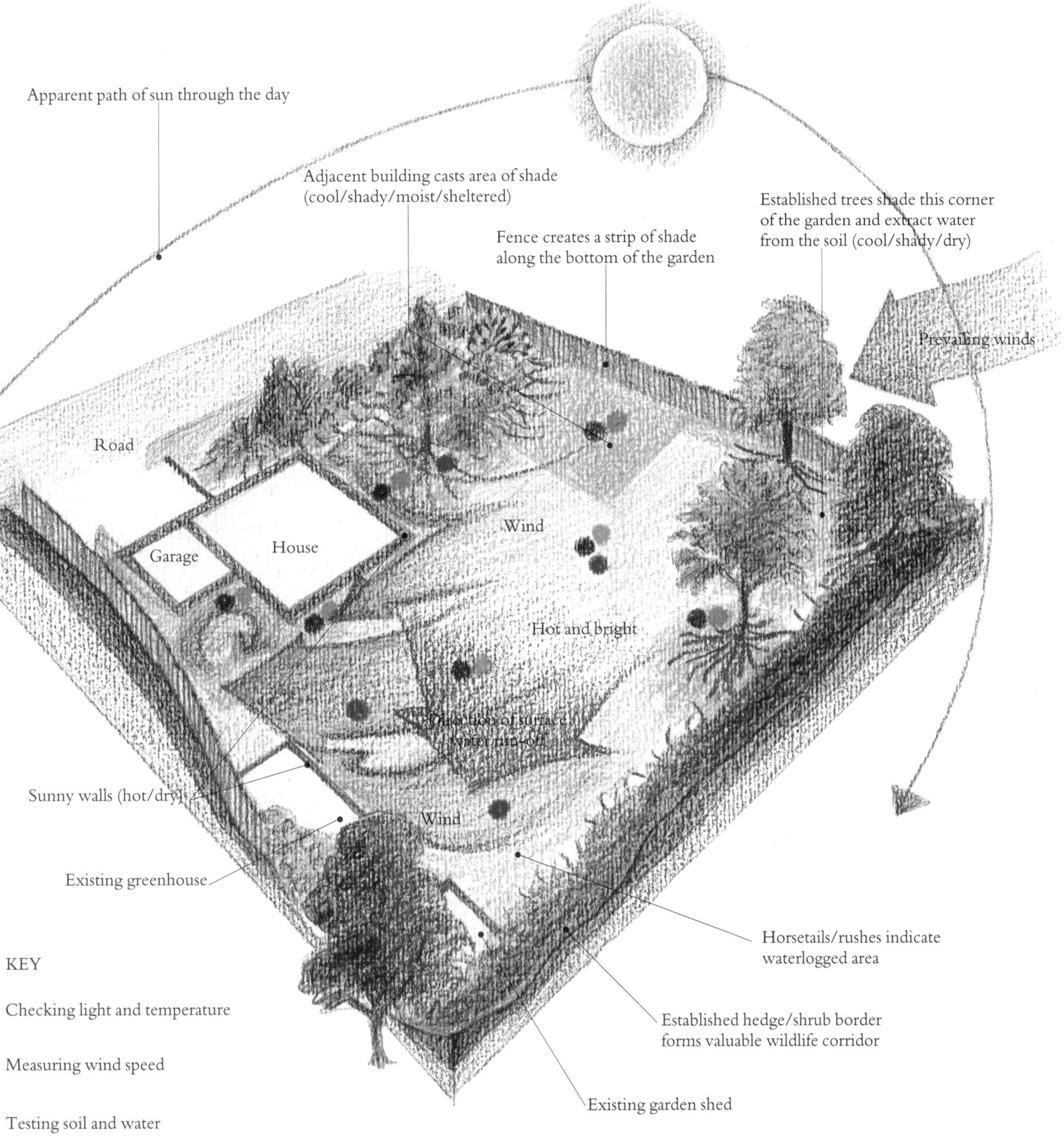
Apparent path of sun through the day
Adjacent building casts area of shade (cool/shady/moist/sheltered)
Established trees shade this corner of the garden and extract water from the soil (cool/shady/dry)
Fence creates a strip of shade along the bottom of the garden
Prevailing winds
Road
Wind
Garage
House
Hot and bright
Direction of surface water run-off
Sunny walls (hot/dry)
Wind
Existing greenhouse
Horsetails/rushes indicate waterlogged area
Established hedge/shrub border forms valuable wildlife corridor
Existing garden shed
KEY
Checking light and temperature
Measuring wind speed
Testing soil and water

Before planning any big changes, you should first of all decide how much time and effort you will be able to devote to garden maintenance (or how much it might cost to buy help and how much you are prepared to pay). Measure this time, not so much in hours and minutes *per se*, but in relation to the size of your garden and to the size of the area on which you are going to concentrate.

As a broad generalization, productive gardening works best if you have more time than space; non-productive gardening works best if you have more space than time. If your garden size outstrips the time you have available, and you still want it to be productive, then consider devoting as much time and effort as possible to redesigning at the beginning in order to save time later. Remember that you do not need to treat the whole garden the same way. It is feasible, and in fact usual, for gardeners to concentrate their efforts on one part, while spending much less time on the rest – so make sure you identify and allocate the intensive parts in advance of any redesign.

The Ecological Status of your Garden

What is the difference between a wilderness and a garden? Truly wild habitats are sometimes in a stable, or climax, state (see p.16), with a particular community of plants and animals. They are also subject to all sorts of extreme or deficient conditions – soil nutrients are often poor, for example. These either limit the rates at which plants grow or restrict the number of species that are able to survive.

Gardens are the opposite. They are deliberately prevented from developing toward a climax state, systematically modified to correct suboptimal conditions, and enriched with nutrients. To tame the wild, to correct deficiencies, to improve poor ground, to draw out the potential, to make something of it, to civilize the primitive, to manage the unruly.... Traditionally, this is what gardening is all about.

The prevailing gardening culture has given us strong notions about how gardens "ought" to be, and we have tended to accept them without much thought. If you want highly productive edible crops, you must largely follow the traditional program. But for other purposes many classic "improvements" are counterproductive. Ask whether constant disturbance is justified; and what is the overall environmental cost of using resources to establish a design that perpetually frustrates a return to the "natural state"?

Moreover, correcting extremes and deficiencies cuts out habitats of the rarer, specialized, native plants and animals adapted to tolerate them, in favor of common generalist competitors. It also creates a dull uniformity among gardens, denying the distinctive features of the locality and bioregion. And nutrient enrichment favors the growth of rank weeds; once applied, it is very hard to reverse its effects.

How does all this affect your strategy? Most established gardens are disturbed and enriched (see p.96). Such a garden will have received a great deal of attention and will continue to require it. If such efforts are needed anyway, they may as well go into useful production. In contrast, a garden carved out of the wild, or consisting largely of subsoil and builders' rubble, may be more stable ecologically, more suitable for wildlife, and less so for growing food.

Your garden's ecological status can then be combined with its size and the time you have available for maintenance. A large and highly cultivated garden will soon become a real headache if you do not devote sufficient time to managing it because it will quickly get out of hand. By contrast, a large but little-cultivated garden should be disturbed as little as possible and should not be "improved" or enriched.

To some extent you will not be able to avoid enriching parts of your garden if you are recycling organic waste and making compost. Since it's there you might as well use it. So designate part or parts of the garden for enrichment and intensive cultivation, and grow something productive or ornamental that will make use of the extra nourishment and attention. Or else give the organic material to someone who can benefit from it – perhaps in exchange for produce.

Strategy Guidelines

The following checklist should help you plan your strategy once you have decided what sort of garden you want:

- Established gardens can hold you back, but also suggest a way forward; how and why did the previous owner or designer solve the problems? Can you take what's there as a springboard for the future, rather than starting afresh? If it's an old garden that has been in the family for several generations, try to discover how it came to be like it is; look for old photographs. If you bought the garden, find what you can from the previous owner.
- Put various items together on your plan and see how they fit. Show preliminary plans to other people for comment.
- Start small and evolve. Keep thinking "process".
- You are collaborating with natural forces, but you are an equal partner; don't let the garden rule you or get you down; don't be sentimental about particular items – look at the good of the whole.
- Re-examine your purposes from time to time. The act of changing the garden will change you, too. Are you managing to achieve what you had in mind at the outset? In the light of experience, do your goals and plans need to change?
- Be humble; don't imagine you know all the answers because you have read this book: as the authors, we can assure you we don't know all the answers either. Read other books, and know that garden writers disagree with each other all the time. Be prepared to discard everyone else's advice and rely on your common sense.
- Careful design and hard work at the beginning can save time and effort later, but quick or cheap dummy runs are often helpful. For example, a sharp change in soil level will erode and slump: it should be retained in some way if you want to keep the sharp change. A temporary retaining method can give you an idea of what a more permanent solution would look like, or whether you would prefer to regrade and make a bank or gradual slope.
- Do the major physical ground works first ("hard landscaping") before the final levels and plants ("soft landscaping").
- If you have a problem, find out if there is a flip-side to it. Can it be turned to advantage if you adjust your purposes slightly? Perhaps you can adapt slightly your plan to flow around the problem.
- Consider the ergonomics of managing your garden and fitting it in to the rest of your life. Are things placed in the best arrangement? Can the same operation, function, or structure serve many purposes? Can the output of one process be transformed into the input of another?
- Working from plans gives a two-dimensional bias. The garden is a space, not a plane. Remember the vertical dimension. It is useful to complement your plans with elevations and sketches taken from various viewpoints. Photographs are helpful.
- Transitions, edges, and boundaries are your garden's skeleton. Visually they are important because the physiology of the eye is designed to pick them out and emphasize them. They do not merely mark the place where different parts of the garden come together and meet; they have their own unique qualities. They are places where change speeds up and where the contrasting qualities of adjacent spaces can be drawn upon simultaneously. They will be reflected in the lines on your plan.
- Walks are important both functionally and visually. It is often useful to lay out temporary walks and see how they are used. A walk may look great, but if people invariably deviate from it, you have obviously violated the so-called "desire lines" and will need to reorganize the layout.
- Your plan will not work out as planned. Be ready for this!

The Three Dimensions

In the chapters that follow in Part II, we shall examine three basic dimensions – efficiency, wildlife, and healing – of garden practice. We have chosen these as "natural" because we believe they can make your garden a positive contributor to the health of the biosphere and the planet.

Chapter Three concentrates on directly useful gardening, using materials, energy, and water efficiently to generate productive crops. Chapter Four deals with nature spaces and wildlife gardening, while Chapter Five looks at healing and enjoyment. Part III shows how the various elements can be put together in the integrated Gaian garden.

THE USEFUL GARDEN

The Resourceful Garden

Consider the wheel. It's so simple, so useful, so fiendishly ingenious. It begins at a certain point, travels along for a while, then starts all over again, and continues to repeat and recycle itself indefinitely. This is how natural systems operate: materials are circulated, used, and fed back into the system to be used again. It's simple, elegant, and self-sustaining.

Modern industrial societies do not work like this. They have moved away from cyclical patterns, where the outputs of one part of the system become the inputs for another, to linear ones in which materials flow only one way. It is almost as if humans have been de-inventing the wheel. Consequently, most industrial processes now have a beginning and an end. Depletion at the beginning, pollution at the end. In fact, pollution is a feature at almost every stage of the process, as untamed materials charge through the environment, from oil field to garbage dump, from fertilizer factories to sewage on the beaches, from coal mines to dying forests.

Because material resources and energy are so readily and cheaply available in modern western societies, it is easy to see how this situation has come about. But the uncontrolled industrial growth which modern lifestyles have spawned is measurably eroding the very fabric of the biosphere.

Ultimately, the answer must be to re-invent the wheel, to make sure that all materials required for human life are made to follow careful cyclical paths with minimal inputs of energy. Only by becoming far more efficient in all our energy and material needs can we hope to reduce our demands on an already stressed and degraded planet.

Reducing our Consumption of Resources

If our problems have arisen through the profligate use of raw materials and fossil fuels, how can we manage to use less of them? And what role does the garden have to play? Compared with the house, the resources used by the garden are negligible, yet there are ways in which your garden can help to reduce your overall consumption. Basically there are three main approaches. One is to recycle and reuse as many resources as you can; in this respect your garden can perform a vital function as a recycling center for many of the waste materials generated from within or imported into the house. The second is to use resources more efficiently so that you get the same benefits with less energy; here, for example, the garden can help you to reduce your energy consumption by deflecting the prevailing winds, or providing an insulative layer between your house and the elements. And third, your garden can make elegant use of the resources that nature provides for free: sun, wind, water, plant material, and biological energies. How you manipulate these resources can have a fundamental bearing on your relationship with your garden.

Modern lifestyles demand a constant throughput of energy and materials in the form of tastefully wrapped goods, and processed and packaged foods; and what leaves your house is often "dealt with" by

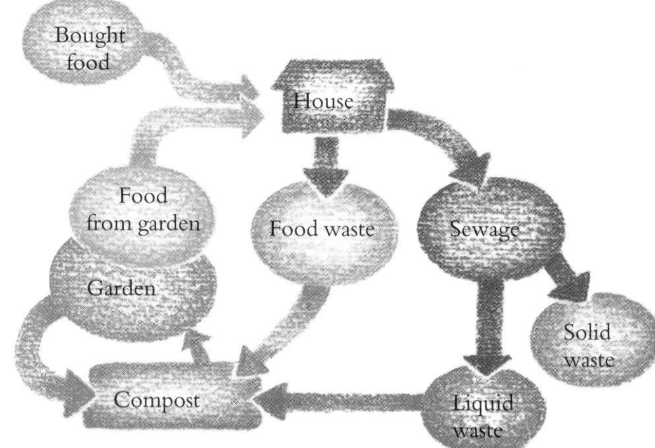

The cyclical organic food system
A cyclical system (above) that produces organic food requires minimal inputs and creates little or no waste since most of the products are eventually fed back into the system.

Energy Use in the Developed and Developing World

In India, the commercial consumption of energy per head is about 15 gigajoules per year, while in North America it is 300, most of which is derived from fossil fuels. We may all aspire to such levels of energy consumption, but as a global standard it is unsustainable, not because coal, oil, and gas are going to run out (although they will in the end) but because the atmosphere will not be able to absorb such quantities of carbon dioxide without severe changes in the climate.

US and UK Waste Production

It is all too easy for your house and garden to add to (rather than subtract from) the environmental impact of modern life. The average household in the US and UK produces about a ton of garbage every year. By contributing to that statistic, you are adding to the problems of disposal and pollution, not to mention the energy wasted in the production of such unwanted material.

Compost bins can be attractive features in their own right. This bin (right) in Wales has two bays for different stages of the composting process, while the fixed roof keeps off excessive rain. Feeding rich kitchen waste to livestock (top right) is not only efficient it also reduces rodent problems.

the public utilities (garbage collection, sewage disposal) or absorbed by the atmosphere. Not even your garden is immune from the products of our industrial society: the shelves of garden stores are bursting with chemicals, tools, materials, containers, potting media, and seeds, most of which you don't need or can make yourself.

Given that you have all these materials flowing through your house and garden, how can you make the best use of them? How can you reduce the quantity of what comes in, and improve the quality of what goes out? Here are three basic guidelines:

- Don't buy anything for the garden until you are sure there is no alternative;
- Recycle all organic material.
- Recycle as much gray water (see p.217) as you can.

Reusing Materials

The best thing you can do with unwanted industrial materials is to find another use for them. This does not so much reduce the amount that ends up in the garbage, as reduce the amount you have to buy. Examples include containers and bottles made of plastic or glass, all of which can be put to good use in the garden (see p.71). Be careful, however, not to become too obsessive in your collection of these items, as you may find that your storage space becomes completely taken over by "potentially useful" materials.

Some biological materials can also be used directly in the garden to avoid you having to buy things. Moreover, when finished with, they become raw input to the decomposer food chains. Examples of such "prime use" materials include:

- Newspaper and cardboard as mulch;
- Paper or centers from rolls of toilet paper as plant pots;
- Coppice shoots for pole bean frames and other rough trellis work;
- Tree brush for support of scrambling plants, such as peas, or for use as windbreaks or light shade.

Many recycling schemes for glass, paper, and aluminum are now in operation in many urban centers throughout the West, so if you can't reuse a material, recycle it. Remember, however, that recycling plants use energy and materials, too, so always try to reuse an item first.

Recycling Organic Wastes

The principle that all organic waste must be recycled is fundamental and underlies all good gardening practice. When you recycle organic waste you generate useful products – this is good for your garden, and for the planet. You are putting something essential and nutritious back into the soil, to compensate (if only a little) for the wastefulness of the mass industrial food system.

You can recycle organic waste in a number of ways, but the two most common methods are either adding it to the compost pile, or putting it directly into or on to the soil. There is a huge mystique about making compost, most of which is unnecessary. Take heart from the fact that whatever you do to it (even if you do nothing at all), it will ultimately break down into brown crumbly stuff. The main problems you are likely to encounter have to do with: the lengths of time different materials take to decompose; getting the carbon-to-nitrogen ratio right; and having all the ingredients available in sufficient quantities at precisely the right time.

The way natural gardeners tend to get round the first problem is by having two piles: one fast one, for dealing with soft wastes (mainly kitchen scraps, lawn clippings, weeds, and other non-woody garden wastes); and one slow one, for dealing with woody and other more resistant wastes (see pp.212–14). The second problem, of having too much nitrogen or too much carbon, can be solved either by adding straw (in the case of too much nitrogen, when the assembled ingredients are too rich), or by adding dilute urine (when the materials are fibrous and high in carbon). In fact, straw is the one thing we can recommend that gardeners bring in to the garden and place next to their compost pile – its fibrous structure helps to keep the pile open and well aerated. Urine, on the other hand, is a freely available commodity which acts as an activator, providing the compost bacteria with a good source of nitrogen and other nutrients to speed up the whole process (see p.215).

The third problem, of not having enough materials to construct a sufficiently large pile, often manifests itself in small- to medium-sized gardens. A large, properly constructed pile operates mainly through the action of bacteria: it heats up and processes its material rapidly. If your pile is too small, then the heat may simply dissipate before it has had a chance to build up, causing the whole process to slow down. In such situations you may also find it difficult to assemble all the right ingredients at the right time, in which case you should call up the services of worms to break down the waste material (see p.216). Worm bins are generally much smaller than normal compost bins and are particularly good at dealing with erratic supplies of sloppy wastes, such as kitchen scraps and grass clippings.

Recycling Paper and Cardboard

Of all the various ways of dealing with paper and cardboard, which form a significant part of every household's waste, the most valuable is to recycle them, so more paper can be made. In the absence of a recycling scheme near you, then find some worthwhile use for it, such as sheet mulch (see p. 221) and plant pots (see p. 71), both of which are important, self-composting processes.

A word of warning: you cannot just dump fresh paper or cardboard on to your compost pile in thick wads – it simply won't rot very well. It needs weathering first. One method of weathering is to line the sides of an enclosed pile with paper or cardboard. This has the added benefit of improving the efficiency of the pile: it provides good insulation by helping to keep the heat in, and is easily incorporated into the compost pile when it has weathered sufficiently.

Recycling Seeds

Multinational seed ownership has had a disastrous effect on the availability of hardy, native species. True, the convenience of a dry, uniform packet of seeds may be persuasive, but you can make good use of your resources by saving, with very little effort, the seeds of many garden plants; and others can be left to self-seed right where they grow.

Any drawbacks and difficulties in saving your own seed are greatly outweighed by potential benefits, not merely economic ones. As a general rule, a plant that sets seed has proved to you it can survive in your garden and is therefore worth saving. Pick out the biggest and the healthiest, and you are on the way to developing a strain that may be uniquely adapted to the precise conditions of your garden. Remember, however, that your seeds must be stored in a dry and cool place (see p.245).

Plastic and Glass

Plastic containers can be put to all sorts of uses, such as rain gauges, wasp traps, and pots for pricking out and potting on. If you cut them about two-thirds of the way down, you can use the top part as a mini-cloche for seedlings and the bottom part as a pot for setting seeds.

Although plastics are useful, they can look ugly in the garden. Glass, however, can be attractive. Vehicle windshields can form low cloches to accelerate germination and seedling growth. Bottles make good edging for beds and, if left alone, develop their own tiny communities of plants, particularly ferns.

To Shred or not to Shred

You can accelerate the rotting of softer woody wastes by putting them through a shredder. This usually renders them good enough for fast composting, but is advantageous whatever process is used. More substantial shredders and chippers can deal with small branches and generate a useful organic mulch.

This raises the question of shredders: should the natural gardener have one? A shredder is an elaborate and expensive industrial product; it also consumes energy and is noisy. Very small or large gardens can manage very well without them: in the large garden there is always somewhere to dump woody waste where it will eventually rot down; and in the small garden, the volume of waste isn't usually a problem. But in the middle-sized garden, especially one with many shrubs, hedges and trees which need constant pruning, a shredder could well be justified. A preferable option would be to share a shredder among several of your neighbors.

The Use of Fire

The main traditional method of dealing with surplus woody wastes is fire (see p.210). Burning turns most of the carbon into carbon dioxide, some of it into known carcinogens, while volatilizing many of the nutrient minerals. Its advantages are that it's quick, kills disease organisms, and leaves a compact, concentrated residue that is rich in potash.

Pots from Paper

Plant pots can be easily made from almost any kind of paper: unwaxed and unglossy works best; laminated paper stops roots from growing through. The origami is simple. Large seeds are sown direct, or seedlings potted on into soil or compost in the paper pots. At planting time, the pots are soaked and planted entirely into their holes. The roots grow happily through the paper, which acts as a reservoir of moisture.

Most of what you need in the garden is available free from natural materials or waste products. The seat (above) uses an ash fork topped with a riven oak shingle. The shingle provides a comfortable perch and also protects the end-grain of the ash, which would otherwise quickly rot. Used wine bottles (right) make an attractive edging and a suitable home for small spleenwort ferns, which are adapted to filtered green light. No-flush composting toilets (top right) save water and allow you to reclaim your own waste nutrients. In this twin-vault toilet, sawdust is added after each use to prevent smells and to incorporate high-carbon and bulky material. The resulting compost, which takes about a year to mature, is ideal for use as a high-nutrient mulch around trees and fruit bushes.

Using Energy More Efficiently

Though your garden's energy consumption is small compared to that of your house, there are ways to reduce it further. These include maintenance with hand tools rather than powered equipment; using few bought-in materials; recycling domestic waste; and altering the microclimates around the house.

You may not have thought of it in this way, but growing some of your own food (see pp.94–109) is actually a way of reducing your dependence on fossil fuels. If you put all your organic waste on to a compost pile, then it makes sense to use your nutrient-enriched garden to grow food and thereby to complete the cyclical walk (see p.68). It also enables you to reduce your reliance on the commercial food system, much of which demands high-energy inputs and damages the environment.

If you live in a cold climate, you can take such obvious measures as draftproofing and insulating your house to reduce your energy consumption. But careful planning of your garden – incorporating a windbreak (see pp.81–2) and a solar greenhouse (see p.79), for instance – can also have an important bearing on energy conservation. If you live in a hot, subtropical climate you probably incur substantial costs on cooling and air conditioning your house. In such circumstances, the planting of shade-giving trees near the house can do much to create a cool and comfortable living space without the need for external energy. Do you have a large lawn? If so, have you thought about reducing its size, or creating a wildflower meadow instead (see p.230)?

Every year millions of gallons of gasoline are wasted on maintaining lawns, the vast majority of which serve no immediately useful purpose, not even recreation. In the US alone there has been a vast expansion in lawn culture in recent years, with a corresponding development of all the equipment and paraphernalia that accompanies such a "crop" system. It is probably true to say that the lawn cultures of the developed world consume more energy and resources than the agriculture of most developing countries. And this is before we take into account the long-term effects of soil and groundwater pollution.

Amplifying light and heat
The reflective surfaces of walls and flagstones in a corner of your garden will increase the light and heat available to plants.

Harnessing Nature's Energies

The energy flows outside your house and garden are not always to your benefit; sometimes you need to encourage them, sometimes divert them, and sometimes you need to do both at once! Sometimes it feels like you're trying to conduct an orchestra.

Energy patterns differ in different parts of the world, and even from one garden to another in the same region. You need to know your own, so during your year of initiation find out what you can about the energy patterns around your garden. The principle energy sources are the sun and the wind; you need to be aware of their effects on plant growth, temperature, humidity, and your own human experience of the garden. Monitor these effects through daily and seasonal cycles, and discover the times when they are too powerful, just right, or too weak.

Light and Shade

Your garden analysis (see pp. 63–6, 194–9) will reveal a pattern of light and shade that follows a daily and a yearly cycle. The daily cycle will change as the year progresses. Imposed on these two inflexible cycles is the weather: predictable in some areas, much less so in others. The cyclical patterns of light and shade make a great difference to your garden strategy because light is not only a source of energy for plants but is also turned into heat. So light and heat tend to go together. Plants, particularly crop plants, can be just like people: in hot, sunny climates the surfeit of light and heat encourages you to seek a certain amount of shade; cool, cloudy climates make you crave more light and warmth, so that excessive shade can become a problem. In those climates that alternate sunny/hot/dry with weak sun/cold, there is the problem of requiring shade in one part of the year and avoiding it in the other.

Maximizing Light

If your garden lacks light (especially if it is in a high latitude), you have the following choices:

- Choose strategies and plants that work in these shady conditions; you may have to abandon plans to grow highly productive edibles, but you can still choose from a wide range of useful crops. Tellingly, the range is much wider at low latitudes!
- Identify the sunniest parts of the garden and concentrate light-demanding species there. In high latitudes you need to identify parts that are sunniest in the growing season.
- Amplify light in sunny spots with light-painted vertical surfaces. This is particularly effective in sun-facing corners.
- Remove elements that cast shade, such as walls, fences, garden buildings, and trees. Be careful because such elements often provide shelter from the winds, privacy, support for plants, and "structure" to the garden. Removing established trees can be a particularly difficult decision.
- Design the garden plantings with a profile that slopes toward the sun, with tall trees at the back, graduating to the most light-demanding plants at the front.
- Tilt productive beds toward the sun. This is particularly useful in high latitudes or where the ground slopes away from the sun side. The effect of a 5-degree change of slope can be equivalent to flat ground 300miles (483km) nearer the equator. The disadvantage of this is that when productive beds are sloped toward the sun, they create an area that suffers a great deal of shade. This problem is minimized by

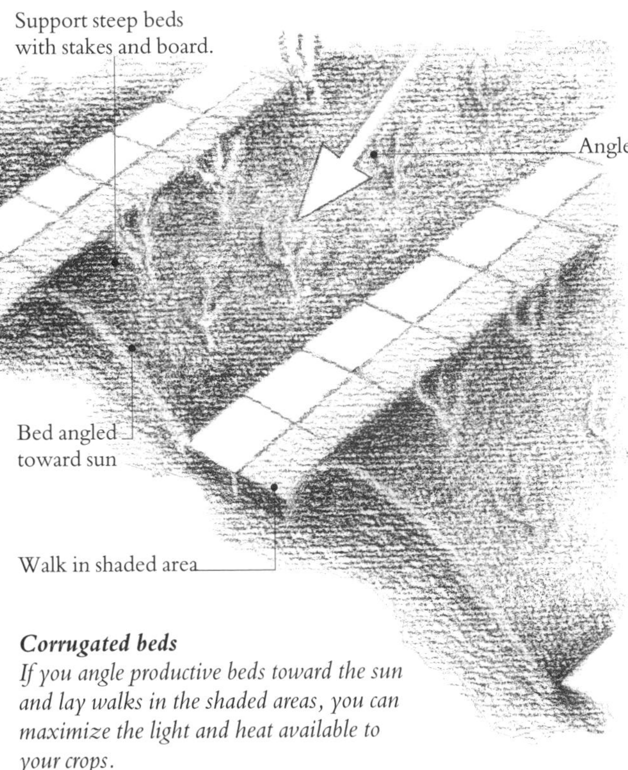

Corrugated beds
If you angle productive beds toward the sun and lay walks in the shaded areas, you can maximize the light and heat available to your crops.

making the back slope very steep and, at a later date, a place for shade-tolerant or taller crops. Probably the best solution is to build a permanent retaining fence or wall, with a walk behind it. The ultimate development of this strategy for maximizing light is a series of asymmetrical raised beds oriented east-west and sloping toward the sun.

- Plant annual crops in east-west rows with small varieties on the sunward side and successions running toward the sun, so that older and larger plants do not shade younger ones.

Designing for Permanent Shade

Some low-latitude climates are characterized by perpetual sunlight with air and ground temperatures that are usually much too hot. Year-round shade therefore becomes a premium. Some plants demand shade anyway; others, though unaffected by strong sunlight, may still suffer from overheating and excessive transpiration.

People too need shade and plants not only provide a cool sanctuary in the garden but they also shade the house. Priority should be given to east- and west-facing parts of the garden and house, for here the sun is low both in the morning and late afternoon. After the intense heat of the day, shading from the western sunshine is particularly important.

When the sun is overhead, effective shading comes from a canopy of leaves and, in this instance, evergreens form a vital part of any plans for permanent shade. They can be supplemented with evergreen vines trained over open frameworks. In general, a permanently sunny climate offers more possibilities than a dull one: you can always reduce high sunlight levels, but you cannot tease more light from the sky than it is willing to give.

Seasonal Light Control

In mid to high latitudes, where you have the additional challenge of designing for seasonal light variations, your best strategy is flexibility and the best plants to work with are deciduous trees and vines. Quite simply, they allow sunlight through in the winter but provide shade in the summer. This attractive strategy needs care because the winter canopy of a deciduous tree can still cut out a significant fraction of the light passing through it. You need to weigh the respective benefits between winter and summer.

Deciduous or annual vines can be trained to cover a trellis or arbor, thereby making a shadehouse for appropriate crops. Furthermore, annuals do not cast winter shade! The winters of many climates are so severe that nothing happens in the open garden anyway and you don't need to worry about creating shade to protect from the deep winter sun. It's the spring you must design for, to give plants an early start and to maximize the growing season in your garden. Here, the sloped-bed system proves to be beneficial.

As far as cropping patterns are concerned, some of the recommendations for dull climates can be simply reversed, with earlier crops on the sunward side shading those behind them. Many crops which need full sun to get them going in the spring will suffer under the full heat of summer sun. This suggests the need for a pattern of shade-requiring intercrops (see p.101), such as lettuce or cornsalad sown between rows of maize.

Air drying to preserve produce, such as tomatoes on a balcony (above), makes use of natural, free energy and the food is not contaminated by preservatives. The produce should not be placed in direct sun but in a spot, such as near a roof vent, where warm air can bathe it. In hot, dry climates the process is simple, but in cooler and damper climates drying in the open air can be unreliable. However, drying in an empty well-ventilated greenhouse is effective.

In hot and sunny climates, creating shade can be essential to the summer comfort of people and plants alike (right); in lower latitudes, overhead shade is particularly important. An open framework of lumber or wire, overgrown with grapevines, usually does the trick. Periodical sprinkling of the foliage and ground with water produces an evaporative cooling effect. If you want the sun to penetrate during the winter, cut the grapevines back or grow annual varieties.

The Importance of Heat

Although sunlight and heat are intimately connected in energy terms, you can often distinguish one from the other in the responses of your garden plants. In mid to high latitudes light in springtime increases rapidly, but the air and soil remain cool. The plants have plenty of light, but the soil is just not warm enough for optimum growth, especially the roots which are so far from the sun. In the fall, the opposite is true: the air and soil are warm but levels of sunlight are declining as the days grow shorter and the sun does not climb so high in the sky. In very sunny conditions plants rarely suffer from too much light – unless they were shade-loving – just heat stress resulting from an excess of transpiration.

The amount of heat which plants need and to which they are susceptible is also determined by many other factors, including air temperature and humidity, wind, the type of soil, and ground moisture. This is the orchestra that you need to conduct to get the maximum benefit. Not enough heat prevents plants from growing properly while too much heat may cause plants to dry out.

Not Enough Heat

The temperate gardener's critical time is spring, because what happens then determines growth for much of the year. Lack of heat prevents germination and slows the activity of bacteria which make soil nutrients available to the plants. There are ways to get round this, which include:

- Pregerminating the seeds;
- Growing on the seedlings in the greenhouse;
- Warming the ground before sowing or planting;
- Providing shelter for the young plants;
- Designing the productive area of your garden for early warmth.

Pregermination

Each species and variety has its own range of optimum conditions for seed germination. Sometimes, it is far easier to meet these conditions in the kitchen or the sunroom than in the ground outside. Most seeds need a combination of warmth and moisture, but some need special treatment such as nicking the seed coats, freezing, or even boiling water.

Growing on the Seedlings

Rather than plant out germinated seeds, grow on the seedlings and let them become established. You can do this by allowing seeds to germinate in pots or flats of soil or potting mix in the house, but as soon as the seed leaves emerge, give them light. So you must have, in descending order of usefulness: a sunroom or heated greenhouse; a sun porch; a cold greenhouse; a cold frame.

A fully heated greenhouse is a great luxury but it is inefficient: most of the heat is wasted. The most natural way to provide heat for germination and seedlings is to make a hotbed (see p.261) – no matter what the scale. For instance, at the New Alchemy Institute in Massachusetts, composting horse manure provides heat, carbon dioxide, and nitrogen for a whole tunnelful of plants.

The benefit of sowing and bringing on the seedlings indoors before planting out is that your plants are guaranteed a good start. It may also protect them from freak frosts, pests, and the fungal diseases that affect weak and stressed plants although this not always the case by any means. They will be bigger and "farther on" than those sown at the same time outside. On the other hand, plants which are sown direct, if they do make it, are often stronger. It is a minor drawback of growing plants indoors that you must acclimatize them or harden them off (see p.261) before planting them out.

Warming the Ground for Sowing

Apart from germinating seeds, temperature increases stimulate both roots and soil micro-organisms – especially the bacteria and mycorrhizas that are so vital in making nutrients available to plants. If the soil is too cold, roots cannot operate effectively, even if the air is warm. This is one reason for growing on plants under cover. And a difficulty with spring sowing is that the

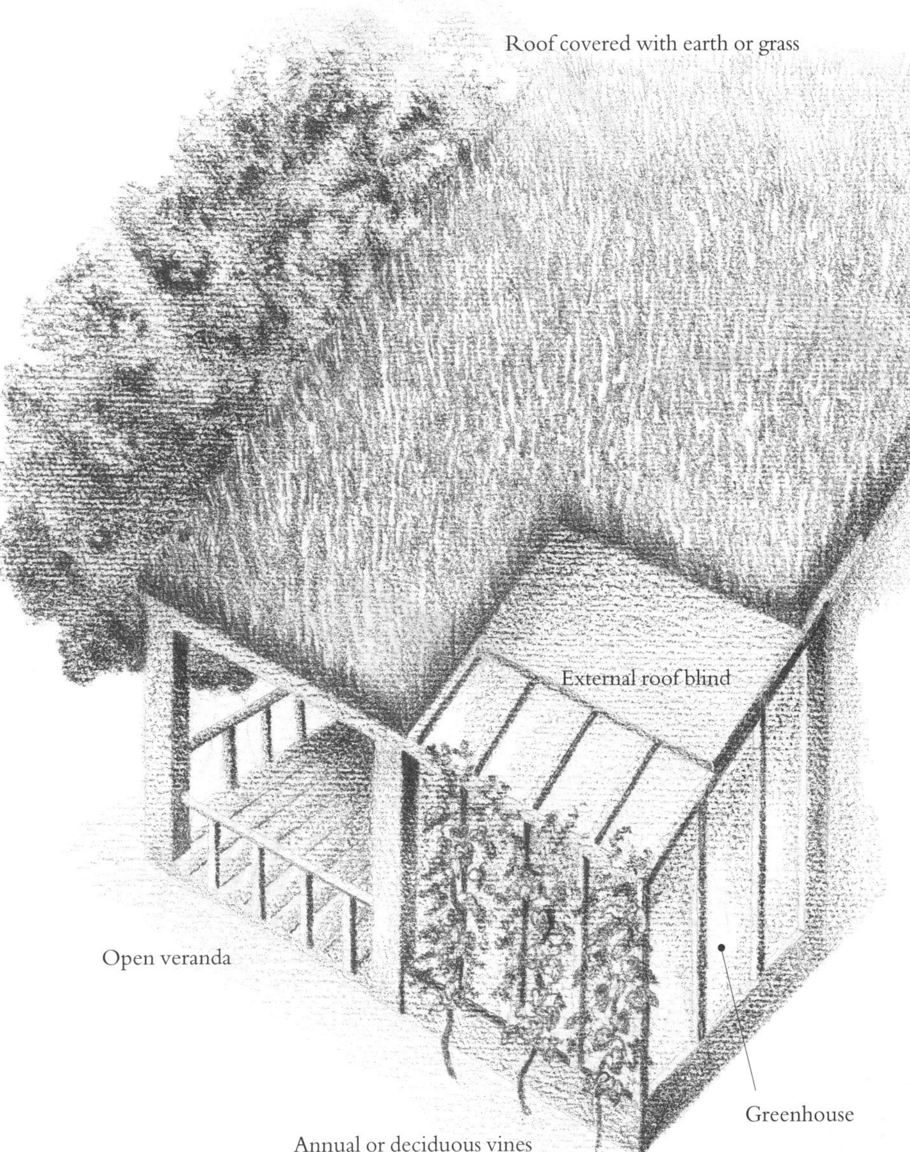

Solar greenhouses
All greenhouses, whether of glass or plastic, use sunlight for warmth. The light passes through the transparent skin, and is partially transformed into heat when it strikes the solid interior. This heat is re-radiated at a different wavelength. In this sense all greenhouses are "solar".

In mid to high latitudes and altitudes, however, ordinary greenhouses lose their heat quickly when there is no sun. A solar greenhouse has a number of features to prevent this:

- *Only the sunward size is glazed; as the sun is low in winter, a glazed poleward side would lose more heat than it gained.*
- *The poleward side is highly insulated and faced with internal reflecting surfaces, which amplify light on to the plants and reduce heat losses.*
- *A large thermal mass stores heat during the night and sunless spells.*
- *Double-glazing and/or retractable insulating shutters (at night) reduce heat loss through the glazed surface.*

In favorable circumstances, solar greenhouses can keep a good internal temperature throughout the winter with no heat source at all except the sun. They work best in climates with a reasonable incidence of winter sunshine, but they are less effective in climates where the winters are generally overcast.

ground is often too wet to prepare a good seed bed. To solve the problems of cold or wet ground, prepare the bed in the fall and cover the soil with an impervious mulch for at least a month before you sow.

Protecting the Young Plants

Once your plants are growing out in the garden, their growth may still be checked by the cold air and soil early on in the season. Moreover, there's always the chance of a freak late frost. This problem is traditionally overcome by cloching (see p.261). This involves covering the plants with mini-greenhouses that will trap sunlight, retain heat, and keep out the cold wind. A cloche (from the French word meaning "bell") was originally an open-bottomed bell-jar or else a square frame with a handle on top. Today, we employ more prosaic substitutes that are just as effective. Cloching can be organized on a plant-by-plant basis, in rows, or even in whole beds.

Designing for Early Warmth

Angling garden beds toward the sun not only increases the incident light, it also speeds up the spring rise in soil temperature. As a general rule, any strategy that increases the amount of sunlight falling on the plants or the soil will be beneficial.

Looking at the wider garden, the main negative influence on the warmth of your beds in the spring will be shade and wind. Depending on the sun's apparent path in springtime and early summer, you could either remove the shade elements or re-arrange the growing area. If trees are the shading features, a knowledge of the daily and seasonal patterns of light and shade will allow you to cull or trim the minimum number. As far as wind is concerned, cloching offers good local protection, while windbreaks protect the garden as a whole. A cheap, temporary means of diverting the wind is to make piles of brushwood along the rows of plants.

Too Much Heat

The effects of too much heat on plants have mostly to do with water. When the rates of both evaporation from the soil and transpiration from the leaves are greatly increased, plants can't keep up so they wilt.

The principal solution is to provide shade (see pp.150, 229). In some climates gardeners supplement this by building massive walls of mudbrick or similar heat-storing material. These walls can absorb some of the daytime heat and re-radiate it during the night, thus moderating the 24-hour extremes. In addition, such walls can support frameworks for shadecloths, screens, or vines.

Trees not only provide shade but they also act as windbreaks and generate a cooling effect as water evaporates from their leaves. You should try to optimize a combination of these two effects – although in hot, humid climates there is a danger of fungal infections if the shade restricts air circulation.

A greenhouse (left) adds an extra dimension to cool-temperate gardening. In this lean-to, the back wall both stores heat and supports climbing plants.

Wind and Windbreaks

On the whole, wind is a form of energy which most gardeners could do without. It brings unwanted cold or heat, dries the ground, carries salt and dust, buffets our plants, and scatters our cloches.

Observe the pattern and direction of winds in your year of initiation. In sheltered, inland areas wind may be of little consequence, but in mountains and coastal regions it may dominate everything. Any physical barrier can act as a windbreak, but on the whole it is better to deflect or merely slow the wind than attempt to stop it dead. Solid barriers, such as walls and fences set perpendicular to the wind, cause eddies on the lee side. As a rule, artificial windbreaks should always be porous.

Trees and shrubs make the best windbreaks, but may take a while to be effective. If you live in a windy area with some established, well-placed trees (even if they are not what you really wanted or cause other difficulties), think carefully before removing them.

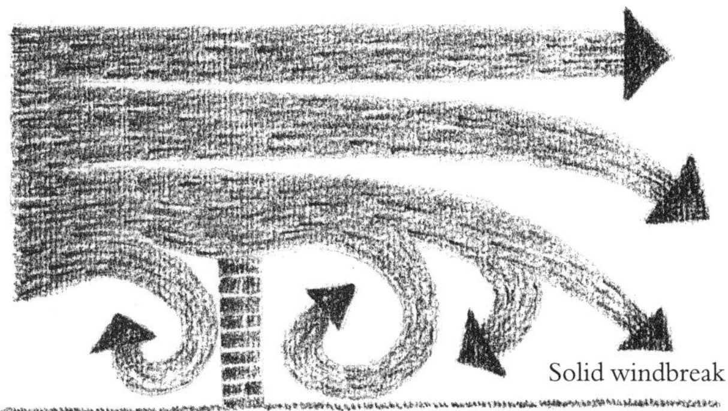

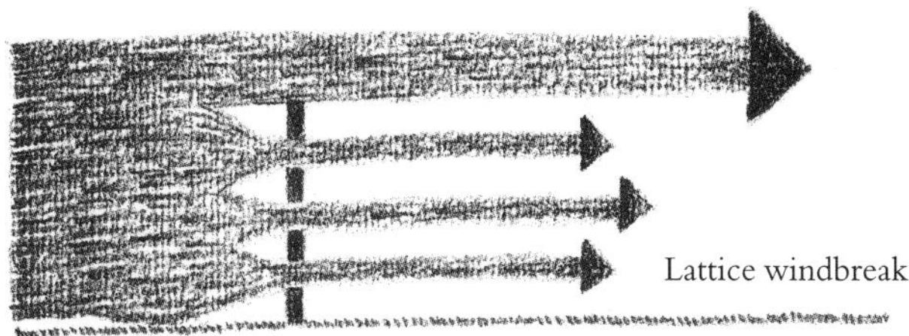

Solid windbreaks generate savage eddies (top) that can damage your plants. By contrast, lattice barriers that are porous to the wind (above) give far more protection – they break up the flow of air and diffuse the wind's energy.

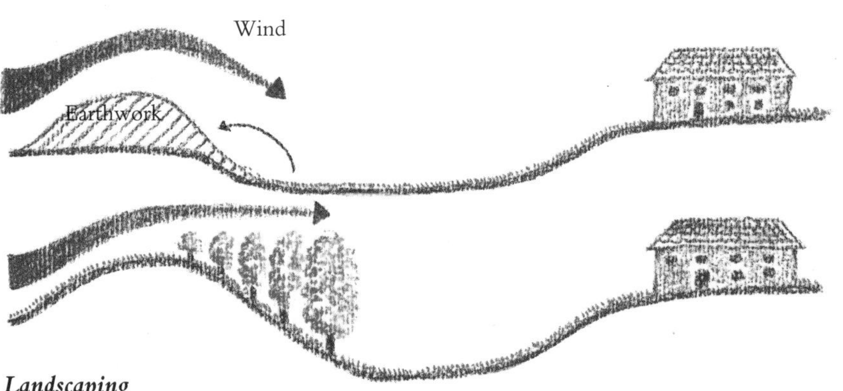

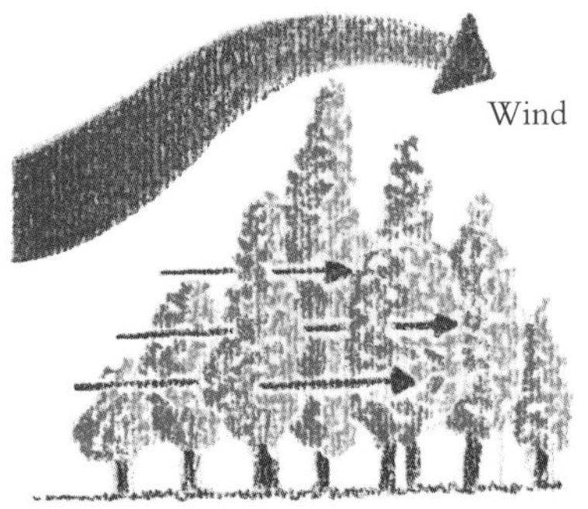

Landscaping
One method of deflecting the wind involves landscaping a windbreak on the windward side of your garden. First shift some soil to build a berm (top) and then plant trees on its leeward side. Select trees with varying heights at maturity – short at the top of the berm, tall at the bottom – so that the top of the windbreak is flat (above).

Profile planting
An A-shaped windbreak created from trees of varying height (above) has two aerodynamic advantages: the slope on the windward side protects the windbreak itself from damage, while the slope on the leeward side keeps turbulence to a minimum.

Windbreak dimensions
The length of a windbreak such as a hedge should be at least 11 times its mature height. This is because the wind will sneak around the ends and generate eddies. As a rule, a windbreak will give protection some 10 to 15 times its height.

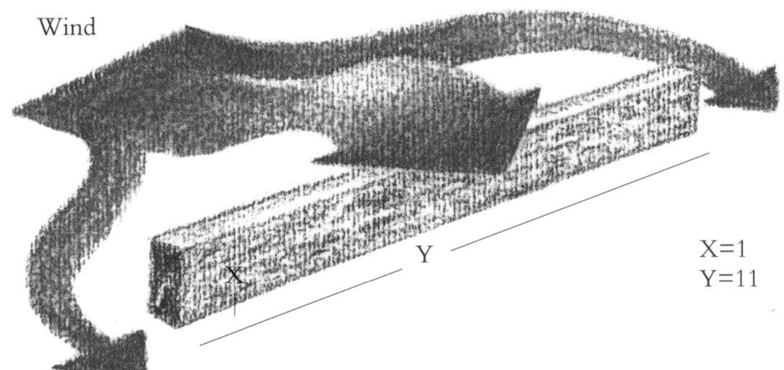

A tree windbreak needs to be long enough and high enough for its purpose. It is usually several rows deep, with a roughly triangular cross-section. Ideally, you should choose trees that have other purposes, such as providing edible fruit or altering the level of the water table. But usually there will have to be some compromise between these and the effectiveness as a windbreak and the speed of establishment.

One serious conflict may arise between the need for a windbreak and the need for light when the sun is low. This may occur in high latitudes and depends on the direction of the prevailing winds. In climates where you need protection against hot, drying winds the shading from trees is a bonus.

A more obvious way for large gardens to reduce dependency on fossil fuels is to provide firewood. Coppicing (the sprouting of trees from the cut stump) was the traditional European method of generating wood for fuel because many trees produce more biomass when coppiced and the wood is more easily harvested on a sustainable basis. From an environmental point of view, it is important to burn this wood efficiently, so it must be dry, and burned in a closed stove, not in an open fire. Cast-iron or Franklin stoves have proved to be the most efficient – they burn a large charge of fuel (preferably air-dried coppice sticks) very rapidly, giving complete and clean combustion.

The row of beech trees (above) acts as the first line of defense against the wind. The beeches protect a row of shrubs, which provide a semi-porous wind barrier for the garden beyond. The grassy strip, which can be grazed, makes a pleasant walk.

Many tree species grow more vigorously when coppiced or pollarded (right). Harvesting the shoots of fresh growth provides material for fuel, fencing, basketry, or general garden purposes.

The Water-efficient Garden

Where does water come from? If you are fortunate to live in a part of the globe where a seemingly unlimited supply of fresh water is piped to your house, you may not have given this question much consideration. Indeed, we live on the "water planet", so what's the problem?

Of this vast global resource, less than one percent is available to us as fresh water (see p.37). Not that this is an insufficient amount. The total volume of water from which we draw our sustainable supplies (the stable runoff from rivers and lakes) is enough to support our present population many times over. However, this water is not evenly distributed throughout the world. Some areas have too much fresh water and squander it; and in many areas where water is in short supply, the demands of agriculture and industry are depleting and polluting valuable groundwater reserves (which are extremely slow to replenish themselves).

Plants vary in their water requirements, but most productive ones like modest amounts in regular doses. They particularly dislike being waterlogged. The perfect food-growing garden, therefore, has a well-drained but retentive soil which, with a regular rainfall, means the gardener need spend no time worrying about water. There are gardens like this, but few that are consistently so. This is because some climates always bring too much rain, others always bring too little, while in many these two situations alternate with the seasons.

For places that are dominated year-round by an abundance or scarcity of water, gardeners may make strenuous efforts to "correct" the situation, or accept it as it is and work around it with minimum intervention. For more details on such extreme gardens, see pages 176–81 (wetland gardens) and 186–91 (arid gardens). However, for those people who have gardens where abundance or scarcity of water only manifest themselves as seasonal or temporary problems, quite simple measures are usually enough to maintain ideal growing conditions.

Water descending too rapidly from clouds (as happens in deluges and cloudbursts) often leads to erosion of the soil and leaching of soluble nutrients. Too much water in the ground leads to waterlogging. Before you try to ameliorate the worst effects of these problems, first find out about the pattern of water arriving in your garden.

If your garden is on a slope, the water may come in from above; or if the garden slopes away from the house, you may be getting a lot of runoff from the roof, patio, or driveway. Tackle these possibilities first. How can you divert this water? First try to channel it into the public storm-water system, via the gulleys into which gutter downpipes flow. If this is not possible, you will have to find some way of ushering the water off your property, or else encourage it to leave through the ground. In an urban situation, merely transferring the problem to your neighbors is not acceptable, so you must either channel the water to a drain or ditch, or else dig a "dry well", or soakaway (see p.207).

Erosion

All soil is eroded by rain. You cannot avoid it, even in the best-managed natural gardens. You must, however, reduce erosion to a minimum – at least to less than what is being regenerated by natural weathering processes. This is typically about 0·2 ton per acre per year.

The most important method of reducing erosion is to incorporate organic matter into the soil. This makes the soil porous, so that rainfall infiltrates easily, rather than rushing over the surface and taking soil with it. Furthermore, organic matter can hold the soil in particles that are less likely to be washed away by the infiltrated water.

The soil on sloping ground tends to be more vulnerable to surface erosion because the water can run faster and create gullies. In this situation the most practical thing you can do is to plant your garden features and crop rows along the contours of the slope, as a means of slowing down the flow. Permanent vegetation, in the form of trees and ground cover plants, will also break up the surface flows and hold on to the soil with their extensive root systems.

Leaching

Leaching is the washing out of soluble soil nutrients, usually by rain but also by over-irrigation. It is the source of some of the environmental problems attributed to those chemical fertilizers that are designed to be soluble in order to make them readily available to plant roots. When it rains they are easily leached away into the ground water (causing nitrate pollution of aquifers) or into water courses (causing algal blooms and eutrophication).

But organic gardens can be just as susceptible to leaching. Well-rotted compost and farmyard manures may not be leached as much as soluble fertilizers, but when the weather is warm bacteria in the soil make nutrients soluble. If plants are growing in the soil the nutrients are absorbed, but if the ground is bare the nutrients will be washed away by the rain. So the rule is simple: keep the ground covered in the rainy season, either by plants or by some other means.

In temperate areas with cold or wet winters, the critical time is fall when summer crops are being harvested and the ground is still warm. If winter-hardy crops are not immediately planted, the ground should be sown with a green manure, or covered with plastic sheeting, cardboard, or straw. In some circumstances the simplest method is not to weed during the last month of the main crops, then let the weeds cover the ground during the down season until you are ready to plant again.

Drainage

Most productive crops need a soil that drains well. If your garden has a drainage problem, tackle it at the outset. Poor drainage is a feature of gardens where water arrives but does not leave fast enough. It hangs around, blocking up the air spaces between soil particles, thereby suffocating plant roots. For some kinds of gardens, poor drainage does not matter. You can just go with it and use plants that are unaffected by it. Free-draining soils allow water to leave downward under the pull of gravity. Waterlogged soils prevent water from leaving for one of three reasons: either the soil itself is not free-draining, an impervious layer lies beneath the surface, or the water table is too high.

Heavy, poorly draining soils can be cured by the steady addition of organic matter or, in really difficult cases, by subsoil drainage. This latter operation requires effort, but is worth while if you are serious about a permanent vegetable plot. The simplest method is the "French drain" (see p.207), which consists of a trench filled with coarse material, running to a ditch or soakaway. Alternatively, if your garden is on a slope, a diversion drain at the top of the slope to carry the water away from your productive plot may be all that is needed.

An impervious layer less than 2ft (60cm) below the surface of your soil might be of two kinds: either a hard "pan" a few inches thick (often caused by over-aggressive cultivation) or much thicker layers of impervious clay. You can break up the pan by digging but, since it is a major undertaking, attempt it only when you are sure the plots are going to be permanent. The operation has the double purpose of removing a cause of waterlogging and allowing roots to penetrate much deeper into the soil.

If you find your soil is lying on layers of stiff clay you can gradually improve the situation by deep digging and incorporating organic matter. It is probably better to treat the situation as you would for a high water table.

During your year of initiation, you should have identified the levels of your water table and suitable areas for crop growing. If, however, the water table is consistently high throughout your garden, then perhaps the best solution is to construct raised beds (see p.239), where you have direct control over the quality of the soil. The effect of waterlogging can then be advantageous: it acts as a reservoir of water which can rise up through the soil by capillary action. The local water table in a chronically waterlogged garden can be lowered by growing appropriate trees, which transpire a great deal of water. For more details of wetland gardens, see pages 176–81.

Several different systems for protecting crops in open ground appear in the photograph (left). At the back are moveable cold frames with hinged lids angled toward the sun. Classical glass tunnel cloches appear in front of these. In the foreground stand unusual cloches made from polyethylene tubes filled with water. These are particularly effective against frost because the freezing of the water in the tubes releases latent heat to protect the crops inside.

A grass berm (right) beside a gravel-lined swale (with a passive, solar- heated house in

the background) provides one effective means of making sure that rainwater goes where you want it to go.

The final stage of a four-step process in a reed-bed sewage treatment system (below) produces clean but nutrient-enriched water. The surface of the pool in the foreground is covered with an aquatic fern that can be skimmed off and composted or used as a mulch. The water itself is used to irrigate crop plants elsewhere in the greenhouse.

Not Enough Water

Your garden often needs water most when water is in short supply. This is certainly true for gardens that suffer from a lack of water for only two or three months a year. Up until now, you may have relied on the public water system to top up the deficit, but this strategy carries an environmental cost. Dams and reservoirs destroy habitats; boreholes deplete aquifers; and pumping stations and purification plants use large amounts of energy and polluting chemicals. While we cannot do without a public water system, we ought to be thinking about ways in which we can reduce our reliance upon it. Remember that the more public water you use, the greater the impact on the environment.

A number of strategies will help you reduce your demands on the public water supply and make your garden more water-efficient. These strategies make a good deal of sense, especially when you realize that many of the purposes for which you use water in the garden do not require high standards of purification. What's more, the flora and fauna in the garden may even hate the chlorine. While we are primarily concerned here with water conservation in the garden, we shall also touch on ways of reducing our overall water consumption.

Here are some basic principles to consider when drawing up your own water conservation plan:

- Reduce water loss from the soil surface;
- Increase your soil's water-retentive qualities;
- Enhance infiltration via earthworks;
- Harvest runoff from hard surfaces;
- Invest in increased water storage;
- Target your water accurately and efficiently;
- Divert your "gray" water (see p.217);
- Use less water in your sewage system.

Reducing Water Loss from the Soil Surface

Water is lost from the soil either upward through the surface by evaporation and transpiration, or draining downward into the subsoil and water table. As a general rule, you want to encourage drainage, but discourage losses from the surface. This might sound contradictory, but good drainage is essential if plant roots are to remain healthy, while loss from the surface is of little benefit, apart from helping to cool the soil and plants in hot weather. The ideal garden situation is a soil which holds water, but still has a good network of air passages for the roots to breathe. To achieve this your garden soil needs to have a good structure, which you can create most easily by adding organic matter (see below).

To reduce water losses from the soil surface, you have to reduce the volume of water lost through evaporation and transpiration. Many methods, such as the use of shade, wind barriers, and translucent covers, affect both these processes at the same time. You can provide shade and wind barriers simultaneously with brushwood, fences, or hedges. One problem with "living" windbreaks and shade plants, however, is that they, too, remove moisture from the soil, especially if they are well-established plants with extensive root systems. Translucent covers, or "floating mulches", are a more recent technical innovation; they reduce evaporation and transpiration by covering both the soil and the crop.

The most important single method of retaining soil moisture must be mulching: covering the soil with a layer of organic or inorganic material. Not only does it conserve moisture, but it also suppresses weeds (which draw water from the soil) and protects the soil from mechanical erosion by wind and rain.

Increasing the Water-retentive Qualities of Soil

Adding organic matter effectively increases the amount of water available to the plants. You can achieve a similar effect by deep cultivation in hard or heavy soil, so the roots can penetrate farther. This is particularly important if there is a hard pan beneath the surface which may prevent water draining away and roots reaching the water. The result will be larger and deeper roots, which need less watering. You can obtain a similar effect by spacing plants farther apart, so their root zones are not restricted by mutual competition.

On the new technology front, a commercial gel which you can add dry to soils absorbs large amounts of water and makes it readily available to plant roots. You may find this particularly useful in light soils that drain too freely, or peaty media that resist wetting once they have dried out. It's fairly cheap, lasts a long time, and is biodegradable.

Enhancing Infiltration Via Earthworks

When it rains, or when you water your garden, you want to ensure that the water gets to where it's needed. The ideal situation is to arrange the earthworks to do your work for you, providing just the right amount of water for each plant. Among the simplest and most useful earthworks are swales and berms (see p.203).

A swale is a simple ditch along a contour, with a bank, or berm, on the downward side that holds up downward-flowing water and creates a long temporary pond. The system may be designed to overflow into a deeper dammed pond and to support a variety of plants on its banks or in the ditch itself. Once the plants are established, they improve its capacity to trap water. The precise arrangement of the swales and berms depends on the shape and slope of the property. The same methods can be used to intercept surface water from outside the garden.

An alternative method of watering is the traditional flood irrigation within barriers. Here, the water is delivered faster than can be readily absorbed but is retained within a bank that entirely surrounds the plot. As a result, the water remains in place long enough to infiltrate the soil. A variation on this method, and a handy technique even in humid climates, is to plant in shallow pits or raise a small dam on the downward side of a slope. Rainfall then fills the pits and waters the plants rather than running away.

Harvesting Runoff from Hard Surfaces

You can easily channel rain water that runs off hard surfaces, such as the roof of your house, greenhouse, or toolshed. The only requirement is that the collecting point is lower than the hard surface. All you then need to do is divert water through downpipes into a water barrel, storage tank, or pond. This water has the added advantage of being soft and free of salt, although in cities and heavily polluted areas the water may be contaminated.

Targeting your Water Accurately and Efficiently

To make the best use of the water available to your garden, you have to know when and how to water. This is especially true if you're watering by hand, when you want every last drop to count. It is a good idea to test your soil routinely by means of a probe-type water meter to find out just exactly how dry it is beneath the surface.

Good watering techniques save time and effort as well as water. "Water thoroughly from time to time, not little and often" is as true now as it has always been. By following this simple rule you encourage plants to put down deep roots and improve their ability to withstand drought. You can reduce your overall consumption of water by watering only at certain crucial stages of a crop's growth when it really needs it – most crops do not need, or even want, plentiful water all the time. See pages 256–9 for more details on when and how to water your garden.

Recycling Gray Water

Gray water is water that has already been used for some purpose, such as washing, cooking, and cleaning, but not for sewage disposal. Sewage water, or black water, can be treated and made safe, but it is not usually practicable on a routine household basis. It's much better to have a composting toilet (see p.217) and not use flushing water in the first place!

In general, gray water is fine for the garden unless it has been previously treated with water softeners, in which case the soil tends to suffer from salinization. Still at the experimental stage, but very promising, are deep soil/leafmold beds for use in greenhouses. Water from bathtubs, showers, washing machines, and sinks is diverted through a coarse filter (that removes debris such as hairs, buttons, and vegetable peelings) and into the beds. Although the water is delivered in large, irregular doses, the soil absorbs it well; and the soil fauna and flora flourish in the warm water, releasing nutrients on which the plants thrive.

Running the warm water into the greenhouse has two advantages: you can make better use of the incidental heat, and the system has the potential to work year-round. Similar systems outside in the garden work well if the ground is not frozen – water is channelled through pipes with intermittent holes or slots. The pipes need occasional maintenance, but are generally kept clear by the soil animals. If you modify your plumbing to divert gray water follow local codes, use environment-friendly washing products, and alternate gray water with that from the water line or another clean water supply.

Getting water where you want it

The classical rain barrel (below left) collects naturally soft, chlorine-free water from the roof. Oak casks are traditional and attractive, but tend to leak if allowed to dry out. Larger tanks, or ponds, are necessary to maintain supplies over a long dry period.

Mulch materials (right) laid on the surface of the ground suppress weeds and conserve moisture by preventing evaporation. Forestry waste products are cheap and widely available. These mulches are, from left to right, chipped bark, sawdust, and ground bark.

Rice terraces in Bali (below) intercept, store, and use the rainwater flowing down the slopes. They also prevent erosion. The system operates entirely by gravity: there no pumps or energy inputs of any kind.

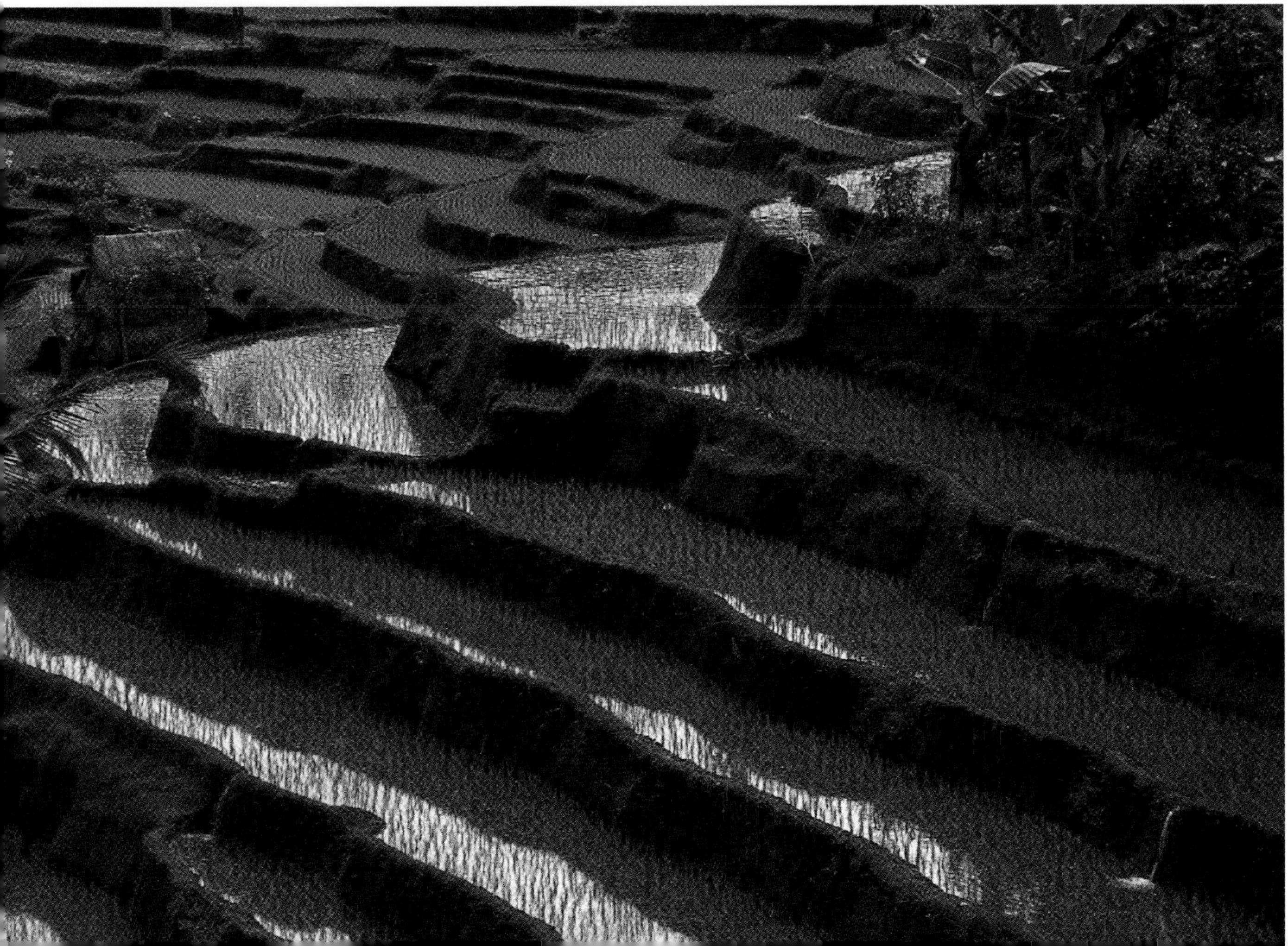

The Water- and Energy-efficient Garden

Although your garden can scarcely be expected to generate a surplus of energy or water, it is essential to minimize its demands on them. You should therefore aim to make the most efficient use of what is freely available. You can, for example, collect rain run-off from hard surfaces and make the best use of light and warmth by the appropriate siting of the various garden elements.

Water collection and storage
In hot climates, underground water storage prevents surface evaporation. In temperate climates, collect run-off in water barrels and distribute in watering cans. Collect gray water from baths and basins, and use it to water trees during the dry months. In drier climates gray water can be diverted through filters and hyacinth/reed tanks, where it is sufficiently cleansed for more general use.

Access routes
Ensure the garden has plenty of paths. These may be composed of various surfaces, such as bark chips, sawdust, or gravel. If you use permanent paving for parking spaces, make sure it slopes toward the garden so water run-off is diverted to the growing areas.

Trees and shrubs
As well as providing shade and chill protection, trees and shrubs act as a sound barrier to traffic and help to clean the air. In urban environments you could help to organize tree planting in your street.

Solar panels on sun-facing roofs heat water, etc.
Sun porch on sunward side of house; fit shades to control heat gain/loss from the house.
Increase solar reflection with water and hard surfaces, such as a pond and patio.
Quiet space
Trees and hedges provide protection against prevailing winds and traffice noise.
A closed porch helps reduce heat loss from the house.
Garage doubles as a shed for bicycles and outdoor toys.
Coal/oil/wood store.

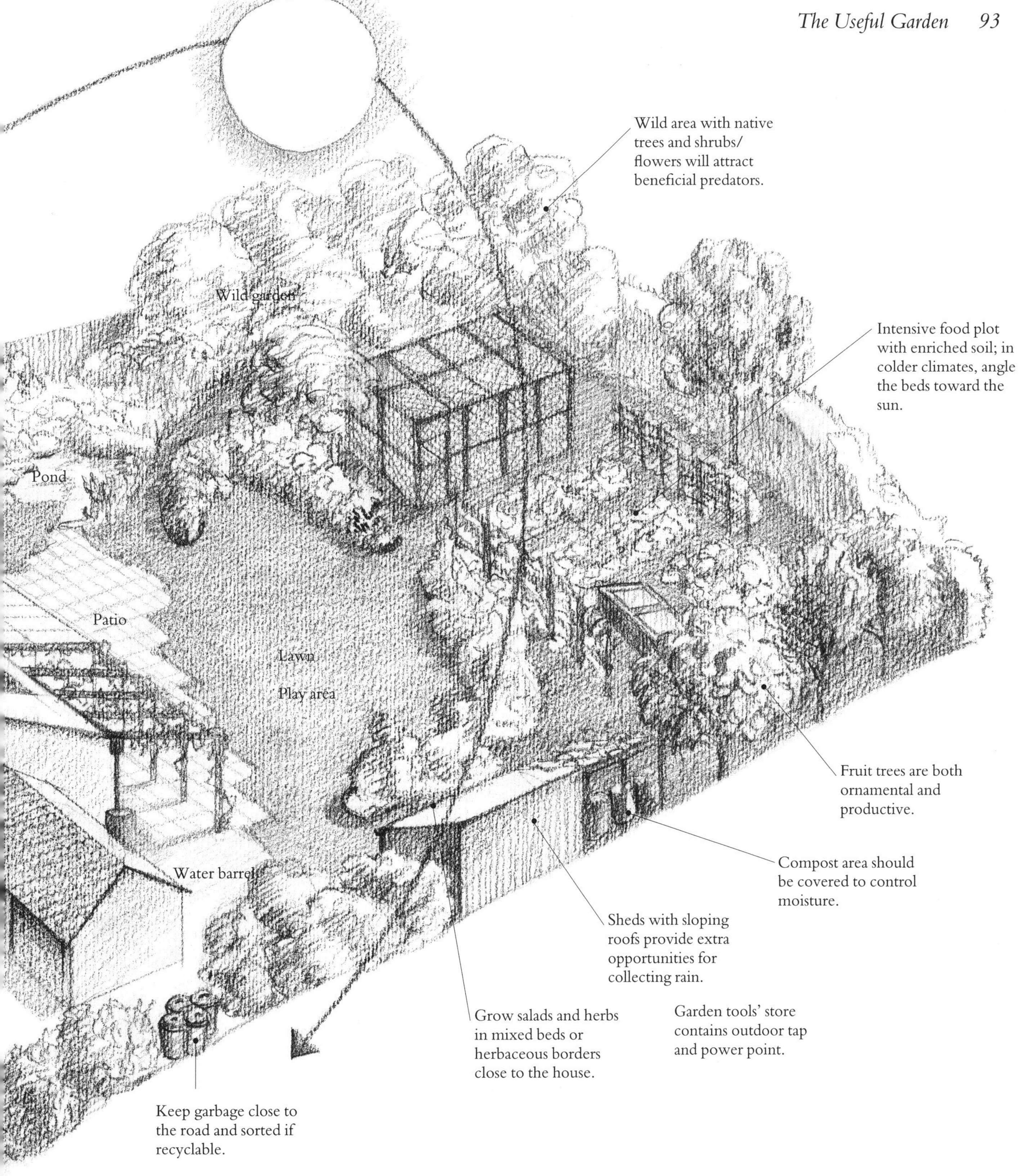

Wild area with native trees and shrubs/ flowers will attract beneficial predators.

Wild garden

Intensive food plot with enriched soil; in colder climates, angle the beds toward the sun.

Pond

Patio

Lawn

Play area

Fruit trees are both ornamental and productive.

Compost area should be covered to control moisture.

Water barrel

Sheds with sloping roofs provide extra opportunities for collecting rain.

Grow salads and herbs in mixed beds or herbaceous borders close to the house.

Garden tools' store contains outdoor tap and power point.

Keep garbage close to the road and sorted if recyclable.

Growing Food

For thousands of years, people in peasant societies have grown enough food to feed their families and at the same time generate a surplus for sale or barter. This works because their income and expenditure are so low that food represents a very large fraction of the whole. In a wealthy, industrial society only those who are short of cash but with time on their hands and access to land would find this economically rational. If you had the skills, and could borrow equipment, growing your own food could be an agreeable way to turn your time into producing something useful.

Why Grow your Own?

On the whole, your modest aim is to grow edible crops that are produced efficiently, appropriate to your circumstances, and complementary to your bought food. You need not incur an overall net cost, and you may even save noticeable amounts of money. The following are some of the reasons for growing your own food and herbs:

- Edible crops are the harvest that complements your efforts in recycling wastes, using your water wisely, and controlling natural energies.
- Gardens can outyield farms and recycle nutrients more effectively. If we all grew our own, the land would be healthier and a tremendous amount of ecologically sound food would be produced.
- Reducing your demands on a food system that has heavy environmental costs (see p.68) is a positive contribution to healing the planet.
- You can save money, especially if you have a low income, a large garden, and time to spare.
- Your own organic crops are rich in vitamins and minerals, free from additives and chemicals, as well as being fresh, convenient, and tasty.
- Vegetable gardening is good exercise; it gets you out into the fresh air and reminds you about the relationship between food and the natural world, and literally puts you in touch with the earth.
- Children can experience and take an active part in the cycle of food production.

You may think that if growing some food is a good thing, growing more is even better, and the height of virtue is to convert the whole garden to producing as much as you possibly can. This is most emphatically not the case. Your food production must complement your garden, the whole food system, and the environment. Remember, you are not trying to maximize, but to optimize.

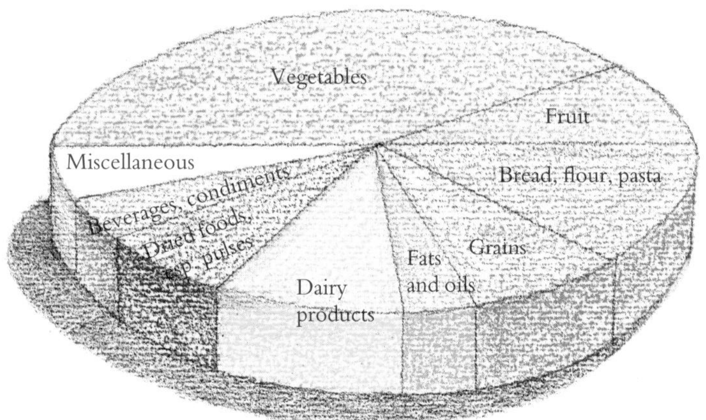

Vegetarian wholefood diet

The right diet
From an environmental point of view, a great improvement on the typical Euro-American diet is one that uses a maximum of local, organically grown produce, and a minimum of animal products, processed and packaged foods, and produce trucked in from a long way away. This is the logic that has given rise to low-meat, whole food diets (above).

The Mesic Garden

It is traditional to segregate the food-growing area from the ornamental and recreational parts of the garden. And the food-growing area itself is organized into vegetable plots, fruit bushes, orchard,

Tree crops may take many years to come to full production, so while they are growing up it makes good sense to give them other jobs to do and combine them with other functions. In the garden above, trained fruit trees make a sheltered walk, are easily reached, and coexist happily with a herbaceous border. In the garden at left, everything is edible but charmingly arranged in the manner of an ornamental garden. The climbing beans on the right were originally cultivated as ornamentals before it was discovered that the pods could be eaten.

greenhouse, and compost piles. If you opt for the intensive method of growing food, you will essentially be creating a vegetable plot that looks like any other conventional vegetable plot with neat, regimented rows of crops. Only there is one very important difference: at the soil or micro-level, you will be encouraging as much richness and diversity as possible. Intensive food production, if it is to be natural and wholesome, relies on careful management of the entire system: composting and maintaining healthy soils using physical, biological, and/or organizational methods (rather than chemical) to deter undesirable plants ("weeds") and animals ("pests").

If you wish to obtain maximum yields from your intensive beds, you must aim to produce "mesic" conditions. Mesic literally means middling – that is to say, conditions which are not excessively hot or cold, wet or dry, acid or alkaline, exposed, elevated, or sloped, shady or salty . . . and in which nutrients are present in ideal quantities and proportions. In other words, perfect conditions for plant growth.

Mesic conditions are what farmers want and strive to create. Gardeners have followed suit, and throughout the ages have striven to file the sharp and distinctive corners off their gardens in order to create the perfect middle ground. This process of "mesification" involves draining, irrigating, cultivating, shading, liming, and fertilizing. However, there are disadvantages, such as attracting pests and weeds, and as a general rule you should only mesify those parts of your garden intended for intensive food production.

Planning your Choices and Strategy

Your year of initiation is essential for you to discover what you really want, what you can achieve, and how best to do it. The measurements and observations will guide you as to what works and what doesn't; how much effort, time, and money certain operations take; what looks unacceptably awful. Remember: don't do anything irreversible!

Traditionally, food and herbs are grown in a rectangular plot that is clearly delimited from the rest of the garden and often out of sight from the house. The location is usually open yet sheltered, freely draining, and not in a frost hollow. Gardeners often set aside a plot for perennial fruit crops.

Separating the productive part of the garden from the rest allows you to focus in one place all the special conditions that promote high yields – the intensive approach. But, alternatively, you can distribute productive crops around the garden, mixed in with all the other plants. Raw yields are much lower, but properly chosen and sited, the edibles may help (and be helped by) other garden plants, and earn their keep by serving other functions, such as shade, ornament, and ground cover. This increasingly popular "integrated approach" can look really good, and suits both large and small gardens.

Locating the productive plot "out of sight" is actually a disadvantage in practical terms. The closer it is to the house, the more exact attention it will receive. Problems are noticed more quickly, harvests are gathered more promptly, and it is easier to fine-tune the crops.

In the traditional approach, gardeners dig or even double-dig (see p.219) the main plot annually, and work in fertilizers or manures. They also prepare new plots by digging or double-digging, and burying or physically removing weeds. They sow or plant crops in straight rows at the beginning of the favorable season, with space between the rows for cultivation and harvesting. As a rule, gardeners arrange these rows in blocks of a single crop variety and weed regularly by hand or by hoeing. At the end of the growing season, they harvest most of their crops and leave the ground bare over the unfavorable season. Finally, they compost any surplus plant material along with their kitchen waste.

While tilling lightens and aerates the soil, and is appropriate in moderate-to-large plots if you have enough time, it is not essential if the soil is healthy, as the many no-till systems have shown. In raised and narrow beds the soil is usually uncompacted and weeds can be easily controlled by light surface cultivation. Otherwise weeds can be controlled by mulches (see pp.211, 221) or by running the chickens over them in a temporary and moveable enclosure. You don't necessarily need to remove all the weeds all the time. Some are innocuous, while others are attractive or even useful. Leaving ground bare in the unfavorable season is not a good idea. If there is no other cover, weeds are better than nothing, and they do it for free.

Gardeners grow most crops from specially prepared commercial seed, but there are other possibilities. You can save your own seeds, which already have the advantage of coming from plants that flourished in your conditions. You can also accept self-seeding from certain crops or the seeding of wild edible plants. These are free, hardy, and worth getting used to. And, in fact, you don't have to sow any seeds at all if you concentrate on perennial and woody plants, although these usually yield less quickly than annual cultivars.

A great temptation is to grow far too much of one variety of crop. It is very easy to do, especially as there are so many seeds in a packet and it seems a shame to waste them. This becomes tedious for the consumers of your produce, and resistance sets in. Better to grow small amounts of many varieties – they add interest and they come to harvest at different times. To keep the costs down, you should arrange seed swaps with friends and neighbors. Traditional gardeners delight in clone-like uniformity of crops, exactly spaced along dead-straight rows. But you can mix different crops in a row, especially if they have different habits and speed of growth (see catch crops, intercrops, and succession crops, pp.100–1).

Appropriate Choice of Crops

Most vegetables are annuals or treated as such, while fruits are mostly perennials. There is a traditional repertoire of these in each climate and garden culture, often strongly influenced by European tastes. They are chosen largely to fit in with the standard diet, and on the basis of received ideas about what is proper to grow in gardens, enlivened by occasional experimentation with new varieties and attempts to carry off prizes at the local fair.

Generally speaking, grow the plants that you and your family enjoy eating, not just what does well, looks good, or comes from the traditional repertoire. And if you're growing crops for the first time, start off by growing the easy plants that do well in your soil and climate. Avoid growing crops, such as peas, that have a reputation for being unreliable. As a rule, choose plants, such as corn, salads, greens, tomatoes, and herbs, where freshness and convenience are paramount. Try to grow crops that displace imported or environmentally damaging products, such as tea or coffee. Become an expert in particular varieties, or better still, grow rare native cultivars that are in danger of dying out, either in your locality or bioregion.

Choose highly productive crops and varieties: those, such as scarlet runner beans, that continue to yield if you keep picking them; plants which have many edible parts; and "cut-and-come-again" crops. Try growing crops and varieties that are either expensive or rarely obtainable, such as white or yellow beets, yellow raspberries, kohlrabi, and Oriental brassicas. At the same time, don't grow big bland crops that can be bought cheaply, unless you have a big garden and lots of time. Finally, grow other crops and varieties to meet your needs when vegetables are expensive or unobtainable: for example, cornsalad, daikon radish, over wintering onions, and Oriental mustard greens. Grow crops that freeze well or can be easily stored, such as root crops, apples, peas and various kinds of beans.

Planning the Productive Plot

By the end of your year of initiation, you should have a fairly good idea about what you are going to do. You will know about the patterns of sun and shade, drainage, soil quality, frost pockets, and desire lines. In a new or undeveloped garden you can plan with great freedom; in an established garden you have to work between fixed elements.

At some point in the garden year, you should make a plan of the plot, and what you want to put in it, with details of all the minor fill-in crops as well, and dates when you intend to sow and harvest. Reality never follows the plan for all manner of reasons, but it's still good to have one. You should also prepare next year's plan to ensure that it dovetails with this

Imaginative combinations of crops and ornamentals give much more interesting results than traditional categories. At Villandry, France (above), box-hedge parterres enclose fruit trees, vegetables, and ornamental bedding plants. In the garden (right), an apple tree stands amid rows of leeks, beans, celery, and flowers.

year's, and to allow you to obtain the seeds, bring on plants in advance, and so on.

You need to decide where to locate the fixed facilities (shed or store, greenhouse, frames, compost, standing faucet or water barrel, storage pond), the permanent plantings (trees, fruit bushes, large perennials), and the intensive beds for annual crops. In a small garden, it matters little where the facilities are placed (but the greenhouse must not be shaded). But taller plants should not shade shorter ones.

The chief ingredients for an intensive plot or a group of narrow beds are: a reasonable amount of sunshine, at least in the main growing season; a site on the well-drained ground well away from large trees or at least sunward of the trees and not in a frost pocket. Make sure the plot is not sited on any desire lines, is accessible to wheelbarrows, and is convenient for watering. Once you have fixed the location of the plot, you can choose the appropriate size, form, and method of "breaking in" from the many alternatives, and apply soil amendments if necessary. You are now in a position to decide what and where you want to sow or plant.

Crop Rotation

You are of course at liberty to scatter mixed seeds at random and see what happens. But it is customary to group plants in blocks or rows of like kinds, because different plants like different treatments. And, because crop type takes different proportions of nutrients from the soil, and suffers from different soil-borne diseases, it is very good to grow each type in a different place the following year, and again the year after that for at least three years. This is crop rotation (see p.234) and is vital if you grow annual crops in intensive beds.

Succession Crops

Most crops are in the ground for only part of the year. When they are harvested it may not be the right time for the succeeding crop to be planted. The gap is usually filled with a non-rotated crop or perhaps a green manure (see pp.104, 222). For example, a single square foot of a vegetable plot in a northern temperate garden might experience the following four-year sequence: kale, celeriac, fava beans, zucchini, green manure, dig over, lettuces, leeks, cabbage.

These "succession" crops are particularly good for providing fresh produce in high-latitude winters when little else will grow. It is a good idea to plan for succession crops to go in as soon as you harvest each summer crop. Direct sowings may not have time to germinate and get established, so where possible you should have potted-on plants ready to go in. These include kale, broccoli, savoy cabbage, cornsalad, mizuna, winter spinach, upland cress, leeks, garlic, chervil, and kohlrabi.

Catch Crops

As succession crops fill a gap after a main-season crop, catch crops fill the short gaps before a main crop is ready. For example, where there is a risk of late frost, snap beans or zucchini cannot be put out until late spring or even early summer in northern temperate regions. Savoys or leeks might have overwintered in the same plot, but since you have been eating them steadily, substantial gaps have opened up. These can be filled with fast-growing plants, such as radishes, baby beets, arugula, and salads, or by a green manure, such as mustard, which is easily hoed in.

A variation on this catch-crop theme is to sow two different types of seed at the same time – one fast, the other slow. Parsnips are usually sown three seeds at a time, in "stations" a few inches apart, but they take a long time to germinate. Radishes sown between the stations come up quickly and handily mark the row for weeding. They are ready to pull just as the parsnips are putting out their first true leaves.

Intercrops

Plants that are destined to be big, but are slow to begin, are usually planted with wide spacing to allow for eventual growth, but this leaves large areas of ground temporarily unused. These gaps can be filled with small or fast-growing plants that are harvested before they are crowded out by the principal crop. Sometimes, these intercrops complement the main crop so well – on account of size or the shape of the root mass, or because they are shade tolerant – that they are simply left in and harvested whenever convenient. This is usually called interplanting, but the distinction is academic. It is by no means essential to cover your plot entirely with edible crops. Flowers and fragrant plants can be slipped in, especially plants that are alluring to insects; and if any attractive wildflowers turn up – leave them!

Spacing

When planting, you may often get better overall yields by closer spacing than the instructions advise, even if the individual plants are smaller. Try it – plant some close, some spaced, and observe the results. You can arrange your plants more densely if the rows are closed up and staggered, so that individual plants occupy a cell in a honeycomb. Each plant has its own space, but more can fit into a unit area this way. Such a honeycomb arrangement has the added benefit of giving more effective ground cover, preventing both evaporation of ground water from the soil and invasion by weed seeds. This is just as well, because it's more difficult to hoe a honeycomb than regular rows.

Herb Gardening

Herbs occupy a special place in the garden because virtually anybody can grow them. Some herbs are grown principally for tisanes, or herbal teas; others, such as sage and rosemary, are medicinal as well as culinary. Many more, such as lemon balm and peppermint, are simply good to drink.

Herbs can do a lot with a little (they are ideal for small spaces) and only by growing them yourself can you get them as fresh or as conveniently. Generally speaking, a family will need, for flavoring purposes, no more than one plant of each of the common culinary herbs. They can easily be grown in containers – in fact, some of the more rampant herbs, such as horseradish and the mints, need containing to keep them out of mischief. Containers can be an advantage in that, if small enough, they can be moved about to suit the season. Chervil, for example, loves a sunny spot in the winter, but can be moved into the shade in the summer. Less hardy herbs such as sage and rosemary, should be brought into a sheltered place in colder weather.

From both a culinary and a horticultural point of view, herbs fall into two, or perhaps three, main classes – flavorings, garnishes, and salads. Most of the sun-loving, aromatic kinds usually used to flavor cooked food are perennials: sage, rosemary, thyme, tarragon, bay, marjoram, oregano, lovage, balm, fennel (which is always grown as an annual). They need permanent places of their own. In severe winters such herbs are better grown in containers, and moved back and forth from sun to shelter.

The softer, fleshy herbs more often used for garnishing are hard to distinguish from highly flavored plants more commonly regarded as salads. Some are perennials: chives, mints, sorrel, and sweet cicely. Like the Mediterranean herbs, they need permanent homes but with a richer and moister environment.

Borage, burnet, celery leaf, nasturtium, Oriental mustard, coriander, and upland cress are annuals you can scatter among other crops in the main plot, or in an odd corner of the garden. You don't need many of any of these, but you can always do with plenty of parsley, basil, and garlic which are used for cooking and garnishing alike. So incorporate these into your plan with a generous provision for parsley. Basil can be tricky; it likes hot weather, but needs to be watered in the heat of the day. In cool summer climates, it may do better in the greenhouse or at least a frame.

Salads

Salads form a vital part of the home garden because their freshness is of the essence: pick them just before use at their point of optimum growth, together with their garnishes. They can be worked in among the main items in your plan: many make good catch crops and some, such as upland cress, cornsalad, and mizuna, are winter-hardy. Many are "cut-and-come-again" varieties that can be harvested over a long period without replanting. And don't forget the wild salads, such as bittercress and sheep sorrel, nor the continental and oriental varieties.

The garden above contains plants that are useful in herbal medicine or homeopathy; they include foxgloves, mullein, monkshood, and poison ivy. The large, thistle-like plants are cardoons. The edible archway (top right) reminds you with a gentle bump on the head when it's time to harvest the marrows. The crop is accompanied by sweet peas, sunflowers, and rudbeckias. The old cartwheel (right) shows one of the many ways of separating and displaying herbs, although in this case the mint is going to need restraining in subsequent years! For most culinary herbs, a few plants is sufficient to meet the needs of a family.

SAGE
RUE
APPLEMINT

Soil Fertility

If you wish to extract the maximum yields from your intensive plot, you must feed the soil with nutrients. Natural processes of nutrient release are normally too slow for the modern-day gardener, which is why so many are tempted to bypass the natural system altogether, and provide the plants directly with soluble nutrients. This is the logical basis for chemical fertilizers, in which the role of the soil is simply to provide water and hold the plants upright.

"Negative organics" (see p.55) uses large quantities of bought-in organic materials (dried blood, farmyard manure, fishmeal, etc.) instead of chemicals. This is better in many ways, but has a "robbing Peter to pay Paul" air about it. In the natural garden you should aim to create all necessary fertility from your own resources. But you will increase yields sustainably only if you increase the rate at which nutrients are made available from the soil reservoir.

A sustainable but productive fertility system, therefore, has two aspects. One is short-term: to stimulate the natural processes to make nutrients available to plants. The other is long-term: to top up the reservoir from which nutrients are drawn. Happily, you can do both at once by the regular addition of organic matter to the soil.

Addition of organic matter is the cornerstone of the intensive approach, and it is hard to overstate its importance. Soil fertility is not just a matter of nutrients, but a complex of chemical, physical, and biological factors: soil texture, composition, structure, pH, and a thriving community of organisms. It turns out that the addition of organic matter addresses all these factors: it adds nutrients and stimulates the microbial activity that releases more from the soil reservoir; it buffers pH; it creates a stable, open structure that improves drainage and water retention; it lightens heavy soils and firms up light ones. If this seems like magic, perhaps it is. But it is a natural magic within reach of us all, and the basis of organic gardening's most famous slogan: FEED THE SOIL, NOT THE PLANT.

There are three principal methods of adding organic matter to the soil. You can grow it right where you want it in the form of green manures, you can introduce fresh matter from elsewhere (see fresh feeding, right), or you can "pre-digest" the organic matter in a compost pile before adding it to the soil (see pp.212–3).

Green Manures

Plants take nutrients from the soil, but they do a great deal in return. Sugars and other compounds from photosynthesis are exuded from the roots and support vigorous populations of microorganisms. Roots die and become food for larger organisms, and the tunnels they leave form channels for water drainage and aeration of the soil. Far from "needing a rest" every now and again, soils actually like having plants growing in them.

So, if at any point in your garden cycle, a patch of bare soil opens up, grow some plants in it. You may then allow such plants to die off naturally, or be killed by frost; or you may kill them by hoeing off the tops; or they may be crowded and shaded out by more vigorous plants around them. In any event they will have done their job and the nutrients they withdrew from the soil will be returned, plus a lot of high-energy carbon compounds, providing food for soil organisms. These plants are called green manures.

Plants grown in between main crops or to fill bare spaces are called cover crops – they are often low-growing and short-lived. More seriously, you can devote part of your rotation cycle (see p.234) to specific plants that feed the soil rather than you. They may be allowed to grow quite large, then are tilled in. Very commonly, they are legumes, which have the power to fix nitrogen from the air, using special bacterial nodules in their roots. Grasses are also frequently used, since their very powerful roots create an ideal crumb structure in the soil (see pp.29, 197).

Not only do cover crops and green manures stimulate soil activity and improve structure, they moderate the soil temperature, suppress weeds, and reduce leaching. They can be sown at most times of the year, in single varieties or mixtures. They are usually dug in before flowering, and it is best to allow a few weeks before planting fresh crops to allow the soil time to digest the material. There are dozens of suitable species.

Nutrients and Soil pH

Nearly all the trace elements in a soil are available to plants if its pH is between 6 and 7. A high proportion of soils fall within this range and virtually all plants will grow in these conditions. The addition of organic matter, especially well-made compost, tends to "buffer" the soil and keep it from straying outside this range, as well as providing a good variety of micronutrients.

So, in most cases, no special attention is needed to pH, beyond adding organic material. Soils which are very rich in lime may have a pH above 7, but most crops can tolerate this, and it may even be an advantage for some, such as celery, cauliflower, asparagus, beets, carrots, onions, leeks, spinach, and Jerusalem artichokes.

Acidic soils are preferred by potatoes, rhubarb, strawberries, cranberries, and huckleberries. Some crops find such soils lack sufficient calcium, so gardeners add lime – this raises pH and can be detrimental to the soil community, causing local deficiencies of micronutrients. Preferable sources of calcium are ground limestone (particularly dolomite, which adds magnesium as well), calcified seaweed, crushed eggshells, and wood ash. The latter three sources are best introduced into the garden via the compost pile.

Fresh Feeding

As an alternative to green manures, bring fresh plant material from elsewhere in your garden and either dig it into the soil or leave it as a mulch layer on the surface. You can use kitchen waste, general garden trimmings, grass clippings, weed tops, or plants specially grown for the purpose. If it looks untidy, or is quickly oxidized by the sun's heat, spread a layer of inert mulch, such as ground bark, wood chips, cardboard or plastic sheeting, over the fresh material.

Rock Flours

Finely ground rock, such as basalt, can make up for deficiencies in a soil's micronutrients. Microorganisms are thought to respond to the influx of micronutrients in the rock powder, or flour, by releasing macronutrients more efficiently. In effect, rock flours mimic the fertility of freshly minted postglacial or volcanic soils.

Dynamic Accumulators

Some plants such as comfrey (see right), have the quality of concentrating, or making available, specific minerals. You can either dig in these dynamic accumulators or harvest the accumulated nutrients by cutting the leaves and placing them on your intensive plots.

Green manures are usually annuals; perennials would develop far larger root systems and exploit a greater depth of soil, but it would not be convenient to have them in the rotating beds of annual crops. So perennials are sometimes grown separately as a source of fresh material for soil food and valuable soil minerals. Such perennials are rather like artesian wells, drawing nutrients from the subsoil up into the living zones of the soil where shallow-rooting plants can benefit from them.

The Virtues of Comfrey

Perhaps the most celebrated of the dynamic accumulators, comfrey deserves a book in its own right. Its roots are very deep; its tissues accumulate potash most strongly, but also nitrogen, calcium, and magnesium. Its vigor allows several cuts a year from each plant.

An easy-to-grow plant, comfrey likes damp, even waterlogged situations, although it will grow perfectly well in any ordinary soil. Unlike most plants it is not "burned" by very strong doses of concentrated nutrients, such as urine or chicken manure, but consumes them voraciously. Its ability to scavenge nutrients in this way makes it particularly suitable for preventing leaching around compost piles, septic tanks, and animal enclosures – in fact, the leaves are rich in protein.

Ladybugs (above) and their larvae have a great appetite for aphids, but hoverflies, lacewings, and ichneumon wasps are more effective predators of undesirable animals. In an ecologically balanced garden with a good variety of native plants and zero use of pesticides, these predators will quietly deal with most pests for most of the time.

The common stinging nettle (left) grows vigorously in rich soil to which it imparts an excellent crumbly structure. A dynamic accumulator of iron and a maker of good compost, the nettle is an important food source for many insect species. When cooked the young leaves are deliciously edible.

Undesirable Animals and Plants

Animals that damage the crops and other plants we are nurturing are a nuisance and so we usually call them pests. Obviously, they did not evolve with the specific purpose of eating our crops but, as with weeds, they have taken full advantage of the new and vast ecological vistas that gardening and agriculture have opened up for them.

In nature, life can be tough for herbivores: plants tend to be heavily defended with repulsive chemicals, forcing a herbivore to specialize in a limited range of plants which it has learned (in the evolutionary sense) to digest. But these plants might be widely distributed, so a specialist herbivore has to spend most of its time searching for its food plant; and when it finds one, the plant may be a poor specimen with little nourishment to offer.

How different the prospect with human crops! They are conveniently gathered together, often in massive stands; they are fertilized to increase growth; and they are bred both to maximize yields of edible parts, and reduce defensive tastes and poisons. For any herbivore specializing in a wild relative of a crop species, it is a bonanza not to be missed. It is not surprising that farmers and gardeners suffer from a "pest problem". As with weeds, we have created the problem ourselves.

The conventional answer to pests is chemical pesticides. However, an increasing number of people believe that pesticides are unnecessary on a garden scale and cause more problems than they solve. The first step, then, in any natural approach to pests is simply to stop using pesticides.

Even though you may have no intention of applying chemical pesticides, you might imagine that the "natural" approach to pests involves some biodegradable, non-persistent product which does more or less the same thing; or even that you can make your own pest-control potions from elder leaves and eco-friendly washing-up liquid. Not so. You need to adopt a completely different approach, with the help of a little biology and a lot of common sense. Although in principle you should be able to work out pest-control programs for each pest from a detailed knowledge of its habits and physiology, this can be completely impractical. There are thousands of different kinds of potential pests, and even more kinds of predator. What is needed is a very general approach to pest control that only becomes specific when circumstances make it absolutely necessary.

During your year of initiation you not only observed creatures visiting your experimental plots (see p.199) but you also watched the creatures that were interested in them. If you continue observing (including the occasional nighttime inspection) you will discover that most pest attacks mysteriously disappear of their own accord. All you have done is to stay out of the way and let it happen. This is the cornerstone of what we call "non-specific biological control" and is the answer to the problem of not knowing what pest is attacked by what predator. For example, the aphid *Myzus persicae* is fatally parasitized by the larvae of the wasp *Ephedrus cerasicola*, but it's not essential for you to know this. All you need to do is to make absolutely sure that conditions are agreeable to *Ephedrus*, so that it will hunt out *Myzus* and do the ghastly deed for you.

Your main concern should be to ensure that whatever pests arrive in the garden, there is always something ready to eat them. Here are some basic rules for doing this:

- Use no pesticides, organic or otherwise: they affect the predators far more than the pests.
- Tolerate a variety weeds and wild plants.
- Create as many different kinds of habitats and microclimates as possible in the garden (see pp.260–5).
- Make sure your garden has a steady succession of plants, such as the members of the daisy and carrot families, with small or very open flowers; these provide nectar for the adults of insect species which have predatory or parasitic larvae.
- As a matter of good practice you should leave at least one plant of any biennial or perennial umbellifer crop, such as carrot, parsnip, parsley, fennel, or celery, to provide a succession of flowers the following year.

These rules should be complemented with three non-specific actions to counter fungal diseases:

- Feed the soil and make sure the plants get enough water. Since healthy plants are known to resist pests and diseases, an extra feed may be all that is needed to see off an attack. However, too much nitrogen can attract scales and aphids. Be conservative!

- Rotate your crops so they grow in different soil every year and keep ahead of fungal diseases.
- Minimize gray mold in humid conditions by keeping plants farther apart and by removing lower leaves to encourage air circulation.

After a year or so, the combination of all these measures will control 99 percent of the potential pest or disease problems. The remaining 1 percent varies from garden to garden. There are always one or two pests for which conditions are so favorable that specific measures are necessary. Here you do have to do some research and think things out.

Ask yourself whether the damage caused to a crop really matters and if it's worth further effort. Are you so committed to the crop – couldn't you grow something else? If you must grow the crop and there are no resistant varieties, then you may have to use barriers, decoys, and/or traps to keep the pests at bay. Barriers simply prevent the pest getting to the critical part of the plant. Common examples include brassica collars against the cabbage root-fly; floating mulch to combat carrot fly; and fruit cages and "humming" tape in fruit bushes to deter the attentions of birds.

Decoys lure the pest away from the plant. For example, since slugs prefer wilting comfrey to almost anything else, a ring of comfrey leaves will protect a crop. Examples of traps include sticky bands on trees to trap crawling insects; daytime traps for slugs under grapefruit halves or slabs of wood; and to combat millipedes, pitfall traps baited with potato.

Another possibility is biological control, where you know both the pest and the predator, and can buy a prepared culture of the predator for release. For obvious reasons this works best in an enclosed space such as a greenhouse. As a last resort, try an organically acceptable spray (see p.109).

Opportunist Plants

A plant community develops from a simple beginning on bare ground to a stable and complex "climax", of which the dominant species tend to be trees (see p.16–7). Most other members of the community are specialists that have evolved to exploit a particular set of conditions and resources within the community as a whole. The various specialisms dovetail together in a broadly complementary way.

Some members of the community thrive on disruption, however. They are opportunists that wait for the settled order to break down. They are, of course, the weeds. There are two main types: the annuals, which specialize in colonizing disturbed soils, and the perennials, which specialize in the rapid and persistent exploitation of fertile soils.

In settled climax situations weeds are rare, but if given the chance, they can grow and reproduce at a colossal rate. This is their forte. The "problem of weeds" in gardens arises because in constantly disturbing and enriching the soil, you are setting up the perfect conditions for both types to do what they are really good at.

Annual weeds are generally less of a problem than perennial ones. The germination of their seeds is mostly triggered by light, so any cultivation brings a flush of green a few days later, as any gardener will have observed. Light hoeing will kill these – too deep and you just bring up more – and you may have to do some hand-weeding within the rows. Rows of crops make a gardener's life much easier in a moderate-sized or large plot.

If crop and weed seedlings emerge at about the same time, you have about two weeks to remove the weeds before serious competition begins. After that time it will be much more difficult, and your crop yields will be affected. Weed competition has more effect early in a crop's life cycle than later on, so don't put it off. Only toward harvest time will your crops be able to outcompete any new weeds.

The dormant weed seeds present in your garden's soil constitute a "seed bank" that is constantly topped up by weed seeds from outside. If fresh seeds are prevented from germinating, regular cultivation will gradually deplete the seed bank. About half the seeds will die anyway each year, so you should be down to a few percent of the original total after about five years.

Established perennial weeds are a different matter. Most of their reserves are in the roots, and hoeing off the tops gives only a temporary check. Of course, if you keep at it for a long time they will finally give up, but it is probably less effort to dig them out once and for all. From the gardener's point of view, tap-rooted perennials, such as dock, dandelion, or horseradish, are easily removed; but those weeds with a network of roots are far more problematic – bindweed, horsetail, goutweed, woundwort, nettle, vetches, quack grass, bracken, and kikuyu. Despite your best efforts to remove them, small root pieces are inevitably left in the soil and from each of these another shoot comes up to the surface. If the infestation is small it is probably worth making the effort to create a clean plot; for more serious invasions, however, you have little choice but to sheet mulch (see p.221) or carpet mulch (see p.211).

Gardeners who don't like the look of sheet-mulches can use organic matter instead to suppress the germination of annuals, but determined perennials will come up through anything loose. Peat and chipped or composted forest bark are common but they cost money (as do shredders). Sawdust is cheap but can temporarily affect the yield of some crops by depleting nitrogen. Rich mulches that both suppress weeds and feed soil organisms are best. Such mulches include compost, seaweed, rotted manure, comfrey leaves, and straw soaked with urine. In fact, loose mulches can be placed underneath sheet-mulches during the off-season to allow the soil organisms to process them and work them into the soil. Loose mulches can also be placed on top of sheet-mulches for cosmetic reasons, but in this case it is preferable to use a porous paper or permeable woven sheet that will suppress weeds but allow rain to penetrate.

Undoubtedly, the most natural way to control weeds is by using well-behaved ground cover plants, and these can be crops in their own right. Low-growing legumes, such as clover and hyacinth bean, are particularly useful.

It is important that you get to know your own weeds, so that you can identify those which are really a problem, and those which just look like they are. It is commonly stated in books that wild plants in cultivated plots act as reservoirs for pests and diseases, but there is very little evidence for this. They are much more likely to reduce the incidence of pests by providing foodplants for their predators, for whom variety is important. So here's a radical rule of thumb: if it isn't a known villain, and it isn't in the way, leave it. If it spoils the row and obstructs cultivation, carefully transfer it to the edge or end of the plot.

An unsung virtue of weeds is their contribution to soil health and fertility. As plants, they grow, fix carbon, and make carbohydrates. When you hoe them off, they die and become food for the soil fauna and flora, which relish fresh organic matter. Larger weeds may have deep roots that bring up nutrients beyond the reach of your crops. Each species picks out a different mix of nutrients, so a variety of weed tops, either hoed off and left on the ground, or put into the compost pile, provides a wonderful cocktail of micronutrients.

Organically Acceptable Sprays

If all else fails (and if you get this far, there's something you're not doing right, or more likely something you are failing to stop yourself doing), you can try the organically acceptable sprays, such as insecticidal soap, rotenone, and pyrethrum. Even though these are non-persistent, they are still wide-spectrum and can do a lot of damage. One of the better sprays is a culture of *Bacillus thuringiensis*, sold under various trade names. A toxin from this bacterium attacks the stomach linings of insect larvae. Since most larvae (caterpillars in particular) are specific to one type of plant, it is easy to target the spray to one offending species.

If, after all, you have still have intractable problems with pests on your crops, remind yourself that you don't have to grow them. It may be an indication that your garden is not the right place for growing food. Give in gracefully, get yourself a good hand lens, and embark on the study of the pests themselves. Soon you will come to know them and become involved in their problems, their innocent cunning, their battles and defeats. You may find yourself growing a crop just because your favorite pests appreciate it so much, and you want to see more of them. Indiscriminate biocide will become unthinkable. At this point you will start to notice that your other crops seem to be managing much better....

THE WILDLIFE GARDEN

A garden is a place where nature and humanity meet. We can see in the history of gardening a rhythmic seesaw of the balance between the natural and the artificial. But in the end the human side of gardening has dominated the encounter: the traditional garden has always been either directly useful or like a work of art, an expression of the gardener's skill and taste. Outside the garden there was always plenty of unproductive, untidy, unimproved nature. No need for more!

All this has turned upside down. Far from seeing farms and gardens as oases of order and plenty in a wild and hostile landscape, we are suddenly aware that nature has shrunk to isolated refuges in a matrix of cities, factories, roads, and mechanized farms. We are beginning to wake up to what we have lost and to realize how little time there is to save the rest.

If anything of the truly natural is to be saved, a great deal must be changed. On the large scale, we have to reorganize farming, industry, transport, and urban life so it is consistent with the health of the wider environment. This is going to take a long time, as these things will. The prospect is not good. What can we do in the meantime to bridge the gap?

Surely a large part of the answer must lie in our gardens. Gardens can reverse their traditional stance of artifice and human-centeredness, and become foci of naturalness, acting as networks of nature reserves and wildlife sanctuaries while we reorganize the rest of our economic life along ecologically sustainable lines. This is very important. Governments and large organizations, if left to themselves will merely designate a few nature ghettoes; we need to bring nature back into our lives on a far wider scale and in far more intimate detail.

Every garden can play a part, no matter what functions go on there. Paradoxically, towns offer the greatest benefits in regions where the countryside has largely been rendered unfit for natural life – modern farming has managed it almost to death. Gardeners have often taken their cue from farmers, whose livelihoods depend on a maximum degree of control. Gardeners too like to display their control, their taste. It is the mark of a "nice garden" that nothing is left to chance. This is the prevailing fashion.

We would like to replace this with another fashion, in which the balance is shifted from control to spontaneity; or to put it another way, nature is allowed to manage more of the controlling function. In this style of garden you can still decide yourself where the balance point shall be. You can still reserve part of the garden for traditional, direct management. You can start as gently as you like, and you can draw back whenever you want. You can do it step by step – in fact, it is very difficult to do otherwise, because that is the way nature works. You can have a really exciting garden, beloved by children and adults alike, far more challenging and complex than the traditional model, but in many ways more forgiving. And you can help the environment at the same time.

Start gently and allow yourself to be drawn in. As your garden changes, you will change yourself. You will learn to experience it in a new way.

Mapping your Bioregion

The garden you see in front of you is part of the world, but also is a world itself. It is like a set of Russian dolls. Outside the garden is the neighborhood habitat, and beyond that the district, the bioregion, the biome, and the biosphere. Within the garden there are millions of microhabitats. Some are more or less obvious, parts which are shaded or dry or exposed – visibly different from the rest. Finer ones lie within the canopy of a tree, the cracks in a wall, between the blades of grass in the lawn. Smaller still, between tiny soil particles, in the hairs of garden animals, and even floating in the air, are communities as diverse as any at the larger scale.

The largest frame for your garden is the biosphere, which is naturally divided up into biomes. These are based on climate and evolutionary history

A partnership with insects to promote cross-fertilization was one of the main innovations of the flowering plants. The bee visiting a sage flower (right) is already covered with pollen from another plant. Its weight on the flower's lower lip levers down the forked stigma to touch the bee's back.

(see pp.38–41). Each biome has a characteristic range of plant types. Within a biome there are bioregions defined by physical features, such as watersheds, or by historic land-use practices. A biome can itself be divided up into more local regions, and into habitat types such as woods, river valleys, mountainsides, saltmarsh, and so on. The "boundaries" between biomes are not abrupt but blend into wide, mixed zones.

Getting a feel for your bioregion is part of tuning in to your environment. Yet this may be remarkably difficult, since the original "natural" conditions and communities of animals and plants in your area may have been altered beyond recognition.

On the large scale, biologists have attempted to reconstruct and map the original vegetation of bioregions. Historical records can also help. In many areas undisturbed chunks may be left: go and see them! Bioregions are not eternally fixed. They move about with climatic cycles, they grow, evolve, shrink, and even disappear entirely. But it is hard to eradicate completely their distinctive features and we can all try to nurture what's left.

During your year of initiation, explore your neighborhood and learn to recognize the characteristic signs of the old bioregion. This can make a practical difference to planning a wildlife garden. Although you can regard your garden as an isolated habitat providing only for its own citizens, this does not reflect the real world. Your garden is part of a web or network in which life, energy, and nutrients move endlessly around. If it fits into this web it will work much better and you will be able to make a more useful contribution to the whole.

Mapping Local Nature Spaces

As a prelude to planning your own wildlife garden try to draw up a map of the local system of nature spaces. Standard maps will help you get the scales and relative locations right. Large-scale topographic maps will give some indications of habitat types but not much local detail. To fill up your maps you will have to do your own field research. In particular, look for:

- Obvious parts of classical habitat, such as streams, rivers, ponds, bogs, woodlands, or rocky outcrops; unused or derelict sites which often present a "tough" environment suitable for rarer species of stress-tolerating plants and offer shelter for animals.
- Corridors that link pieces of habitat too small in themselves to support diverse flora and fauna – small streams, canals, drainage ditches, railroad embankments, road sides, lines of trees where the canopies touch, hedgerows, or banks.
- Managed ground, such as gardens, farmland, parks, playing fields, that may benefit nature in spite of the efforts to manage it.

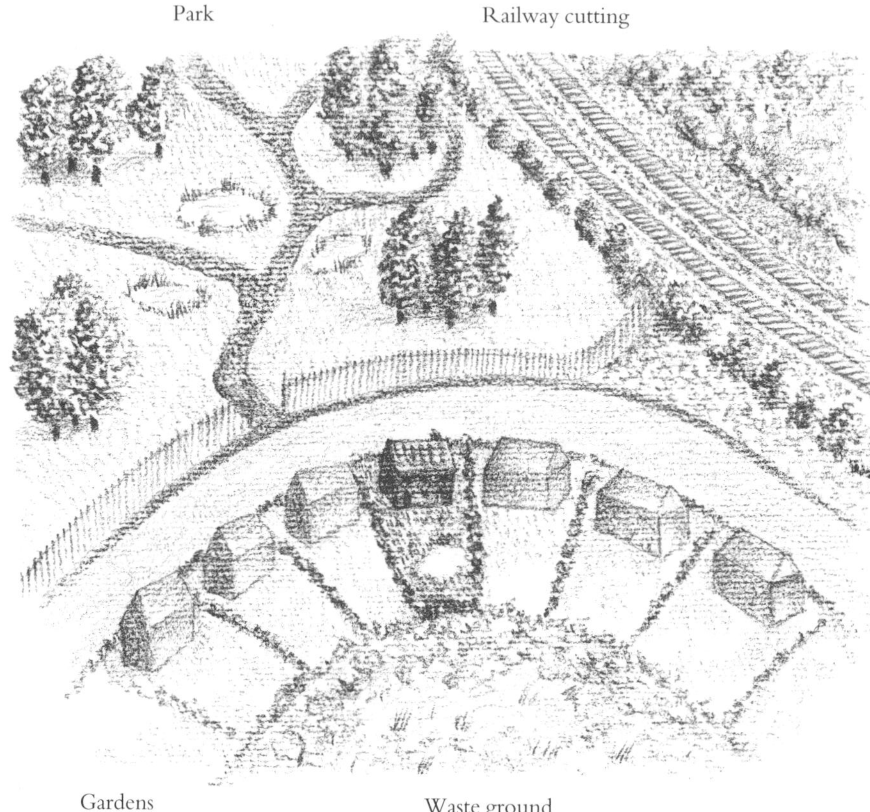

Of all the garden developments you can undertake to increase habitat diversity, ponds are probably the most effective and the most gratifying. If you have the space, a large pond (above) offers a wide range of possibilities, but even a tiny pool can make a noticeable difference.

A much more intimate view of a pond comes from a large mirror set at an angle of about 45 degrees near the edge (right). The mirror reveals not only the horizontal perspective but also the water's undersurface, itself a habitat for many pond creatures.

Planning a Wildlife Garden

Before undertaking any major developments in your garden, contact other people or groups who think along the same lines: then you can plan together, remembering that the maximum diversity is in the network, not the individual parcels of land. Then ask yourself four fundamental questions.

Firstly, is your garden suitable for a nature space? Any garden can be, at least to some degree, but is this the best use of your garden? Look at all the things you would like to use the garden for. If you have plenty of time and a moderately sized, well-situated, highly cultivated and enriched garden, you should really grow food. In a small garden, too, you may need most of the space for functional and recreational facilities. However, if your time is limited and your garden is large or "problematic" in a way that makes productive growing difficult, then think about creating a nature space. It does not need to occupy the whole garden; in fact, since nature will inhabit the rough, poor, and uncultivated bits, a nature space can pleasantly complement other purposes.

Secondly, how does your garden fit in with the outside network? An analysis of your local habitat network may suggest something you could usefully do to complement it. This may involve more of the same: for example, if you found that your treeless garden was a broken link in a chain of trees acting as a corridor, it might be most useful to add back that link. Or you may collaborate with neighbors to create a "critical mass" of a particular type of habitat. Alternatively, you could provide a contrasting habitat that is locally scarce: ponds in an area too rigorously drained, trees where there are few, or special shelters, such as bird houses or underground holes.

Thirdly, are you going to specialize? You may decide to create as large an area as possible of one kind of habitat, or concentrate your encouragement of a particular group of animals or plants – for example, prairie flowers, ferns, amphibians, or butterflies. You may prefer the little-bit-of-everything approach to start with, and allow the succeeding years to suggest a preferred direction. This is often the best way forward, especially if your local survey gives ambiguous results and does not indicate any obvious and decisive role for your garden.

Finally, how far are you prepared to go? There is no need to plunge straight into a total rethink of your garden. The great thing about a wildlife garden is that it can be very small and you can develop it bit by bit, and have as much or as little as you wish.

Simple Measures for your Year of Initiation

However you answer these questions, there are simple things you can do that will combine easily with almost any other function and will not greatly affect the appearance of your garden. Moreover, they are straightforward and rewarding projects to try out in your year of initiation. Real enthusiasts for nature spaces can, at the same time, contemplate taking wholesale redesign measures that will seriously change the appearance of their gardens. These include restoring original habitat conditions and communities of organisms, leaving the garden (or parts of it) to evolve with the minimum of intervention, and creating major habitats, such as ponds (see pp.262–3) and woods (see p.123).

Providing Food and Water for Birds

Birds are probably the most visible and charming of the garden's inhabitants and visitors. They can of course feed themselves, but more birds will come more regularly if extra food is provided. Bird-feeders of many kinds are readily obtainable, or you can make you own. Placed on or just outside a window, they guarantee hours of entertainment, the house becoming a convenient and comfortable "hide".

A bird-feeder can be extremely simple, but it does not take much greater effort to make an advanced model that works better and provides for a greater range of bird needs. The feeder should be placed near the house to ensure it is cared for. Regular re-stocking is important, especially in unfavorable seasons, when the birds may come to depend on it. And remember to brush off left-overs before providing new food.

Put out a variety of foods to attract a variety of different birds: wholewheat bread, seeds, nuts, fats, berries – but no salty foods. The most important times are seasons when food is scarce and when migrant birds are passing through – they need a lot of energy for their journeys. Water is just as important, especially in a dry season. So make sure you have either a small pond or a removable water-dish on the bird-feeder.

Many birds need water for cleaning their feathers, particularly in cold winters when they have to keep themselves well fluffed-up to stay warm. A bird-bath must be kept fresh and topped up, so make sure it's light enough to lift and tip the old water out. Any shallow vessel will do, the larger the better – self-standing casserole dishes or tart pans are fine, as are garbage can lids when they are supported by three bricks or stones.

In climates with very cold winters, snow will usually provide water for drinking, but not enough for "feather-fluffing". When the water in your bird-bath freezes, knock the ice out and give the birds at least a few hours of water each morning.

Plants for Wildlife

Most other animals are best fed with flowers, seeds, fruits, or decaying matter from the garden. The simplest and least obtrusive step you can take is to grow flowers that provide nectar and pollen for insects (and some birds, too). Nectar and pollen feed many of the most attractive insects, such as butterflies, hoverflies, and bees. You can discover by observation which plants supply which animals – the species are likely to be different in each bioregion. As a rule, you should try to cultivate a wide variety of single-flowered, non-hybrid plants.

Seeds and berries are an essential food source, especially in unfavorable seasons. Again, you can provide these with ordinary garden plants, such as sunflowers, ornamental grasses, and wild irises, and shrubs and trees, such as sumac, dog rose, mountain ash, holly, serviceberry, pyracantha, snowberry, and cotoneaster. These not only feed birds and insects, but some small mammals as well.

You can also grow attractive wildflowers for their own sake, either on their own, in a wildflower meadow (see p.230), or in a herbaceous border. You can also gain great satisfaction by growing species which are rare or endangered in the wild. You can buy wildflower seeds from local suppliers. If you are collecting from the wild, be careful not to contravene any local or national conservation laws.

Animal Shelters

The easiest shelters to provide are houses for birds and bats (see pp.264–5). These can range from tiny titmouse houses to substantial chambers for owls. They are best placed in trees with cover, but if you have no trees, fit them to walls and fences. Make them inaccessible to such predators as cats and give them a fringe of foliage from a climbing plant to afford some protection. Don't take it personally if the birds you are trying to attract decline your kind offer and choose another nearby place to build a nest. A dry, covered house composed of old leaves or straw can be useful for such small, hibernating mammals as hedgehogs or field-mice.

Creating Microhabitats

The richest habitat you can create is probably the compost pile. However, since you will frequently disturb the pile long-term populations of animals will not build up. A rotting log left in a quiet corner provides a more stable habitat. After a year or so, algae and mosses will cover it. Meanwhile, furious successions of beasts and fungi will work the log over, attracting the attentions of larger garden animals. Occasionally, break pieces off to see what's going on inside, and add other types of log from time to time.

Another easy and attractive small habitat you can construct is the mini-pond. The classical vessel for this is an old stoneware sink, but unless you insert a ramp its steep sides prevent some animals from getting in and out. Whatever vessel you use can be stocked with animals or just left to its own devices to see what turns up. For more details on microclimates and microhabitats, see pages 262–5.

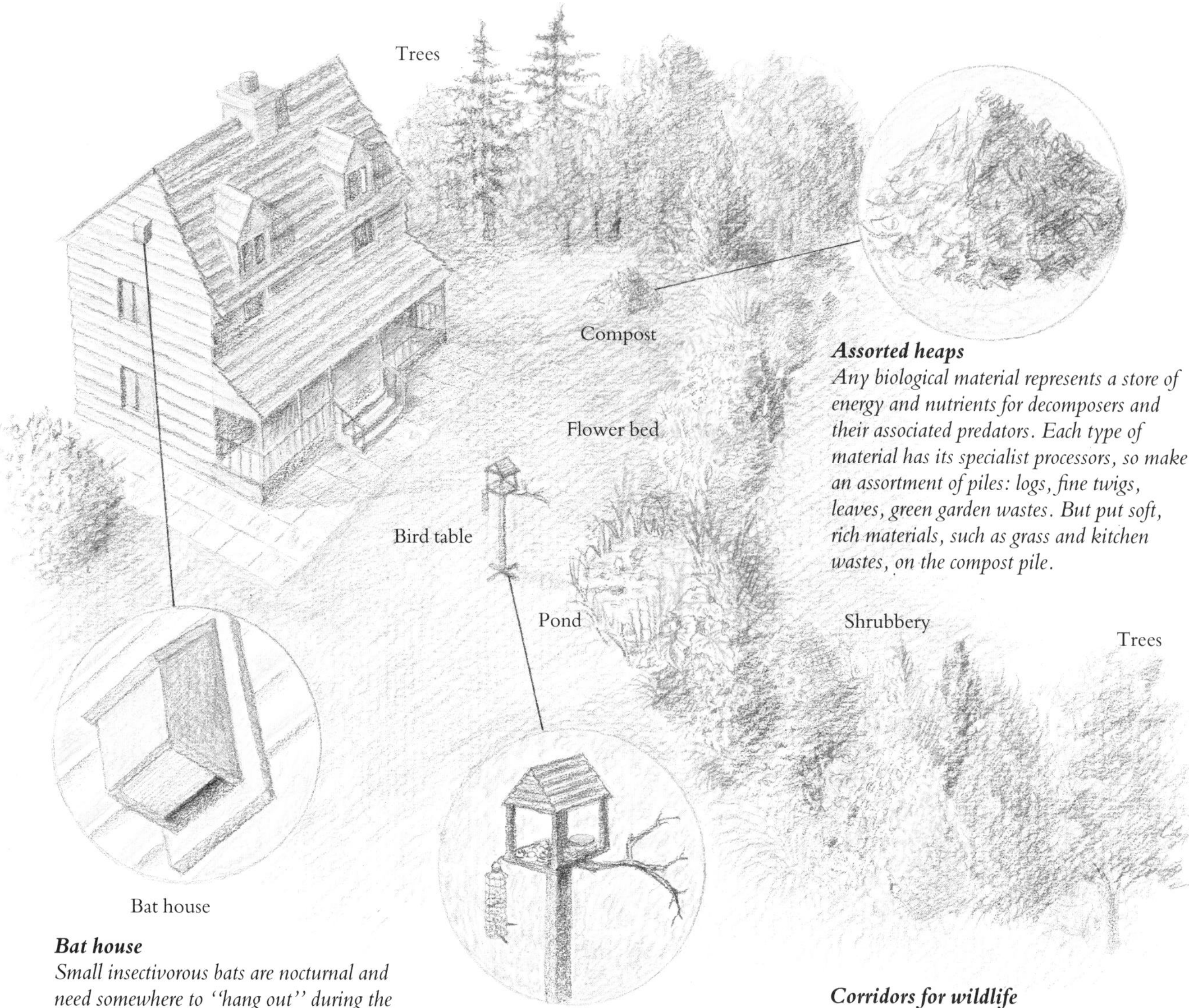

Assorted heaps
Any biological material represents a store of energy and nutrients for decomposers and their associated predators. Each type of material has its specialist processors, so make an assortment of piles: logs, fine twigs, leaves, green garden wastes. But put soft, rich materials, such as grass and kitchen wastes, on the compost pile.

Bat house
Small insectivorous bats are nocturnal and need somewhere to "hang out" during the day. A bat house fixed to a west-facing wall provides as good a place as any, but ideally you should locate them in various spots and let the bats choose. Make sure there is a full-width slot on the underside of the structure to give bats easy access.

Bird table
The ideal bird house is equipped with:
- *A slightly sloping floor*
- *An open cover with shelter on the windward side*
- *An extension of twigs for shy birds and for "waiting in line"*
- *A removeable water container*
- *Feeders that hang below*
- *A brush ready for daily cleaning*

Corridors for wildlife
Your garden may contain a wonderful collection of special habitats but their value to wildlife will increase if they link up with similar habitats nearby (see p.112). Such links are provided by linear "corridors" of sheltered and undisturbed habitat, such as trees, bushes, hedges, old walls, and tangled undergrowth.

Relinquish Control

The purpose of most traditional practices is to control the garden and make it behave as you want it. To create a true wildlife garden you deliberately relax this control and hand over the "running" of the garden to the much more complex checks and balances of natural systems. This may sound straightforward enough, but goes against the grain of activities which are usually thought of as essential, worthy, and almost sacred. So you may need courage here....

Relinquishing control consists simply of not doing things. You don't have to follow this approach everywhere in your garden, of course. It is best at first to designate a particular part of the garden where you can practice not doing things and then observe and monitor the results.

Don't Use Pesticides

This is the single, most helpful thing you can do. "Pests" are part of the ecosystem and are somebody's food. If you kill one species you've broken a link in the food chain. Furthermore, the pesticides tend to move indiscriminately through the food chains, killing at random, breaking more links, and weakening the whole system. Pesticides often concentrate toward the top of a food chain: this means that in your attempts to get rid of undesirable invertebrates you actually damage the big, "friendly" vertebrates more.

In the wildlife garden it really doesn't matter what happens, and who eats what or whom. There may be temporary population explosions of one organism or another, but this is all part of the game, and predators and parasites will soon catch up. If you are not trying to grow productive crops, the "pests" are usually far more interesting than the plants they are consuming, especially if you take time to observe them and understand their biology. They may, in fact, completely wipe out some of your favorite plants. The best strategy is to shrug your shoulders, have patience, and allow a riper ecological equilibrium to evolve.

If you have used pesticides extensively, the act of suddenly giving up may affect the garden rather like the abrupt withdrawal of drugs from an addict. The system may be very unstable for a while, with feverish infestations of one species or another. Resolve not to mind. Observe all this with interest, and notice how the system eventually calms down to a more "damped" equilibrium and much greater diversity.

Don't Improve the Site

If the purpose of gardens is useful production, very few sites are ideal. So we strive to make them ideal – we try to mesify them (see p.96) by amending and fertilizing the soil, digging, draining, watering, weeding, and pruning. Most plants appreciate this treatment by growing bigger and better, provided they are on their own and free from competition.

But these conditions are rare in nature. When they do occur they are dominated by "generalist" competitor plants that gardeners consider rank weeds: docks, thistles, nettles, buttercups, bindweeds, many grasses, plantains, brambles, and dandelions. We have taught ourselves to find these plants disagreeable and ugly, and they are indeed badly behaved: if left to themselves in ideal conditions they will certainly crowd out "nicer" wildflowers to the detriment of overall diversity.

Most "nice" wild plants are specialists of one kind or another, each able to hold its own in a specific type of habitat and soil condition, and to tolerate particular lapses from the ideal. We get more diversity and a more attractive appearance by encouraging these specialists, and that means not encouraging the generalists, not enriching, and not improving the growing conditions. Let there be stress and difficulty!

It is not a question of eradicating the rank weeds: they have a role to play in the scheme of things and anyway they will always be there. Just don't make it easy for them to take over. So find the roughest, poorest, least developed parts of the garden for nature spaces, and transfer nutrients in surplus growth away from these areas into the more useful sections of the garden or into localized piles of decaying matter.

Don't Cultivate the Ground

Bare, disturbed ground is another rarity in nature. Usually the soil is covered either with vegetation or a mat of decomposing material. Only when trees fall or the ground is scuffed up by animals is soil exposed to the light and air. When this happens, the seeds of specialist annual plants, which have either been waiting in the soil or parachuted in, germinate quickly. Gardeners inadvertently spend a lot of time creating the ideal conditions for plants such as chickweed, knotweeds, and poppies. Although annuals, these plants are highly competitive and can crowd out the choicer specialists, again reducing diversity. Abolishing these annual opportunists is almost impossible. All you can do is stop yourself making life too easy for them by gratuitous cultivation of the soil.

Don't "Weed"

Traditionally, "weeding" is the physical removal of all plants incidental to the main purpose of a garden plot. It is necessary to prevent the success of highly competitive wild plants. The well-controlled garden then becomes one in which the only plants are ones intended by the gardener.

From a wildlife point of view, "proper" garden plants are not ideal and you can foster the greatest diversity by allowing the wild plants to emerge. Some control is desirable to prevent the obliteration of specialist wild plants by their aggressive competitors, especially in the early stages of establishing a nature space. Remember, it is essential that the widest possible range of local native plants be allowed to emerge of their own accord. In the wildlife garden, "weed control" is best accomplished by mulching with relatively inert (nutrient-poor) organic materials, such as ground bark.

Don't Remove Junk

Unsightly old furniture, household appliances, scrap metal, containers, and building rubble would normally be recycled or carted off to the local dump. However, the complex structure of mixed junk provides a fine range of spaces and microclimates suitable for homes and hunting grounds for wild animals.

To overcome the problem of how ugly it looks, combine scattered junk into one or two large piles, cover with brushwood, and simultaneously plant fast-growing annual scramblers, such as bryony or nasturtiums, and perennial or evergreen rambling plants, such as rambling roses, clematis, jasmine, periwinkle, or ivy. Make sure, of course, that your piles of junk have no sharp edges or features that pose a danger to children.

Don't Get Rid of Decomposing Garden Waste

Another reflex of conventional gardening is that decay is unhealthy and must be sanitized. But for the wildlife garden decay is essential and the cornerstone of the food chain. Much more energy and material passes through the decomposer system than either the herbivore or carnivore parts of the overall food chain. Many larger animals depend on a flourishing population of scavenger organisms.

So never throw out garden waste unless it is diseased and a threat to your vegetables. Put it into the compost pile, or leave it in small piles around the garden, preferably in cool, damp spots where the various decomposer organisms will process it. Allow the benefits to work their way up through your garden's food chains.

Don't Remove Spent Growth

At the end of a growing season, gardeners usually "tidy" the garden by removing dead straw and leaving the ground clean. However, the dead growth is useful food and provides a protective layer over the ground. At the start of a cold season, it traps air and keeps the ground warm, while before a dry season it traps moisture and keeps the ground cool.

Don't Keep Mowing the Grass

Many gardeners try to create and maintain a perfect billiard-table lawn and will go to great lengths to suppress wildflowers. Wildlife gardeners prefer the opposite strategy. Wildflowers can be deliberately introduced into grassland and green swards can be sown with mixed seed. However, wildflowers are either already present in your garden or will arrive spontaneously: you can reveal them merely by altering your pattern of mowing. As a general rule, set the mower high and use the clippings as mulch or put them on the compost pile.

Spring flowers in grassland are adapted to rapid growth and flowering before the grass overtops them. To reveal these plants mow the grass high year-round except in late spring and early summer. Hay-meadow flowers can hold their own with spring growth, so you can leave the grass until early summer and cut thereafter. For summer meadow flowers, mow the grass until the end of spring, then once in early fall.

The benefits of long grass are not restricted to wildflowers. The grasses themselves have beautiful and varied forms and flowers. Grasses feed the soil with dying fragments of root, so there is usually a flourishing fauna under the ground.

Restoration Ecology

The bioregion is your touchstone. By shrewd detective work in your year of initiation, you should have gained some idea of the kind of natural vegetation and wildlife that occupied your garden before it was developed hundreds of years ago. Your bioregion is unique in the world and should always inform your plans.

Restoring the original habitat is an inspiring goal that conservation groups in many countries work hard to achieve. But it is not easy. Human settlement has often changed the land so profoundly that the original habitat and community of organisms have changed beyond recognition. Even if we can identify the original habitat, restoration is a bit like trying to re-create an ancient human culture through archeology, descendant languages, folk tales, and cultural habits. Sometimes it seems to work, yet you never really know how near you are to the real thing.

Using Native Species

You may not be in a position to restore your garden to its original habitat but you can cultivate species that are native to your bioregion. The term "native" can be misleading. A native plant may grow elsewhere in your country or state but still be inappropriate in your neigborhood. You would not, for example, expect chapparal flora to grow naturally in the lusher parts of California. The term native, therefore, depends on the overall conditions of soil, climate, atmosphere, and so on, of the neighborhood being considered. Plants introduced from other parts of the world can become naturalized if they grow naturally and without the need for special conditions or constant maintenance.

Can plants that have vanished from your neighborhood be reintroduced? The answer is probably yes if the conditions in your neighborhood have not radically altered. Before the last Ice Age, for instance, many species now considered exclusively American – tulip-trees and magnolias, for example – were common in Europe. Even southern hemisphere trees, such as the monkey-puzzle, were not unknown. Such species have been re-introduced and are now accepted features of garden landscapes.

Obstacles to Restoration

On the garden scale, completely authentic restoration ecology is unlikely to succeed because:

- The community may have required a much larger minimum area than is now available for restoration;
- The soils will have been irreversibly disturbed and "improved";
- Particular conditions for the community, such as fire, specialist soil fungi, intensive grazing, or co-evolved species, may be absent;
- Vigorous aliens may now be present and impossible to eradicate;
- Restoration efforts may be technically illegal or socially unacceptable;
- Constant intervention may be needed to maintain the restored ecosystem.

Generally speaking, native plants improve the overall diversity of the garden because they are adapted to the climate, and over time have developed relationships with each other or with native animals and fungi. Therefore, they "work" and don't need a lot of looking after; they also support a larger number of wild animals.

But this is not always the case. Some true local natives do not do well in garden conditions and may need a lot of fussing over. It's often a challenge to try, but overall is not worth the trouble. Conversely, some exotic species, such as buddleia, nasturtiums, teasel, wisteria, evening primrose, petunia, and nicotiana, do very well in a new context and can be valuable wildlife plants. However, exotics can become problem weeds once they are away from the factors that control them at home. These include Japanese knotweed and *Rhododendron ponticum* in Europe, brambles and "Patterson's curse" in Australia, multiflora rose in North America, and water hyacinth in Africa and Asia. So watch out for badly behaved exotics!

It seems to be a universal rule that wherever they live, people regard their own native flora as rather dull and quiet, and hanker after gaudy aliens. In fact, the places from which exotics are drawn also appear dull and quiet most of the time. The plant world is everywhere just green and brown for the most part – nowhere on Earth will always look like a flower show. But every region has its special peak seasons when unusual numbers of plants are in flower; ornamental gardeners contrive to combine these peaks to give a steady show of dense color, helped by breeding and hybridization.

If you stick to the native plants of your own neighborhood, district, and bioregion you will not get the brilliant effects of cultivated flower gardening. The result will be far more subtle and you may have to adjust your tastes. The same is true if you pick plants especially for their feeding value: they may not be "garden worthy" in the traditional sense. For example, the members of the carrot family (Queen Anne's lace, hogweed, fennel, alexanders, angelica) are not famous for their brilliant colours, but they are outstanding as nectar plants. Teasels trap rain water in their leaf axils, providing a useful service in dry weather; their seeds feed such small birds as goldfinches. But nobody could say they were "pretty". Grasses are immensely valuable sources of pollen and seeds; their flowers are truly beautiful when you look at them closely, but most people find them dull, green, and all the same.

You will contradict convention even more by providing plants whose leaves are eaten by animals – many are considered noxious weeds and nibbled leaves tend to look ragged and untidy. Yet because most leaf-eaters feed on only a few kinds of plants, and are adapted specifically to the bioregional natives, you need a good range of wild plants to attract a wide range of wild animals. Caterpillars of the nymphalid butterflies, for example, depend entirely on the leaves of stinging nettles. Therefore, without nettles there would be no peacocks, tortoiseshells, or red admirals! Similarly, the figwort gives life to the figwort weevil and ragwort feeds the cinnabar moth.

If you want big animals, you must provide for the small ones that feed them. The rule here is: look after the bottom of the food chain and the top will look after itself. If you provide plenty of material to feed the invertebrates, then plenty of vertebrates will turn up to eat them. The plant-feeding insects are a food source for the carnivores, such as spiders, scorpions, centipedes, ground beetles, dragonflies, amphibians, reptiles, bats, moles, gophers, hedgehogs, echidnas, foxes, and badgers – not to mention all those birds that dart about catching flying insects on the wing. But the most important food source for the carnivores are the small scavengers that live off decaying materials: insects, grubs, pill bugs, worms, snails, and slugs.

A Practical Approach

Left to its own devices for several years, your garden would be dominated by just a few very aggressive species. To avoid this, you must design and manage your garden with the specific purpose of creating diversity. Essentially, this involves the deliberate creation of miniaturized habitats which complement the local range outside the garden. In particular, try to create the maximum number of transition zones between habitats. These zones allow organisms to exploit the qualities of more than one habitat and adjust more easily to the changing conditions of weather, seasons, day-night cycles, availability of food, and so on. Some typical transitions are: light-shaded-dark; open-sheltered-enclosed; wet-damp-dry; steady

This scenario shows what you can achieve with minimum intervention or very light "editing": a miniature textbook of the habitat flora in which repetition is balanced by diversity – with impeccable taste. With one exception, the plants here are all native to Britain.

Succession and Editing

If you set aside an area of your garden and leave it to its own devices, you can discover the variety of species potentially present in your garden. Furthermore, by simply "editing out" plants you can maximize the overall diversity of the flora.

During your year of initiation, try out the following experiment. Mark out two plots, at least 10 square feet in area, on ground that has not been cultivated intensively. Dig a trench in one of the plots, remove the dark layer of topsoil and put it to one side. Then dig out an equivalent volume of subsoil and stack it. Remove the topsoil from the other plot and put it into the first plot. Then put the original topsoil back on top. Finally put the subsoil into the second plot.

You now have two more or less identical plots, one with rich topsoil, the other with poorer subsoil. Divide each plot into two with a permanent marker, such as a plank on edge. Leave the plots and note each week what happens. Do not water, feed, or plant anything in, the plots. Weeds will germinate rapidly in the enriched plot, less so in the poor plot.

In one half of each plot, leave the plants completely alone for a whole season. In the other half, gently remove plants you don't want as soon as you can identify them as well as those plants that threaten to take over. It's up to you to decide what you want there, but remember you are aiming for maximum diversity. See how many different species you can log in the course of a single year.

From this simple experiment you can discover:

- The plants present in your local "seed bank";
- The difference between species emerging from enriched and poorer soil;
- How the same species fares in rich and poor conditions;
- What the plants look like when they are mere seedlings;
- The succession of plants – which ones are aggressive and which ones suffer as a result.
- The effect of slight management or "editing" as opposed to a total hands-off approach.

These plots are a microcosm of the sort of things that could happen in your garden with minimum intervention. If you leave them for succeeding years, they will continue to evolve and the "unedited" plot acts as an experimental control for the "edited" plot. "New" plants will appear, while others vanish. Some will arrive on the wind, others deposited by animals. In one experiment at the Centre for Alternative Technology, Wales, 42 different species in 20 different families of plants were recorded by the second year in what appeared to be completely barren clay subsoil.

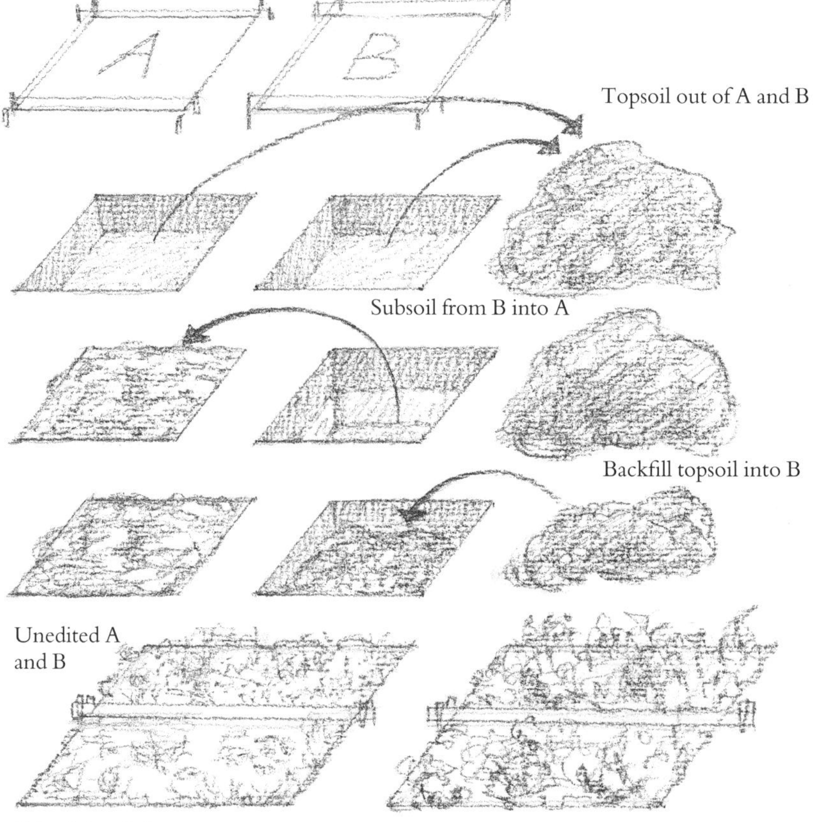

temperature-variable temperature. For most areas, the richest possibilities are usually provided by trees/woodland and ponds/wetlands (see pp.176–81, 262–3).

Trees and Woodland

If your garden is large enough to take them, trees are a great asset because they extend the volume of protected space, provide shelter, and create micro-habitats, especially for insects. They need little maintenance, are particularly valuable in hot and dry climates, and can fix large quantities of carbon dioxide, thereby helping to counter the greenhouse effect. In creating a tree garden, you are trying to speed up the process of succession.

However, trees are not always advisable. If your garden is already wooded, and surrounded by forest, the greatest diversity of plants and wildlife will come from *clearing* trees, not growing more. By competing with plants and crops for light, water, and nutrients, trees may reduce yields. Moreover, trees take a long time to grow, often cast dense shade near a house, and may pose a fire risk.

Moving and Planting Trees

The following guidelines will help you create a tree garden:

- Retain already existing trees, at least early on in a planting plan.
- Use self-sown, native seedlings in preference to transplants from off the site or from elsewhere on site.
- Estimate the effect new trees will have on the garden in 5, 10, and 50 years' time.
- Arrange the different types so that their final canopy heights complement one another.
- Plant several different species with contrasting qualities.
- Plant slow-growing trees at the same time as fast-growing "pioneers".
- Plant more than you need and thin out later.
- Plant taller trees on the poleward side, shorter ones on the sunward side, of the garden.
- Group like trees together, not as isolated "specimens".
- Plant trees that are three years old or less.
- Don't let tree roots dry out, even for a few minutes.
- Keep new plantings well watered in the first season.
- You can plant direct into stony ground or garden rubble.
- Mulch around the base of the trees to suppress competitive growth and retain moisture.
- If overshading is likely to be a problem, choose species that can be coppiced.

Experiencing Nature

Pre-digested television and magazine images have blunted our direct experience of the natural world. In creating a wildlife garden we start to recover what we hardly knew had been lost and to perceive the living world on our doorstep in a completely different kind of way. But it takes a little effort. Here are some hints on how to help the process along:

- Be quiet, patient, and prepared to sit still for long periods not only because animals are shy, but because the natural patterns are subtle.
- Plants live at a slower pace than us, while birds and small mammals are faster, and insects faster still.
- Use all your senses.
- Dusk, night, and especially dawn are the best times to study animals.
- Be aware of the small: for each thing you can easily see there are ten times more you cannot.
- Be aware of the hidden: look for the creatures in the soil, rotting wood, or leaf-litter.
- Look for signs: tracks, molehills, worm casts, dung, hair, seeds, cast skins, shells, scratch marks, grazing patterns, and nests.
- Be aware of your cultural biases in favor of "nice" (large, attractive, cuddly, rare) organisms and against those that: seem dull or common; sting or are poisonous; are called weeds, pests, and creepy-crawlies; are associated with death, decay, and excrement.
- Prepare handy vantage points from which to observe: a chair by the window with binoculars at the ready; a tree-house; a comfortable seat in the wood; a tent with viewing-hole.
- Keep a log of your observations.
- Read up on the biology of the garden organisms; the scientific approach will tell you things you won't find out any other way. Latin names aren't essential, but sometimes they help.

THE HEALING GARDEN

In 1989, the Kogi, an isolated and little-known tribe of Indians from the Andes in South America, made deliberate contact with the outside world. They had an important message to convey. In a moving film made at their own request, the Kogi astonished the modern world with a stern lecture about the state of the planet. For many people, the film represented a turning point in their attitudes to the global environment. The reality of a threatened biosphere was brought home to them by a lordly and ancient culture that had remained utterly immune to the influence of "civilization" – a word which the Kogi used with heavy irony.

Kogi society is an ecological theocracy totally dedicated to the wellbeing of life on Earth. Kogi priests, some of whom spend up to 30 years in complete darkness communicating with the biosphere, brought an air of absolute authority to the film. Their chilling message was simple: The Earth is dying. You are killing it. Please stop.

If the Earth really is in trouble – and an increasing body of scientific evidence seems to support the Kogi in their fears – what are we to do? How do we "stop"? The orthodox view is that science must analyze the problems, and governments and technology must solve them. Albeit a necessary part of the solution, as a panacea this approach is looking distinctly threadbare. What is equally necessary (but scorned as impractical) is a substantial overhaul of human lifestyles and attitudes to the natural world.

The reason for this is straightforward. The Earth's malady is not catastrophic, but rather like a stress-induced disease or AIDS: the illness destroys the body's natural capacity to heal itself. It is caused by billions of tiny actions, each insignificant in itself, which accumulate so fast that the natural healing processes cannot cope with them. These tiny actions are nothing sinister, just us trying to live modern, sophisticated lives. The problem, then, is that to allow the Earth to heal itself, we must change the way we live. And if the Earth has problems today, they are really *our* problems; it is *we* who need healing.

But what sort of healing is this? Obviously, we are not individually "ill" in the ordinary sense. It is a kind of collective illness that springs from the lust for modern life: eating hamburgers from ex-rainforest ranches and imported foods year-round; travelling about in airplanes and cars; consuming vast amounts of goods and throwing away the packaging; wanting to be free to walk around in our shirt sleeves in winter; or wanting to live without constraints. That's modern life and it's going to be a hard act to follow. But weaning ourselves off it is almost certain to bring withdrawal symptoms.

The conventional medical approach – to identify a discrete disease or malfunction and cure it – cannot be expected to work on this illness, either at the individual or the planetary level. The ills of the Earth and of our collective madness cannot be cured as such, but they can be healed. Healing, we now see, is not the same as curing, even though it may bring about cures. Healing is more like growing, unfolding, balancing, reconciling; more to do with *letting* things happen than *making* things happen. It is not a mechanical or even a rational process, but more like magic or alchemy, appearing in disguise or when you least expect it. Our health, and the health of the Earth, are bound together in many ways, some direct and physical, some far more subtle.

As the place where you and the biosphere are likely to engage most intimately, your garden provides a unique opportunity to explore the mutual healing between you and the Earth. It is a model of the universe, a microcosm of the biosphere, and a metaphor for yourself. Your garden can help you deepen your senses and offers a sanctuary where you can be at peace with yourself and the world. It is your window into the natural world, and also your workshop, textbook, medicine chest, sanctuary, mentor, and confessor. It's all there – go for it.

The chief purpose of most gardens is recreation, play, and fun. If children love the garden, then you know it's doing a good job. There is plenty of scope for the imagination in combining children's play with the other functional aspects of the garden.

Deepening the Senses

Our sensory experience of the world is often straitjacketed by habit and customs. The first step in deepening the senses is to try to appreciate the world on its own terms, as children do: the softness of dandelion seeds, the magnificent wreckage of spent teasels, the stately gliding of slugs, the smell of the compost, the sound of wasps in the jelly, and the feel of wet grass beneath your bare feet.

Of all the senses, vision has dominated our view of the garden: what the garden looks like is our principal concern and most vivid experience. But just as moonlight washes out the stars, so the brilliance of vision eclipses our other senses. Try restoring the balance by simply closing your eyes. Do it again and again; make a habit of it and cultivate the precious and unremarked ability of shifting and focusing attention to other senses. These include the quiet, unlauded, and reassuring sense of kinesthesia, which tells you where your limbs are and the weight of, say, the wheelbarrow you're pushing.

Another "hidden" sense signals the balance of heat radiation between yourself and surrounding objects. You will feel comfortable when the balance is right, even if the thermometer – responding only to air temperature – says otherwise. You can use this quiet sense to identify good spots for the location of seats and playspaces.

The Sense of Touch

To deepen your sense of touch, stop using your hands so much and use other parts of your body for making contact. Going barefoot in the garden cannot be recommended too highly (but beware poisonous creatures and sharp edges). Let your feet learn the different textures of the lawn, soil, walks, leaf-litter, and gravel. And lie down on the grass, or in the pond, mud, sand, or in a bed of ferns. Feel it and let your body remember!

Children love to stroke the woolly leaves of plants such as "bunnies' ears" and mullein, feel the sticky buds of horse chestnuts, or tease each other with spiny things. A whole host of textures wait to be explored: leaves, flowers, bark, grass, earth, lichens, mosses, and fungi. So make a point of growing plant species that offer a variety of textures in their leaves, flowers, seeds, and stems.

The Sense of Smell

Touch is a very immediate sense that requires an intimacy with an object. By contrast the sense of smell gives no spatial or directional clues to the world around. Yet scents and aromas can evoke memories more vividly and instantly than any other sensory stimulus and, consequently, can create a particular atmosphere in your garden.

Gardens are famous for producing deliberately managed scents, but they also generate a range of other evocative aromas: freshly turned soil, after-rain smells, humus, freshly cut oak wood, the resin of conifers, and newly mown grass. Rotting smells, while disagreeable, can help the alert gardener to discover and diagnose what's happening to the chemistry of the compost pile.

Some living things deliberately produce bad smells. Insectivorous plants, such as pitcher plants, give off a putrid smell to attract carrion-eating flies. Although fungi often smell peculiar, some have a delicious bouquet – chanterelles, for example, smell "like apricots". The flowering currant smells unpleasantly of cats, skunk cabbage of skunks, and worse still, red valerian stinks convincingly and disgustingly of a dog's feces.

But most plant scents are positively agreeable to us. Many come from aromatic compounds in leaves, where they deter grazers, and in flowers, where they attract pollinators. Smell and taste are directly connected so many garden smells are part and parcel of the taste experience – think of tomatoes, basil, coriander, lemons, and quinces.

Leaf smells are sometimes given off freely by plants such as cypress, eucalyptus, and lemon plant, but are usually stimulated by gentle brushing or bruising. So it is a good strategy to put plants with aromatic foliage along the sides of walks or in tubs on patios where you touch them regularly. You can grow small aromatic plants, such as Roman chamomile, Corsican mint, and thyme, on paths – when you walk on them they release their aromas.

A common planning mistake is to organize all the scents for the daytime. So grow nicotiana, night-scented stock, honeysuckle, and some viburnums, for evening and nighttime perfumes – especially beside windows that are open on warm evenings.

Many scented flowers and leaves retain their odor after harvesting. In days gone by, lavender, tansy, meadowsweet, and other large plants were strewn about the floors of houses – they still are in greenhouses and garden sanctuaries. As an alternative to strewing, dry the scented parts of plants and put them to good use around the house: sweet woodruff, lavender, or southernwood for cabinets and closets; and fill herb pillows with hops, lavender, rose petals, rose-geranium, thyme, or lemon verbena.

The Sense of Hearing

A healthy garden is full of sounds, but for most of us silence is just as precious. It is difficult to keep out unwanted sound (particularly from traffic) but massive walls and trees are usually the most effective means of doing this. The simplest barrier you can build is an earthen berm reinforced with fast-growing trees, such as willow.

Birds are undoubtedly the stars of the garden sound system. As a rule, they are fairly quiet in the middle of the day and night. Evening is better, but dawn is the best, especially in the breeding season. So find out which birds frequent your neighborhood and attract them to your garden by growing the plants they like. And the same goes for insects which hum and buzz during the high season.

The sound of the wind varies with its strength and direction, and is amplified by the rustling foliage of trees. Wind tends to come in gusts and eddies, creating a natural variation that forms the basis for various "wind instruments" (see p.29).

Sounds of water are always special, but require some cunning or electric hardware to produce. With an electric pump (conveniently driven by solar cells) you can circulate the water of a pond and create fountains or waterfalls. The range of sounds is surprisingly large, from a simple ripple to rushing, splashing, deep gurgling, the hiss of a non-turbulent waterfall, and the intermittent "plink-plink" of individual drops.

Looking and Seeing

Human beings are a visual species. But although we have acute, stereoscopic color vision, we often look without seeing. Try manipulating your vision so as to see in new and different ways. Start by lying under trees or in the undergrowth and look vertically instead of horizontally. Alternatively, you can put a mirror on the ground and gaze at the reflections. For scrutinizing small details and microlandscapes, such as lichens on branches, arrays of dried seed-cases, or creatures in the lawn-jungle, let your eyes be aided by a good hand lens or a close-focus monocular lens. To encourage movement, either keep animals (bees, fish, or fowl) or attract wildlife. In addition, let the wind play with something – a wind instrument, prayer-wheel, or shimmering tree, such as aspen and white poplar.

During the day, we automatically focus what we're looking at on an area, called the macula, in the middle of the retina of each eye. In bright light the macula gives a sharp image in full color; the rest of the visual field is just context. In dim light we rely on the non-macular retina, which forms 95 percent of the total retina and is designed for night vision, to give us visual information. Turn off all lights for ten minutes and but keep your eyes open: you will soon be aware of the objects in your peripheral field of vision. Don't swivel your eyes to see the objects better. Instead, stare straight ahead and use your peripheral, non-macular attention on the world around. This skill adds a new dimension to seeing.

Subtle Energies

The shapes of the main plantings, large features, or walks in your garden greatly affect your feeling of its form. Tensions between these elements are almost visible and a peculiar energy seems to flow along walks and through openings, gates, and lines of sight. Shaping these subtle energies and making them work for you in your garden is not something that happens overnight. Like the ancient Chinese art of feng-shui (see p.54), working with the fundamental elements of the biosphere is not something that can be measured on instruments or reduced to a formula. Also like feng-shui, your overall aim is to make your garden feel good by freeing, diverting, and harmonizing these subtle energies. You can begin by tuning in to your garden and feeling where these energies are flowing.

Turbulent, directed water communicates excitement (above). Its rapid movement defeats the eye and becomes not just water but a waterfall or fountain.

Making Potpourri

Flowers, leaves, and seeds are the basic ingredients of a good potpourri, which helps to spread the fragrant season throughout the year. You can choose from a large range. Flowers include roses, sweet peas, pinks, wallflowers, jasmine, honeysuckle, and lily-of-the-valley; aromatic leaves include bee balm, choisya, sweet woodruff, scented geraniums, melilot, coriander, thyme, and verbena; and seeds include sweet cicely, alexanders, coriander, parsley, anise, and cassia. A potpourri needs some kind of fixative to help release the fragrances steadily over a long period. You can make your own from two rather severe types of iris: orris and sweet flag – always a sign of the serious herbalist.

The sound of trickles and individual drops of water creates a rich, lively, and tranquil atmosphere, as expressed in the Japanese garden (right).

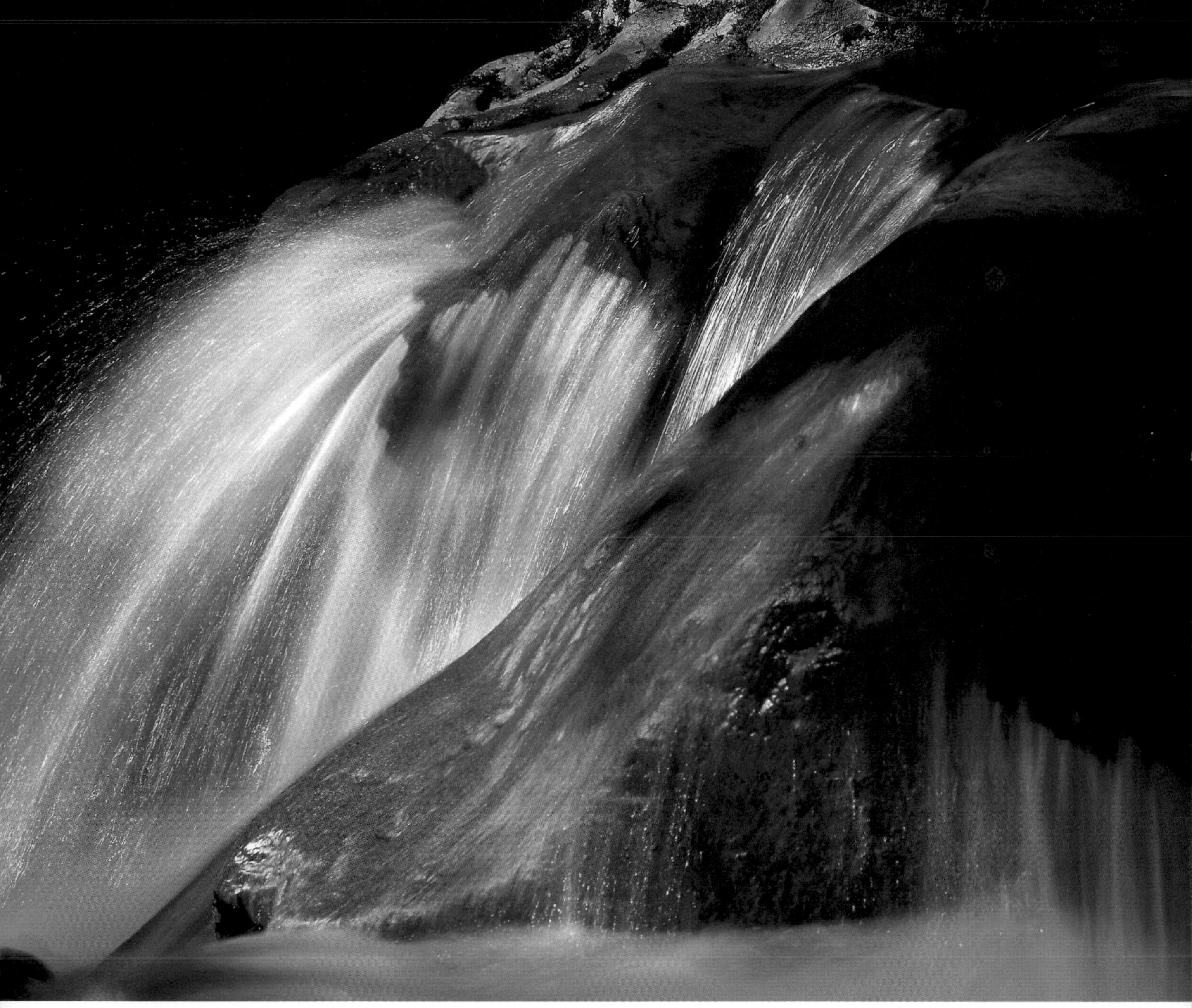

Natural water flows reflect and refract light in ever-changing ways.

Wind Instruments

The wind chime is the commonest and easiest wind instrument to make. A less percussive and more responsive effect comes from the wind flute, which is simply a hollow, horizontal tube with a hole drilled underneath – when the wind passes across it, you can hear moaning harmonics. Sets of tubes, each with a different pitch, create more complicated sounds. The most sophisticated wind instrument is the aeolian harp, essentially a series of tunable strings stretched over a sound box. As a wind eddy passes over the strings they vibrate. Like the wind flute, the harp needs a strong breeze to work well – and it must be brought in at any sign of rain.

Wind chimes, usually designed for sound can also have a visual appeal, as this amusing Balinese chime illustrates.

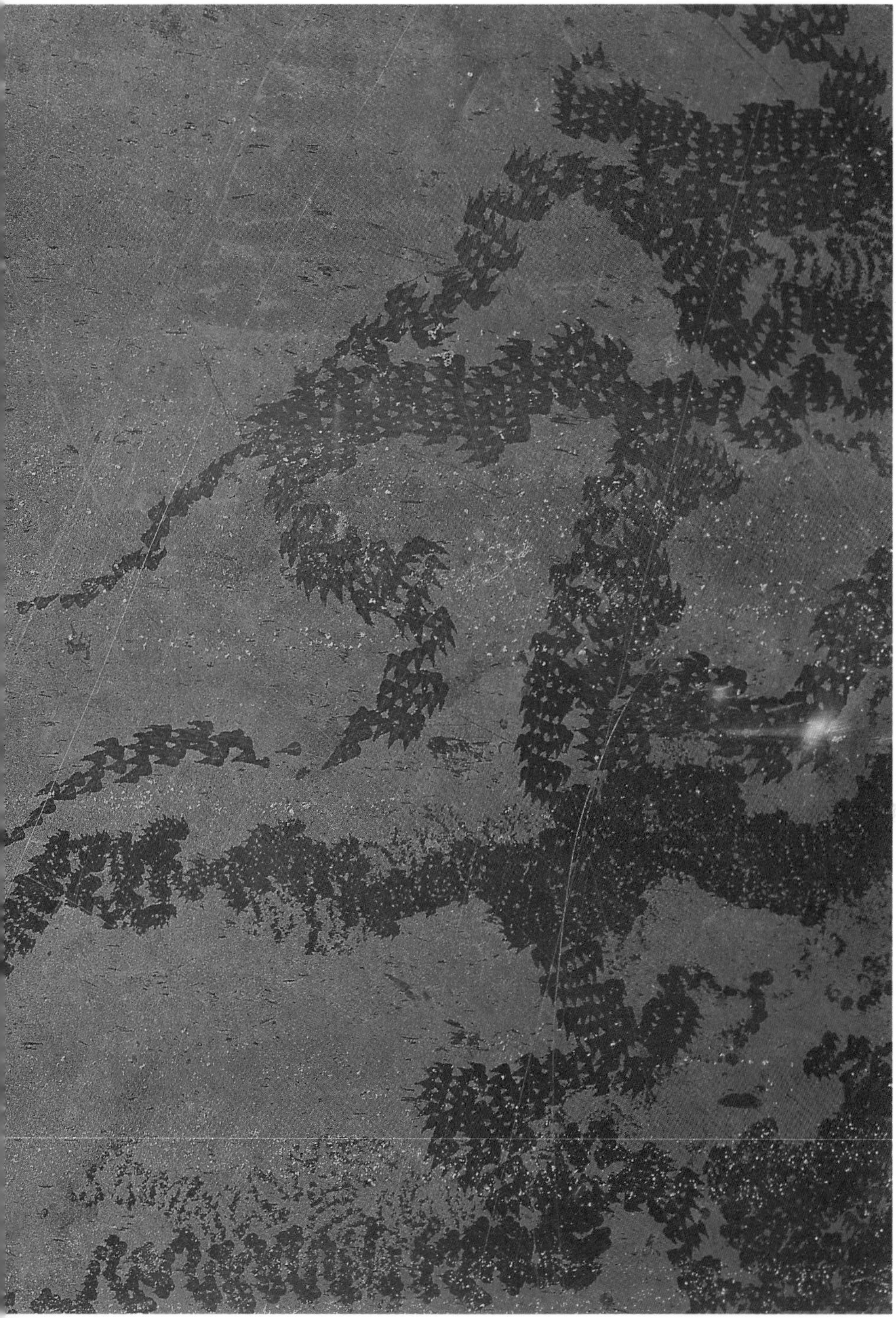

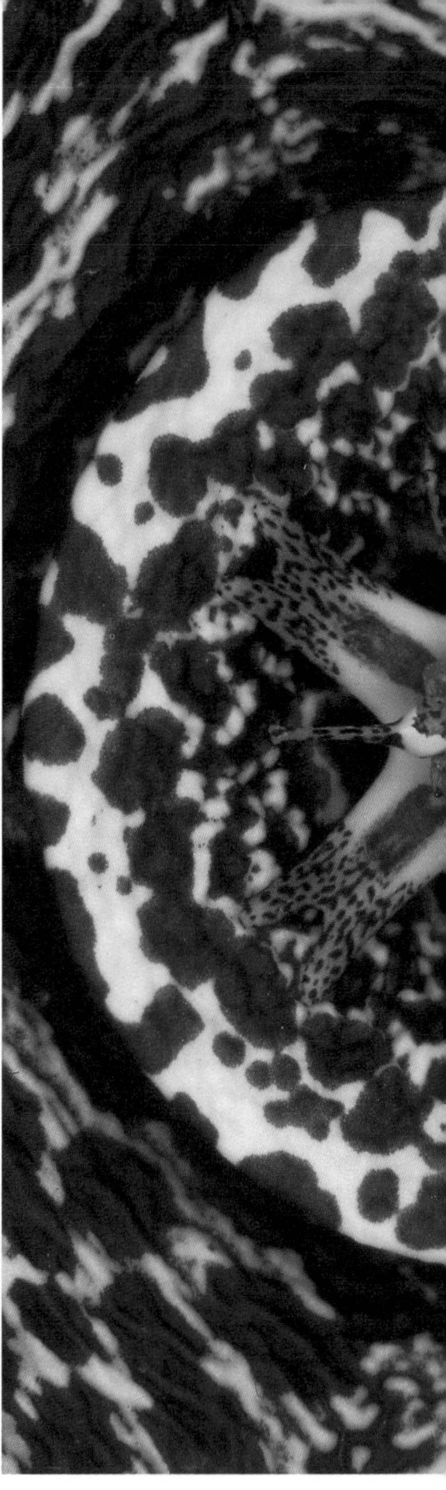

Slugs create beautiful patterns (left) like Chinese dragons as they graze algae with their rasping tongues. Stapelia variegata (above) exudes a scent of rotting flesh to attract carrion feeders for pollination.

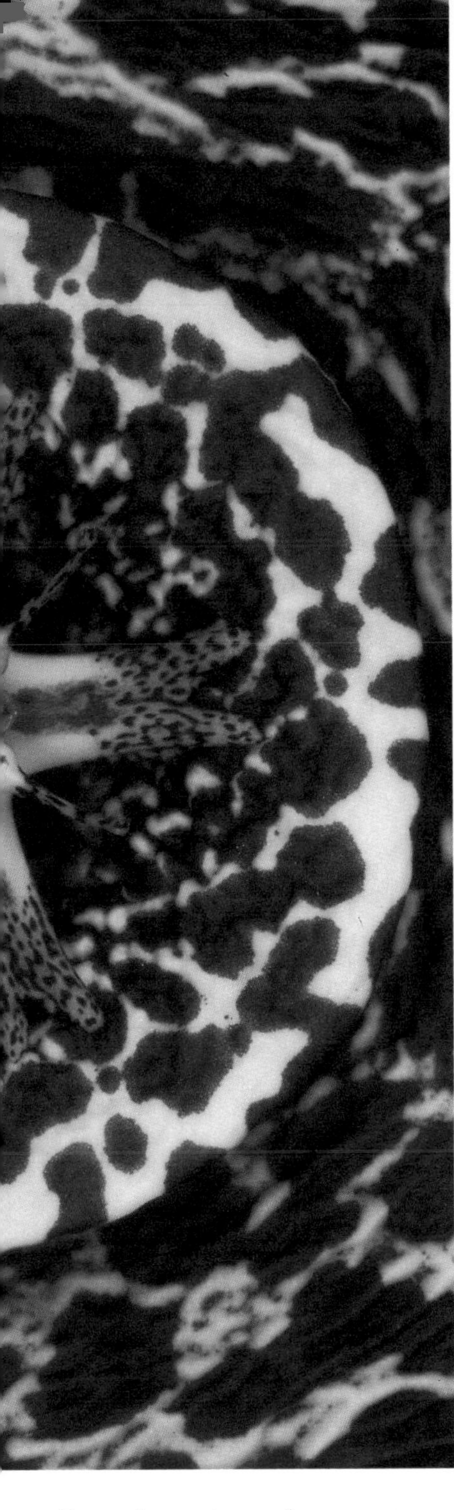

Frost and vegetation together can create a spectacular natural artistry (above right), while the silent beauty of fallen autumn leaves (right) combined with still water suggests hidden depths.

Healing the Body

The garden's main contribution to routine health is through eating fresh salads, herbs, and vegetables – both cultivated and wild – in as great a variety as possible. They provide minerals and vitamins, and are known to reduce the incidence of cancer.

The sheer weight of tradition and mythology surrounding medicinal herbs is enough to create an aura of wellbeing in the herb garden. Although self-prescribing is not always advisable, it is good to take command of your own health and proper use of the most common herbs forms an important part of your bond with the healing garden.

You cannot grow every plant with a medicinal use – there are far too many. A good herbal textbook will advise you about what will grow in your region, and what is suitable for self-medication. Your choice will also be guided by the kinds of ailments to which you or your family are prone. Incidentally, when gardeners in France were asked which herbs they grew themselves, the following 12 herbs emerged in order of popularity: thyme, linden flowers, sage, mint, vervain, rosemary, balm, lavender, green anise, horsetail, meadowsweet, and hawthorn.

Herbs and their Uses

The following is a list of herbs that are easy and useful:

Sage (leaves: sore throats, flu)
Garlic (cloves: colds, flu)
Rosemary (leaves: cleaning wounds)
Feverfew (leaves: chronic migraine)
Borage (flowers: fevers)
Comfrey (leaves: poultice for sprains)
Coltsfoot (leaves: cough, sore throat) W
Chamomile (flowers: relaxant, soporific)
Chickweed (whole plant: poultice for drawing splinters) W
Lavender (dried flowers: calming, esp. children)
Hops (dried flowers: calming, esp. for children)
Mint (leaves: digestion)
Greater celandine (sap: warts) W

The herbs marked W may grow wild so you do not need to grow them. Other useful wild plants include elder, yarrow, meadowsweet, dandelion, St John's wort, nettle, goldenrod, and shepherd's purse.

A typical temperate herb garden (above right) contains a range of herbs, from mint to chives.

Bath Herbs

One unsung use of medicinal herbs is in the bath, where they act as stimulants, relaxants, and skin tonics. Effective bath-infusions can be made from the leaves of common wild plants, such as blackberry, nettle, or dandelion.

Fragrant types make the experience more invigorating – the best is lavender (from the Latin 'lavare', which means to wash). Fill a bag of cheesecloth or muslin with your chosen herbs (fresh or dried). Tie the neck securely and hang the bag around the hot tap so the water runs over it. When the bath is full, squeeze the juice out of the bag and leave it in the water.

- Stimulating herbs: lavender, basil, bay, fennel, lemon verbena, rosemary, meadowsweet, eau-de-cologne mint, sage, ginger-mint, thyme, eucalyptus.
- Relaxing herbs: catnip, chamomile, jasmine, linden flowers, vervain.
- Tonic herbs: blackberry, comfrey, daisy, dandelion, lady's mantle, marigold, nettle, yarrow.

The sandpit is a child's domain in an adult's garden (top), while a vegetable man symbolizes harvest. In a feast of the senses (above), hollyhocks and French marigolds give colour, nicotianas spread their scent beside a window, and in the fullness of time ripe grapes will be tasted from the vine.

Healing our Relationship with the Earth

The universe is like a great hologram: the whole is to some extent represented in every piece. But the universe is easier to see in some places than others. The garden is an especially rich and accessible channel: it is your window on Gaia and, in a remarkably direct way, the rest of the solar system, too – and even the stars in our galaxy.

The stars and planets have a way of putting things in perspective, probably because they seem to us to be essentially eternal and to pace the recurrent cycles of time. Try to find out about the heavens during your year of initiation. Your garden gives you a ringside seat – a low-set deckchair will save craning your neck. Tune your vision into the realization that what you see are real bodies of varying sizes, at varying distances, following precise orbits.

Start with the Moon. Log its phases through the lunar month and picture where it is in its orbit around the Earth. Remember that moonlight is reflected sunlight so keep the Sun in mind, too. Notice that the Moon rises later each evening as it waxes. Spend time in the garden at night as it comes to the full. Use your peripheral vision. Be aware of your moods and dreams. What is the garden trying to say?

Next, get to know the planets. When the Moon is strong it blanks out most stars but the brighter planets remain – Venus, Mars, Jupiter, and Saturn, although they are not usually all visible at once. The planets follow an invisible line called the plane of the ecliptic; as you look at them you are looking out through the remains of the great disc from which the solar system evolved, and in which all the planets now move – including the Earth.

The plane of the ecliptic is a useful reference point. It appears to swivel around as the Earth rotates on its axis hour by hour, and will go up and down with the seasons. Keep a track of where the planets are on the ecliptic. Constellations of stars behind the ecliptic make up the 12 signs of the zodiac and as they progress along their orbits around the Sun the planets "enter" (move in front of) or "leave" (move away from) the different constellations. The positions of the Moon and the planets in the sky, and their relationship to one another are of crucial significance to the practitioners of biodynamic gardening (see p.254).

The seasons have their own qualities and affect your feeling for the yearly cycle. Try to pick up also on the Moon cycle, feeling for changes in yourself and the garden. Finally take some time to contemplate the daily cycle. The day/night contrast is absolute: watch how the light changes in color, intensity, and direction from dawn through to dusk, and see how your garden's quality – and the behavior of its inhabitants – alter accordingly.

To observe the apparent movement of the sun, try making a temporary sundial. First fix a long stick or cane firmly into the ground, leaning somewhat toward the nearest geographic pole. Set an alarm clock to ring on each hour of a sunny day, and when it rings put a stone or a small marker stick on the shadow of the central stick. In low latitudes, where the sun is high all summer, mount a permanent sundial vertically on a sunward surface, with the pointer sticking out horizontally.

The rhythms of planetary, solar, and lunar time cycles are complemented by evolutionary time. This is the unfolding, linear history of your continent and bioregion, of the rocks, soils, plants, and animals that have occupied your garden. More recently, this history includes the people who have created your garden and cultivated it before you, and the kind of changes they wrought. By familiarizing yourself with the history of your garden you will be much better placed to heal your relationship with the Earth.

On an ordinary time-scale you can note the evolution of your garden in various changes you make, but principally in the growth of trees. The life-span of trees is broadly similar to that of people, and it gives a special perspective to children if over the years they can observe the growth of a tree that was planted in the year they were born. So if you have the space plant a tree for each child. Even if you move house, it is always a pleasure to return and marvel at the growth of "personal" trees.

In a volcanic garden (top) at Beppu, Japan, the shrubs are clipped to reflect the rounded shapes of the boulders. A sundial becomes the focal point of a formal garden (right); a small dial such as this can be adjusted to allow for daylight-saving time.

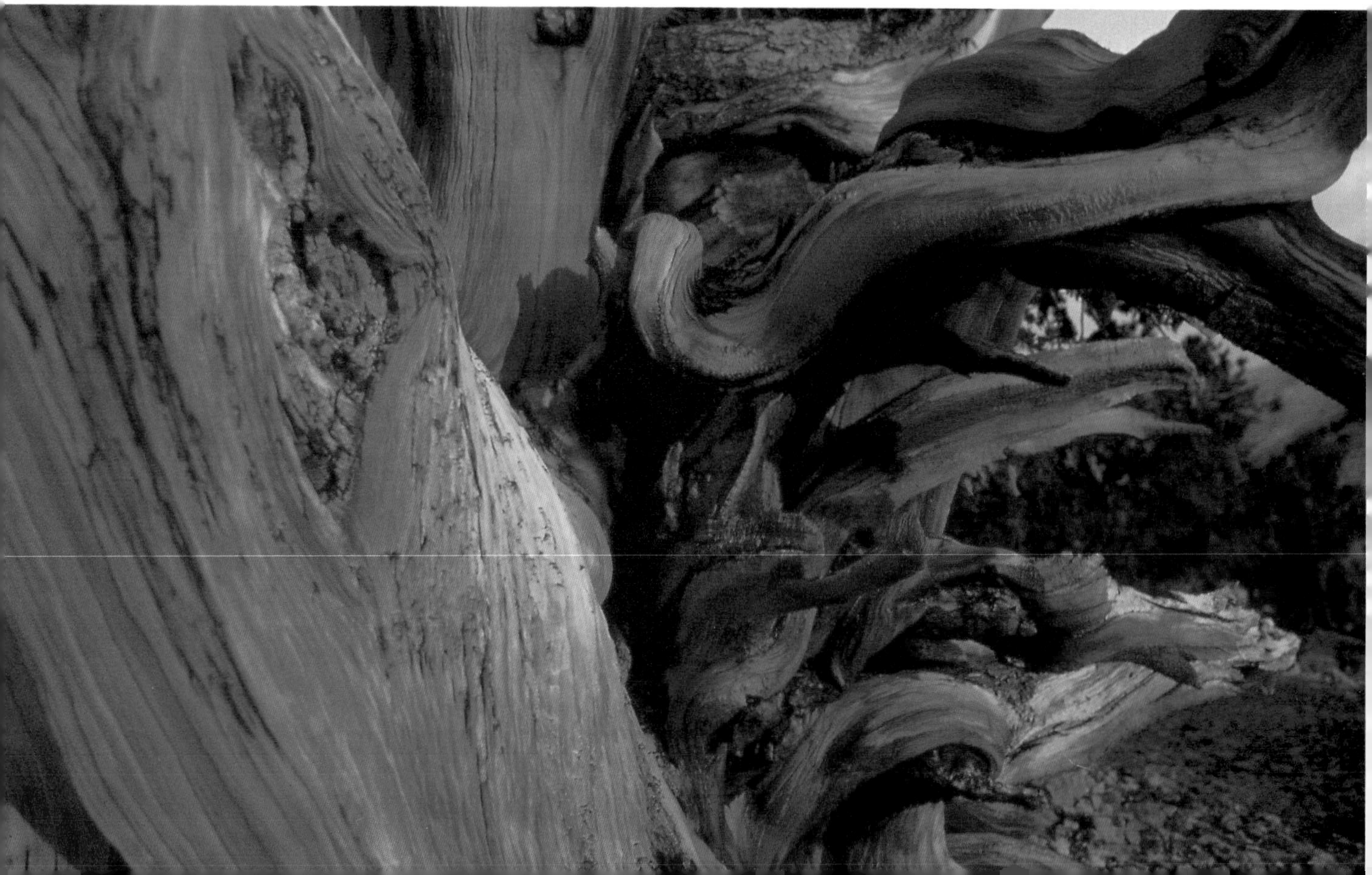

Healing the Spirit

Gardens crop up in the tradition of many ancient religions. The biblical Garden of Eden represented static primal innocence and perfection, that yet contained the seeds of innovation and creative risk. Muslims and Christians inherited the myth of Eden and also a Persian invention: paradise. In the form of a walled garden with lakes, fountains, and fruit trees, paradise became a place for healing the human spirit and, very naturally, the model of what the righteous could expect after death.

It is no accident that monotheistic religions emphasized the model of a perfectly designed and regulated garden rather than raw nature. Those that believed in an Earth Mother, and in a pantheon of nature spirits who inhabited rocks, trees, rivers, and so on, were ruthlessly persecuted. Yet in the East, pantheism reached an ineffable sophistication in the philosophy of Lao Tzu, while in the West the Druids embraced it. In fact, indigenous peoples the world over remain pantheistic in their beliefs. And it is no surprise that, at a time of environmental concern, the sacredness of nature is taken seriously once more.

Back in the East, Buddhism has generally been one of the contemplative religions that emphasized detachment from the world. Zen, however, developed practices that used everyday events, tasks, and crafts as tools for spiritual development. Zen gardens are famous for a sense of peace, order, and simplicity, in which all extraneous and distracting elements have been removed. Single rocks and pools with slow-moving fish serve as aids to meditation. The same spirit is found in the fastidiousness and restraint of traditional Japanese gardens. The undisturbed surface of a body of water is the commonest metaphor for the mind that is truly still and receptive in meditation. "The still mind of the sage is the mirror of heaven and earth." There are places, such as the wonderful Findhorn Garden in Scotland, where nature spirits are consciously invoked. But you do not have to be a practising pagan or pantheist for your garden to become a place for spiritual growth and healing. Set aside a quiet spot where you feel right and are least likely to be disturbed. This is your sanctuary.

In a resurgence of life, the storm-felled beech tree (top) in the New Forest, England, has struck new roots and rises from its knees toward the light once more. An emblem of endurance, the bristlecone pine (left) from California is among the oldest living things in the world. Its blood-red heartwood reveals the ravages of both time and a harsh environment. When this pine was a mere seedling, human beings had only just started to use iron tools.

The Garden as a Mirror for your Self

Really, you and your garden are astonishingly alike, and the similarities, once realized, should help to accelerate the healing process. In your garden, as in yourself:

- Far more is hidden than reveals itself to the superficial gaze. In other words, the more you seek, the more you find.
- Secrets are not discovered, nor results achieved, in any single way. Some need effort, discipline, hardheaded analysis, and painstaking investigation. Others come through patience, not striving, just letting things happen.
- There is a bright side and a dark side, equally essential and interdependent. Above, all is visible, conscious, light, sun, color, movement, and reason; below, all is invisible, unconscious, dark, and cool; a world of dissolution and of alchemical processes of transformation.
- A boundary marks the border between an inner world and an outer world. While you have control and responsibility for what goes on within the boundary, you also affect the environment outside the boundary.
- Periods of dormancy alternate with periods of growth. Progress cannot be made unless these periods are identified and recognized. Part of the healing process is choosing the right time to take action. "For everything there is a season, and a time for every purpose under heaven".
- Failure and loss can be dispiriting, but the healing processes spring perennially, and it is gratifying to watch them at work. It will be easier next time. What did you learn? And what is now possible that was not before?

- A good, organic, high-fiber diet maintains health. Junk food/chemical fertilizers or drugs/pesticides undermine it.
- In the end, the process is more important than the product.

All this is hardly surprising, for all living systems are similar. Perhaps the whole planet – even the whole universe – is like it, too. When we heal the part, we heal the whole.

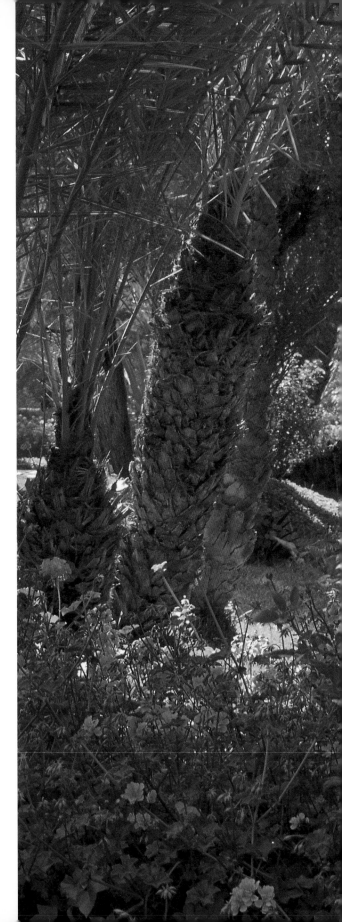

When humans appeared on the Earth, the land was dominated by flowering plants such as the pelargoniums in the foreground of the Moroccan paradise garden (right). But the ancient heritage was not forgotten: the "living fossil" cycads in the background survive from the time of the dinosaurs. "Paradise" was an ordered, humananized vision of nature, with streams and fountains (above).

PART III

THE GAIAN GARDEN

Introduction: Planning an Integrated Garden

Traditional styles of gardening have evolved a well-established horticultural language, with a syntax that sets the tone and layout, a standard vocabulary of plants, and a fixed grammar that specifies how the flora should be deployed. The language is rich but stilted – a baroque creation, in which excessive ornamentation and moribund conventions stifle the spirit of all the participants in the garden.

We can improve on this by learning, or indeed inventing, a new language that is relaxed and immediate – more like speech than writing. The old vocabulary would be enriched with hitherto forbidden phrases – earthy vulgarisms in the form of wild and native plants. Rather than strive for standard speech, the new language would embroider a vast patchwork of dialect and patois, as both human and plant communities are reacquainted. A different syntax would evolve from garden layouts designed around natural criteria, not those determined by fashion or convention. A looser grammar would emerge to emphasize communication, expressiveness, and usefulness instead of a desire to be correct.

We can capture the essence of the new language in the word integration: integration of different features, functions, and qualities within the garden; integration of the house and garden; integration of the garden with the neighborhood; and integration of the garden with the wider environment. Through such integration, your garden will cease to be an artificial stereotype propped up by technological main force and become a valuable part of the biosphere and the planet, a link between you and Gaia.

Planning the Gaian Garden

First and foremost, take it easy. Whether you are starting from scratch or inheriting a fully formed garden in the standard tradition, your year of initiation will give you plenty of time to work out alternatives. You may need time to break down stock assumptions and old habits of thought. As a useful planning exercise, consider various features, practical functions, and qualities of your garden and ask as many awkward questions about them as you can. Take each heading and make a list such as the that follows:

Features	Practical Functions	Qualities
Boundaries	Play	Visual
Walks	Washing/drying	Privacy
Seats	Storage	Sanctuary
Trees	Composting	Healing
Slopes	Growing food	Wildlife
Structures	Vehicle maintenance	Security
Water	Watering	Sounds

By considering each of these and how they relate to each other, you can come to view your garden in a new and different light. The aim is to integrate the various aspects so that they support one another. There will of course be conflicts, but look for ways in which these can be creatively resolved or bypassed; or for situations where a 10 percent sacrifice on one side may yield a 50 percent benefit on the other. Try turning problems into opportunities by a some lateral thinking or a simple shift of perspective.

Questions and Answers

Take each item on your list and interrogate it. The sort of questions you might ask about a feature are: what roles does it play? What else could you do with it? How else could the role be served? How valuable or important is it to you, your garden, or the environment? Do you have another problem that could be solved by modifying this feature? What small changes could bring about a large improvement?

Take boundaries, for example. They are important because they define the frame of your garden. They may exist only as lines on a map or as the limits of agreed territory between neighbors, while others are marked by a fence, wall, or hedge – in other words, a feature with near-vertical sides. Although

Keeping the soil unfertilized, selective mowing, and the use of special seed mixes are all ways of combining lawn, flowers, and wildlife value.

you can screen such a notable feature out of your immediate perception – much as one ignores the frame of a painting – you could transform it into something significant. Think of all the things a boundary feature could do: • Keep out grazing animals, dogs, and people • Prevent people seeing into the garden • Define a view • Give the garden a vertical dimension • Become attractive in its own right • Direct the eye in various ways • Give a sense of enclosure • Provide secure support for nests and bird houses • Constitute a system of microhabitats • Support climbing and trained plants • Provide backing for seats • Reduce ambient noise • Provide shade or shelter from wind • Reflect light • Store heat.

The potential problems a boundary feature may cause include • An oppressive sense of enclosure • An overwhelming visual element • An obstacle to views or cooling breezes • Turbulent air flow • Competition between the roots of hedges and other plants • An unattractive appearance • Excess shade • A hindrance to the free passage of wild animals.

You will have to weigh up the advantages and disadvantages of a feature, according to your needs. For example, turning a boundary into a windbreak may block cooling breezes when the weather is hot; erecting a high boundary to give privacy might create too much shade; and a solid structure may exacerbate wind turbulence. These conflicts provide opportunities for creativity.

Start thinking about the balance between what you want and what changes are possible. If, for instance, the roots of a hedge compete with edible plants you want to grow, why not then make the hedge itself edible? Or have a fence and grow climbing edibles? Or lay a walk next to the hedge. Or use functional elements (sheds, compost bays, garage) as boundary features.

Walking through a gateway (left) is a rite of passage in which you cross a boundary between domains. You can make such gateways conspicuous and even cultivate them. If the gate is an arch (right) the subtle effect is accentuated: at first there is a tantalizing frame through which you view one domain from another; on emerging from the arch there is a gentle, symbolic rebirth.

You can perform a similar exercise with garden functions, although the questions are different. Take play, for example: • Who's playing? • When and where do they play? • Is the play quiet, clean, messy, wet, rambunctious, adventurous, open-ended? • How does play relate to other functions and activities? • Is it safe? • Does it need supervision?

Small sand/gravel boxes or paddling pools placed on a firm surface outside the kitchen window are easy to incorporate into most gardens. Ball games that need a lawn may conflict with crops or herbaceous plants. Screens, frames, arbors, or internal hedges/shrubs may contain play areas. Trees can accommodate swings and climbing frames without the need for special equipment. Structures, trees, and changes of level are essential for stimulating children. Ponds are always a winner and play-houses can double as blinds for watching wildlife.

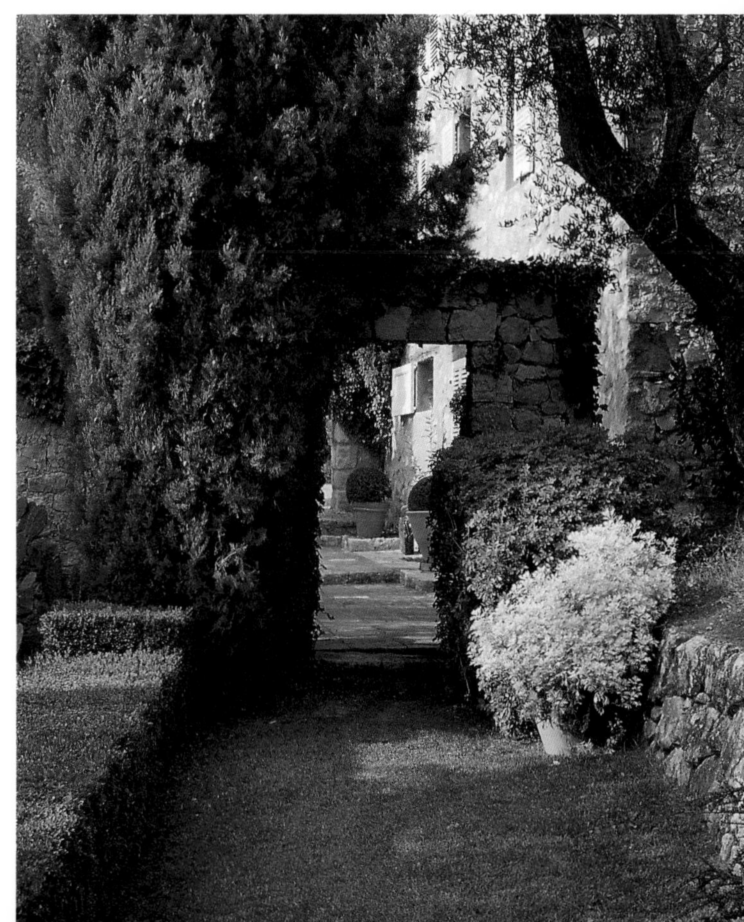

Unlike features and functions, garden qualities are often vague and consequently generate huge lists of possible angles for consideration. The visual aspect of the garden, for example, concerns: • Balance • Depth • Texture • Views within and without • Unity • Interest and surprise • Daily and seasonal patterns • Jarring elements • Aesthetics • Illusions and trompe l'oeil.

Serve Many Purposes

Books on garden design are full of such resonant checklists. Gaian gardening encourages you to combine elements and so serve many purposes, visual and otherwise. In this respect your garden's aesthetic may be unusual in that it lacks the crisp control of traditional gardens. You can, for example, site productive plots near the house; tolerate, or even choose, dowdy or scruffy natives for their wildlife value. You could allow bizarre edibles to jostle with ornamentals in the borders or deliberately neglect some parts of the garden for months of the year. Why not eschew bedding plants altogether as a waste of space and effort, or because they require excessive resources to sustain them. Finally, you could and tolerate and incorporate what others call "weeds" and "pests".

All this may require a certain retraining of your eyes and brain. Yet clever design can resolve most of the apparent conflicts. Many edibles are visually spectacular and good enough for any border; ornamentals may earn themselves a place as companions in the vegetable garden – precisely because they are good for wildlife; and careful management and choice of plants can reconcile minimum intervention with neatness.

It may be helpful to exaggerate the differences between the Gaian approach and the traditional style. For instance, Gaian gardening seeks to integrate not segregate, to make choices according to ecological or natural criteria instead of precedent or custom, and to be design not management intensive. In practice, though, any Gaian gardener must acknowledge a debt to the traditional gardening, and traditionalists are becoming more Gaian without realizing it.

Making a Difference

A Gaian garden should emphasize a difference from its surroundings wherever possible. If your particular neighborhood has been "homogenized" in the standard style, the creation of a bioregional, minimum-intervention garden will be sharply different and worthwhile. But think of, say, a remote house in a desert or on a foggy moor, surrounded by millions of acres of natural habitat. A garden that merely imitates the habitat will be contributing very little to the diversity of the bioregion. If you followed the Gaian approach you would seek to enrich the local

Creating places of shady repose
Wild plants congregating around a stone seat (above) give a cool and secret space. Hammocks supported between neighboring trees (left) offer simultaneously both shade and an open prospect. A pergola (right) surrounded by roses on all sides delivers a delightful combination of scent and dappled shade.

habitat by providing conditions that are complementary but still within the bioregional framework.

In "making a difference" the range of approaches runs from the minimalist and hands-off method to the elaborate design and construction style. But, of course, you can vary your approach in different parts of your garden. Extreme minimalism applied across the whole garden is usually unsatisfactory – you tend to get a mess of weeds, little diversity of flora or habitat, and very few wild edibles. The "editing" approach (see p.120) gives better results, and you could complement this by deliberately planting native species, or plants from similar bioregions to your own. For serious food growing you must use "proper" edible cultivars (preferably those that will flourish without too much input) and local land races wherever possible.

Habitat and Climate Gardens

The following pages of Part Three address the problems and opportunities of gardening in a number of specific situations. Most gardens will not fall neatly into any of these categories but they are bound to share various qualities or potential problems to a greater or lesser extent.

HABITAT GARDENS

The Urban Garden

In its popular form, the traditional approach works best in a fairly large, open garden with gentle slopes, favorable orientation, and a good, deep soil. This is the middle ground, the ideal mesic garden (see p.96). Furthermore, the approach is assumed to work in isolation from its surroundings, as if the garden were located in the middle of a rural environment.

Few gardeners enjoy this happy situation. Most, in fact, live in cities where factors outside the garden, for better or worse, exert a strong influence. We can list potential benefits and problems of gardening in the city, bearing in mind that what seem at first to be problems can often be turned to good account. Potential benefits include: • Range of microclimates • Warmer temperatures than hinterland • Waste and scrap materials available • Good possibilities for cooperation. Potential problems include: • Poor or non-existent soil • Air and/or soil pollution • Restricted size • Overshadowing • Lack of privacy • Unsympathetic neighbors • Noise • Dogs and cats.

In general, the Gaian approach seeks to harmonize the garden with the character of the local habitat. But in an urban environment it would usually strive to contradict its surroundings rather firmly. For those who want little more than an extra room for their home, nothing is simpler than to recreate an utterly artificial garden: completely cover the soil with paving stones; set up spotlights (sodium lights are the most efficient) and wire the space for sound; erect steel and aluminum railings; and use plastic plants, plastic awning for shade, and plastic furniture. You can leave concrete block walls bare for the really brutal effect, or else you can modishly paint hard-edged abstract or social-realist murals on them.

An open canopy of deciduous trees around urban buildings can moderate the summer climate without being oppressively dark in winter. The fresh white dogwood flowers (top left) are always a welcome sight in spring. For low maintenance you can pave, grass, or stock the space between trees with ground cover plants (left).

Old city gardens may be rich in organic matter from generations of pre-chemical fertilization. The soil structure may also be good and you can grow just about anything – especially weeds! But most often, city gardens have poor soils or no soil at all.

Poor soils are most common in new gardens which builders, who are notoriously cavalier with soil, have created. They excavate subsoil and dump it over the original topsoil; after compacting the structure with heavy machinery, they bury rubble and other refuse in it. Can you use it? Some plants, especially trees, like a bit of rubble to open things up, and the lime in mortar can provide a lime-rich zone. And such nutrient-poor soils can make an excellent site for many wildflowers. Fussier plants will need their own pockets of compost-enriched soil. As your compost supply builds up you can "restore" as much of the garden as you like, little by little.

In the most extreme situation, you may have no soil at all, because your garden is entirely paved. Here, you can create the most flexible system of all – the container garden. Don't forget the possibility of breaking through the paving stones in places to provide pockets for trees and climbers. Make sure they can get enough water. The growing media can be provided either by bringing in natural soil or by commercial materials, supplemented perpetually by household compost.

Thinking Vertically

A small urban garden may have far more wall space than ground space, so think vertically. If space is at a premium, clothe the boundary walls and fences with climbing (or in some cases, trailing) plants, or hang containers on them. Even in very small gardens, tall but lightly shading trees can fill a huge, vertical volume with foliage at different levels. One of the best places to appreciate these trees is from a balcony facing the garden.

Creating Shade

In hot climates, houses are deliberately designed with yards to increase shade and provide comfort. If your summers are intolerably hot, develop cool, shady areas with dense foliage, arbors, and pools. These will suit the many climbers that enjoy shady roots, yet can reach up to the sunlight.

If you feel oppressed by the lack of light, try painting the garden walls white, or with light hues. Hanging large mirrors on the walls may also help while at the same time appearing to enlarge the garden – they also help plants to grow straighter. Remember to take the sun's path into consideration before positioning the mirrors.

Urban gardens in temperate climates may suffer from too much shade and you may find you have to take measures to admit as much sunlight as possible for your plants. A roof garden presents the most radical solution to overshadowing. Many buildings have flat or partly flat roofs, which are specified to take light foot traffic and are suitably drained. You may need to reinforce the structure, but at the very least you should be able to grow plants in containers. Roof garden plants may need protection from the wind and plenty of watering.

Available Materials

One advantage of gardening in a city is the ready availability of a wide range of materials: cardboard or old carpets make good sheet mulches; vegetable wastes from supermarkets are excellent for composting; and, unusually perhaps, hair clippings from hairdressers act as slow-release nourishment for trees and shrubs. And you can collect materials for containers (tires, paint tins, oil drums, scrap wood) almost at will.

The Problem of Pollution

Most plants remain unaffected by pollution, either in the air or the soil, unless it is severe. Slow-growing lichens are the most sensitive to pollution – if you know how to read them, the species present can tell

The orderly, rectangular patterns of the Dutch garden (top left) are broken up into little "rooms" and complemented by a wide variety of plant forms. In the British garden (left) flagged paths meander through thickets or herbaceous perennials, giving a "cottage garden" atmosphere. In both these temperate, oceanic-climate situations, openness to light and sun in important, so tall trees are kept to the sides. By contrast, in the Venezuelan courtyard garden (above) a pool and shade trees combine to create a cool space; house doors and windows may be opened to encourage through drafts.

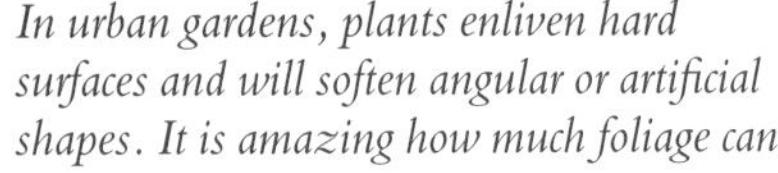

In urban gardens, plants enliven hard surfaces and will soften angular or artificial shapes. It is amazing how much foliage can produce when grown in small containers, which may themselves be a pleasing part of the overall garden design. Climbing and hanging plants are particularly effective – but be careful to keep them well watered in dry weather.

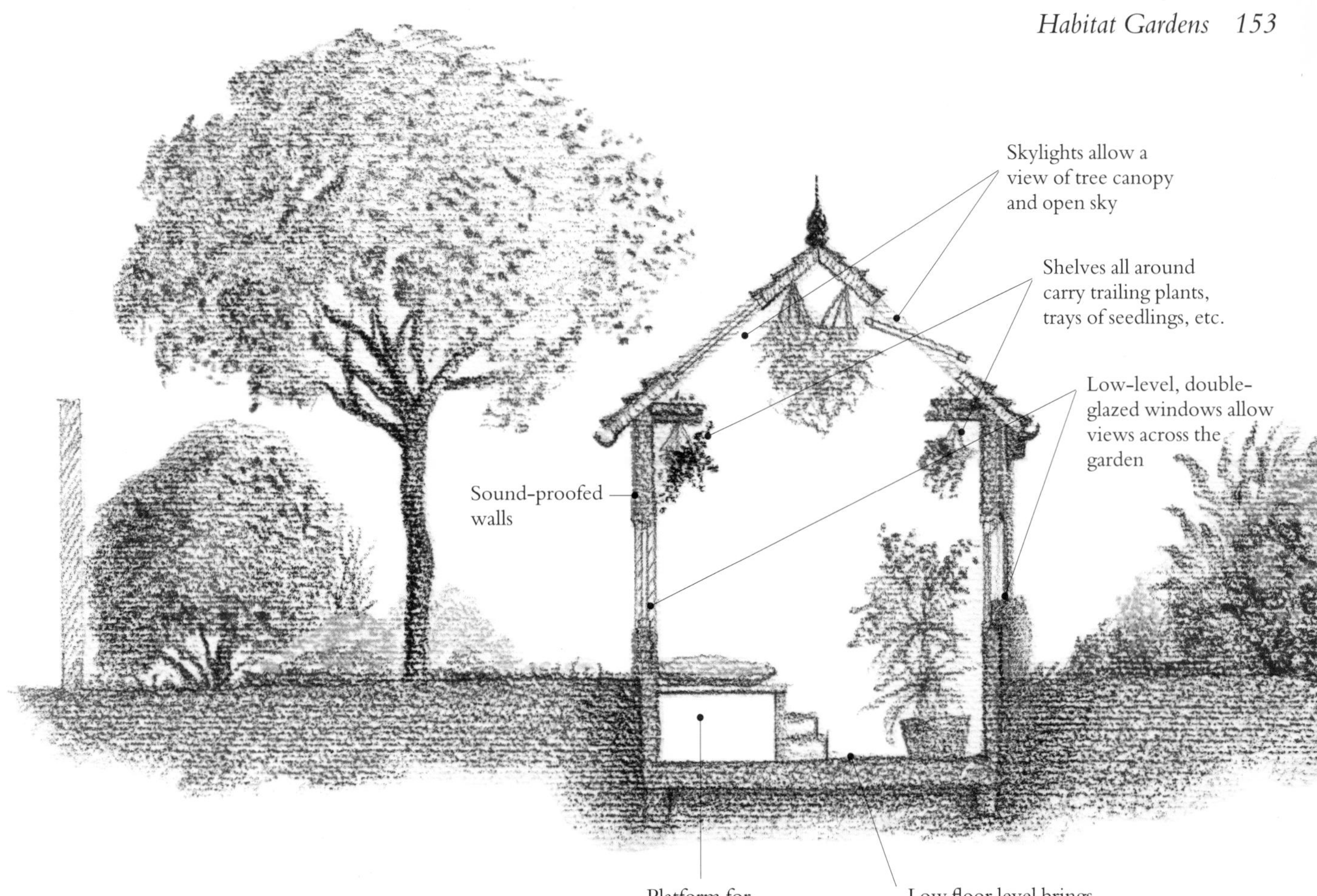
Skylights allow a view of tree canopy and open sky
Shelves all around carry trailing plants, trays of seedlings, etc.
Low-level, double-glazed windows allow views across the garden
Sound-proofed walls
Platform for relaxation and meditation
Low floor level brings windows to eye level when person is standing

Skylights, plants, and low-level windows are the key elements of an urban retreat (above). They help you become intimate with nature and bring you peace from the busy world outside. Amid trailing plants and comfortable surroundings, you can relax and meditate, thereby healing your spirit.

you how polluted the air is. Lead, the most damaging air pollutant to humans, may be deposited on leafy crops grown beside a busy road. Only 50 percent of this can be readily washed off, so it's best not to grow leafy crops in such situations. Fruit, root, or seed crops do not absorb lead in significant quantities from the soil so long as the pH is between 6.5 and 7 and there is plenty of organic matter present.

A Warmer Temperature

A city generates a huge amount of waste heat and is always a few degrees warmer than its hinterland – no help in hot climates, but a measurable benefit in cold ones. The variety of warmer microclimates in sheltered nooks and beside poorly insulated buildings means you can grow a greater range of more tender crops than is considered "normal" in your region. They may need extra protection in very cold weather, but next to the house they stand a reasonable chance, and even more in a sunroom.

An Urban Retreat

Quietness and greenness are the priorities for a city retreat. Glazing should be low enough to give you a view of a foreground you are able to control, a view of greenness that helps to restore your spirits and to heal your urban frustrations. Insert skylights so you can see the sky and overhanging trees. Inside the retreat, hang plants near windows and propagate seedlings on high shelves. If you cannot guarantee views at least seal the retreat well with sound-insulating materials.

Urban solutions

The patio garden in Spain (left) clothes all the vertical surfaces with rampant climbers, while citrus trees provide shade, scent, and fruit. Plucking oranges off the tree is one of the great delights of a frost-free garden. The rooftop garden (top right) boldly solves the problem of shade in a densely built environment. The different levels and complex layout prevent any overall view and give a sense of indefinite space while plants around the skylights, viewed from within, soften the hard urban roofscape. In the tiny garden (below right) greater size is suggested by small details and fine-leaved plants, while the classic trompe l'oeil (near right) achieves its ends by style and chutzpah.

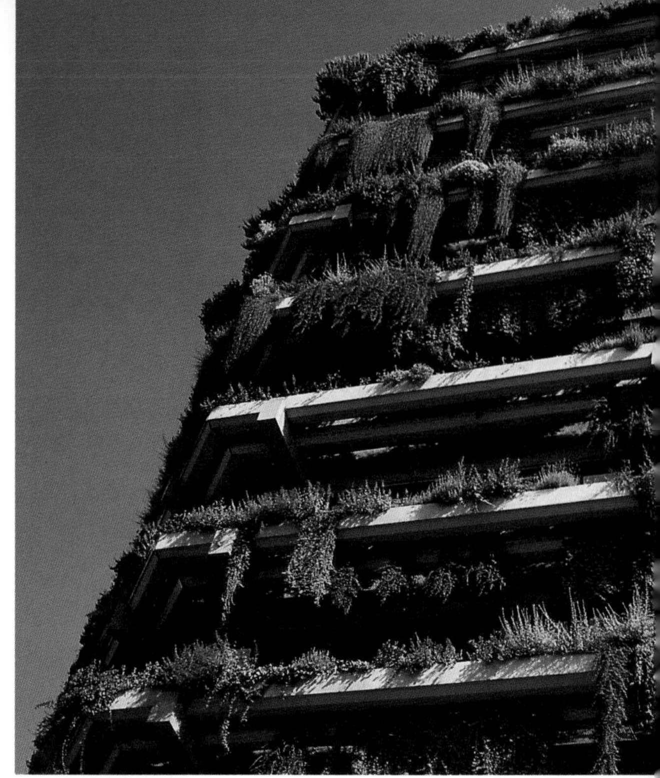

CATS AND DOGS

These domestic creatures can cause problems digging up plants and leaving droppings, rummaging through the compost pile, and terrorizing birds and their nests. Digging is less of a problem with permanent plantings, but you should protect sowings with chicken wire until established. Enclose and cover compost piles or use a worm bin instead. Dogs can be kept out of your garden by good boundaries but cats are a law unto themselves – they do serve some purpose by keeping rats, mice, raccoons, and rabbits at bay.

RELATING TO THE NEIGHBORHOOD

For many people, their garden boundary defines a territory which almost becomes a second skin, an extension of themselves. As the wider environment recedes, they behave as if their garden exists in isolation. This deserves some challenge. The Gaian gardener needs to explore the social dimensions of gardening, and greater integration with the neighborhood and the bioregion at large.

Lack of privacy in the city is to some extent a state of mind. Some people are able to ignore "the public" or their neighbors; others positively relish being on show; yet others will go to any length not to be seen. Although tall boundaries prevent people from looking into your garden from ground level, they cast a great deal of shade and can give a restricted feel. As an alternative, create a smaller, private space. Arbors clothed above and around with vines will screen you from both ground level and tall buildings.

COMMUNITY GARDENS

The restrictions of urban gardening can often be relaxed by turning to the resources of the neighborhood, or collaborating with friends and neighbors. Community gardens offer space for growing food crops, while city farms could become the hub of local community life, with cafe, farm shop, gardens, playgrounds, workshops, and animals, as well as somewhere to do a bit of gardening. Such farms could develop into centers for recycling, for renting tools and machinery, for buying seeds and supplies in bulk, and for borrowing such useful animals as pigs for plowing or goats for clearing scrub, and so on.

Cooperation with others can start very simply with swaps of seeds (because you usually get too many in a packet), exchanges of produce, or bulk-buying of materials. Costs can be cut when you share your equipment with those around you: if you and your neighbors each buy a machine, such as a rototiller, shredder, hedge trimmer, or brushwood cutter, you can then borrow from others when you need to. Also, look for seed companies that offer discounts to members of garden clubs.

Greenhouses, too, work better if they are larger. Why not share potting and propagation facilities, and have private plots in a large, plastic tunnel which will work much better and cost very much less per square foot than a dozen individual greenhouses. Temperature fluctuations can be kept to a minimum in a large, cool greenhouse. The ultimate development of collective gardening is found in permaculture villages, such as Crystal Waters in Australia, or Village Homes in Davis, California. At each of these locations, strong and deliberate ecological principles guide the design of both public spaces and private homes.

Public urban gardens
Plants improve the atmosphere of public buildings and townscapes both literally and metaphorically. They can moderate temperature, clean the air, save on air-conditioning, and make everyone feel better. Trailing plants are particularly effective, either in the open – as in the building in Barcelona (top left) – or in enclosed areas (left). The Village Homes development in Davis, California (above), is probably the most advanced urban landscape project anywhere. Here, passive solar houses with conservatories are surrounded by plantings of fruit trees and swards of self-fertilizing, low-maintenance Dutch clover.

The Mountain Garden

Height above sea level is not the sole criterion of a mountain garden. A windswept, craggy hillside in Scotland, some 1640ft (500m) above sea level, might qualify, but a warm and fertile plateau in Ecuador, situated at many times this altitude, would not. A true mountain garden has steep slopes which are exposed to severe winds and thin soils prone to both erosion and alternate waterlogging and drought. Apart from stunning views, its advantages may include a distinctive local flora, clean air, and some dramatic natural features.

Steep slopes have secondary effects: rapid erosion in heavy rain and exaggerated patterns of light and shade. The orientation of the slope with respect to the sun has a profound influence on a garden at higher latitudes: a sunward slope brings many natural advantages, while a sunless slope will limit the possibilities of most sites.

Trees, Shrubs, and Herbs

Mountain soils are often poor because nutrients are scarce or else there is little organic matter. On heathland, the light soil can be amended by leguminous and cover crops, and by adding organic matter. On acidic moorland, the soil is peaty and organic matter is plentiful, but the nutrients are locked up by the particularly low pH. Here, you can grow various ericaceous, low-shrub, berry crops, such as blueberry, huckleberry, whortleberry, cranberry, cowberry, bilberry, crowberry, elderberry, and salal. You can also cultivate a range of and acid-loving crops, such as rhubarb and strawberry.

In mountainous areas of the humid tropics erosion can quickly deplete the soil on cultivated land. Terracing the hillsides slows the downflow of water, allowing eroded soil from higher up to be trapped and saved in the lower terraces. In the absence of terraces, it is essential to maintain tree cover in order to minimize erosion.

If the ground of your mountain garden slopes steeply toward the sun, you can locate trees almost anywhere without causing undue shade. The direction of the most problematic winds could be the critical factor in determining where they are planted. If the ground slopes steeply away from the sun in mid and high latitudes, any trees on the sunward side will shade both garden and house; tall trees are most suitable at the bottom or sides of the garden, and wind shelter on the sunward side must be provided by fences and hedges.

Trees and shrubs play an important role in soil stabilization and creation. Without compromising your other goals in the garden, keep existing trees and plant others if necessary. The minimalist mountain gardener relies entirely on plants which can tolerate the conditions. Some produce edible fruits – juniper, mulberry, olive, carob, almond, bayberry, and gooseberry; others are woody aromatic herbs, such as thyme, sage, and marjoram.

Water Management

The relation of the slope to the house is of daily importance not only because it is you that has to go up and down the garden, but also because you have to manage the water supply. Water from a pressurized supply will reach all parts of the garden; but in the absence of such a line, or if you wish to use gray water and runoff, it's obviously much easier to run the water downhill!

Surplus runoff from the main body of the garden, collected via diversion drains in a storage pond, will give the greatest yield at the bottom of the slope. But if you need the water for irrigation, site the pond near the middle of the slope, with plants that need watering below it. Set up another pond at the bottom for use in dire emergencies. Similar logic applies to the movement of other bulky materials, such as compost, much of which arises within the garden itself and is concentrated on intensive crops.

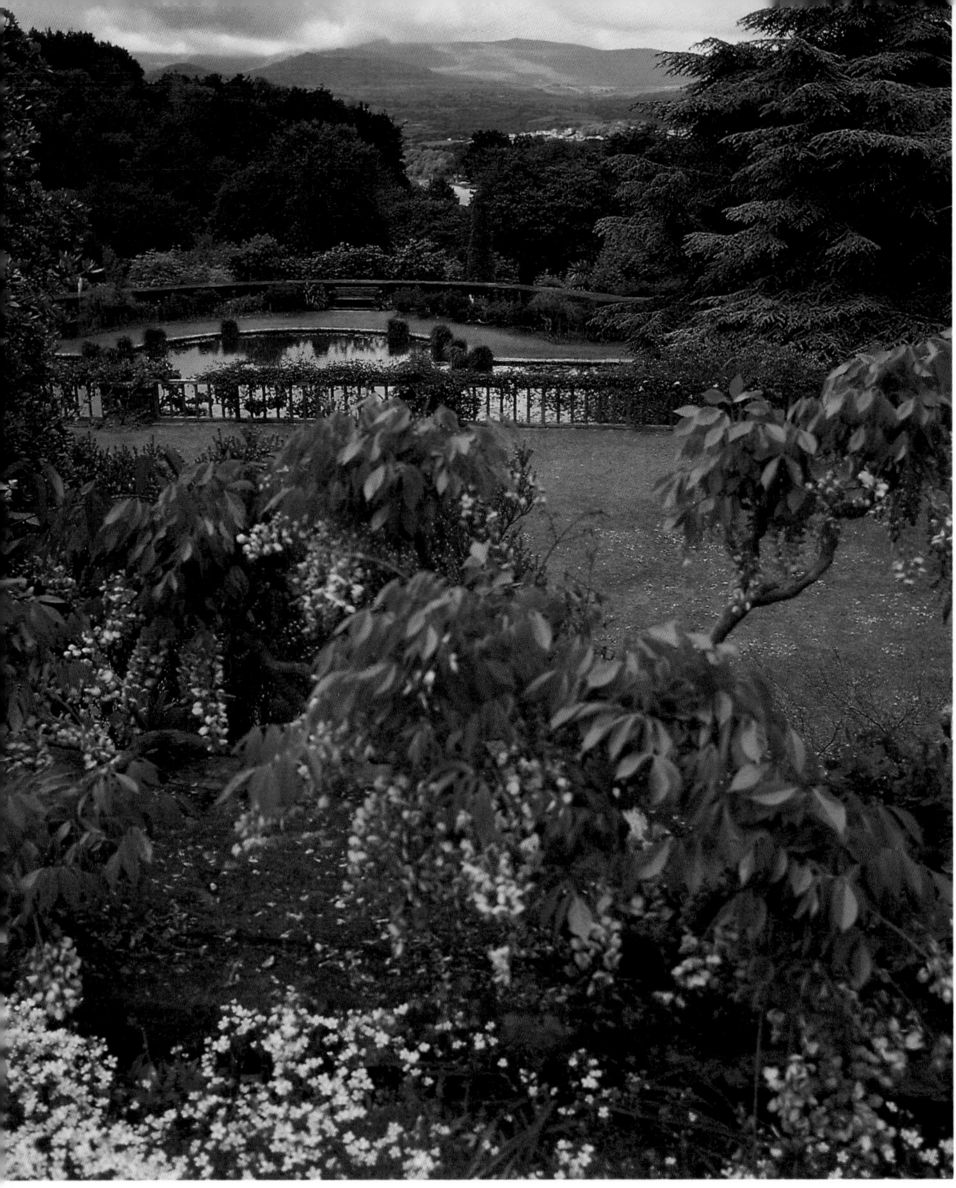

The gardens at Bodnant, Wales (left), are built on the steep side of a valley in a series of broad terraces, each with a different prospect, giving way finally to a deep ravine. The differences of level are exploited for dramatic effect. In the Venezuelan garden (right) the house is sunk into the hillside so that the upper garden flows on to the roof. At high altitudes with a short growing season, vegetable gardens can still flourish, as in this example from the Swiss Alps (below right). Although the winters are severe, the heavy snow cover protects many perennial crops from fatal damage. The so-called "alpine" plants thrive on the regime of sharp dry winters, well-drained soil, and a resolute thaw. They may not do well in the erratic weather of milder oceanic climates.

Steep slopes often have thin soils simply because the soil falls, or is washed, off the underlying rock. Rain gathers into rapid rivulets and streams, washing the soil into the valley or plain below – which is one reason they are so fertile. To avoid losing your soil, slow the water down – the simplest way is to break up the flow with rocks and cascades.

An alternative approach (you would probably need to do both in reality) involves creating what are in effect miniature valley bottoms. These intercept the flow of eroded soil and nutrients, and at the same time slow down the water runoff. To this end, permanent landform features are constructed across rather than down the slope. Such features include ditches, swales, berms, terraces, and retaining structures.

The Value of Terracing

At its simplest, terracing just cuts into the upslope and spreads the excavated material below the cut. This results in a level area at the expense of even steeper slopes above and below – these need to be supported or retained in some way. It is traditional, obvious, and appropriate to use the features and natural rock of the mountain for the retaining walls of terraces.

The effect of terracing is to increase the depth of soil, and trap water and nutrients flowing from above. You can grow the more demanding crops in the richer soil of the terraces. Always look for opportunities to solve several problems at once: steep slopes can, for example, offer the tree shade and

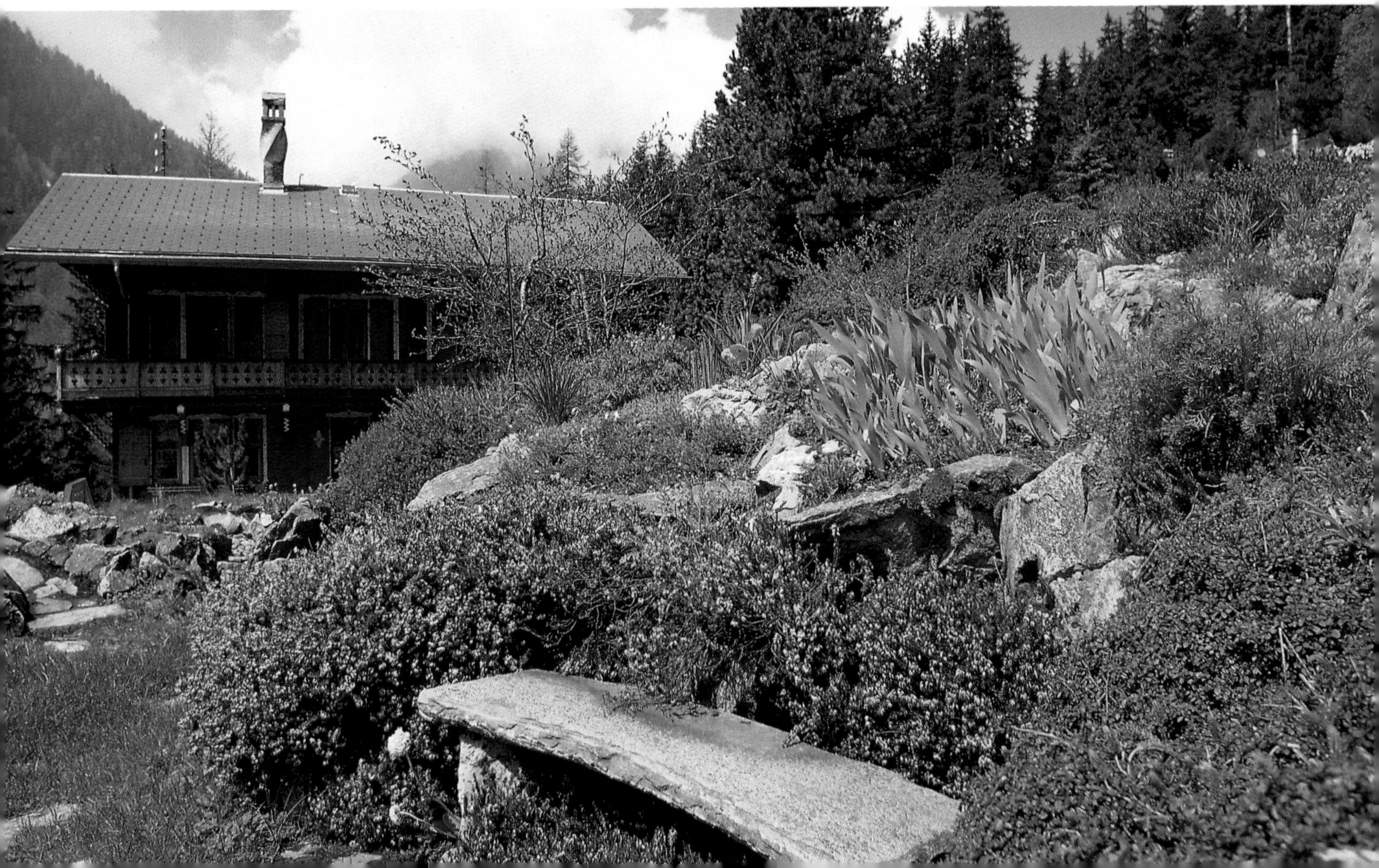

shelter without root competition, together with easier harvesting of fruit.

Access to very steep terraces can be a problem. Steps are best for retaining soil; they use the least space, but present a serious obstacle to wheelbarrows. A good pattern is a slow zigzag of gently sloping terraces, using the retaining walls as pathways. If there is road access to the top of the slope, make sure all materials are delivered and stored there, so they can be carried downwards.

A Mountain Sanctuary

The garden cave is the mountain equivalent to the garden shed. But such a cave suggests designs for a mountain sanctuary, sunk into the slope to provide some moderation of temperature. On a sun-facing slope, the sanctuary could be warm for much of the year, especially if glazed. A skylight that opens gives you the chance to stargaze: the skies get clearer with greater altitude, especially if not disturbed by smog and light from nearby cities.

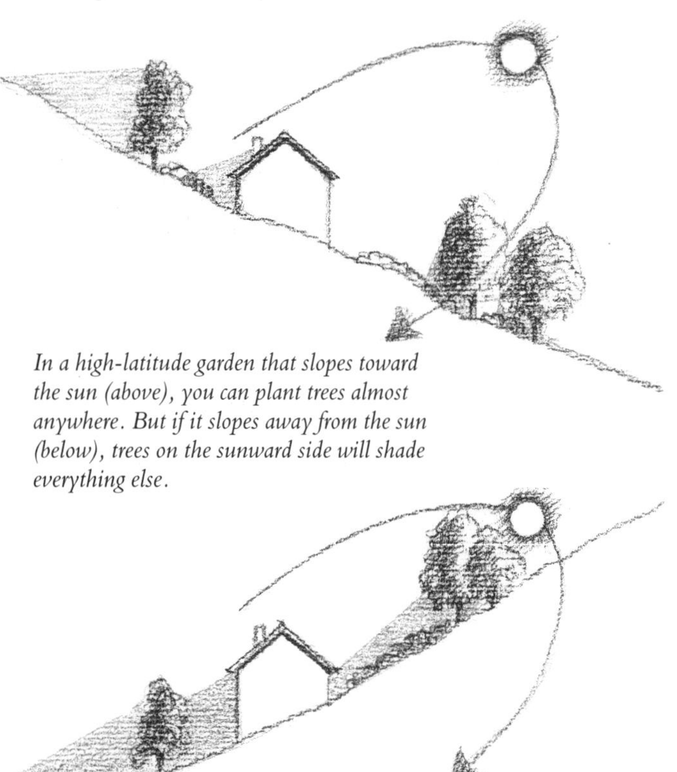

In a high-latitude garden that slopes toward the sun (above), you can plant trees almost anywhere. But if it slopes away from the sun (below), trees on the sunward side will shade everything else.

Earth tanks and wells collect water run-off

A mountain garden exposed to strong winds needs to be protected by windbreaks on at least three sides (right). In the summer months at high latitudes, you could choose to concentrate on the short but intense growing season.

To make a terrace from a mountainside, you need only use the soil and rock that is already present (below). When you plant trees in the soil of the terrace remember that, when mature, they will cast shade on the crops growing on the terrace above.

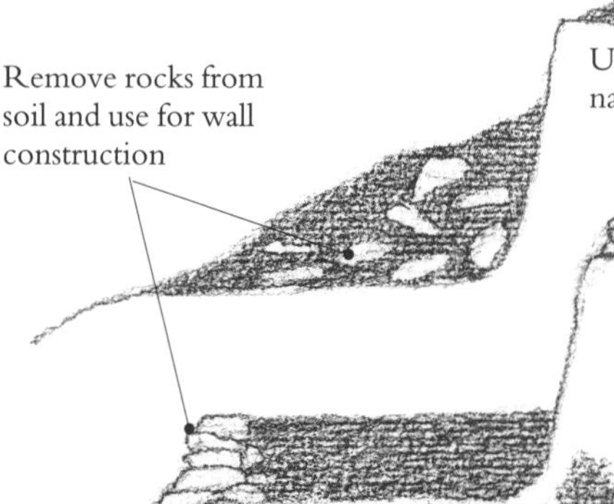
Remove rocks from soil and use for wall construction
Use rockface as natural retainer

Fruit can be easily picke

Terrace wall provides suppo for fan-trained and nut trees

Tree roots invade rock fissures

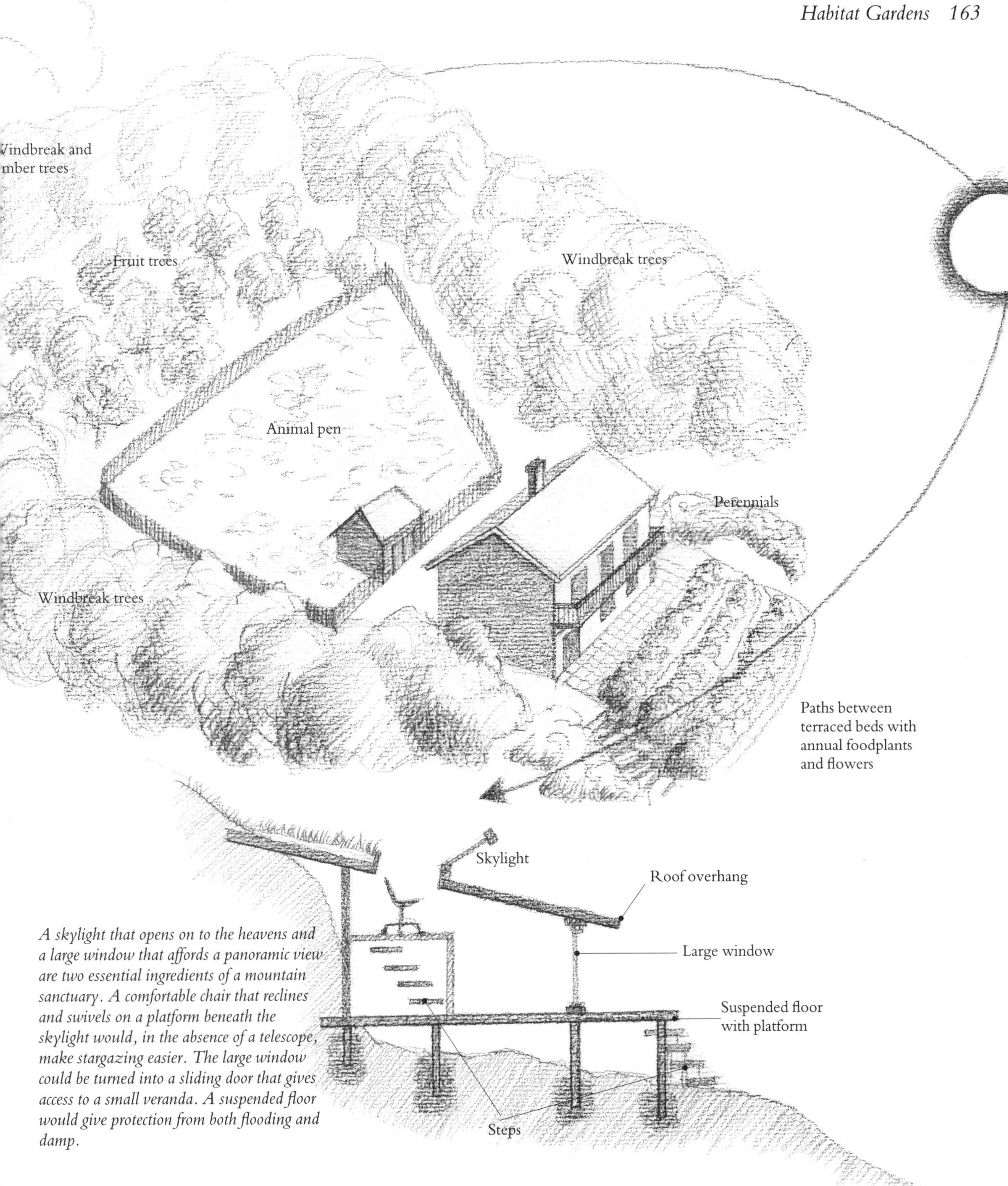

A skylight that opens on to the heavens and a large window that affords a panoramic view are two essential ingredients of a mountain sanctuary. A comfortable chair that reclines and swivels on a platform beneath the skylight would, in the absence of a telescope, make stargazing easier. The large window could be turned into a sliding door that gives access to a small veranda. A suspended floor would give protection from both flooding and damp.

The Coastal Garden

It might seem slightly ridiculous to consider all coastal situations at once, ranging from palm-fringed beaches and mangrove swamps through mudflats and estuaries to fjords and storm-tossed cliffs. However, they do share some features: a milder climate than the interior, with extremes of heat and cold moderated by the sea; exposure to wind and salt spray; sandy or rocky soils with little organic matter and a proneness to drying, compounded by salt. These might be combined with steep rocky slopes facing the sea and the elements.

Coastal regions have useful resources: fish, shellfish, edible seaweeds, seashore plants, such as samphire, and fruits from seashore trees, such as elder or beach plum. However, pollution from sewage or oil is an ever-present danger. Local native species offer a good guide to your choice of plants. Watch out for halophytes – they tolerate drying out and share a great deal with many desert and mountain plants. They usually have silvery or fleshy leaves and a bushy, dwarf or creeping habit; they do well in garden soils but will survive salty onslaughts better than other plants.

"Ordinary" plants need shelter from the wind and from the salt and sandblasting it can bring. You can provide this shelter either by sinking parts of the garden and using the excavated material to raise a bank on the windward side; or by erecting windbreaks (see pp.81–2). Solid walls generate turbulent gusts on their leeward side and so cause more problems than they solve. If they already exist, they should be complemented with trees and shrubs to break up the force of the wind.

A high wall with climbers breaks up wind eddies on the lee, sheltering a coastal garden (top left). Naturally tolerant plants, such as Sedum spectabile, Achillea, *and* Gypsophila, *are best for typical sandy coastal gardens. Some coastal habitats, such as dune slacks, encourage moisture-loving plants, such as* Astilbe *and* Filipendula *(left). Bark mulch helps to conserve moisture and slowly builds up organic matter in sandy soils.*

You need to soften a windward bank by growing appropriate plants on the lee – you will never find a better use for a thick bramble hedge. If there is no bank, new windbreak plants will need protecting with a wind-porous fence of some kind, or at least a screen of brushwood supported by stakes driven into the ground. Plant them densely for mutual support and fertilize, water, stake, and mulch them for the first year or two. You need to think ahead to the final height of any trees if part of your reason for living where you do is the view of the ocean.

Most trees which are suitable for windbreaks do not produce edible crops – although they can look good. These include various willows, black pine, wild privet, *Escallonia*, *Griselinia*, and *Eleagnus*. Behind them you can plant conventionally useful trees and shrubs, such as Spanish chestnut, sloe, strawberry tree, sand cherry, beach plum, *Sambucus racemosa*, *Sorbus domestica*, and *S. aucuparia "edulis"*, and aromatics, such as rosemary, bay, and lavender.

Within the protected zone, the easiest edibles to grow are often those with wild cousins on the other side of the hedge: carrots, cabbage, seakale, asparagus, fennel, and almost any member of the goosefoot family such as spinach, beetroot, and purple orach. In addition, if the soil is light you can plant garlic, onions, shallots, potatoes, and horseradish. But these will still need mucking, watering, and weeding/mulching to get good yields!

It is a good general principle to grow dwarf varieties, rather than ones which might get blown over, although a good thick clump of Jerusalem artichokes will survive strong winds and will serve as a windbreak for other crops. Another idea is to erect a very sturdy frame for a climbing crop on the windward side, ideally in a V-shape with the point facing the wind. The frame can support such climbing annuals as scarlet runner beans or vining squash, or such perennial vines as passionfruit, kiwi, hops, grape – or soft fruit canes.

Coastal Sanctuary

A prospect of the sea makes one of the best views from a sanctuary. The endless changes of sea and sky (here, the "oceanic" climates have the edge) are an unfailing balm for the soul. At the same time, the wildlife of coastal regions is especially rich. Build yourself a blind sunk partly into sand dunes or a cliff ledge, approachable from the rear, with a wide but narrow window facing the sea and a single-pitch roof facing the wind. And further back from the seashore you will almost certainly find a number of other interesting habitats, such as salt marsh, dune slacks, and brackish wetlands, to explore.

One aspect of integrating a coastal garden is the unique opportunity it gives you to create a view with the sea as a permanent feature (right). So choose your plants carefully, and remember that the wind is the element that will cause you most problems.

Cross section of sanctuary

A wooden blind sunk partly into the sand dunes is a perfect spot for observing the eternal movement of the sea. In hot weather, a skylight with wind-catcher frames made of wood or zinc directs the air (above) into the sanctuary. Wooden shutters and mineralized roofing felt afford a fair amount of protection when the weather turns stormy or the wind reaches gale force.

Windbreaks are a vital feature of any coastal garden because they protect the house as well as the garden's crop plants and flowers. If the garden has sand dunes, they should be stabilized with plants such as beach grass, with bramble thickets grown in the lee. Windbreak trees should be chosen to diffuse the force of the wind and create a calm area in front of the house for cultivation.

The Woodland Garden

If your garden is either wooded or surrounded by dense trees, it will benefit from a perpetually moderated climate that is warmer in winter and cooler in summer. Its three fully developed dimensions – its volume – offer potential supplies of leaves, woodfuel, animal forage, perhaps fruit and nuts. However, the soil will be dominated by tree roots and parts of the garden may be heavily shaded. You may also find that the winter sun cannot reach your house, thereby increasing the need for heating and lighting.

Living in a wood may be just what you want, especially in hot or arid conditions. It offers abundant wildlife and edible products from wild plants, such as elderberries, persimmon, papaw, juniper, hickory, honey locust, mulberry, hazel, walnut, and honey mesquite...although you would be lucky to have more than a few such trees in a garden randomly stocked with natives or typical ornamentals.

If your garden is new but complete with trees, or was abandoned long ago, the wood will have an undergrowth of shrubs and a tangled understory of semi-woody and herbaceous plants. Some of these may be edible, such as blackberries or cloudberries, or useful in other ways. The fungi growing on the ground, on trunks or on rotting wood, in great abundance at certain times of year will prove to be most valuable; few other epiphytes are edible, but like mistletoe have their uses.

The trouble with non-edible varieties of trees and shrubs is just that: you can't eat them. Their potential yields are also difficult to harvest on a sustainable basis without killing them, although twigs for kindling, leaves or needles for mulch, and leafmold are notable exceptions. To manage a miniature forest effectively with minimum interference you are really obliged to get some help from animals: goats, pigs, chickens, turkeys, doves, and bees.

A compromise would be selective thinning. You could send the goats in to clear the undergrowth: they would not harm established trees. Then you could fell trees such as willow, birch, hickory, maple, mountain ash, ash, elm, or linden; convert the heartwood for lumber; leave offcuts for firewood; feed brush to the goats; and stockpile a good supply of bean poles, small-plant supports, and brushwood for miscellaneous purposes. The pruned trees could become permanent goat forage without the need to cut them: the goats would become self-catering. Further harvesting of tree products could be achieved by chickens feeding on soil macrofauna, which feed on fallen leaves; and doves feeding in the tree canopy beyond the garden, but housed in quarters that would allow convenient culling and collection of guano. Most animals need fencing, either permanent or electric, and you need to put this cost into your calculations.

The overwhelming feature of the herb layer in woodland gardens is shade. Dry shade is always a difficult habitat; greater variety comes from damp shady habitats: dwarf palms and arum lilies grow in a subtropical climate (left); ferns, irises, and candelabra primulas thrive in a temperate situation (top left).

Shade-tolerant Crops

Growing edible herbaceous crops in a woodland garden is hard because shade and root competition from trees inhibit growth; and you would need to keep the animals away somehow. But it is possible. One method is to borrow a pair of pigs to dig up the roots of the understory and prepare the ground. Complement the work of the pigs by cutting any tree roots off down to at least a spade's depth, around an area designated for crops.

These crops would have to be shade-tolerant edibles or otherwise useful plants, preferably native perennial species that can hold their own against the tree roots. What counts as "shade-tolerant" varies considerably from one part of the world to another. In seriously sunny climates, you will be able to grow

An example of how a productive garden that integrates trees and animals might be laid out is shown below. Note the position of the animal house, the stockproof fence, and the coppiced area for animal forage.

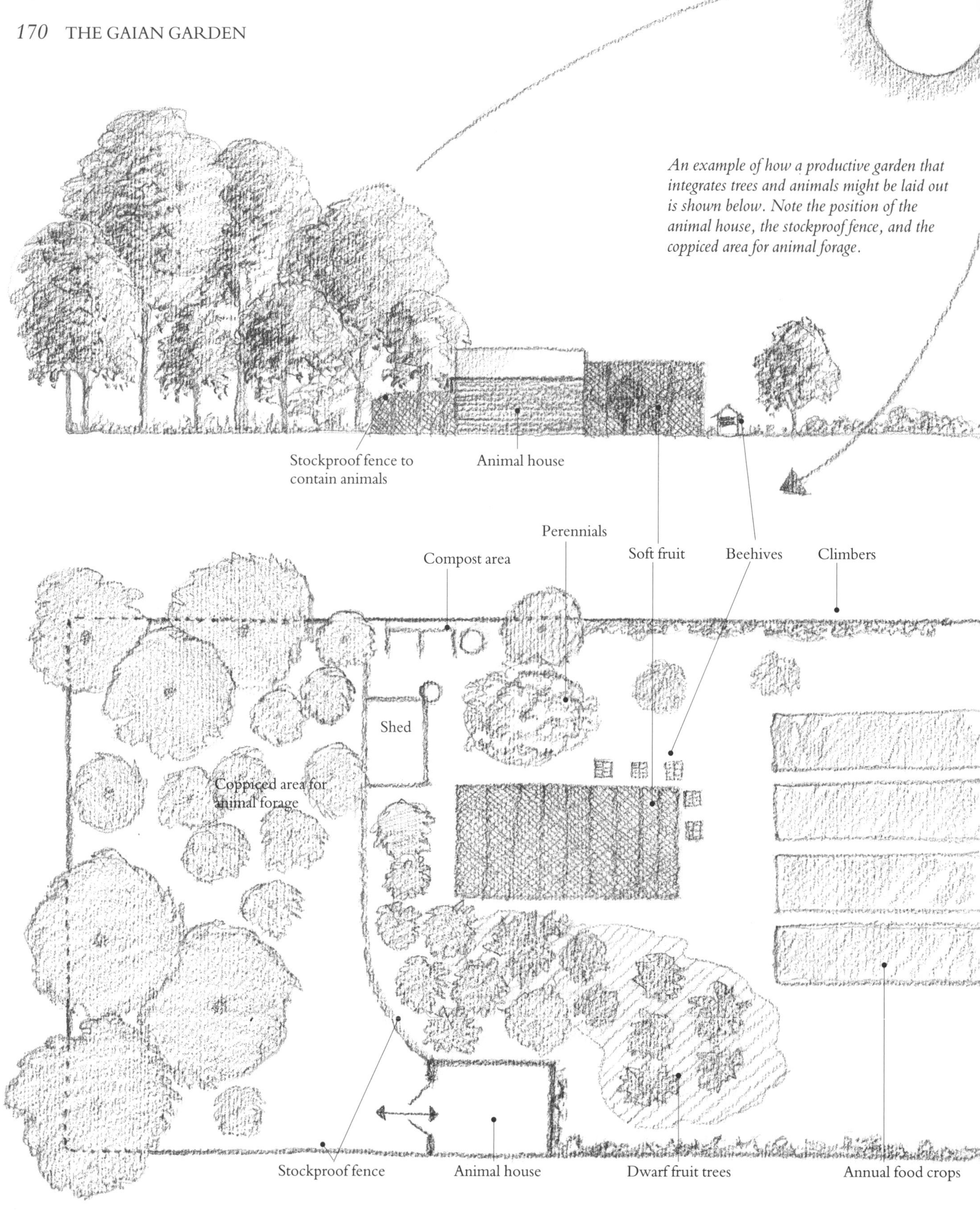

"proper" vegetables, and indeed they may thank you for the shade; while in the gloomier parts of the world, leaf crops and herbs may be all that you can grow and harvest under an established tree canopy.

If you want highly productive conventional crops, or sunloving ornamentals, your only option is to clear some trees to let in the light. You must do this on the sunward side: trees and annual crops may then happily coexist, provided the trees are far enough away not to steal the moisture and nutrients with their greedy roots.

Unexpectedly, trees do not have deep roots on the whole. Instead, the roots spread far beyond the drip line in the top 18in (0.5m) of soil, typically covering an area greater than that of the canopy. This means that you should plant your annual row crops as far away as possible from the trees or else install some kind of root barrier. And focus activities other than growing under the trees – walks, compost, animal housing and foraging, storage, sheds, or seats.

Integrating Trees

All the foregoing assumes you have inherited a woody garden but are determined that the snarl of the chainsaw shall disturb the peace as little as possible. But perhaps your garden lacks trees and you want some; or you have some and you want more. This is, in many ways, a happier situation because you can choose trees for productivity, wildlife, scent, or appearance, and so fit them into your garden design.

A wonderful example of such an integrated forest garden grows in Shropshire, England. Here, Robert Hart has set aside 5400sq.ft (500sq.m) and designed a Forest Garden with seven distinguishable vertical layers containing over 70 useful plants. The rest of the garden hosts an even greater variety of annual and perennial crops, fruit and nut trees, vines, experimental crops, and a miscellaneous collection of rare cultivars.

The following guidelines should help you to integrate trees into a mixed-purpose garden:

- Move small trees that are in the wrong place. They may not like to be moved, and may sulk a bit, but it could give you a head start.

A tree house in the unique world of the canopy makes a perfect woodland sanctuary. The geometry is often haphazard and naturalistic as the structure follows the form of the branches. You can erect walkways between trees, and platforms to sit on.

- Choose trees which are not aggressive rooters, particularly for small gardens.
- For some kinds of productive tree you need more than one individual to assure pollination. In a large garden, try matchmaking various complementary varieties; in the small garden, however, choose self-pollinating varieties.
- Fruit and nut trees on dwarf rootstocks, or genetically miniature varieties, have tremendous advantages in almost any garden. You can plant more in a given space, with an increase in overall yield; you can grow more different types; they are far easier to look after, prune, and harvest; they bear fruit quicker; they can be slipped into odd corners; there is less root competition. However, they are expensive – but you may well consider it money well spent.
- Bees are very good pollinators for all your fruit and nut trees; they are probably the one domesticated species capable of harvesting useful products from inaccessibly large trees – and they may forage far beyond your garden, too.
- Group together plants with similar requirements. This implies a certain planned segregation that

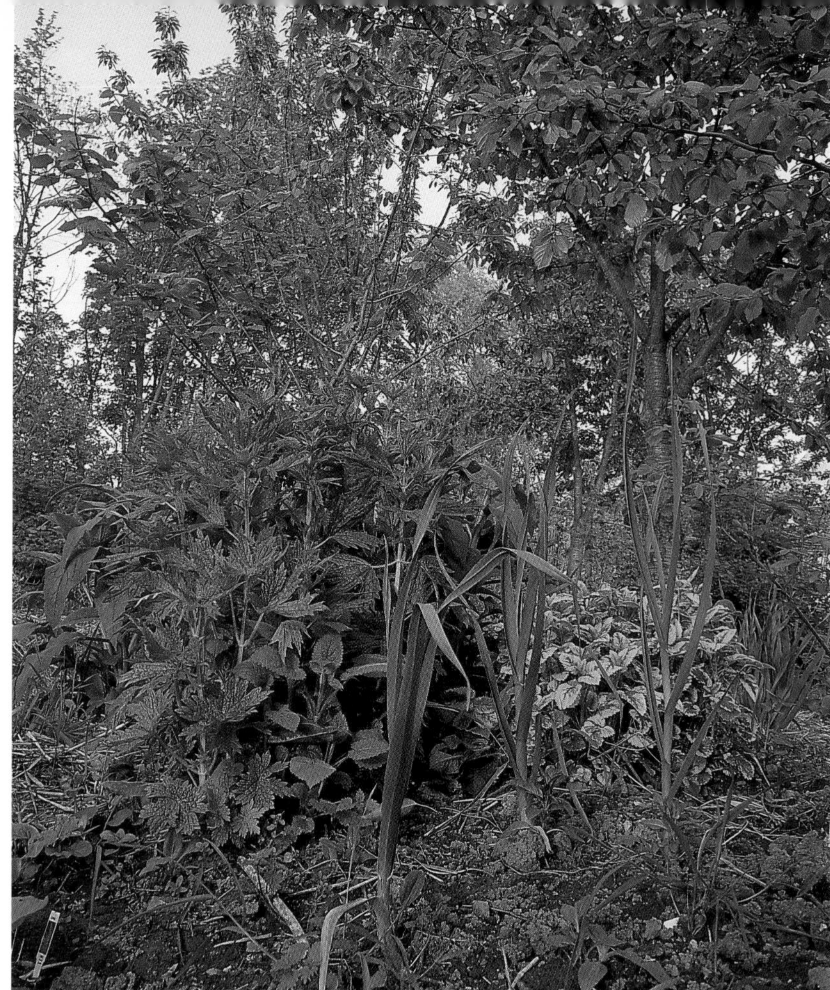

Robert Hart, a veteran writer on tree crops, has developed an inspiring "forest garden" in rural Shropshire, England (left). Spacing and choice of varieties maximize the diversity and productivity of useful plants in three dimensions. Nearly all the plants are perennials so there is no need for tilling. The only maintenance required involves light pruning, weeding, and occasional "editing". This is not a good method for growing staple crops or annual vegetables, but it does produce all the "extras" in an elegant and sustainable way.

contrasts with the riotousness of natural systems. The most common pattern in mid to high latitudes is almost certainly going to take the form of a linear sequence from the sunward side, starting with annuals, through herbaceous perennials, bushes, shrubs, and dwarf trees and backed up by standard trees. Such a pattern minimizes conflicts of shade and root competition. It also means you can site functional processes, such as storage, compost, leafmold, paths, and animal houses within the root zones of larger trees; and stockproof fencing along the same lines allows animals access to the wood and thicket, but protects the more "delicate" parts of the garden (see illustration, p.170).

- To some extent, you can compress segregation patterns by "stacking" vertically, with smaller plants growing under larger ones. There is some competition for light, water, and nutrients, but by suitable spacing and choice of varieties you can increase overall yields and diversity.

Designing an Orchard

The orchard is a classic and tested pattern: well-spaced fruit or nut trees combine the qualities of an open wood with those of a meadow. The small trees, grouped together in rigid rows or more pleasing naturalistic patterns, are friendly places with grass that is grazed or cut for hay. The hay becomes mulch for the trees, fertilizing them and suppressing weeds.

Orchards may be tremendously varied: more than one of any species may give you a glut that's hard to cope with. You can play your part in conserving old and rare varieties, too. These heritage species can be combined with bush fruit, perennial or self-seeding ground crops (as in Robert Hart's Forest Garden pattern), or with strips or islands of more conventional annual row crops. You can protect the orchard with fruiting hedges of semi-wild types, such as elder, serviceberry, mayhaw, damson plums, sloe, brush cherry, and flowering quince.

Tree houses are difficult to anchor securely without some damage to the tree, which makes the use of stilts (above) an inventive detail. Stilts also allow the tree to continue growing, with little damage either house or tree. Many trees are an important source of pollen for bees so it makes good sense to site beehives in woodland (top right). Coppiced woodland (above right) makes an excellent habitat for wildlife, especially dormice.

Coppicing also permits sunlight to penetrate to the floor of the woodland, which means that spring flowers are then able to proliferate.

Planning and Planting a Woodland Edge Habitat

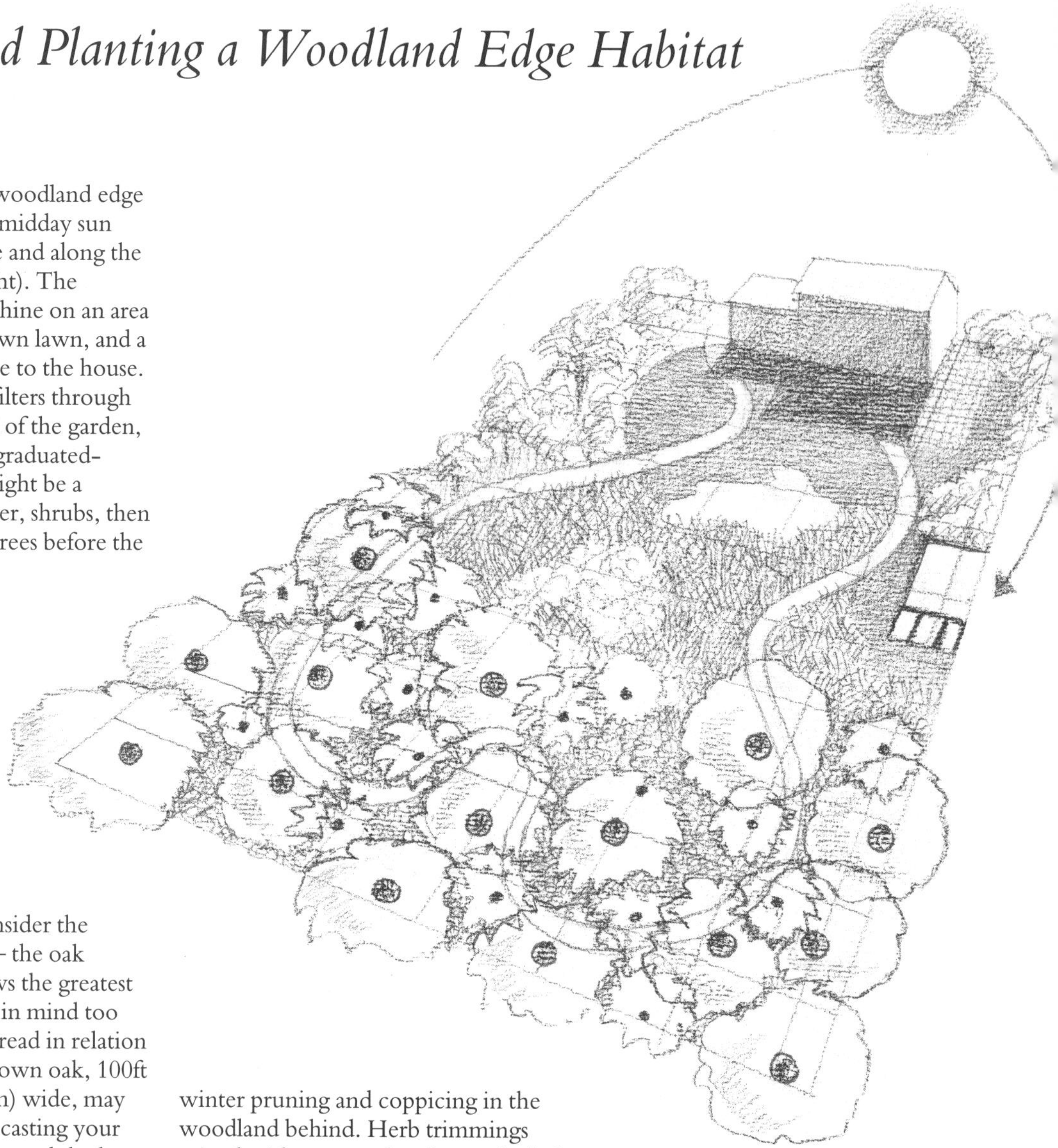

The Site

The ideal position for a woodland edge habitat is one where the midday sun will shine over the house and along the length of the garden (right). The afternoon sun will then shine on an area – containing a patio, mown lawn, and a pond, for example – close to the house. To ensure that sunlight filters through to the trees at the far end of the garden, you will need to plant a graduated-height sequence. This might be a meadow, then a herb layer, shrubs, then coppiced and pollarded trees before the large trees begin.

When planting trees, consider the animals they will attract – the oak family, for example, draws the greatest diversity of species. Bear in mind too the mature height and spread in relation to your garden. A full-grown oak, 100ft (30m) high and 70ft (20m) wide, may need pollarding to avoid casting your neighbor's garden in perpetual shadow. Maples can be coppiced every seven to ten years. Smaller and faster-growing species, such as birch or thorns, may reach around 30-60ft (10-20m) but do not live so long.

Access

For constant use you will need a path of gravel or bark chips. A few smaller paths through the herb layer will help to protect flowers and wildlife, especially in the spring. After the herbs have flowered and the seeds dispersed, you can clear the area to give access for winter pruning and coppicing in the woodland behind. Herb trimmings mixed with cut meadow hay and piled up in the woodland make an attractive habitat for many species.

Planting and Maintenance

If you can, buy container-grown trees when they are about 6ft (2m) tall and plant them at 10ft (3m) intervals. They will need to be staked and mulched every year with a layer of coarsely chopped forest bark. If you buy saplings, plant them closer together and protect them with growing tubes or cones, particularly if rabbits or squirrels are common in your neighborhood. At the height of the growing season you may need to cut back many of the tall-growing herbs.

Shrubs are best planted about 3ft (1m) apart and in groups, leaving glades for lower-growing herbs. Prune lightly if necessary in the early years, but wait until shrubs are established before first coppicing. You may want to wait until late winter before pruning some seed- and fruit-bearing species of shrub in order to leave a varied diet for overwintering birds.

A Mature Woodland Edge

A rich and varied habitat will develop over the years. In early spring, the woodland floor will be smothered with native flowers you have introduced. Birds and insects, such as butterflies and bees, form a vibrant part of the evolving ecosystem. They help to build up other species – birds, for example, may bring in new seeds from the surrounding habitats. During the summer, cut grass helps to replenish the habitat. The fall brings the display of fruits. Rambling berries and the smaller nut trees you coppiced earlier will be bearing fruit. Trees and shrubs, now well established, will be supporting climbing plants, such as ivy and honeysuckle. Rotting logs will be host to mosses, lichens, and flying insects. The tightly woven heaps you have made from coppiced branches and annual prunings will, as they rot down, offer refuge for insects, small birds, and mammals. In spring, the cut grass and herb pile become a home to small reptiles, mice, and bees.

A 30-year-old English wood (above) contains a diversity of trees, shrubs, and flowers. From left to right you can see a white birch, a mountain ash, Prunus padus, *a European hornbeam, a second silver birch, and a hawthorn. The hornbeam was pollarded after 20 years to prevent it overshadowing other species. In the shrub layer you can see holly, elder (coppiced every 4 years), and hazel (coppiced every 7 years). In the background behind the* Prunus *lies the habitat pile, while in the foreground a rotting, ivy-covered log provides a variety of insect food for birds.*

The Wetland Garden

The difficulties plants face in chronically wet soils are obvious: excess water and lack of air mean that the great majority just won't grow. But, in fact, wetlands can be immensely variable, with a wide range of plant and animal life. And since a number of plants are well-adapted to the rigours of wet conditions, the minimalist asks: why not accept fate and grow what does well? In natural bogs and fens, however, biological productivity and species diversity is low, offering the gardener a good opportunity to enrich the habitat range.

Many wetlands respond well to relatively small interventions. The crucial change is to alter ground levels so that, instead of uniformly waterlogged ground, you have some drained soil and some open water. At a stroke you have multiplied tenfold the habitat diversity and productive potential of your garden. At the very least, the raising of soil above the water level will allow the growing of mesic plants, without diminishing the contribution of the water's edge and the water itself.

The possible variations of this principle are endless; it has been the basis of many sustainable polyculture systems in the humid tropics, but can be applied anywhere. In these traditional systems, the greatest effects are achieved by simple geometry: the arrangement of raised and lowered levels both in plan and section. Generally, large open bodies of water are avoided in favor of intricate patterns of small pools, promontories, islands, bunds, and channels. This does not require any greater excavation than a single simple pond, but gives rise to a greater range of microclimates and the possibilities of radically different treatment in different parts of the system.

These possibilities include (but should not contravene local or national clean water regulations):

- Siting animal housing partially over a pond to allow droppings to fall in the water directly.
- Raising the calcium level in some parts of the system with eggshells, calcified seaweed, or ground limestone.
- Oxygenating some parts with cascades or fountains. Pumps for remote fountains can be operated by photovoltaic panels.
- Running gray water into a pond system.
- Using aquatic animals to convert food waste into useful flesh in place of more usual domestic animals; fish and crustaceans can also eat pests, such as slugs and caterpillars, collected from the garden.
- Covering part of a pond system with a greenhouse to provide a warmer microclimate and a source of irrigation water for greenhouse crops. This combines well with a gray-water treatment system.
- Providing shade by floating vegetation where overheating is a danger. Alternatives include screens over narrow channels, or rafts – either of which can be combined with animal housing. Deep sumps provide refuge for fish, and barrels or undercut caves shelter fish from direct sunlight.

Wetland systems are often rich in nutrients because everything runs into them. In fact, they may become too rich, leading to algal blooms, loss of oxygen, and the death of larger organisms in the water. A complete food chain is necessary to allow the nutrients to be turned into useful biological material: you must keep harvesting and recycling the nutrients. Rake out and compost green matter and algae, and from time to time dig out the rich mud in the channels and use it to fertilize the banks.

In a warm, humid climate, molds present the principal problem for edible crops. To counteract this, create raised dry zones and complement them with good, natural ventilation – encourage breezes by open planting, remove foliage near the ground, and restrict the sheltering effect of nearby trees.

The water in this pool (right) is more implied than visible: the surface is covered with duckweed, the smallest of all flowering plants; flag irises and arum lilies crowd around. The overarching dogwood and cotoneaster reinforce the sense that this mimics a rich primeval swamp.

Wetland Sanctuary

The water-garden sanctuary needs to be dry and yet close to the wetland world. One possibility is a roofed jetty, fixed firmly to the bank and supported on stilts over the water. Looking somewhat like a boathouse, the structure could be clad to keep it snug, with blind windows on three sides and a trapdoor for peering directly into the water beneath and watching the aquatic life. If your garden receives a good deal of rain, collect runoff from the roof and let it run over a rain sculpture. You could make this from a series of surfaces, shallow containers, tiny runnels, cataracts, and minature landscapes that play with the rain before it reaches the main body of water.

A waterproof membrane isolates a constructed water feature from its surroundings so that it has no influence on the surrounding plants. In fact, drought-tolerant plants may flourish here (right), which looks ecologically odd. In the natural wetland (below right) the influence of the water extends beyond the banks to encourage characteristic water species.

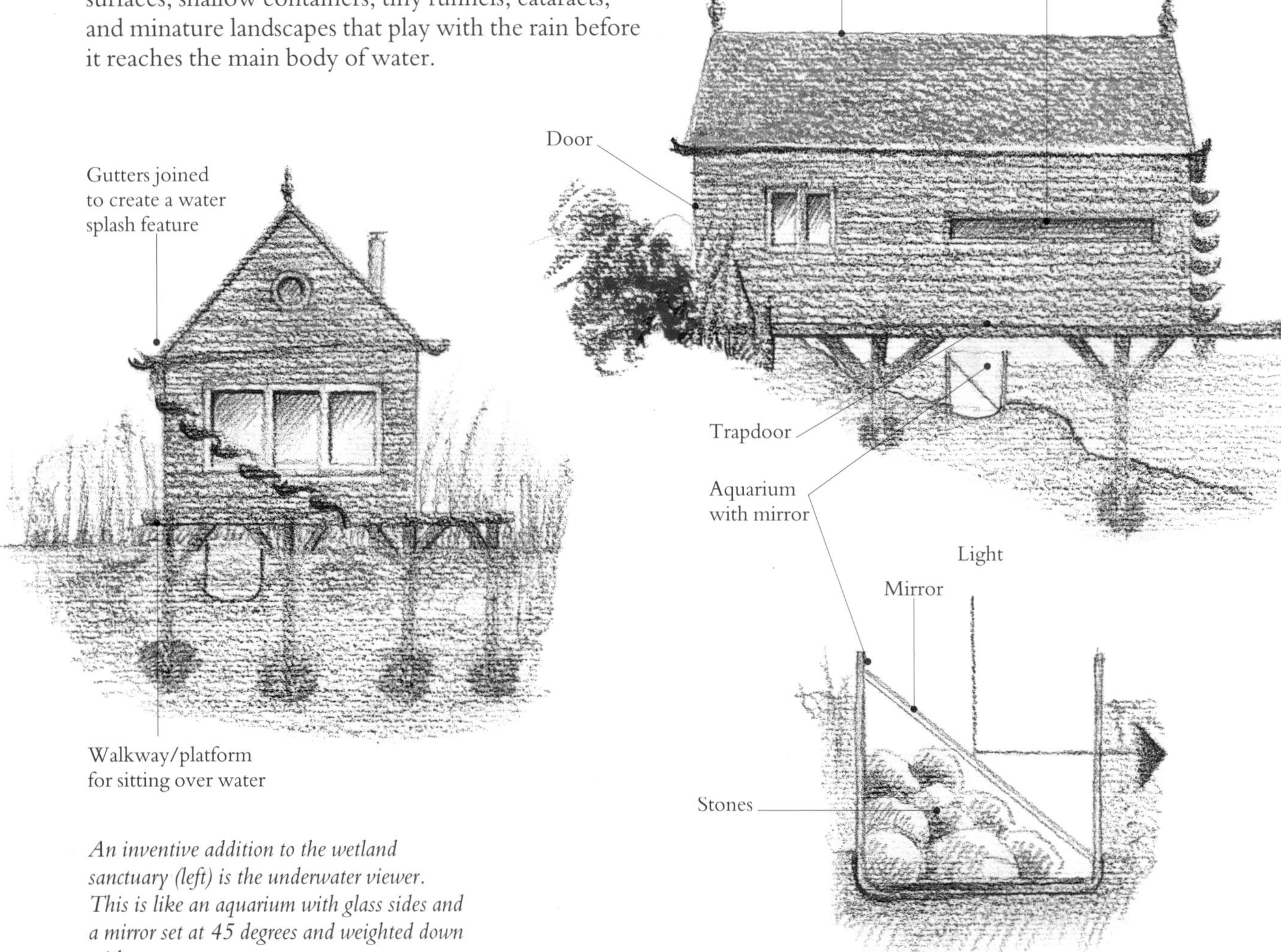

An inventive addition to the wetland sanctuary (left) is the underwater viewer. This is like an aquarium with glass sides and a mirror set at 45 degrees and weighted down with stones.

Emergent water plantains and irises punctuate the surface of a large, plain pond (left). Sedimentary rocks laid horizontally create a feeling of stability and repose. Rounded, water-worn stones (below left) usually look appropriate in any wetland landscape, however they are placed. The large dark leaves of the Ligularia *in the foreground contrast with the more delicate foliage of the other poolside plants. The other ponds illustrated here all feature moving water. Where a steady trickle falls from a height into a small space the noise can be surprisingly loud, especially if the pool is backed by a resonating cavity (below). The rocks in the Japanese garden (top right) are volcanic tufa – symbolically, we can see earth, air, fire, and water at one glance. The garden (below right) shows how a wetland and a dry mountain rock garden can exist happily side by side.*

CLIMATE GARDENS

The Cool Temperate Garden

A certain environmental catastrophe plagues some parts of the world with a terrible regularity. A defoliator of trees, a decimator of perennials, and a killer of many annuals and animals, this recurrent catastrophe is frost. Less than 10 percent of plant species are resistant to it, yet gardeners have come to accept this frozen reaper as a fact of life, working their plans around it with stoical resignation. Frost has such an overwhelming influence that if only one climatic map appears in a garden book, it is that of the "hardiness zones". Such a map indicates which plants can be grown outside without protection. As a result, we speak of "hardy" and "tender" plants.

The minimalist in a cold climate will grow fully hardy plants. Although the growing season may be short, plant materials can be harvested and stored. In winter, even hardy species become dormant, leaving little to be had directly, except timber, fuelwood, and roots. Perhaps it is surprising that humans – originally a tropical species – should ever have bothered with the cool temperate parts of the Earth. Only with the help of animals did they get through the winter, the more so in the circumpolar regions. From the point of view of environmental sustainability the hunting/herding strategies of the Inuit, Lapps, or Mongols are admirable, but are not possible in the garden!

The determined minimalist will look out for edible weeds that grow in the winter and for perennials that will give a spring crop earlier than their delicate annual counterparts. One common northern-hemisphere weed that defies extreme cold and is always ready to be picked in the middle of winter is the bittercress, *Cardamine pratensis*. Despite its name this plant tastes like watercress and is available with no effort bar the picking. Another is sheep's sorrel, *Rumex acetosella*. Of the perennials, Good King Henry sprouts before any spinach, while the tree-onion may be giving juicy greens in late winter.

Another easily harvested cold-climate product is sap, which rises in early spring. You can tap sap by drilling a shallow hole in a tree trunk, inserting a tube into the hole, and collecting the runoff in a bucket or tub. Though maple is the most famous, birch sap makes the earliest and most ferocious of all the wild wines.

In cold climates, vegetation enters a dormant state at the beginning of winter and looks for all the world to fall asleep. Deciduous trees, such as the silver birch (left), drop their leaves while ferns and herbs retreat to their rootstocks. Only the spruce keeps one eye open.

Improving Productivity

Like gardens in other extreme climates, those with a severe winter and short growing season need substantial modifications to improve productivity by more than a token amount, and nearly all these are aimed at increasing temperature. As in other cases, the strategy is to try and modify the overall garden (and if possible, the house) climate with little cost and effort, while concentrating the more expensive or time-consuming preparations on the most useful crops or garden products.

In cold climates, the cost of heating could be almost as much as the cost of essential food, so it is worth considering whether the garden should really concentrate on reducing fuel bills instead of growing food. The simplest way to reduce heat loss and wind chill is to clothe the house with a heavy evergreen vine, such as ivy, that traps a layer of air next to the wall. Erect windbreaks, at least on the side of prevailing winter winds, but also on the poleward side. In fact, a horseshoe windbreak around the house is best since it leaves the sunward side open to the low winter sun, which in some climates can substantially reduce the heating load. Trees on the sunward side should be deciduous to let light through the bare winter canopy. Earth berms and appropriately shaped roofs can amplify the effect of a windbreak.

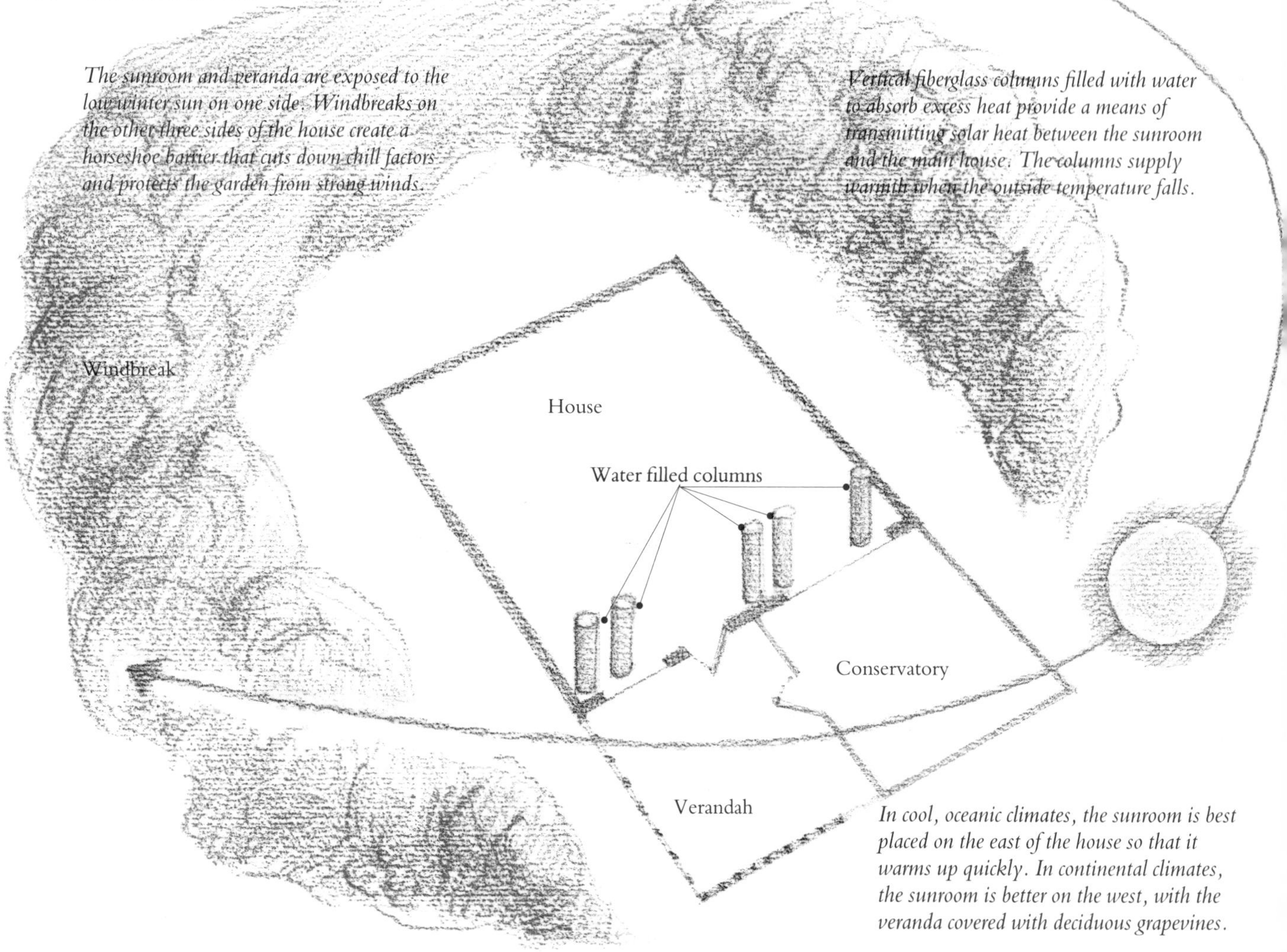

The sunroom and veranda are exposed to the low winter sun on one side. Windbreaks on the other three sides of the house create a horseshoe barrier that cuts down chill factors and protects the garden from strong winds.

Vertical fiberglass columns filled with water to absorb excess heat provide a means of transmitting solar heat between the sunroom and the main house. The columns supply warmth when the outside temperature falls.

Windbreak

House

Water filled columns

Conservatory

Verandah

In cool, oceanic climates, the sunroom is best placed on the east of the house so that it warms up quickly. In continental climates, the sunroom is better on the west, with the veranda covered with deciduous grapevines.

Valuable methods of lengthening the growing season include cloches (see p.261), cold frames, and greenhouses for productive crops. A greenhouse is a place that benefits many other activities in a cold climate – it can even be a sanctuary. The cheapest form of greenhouse is the plastic tunnel, an ugly structure with great potential on account of its size. It can act as a workshop, garage, playspace (sand box, badminton, volleyball), laundry, picnic area, compost, outdoor washroom, plunge pool, bathroom, dry storage, or toolshed.

Cool-climate Sanctuary

The main priority of a cool-temperate or a cold-climate sanctuary is warmth! In cloudy, northern oceanic climates even the summers can rarely be described as hot. But many climates that experience severe winters also have hot summers. Hence, the sanctuary will need to be flexible enough to create cool conditions in summer.

A possible resolution for gardens with mixed requirements is a series of covered zones centered on the house. A combined sunroom/veranda built on to the sunward wall at the front of the house, or to the east if you have a choice, is a priority. Adjoining the sunroom, inside the house, a small antechamber with a view provides the sanctuary during the coldest weather. For several months of the year, the sunroom itself will be at a comfortable temperature in the day through solar gain and incidental heat from the house. When the weather turns really hot, a covered, open veranda surrounded by vines or deciduous shade trees will provide the required coolness.

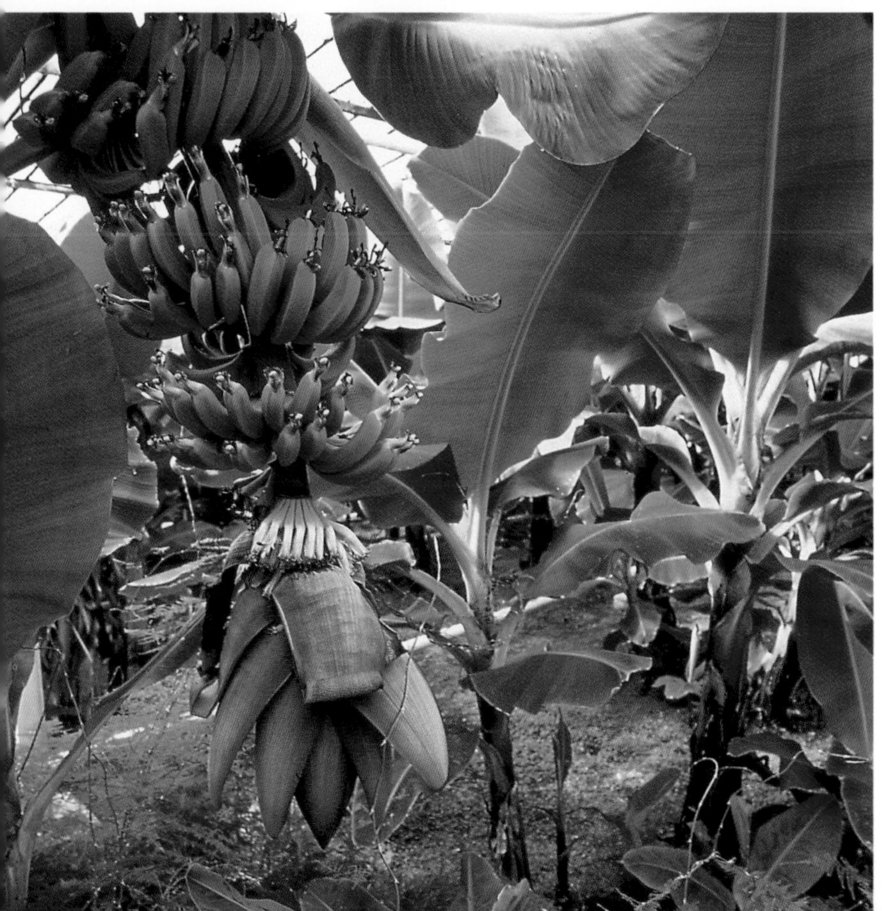

The unheated greenhouse (above) has a number of features that help moderate temperature extremes in cool climates. An internal pool and massive insulated stone walls on the poleward side absorb heat and release it slowly during the night. At the top left is a raised growing bed which, during the colder parts of the year, is given additional protection with glass frames. In winter, ground heat conducted to the empty space below the bed allows the growth of tender crops. In the spring, it is used as a hotbed, with compost heat permitting the rapid germination of seedlings in trays. In summer, the bed is perfect for warm-climate crops, such as melons and egg plants. Even in high latitudes, tropical crops, such as the bananas grown in a geothermally heated greenhouse in Iceland (left), can be viable so long as sufficient heat is available, and the long hours of daylight can give good, rapid yields.

The Arid Garden

Some parts of the Earth rarely see rain, resulting in total deserts. But such a stark situation is exceptional. More commonly, the rain comes only at certain times of the year, leaving long periods of drought. So, just as high latitudes have an annual cycle in which a favorable warm season alternates with an unfavorable cold season, so mid latitudes often have a favorable wet season alternating with an unfavorable dry one. Curiously, plants respond to the wet/dry and the hot/cold cycle in rather similar ways: as the unfavorable season approaches, annuals flower set seed and die; perennials retreat to their rootstocks; deciduous trees lose their leaves and go into a dormant state; and evergreens attempt to survive using their specially adapted leaves.

Gardeners in seasonally arid climates will know their own variations. In warm areas where the rains come in the summer (eastern coastal zones), life is easier than where the drought coincides with the hottest part of the year (Mediterranean, savanna, and some monsoon regions). Perhaps the most difficult of all are continental interiors with both cold winters and dry summers – yet these contain some of the richest farmlands. And, as a footnote, those parts of the temperate world that believe they are well watered may now need to pay more attention to dryland growing strategies as the greenhouse effect starts to shuffle the climatic pack.

Pros and Cons of Arid Climates

Gardeners can turn the conditions that prevail in arid climates to their own advantage: water may be available in sufficient quantities if it is managed properly; if conditions are right, plants can grow extremely well in the abundant light and warmth; weeds may not be so much of a problem – neither are slugs and snails! Furthermore, earth, mud, and stone are readily available for construction purposes, and the weather is perfect for drying crops, such as raisins, figs, and apricots.

On the down side, dry climates may suffer strong fluctuations in temperature – on occasion, the heat may be so intense that there is a risk of fire. The soils are often problematic, too. They are either too acidic or alkaline, with deficiencies of some trace elements and toxic levels of others; a hard, impermeable layer may lie a little way below the surface; and they may contain a high level of salt. Sometimes, the rain comes in such a deluge that it causes gully erosion in the fragile soils.

The resource cost of maintaining a standard mesic garden in an arid climate is inappropriate and unsustainable. One logical alternative, dubbed "zeroscaping", is to replace mass vegetation with hard surfaces and occasional specimen plants. This reduces the horticultural maintenance load but has a drastic effect on the local microclimate, causing discomfort and a huge increase in the need for air conditioning. The minimalist, of course, accepts what's there and grows drought-adapted native plants. This impulse has inspired a novel but rational approach to arid landscape design called xeriscaping. Gardeners grow a rich array of drought-tolerant plants that need little maintenance yet mollify the microclimate and uphold the integrity of the bioregion.

In arid climates, the dryness is due not only to the lack of rain, but to the rapid evaporation of soil moisture, and to the lack of infiltration into, and retention by, the soil. There is not much gardeners can do to make it rain more, but they can use the rain that does come as efficiently as possible, taking measures to reduce evaporation and increase the water-holding qualities of soils. Much of this has to do with trees, which control erosion, and provide shade and screening. Apart from their water management

The cacti are a uniquely American family and the saguaro (left) is an instantly recognizable symbol of hot arid regions. Its knobbly curves are reflected in the molded shapes of adobe buildings.

qualities, trees also provide stockproof barriers, promote nitrogen fixation, and supply fuel, forage for animals, and fruit.

The key design points for an integrated approach to gardening in arid climates are: planting drought-tolerant species; creating shade and shelter from the wind; harvesting and storing water; preventing water loss; and targeting water for maximum benefit.

Drought-tolerant Plants

From the point of view of useful crops, we can imagine a "seasonal minimalist" harvesting what grows abundantly in the wet season and giving up with good grace in the dry. More seriously, there are plenty of drought-tolerant tree crops that, once established, yield during or at the end of the dry season. These include olives, carob, grapes, date, doum palm, pistachio, pomegranate, walnut, fig, bearberry, hickory, piñon nut, jujube, cashew, stone pine, and all manner of Asian, Australian, and African trees that have no common names in English. And we should not forget that, as the first rains come, so do the mushrooms. As for ornamental trees and herbaceous plants that tolerate drought conditions, the available choice is enormous.

Your choice of plants depends to some extent on the precise nature of your climate, and how much you are able to irrigate. In addition to the drought-tolerant productive trees mentioned above, others will do well in frost-free areas during the wet season: citrus fruits, avocado, persimmon, coffee, guava, apricots, quince, almond, mango, mulberry, loquat, and cherry. Among perennials, the aromatic "mediterranean" herbs are an obvious choice: sage, thyme, rosemary, bay, fennel, savory, and myrtle. In a warm wet season, you can probably proceed like any "normal" gardener, with the advantage that crops, such as onions and garlic, that like a warm dry finish will enjoy the onset of the dry season.

Protection from Sun and Wind

Soil moisture evaporates equally in hot sun and drying winds. Mulching is therefore essential in a dry garden.

A garden in an arid climate (right) needs to be carefully and rigorously planned. Of prime importance is a sequence of almost constant crops that are self-shading. Rows of evergreen trees and rellises covered with thick-leaved grapevines or other crops provide permanent screens and all-round shade to the house. Water run-off and gray water are diverted into swales that provide irrigation for fruit trees in orchards.

It is often worth growing drought-tolerant plants specifically to provide mulch material throughout the dry season. Such plants include acacias, *Leucaena*, *Casuarina*, tamarisk, and coarse forage grasses. Ground cover plants, especially legumes such as hyacinth bean and annual lupins, can greatly reduce moisure losses from the soil if they are established in the wet season.

You can create temporary windbreaks from fencing and brushwood, but any permanent structure must have the right sort of profile, several trees deep. The integrated approach to gardening requires that these trees take on other useful functions, such as nitrogen fixation, forage material, lumber, livestock barrier, honey production, and so on.

Sunken Lawns

If you insist on creating a lawn, you will have to deal with a perennial problem in dry, or seasonally dry, areas. The grass grows well enough in the cool, wet season but withers in prolonged hot, dry weather. It is not killed, merely retreats to its roots: but its effectiveness as a lawn is lost. Some grasses tolerate dry conditions, but they are not usually favorites for the classical purposes of a lawn. The only way to maintain lawns in these hot, dry conditions is to provide the grass with constant irrigation, which consumes an immense amount of valuable and much needed water.

In marginally arid climates, you can maintain a lawn by standard drought-defying techniques: choice of a grass species, generating a high organic content in the soil, shading, windbreaks, but not mulches.

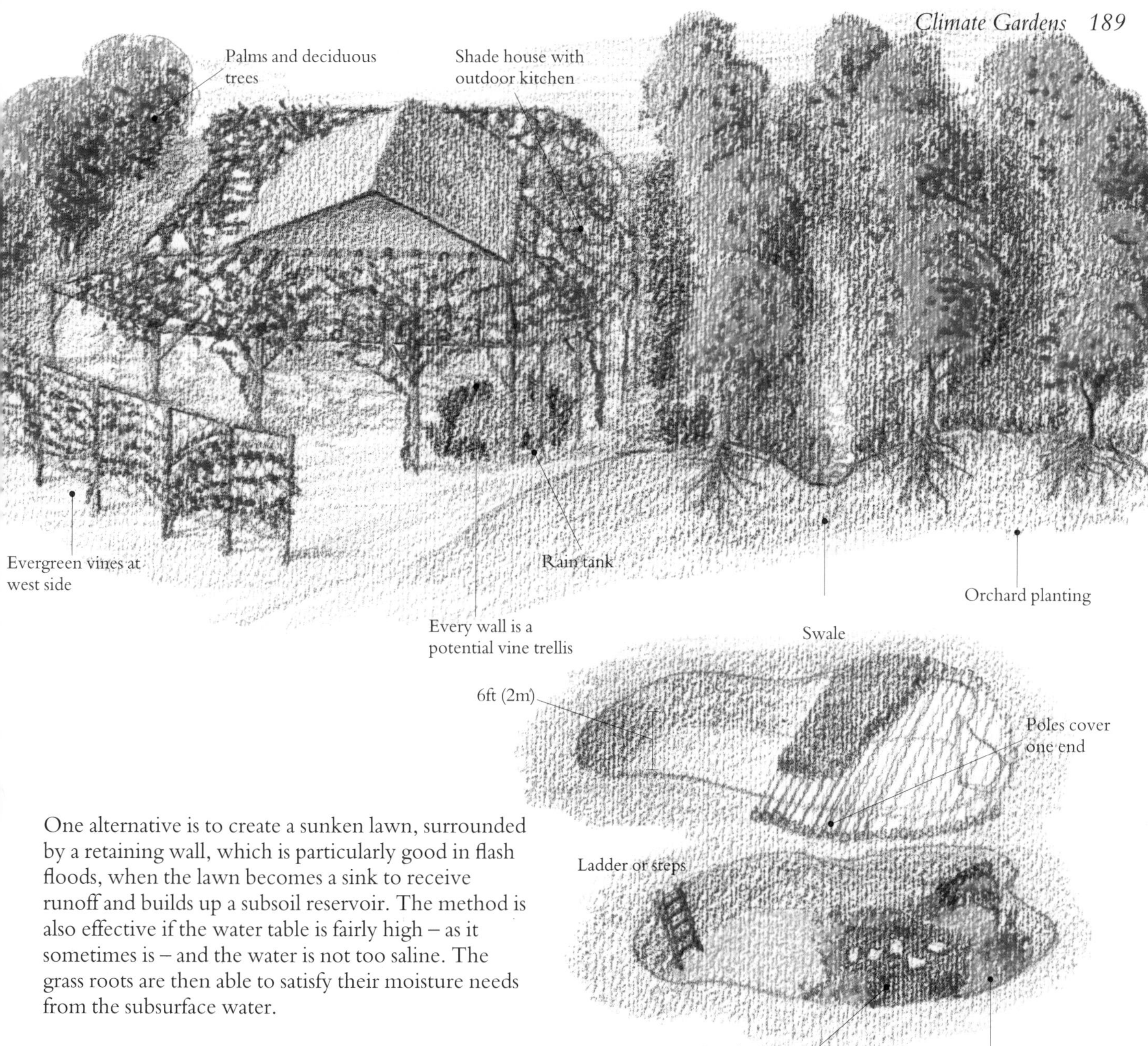

One alternative is to create a sunken lawn, surrounded by a retaining wall, which is particularly good in flash floods, when the lawn becomes a sink to receive runoff and builds up a subsoil reservoir. The method is also effective if the water table is fairly high – as it sometimes is – and the water is not too saline. The grass roots are then able to satisfy their moisture needs from the subsurface water.

Arid-climate Sanctuary

Above all, a successful retreat in any dry climate must provide coolness and be kept supplied with water. To achieve these aims without resort to technological overkill, you will have to create shade either by trees, arbors, or screens, by wind-funneling, or by constructing an underground shelter. In addition, water circulated into a pool and intermittently sprayed on to foliage will evaporate into the local atmosphere and provide a strong cooling effect.

The first step in creating a hot dry sanctuary is to excavate a longish hole about 6ft (2m) deep (top). Span one end with round poles or something similar. Fill the gaps between the poles with twigs and adobe. Then pile on more adobe and earth. Make a pond (above) as wide as possible, leaving a sanctuary space at the covered end. Set stepping stones in the pond and erect steps or a ladder in the open part. Fountains or waterfalls are optional extras.

In a seriously arid climate, the obvious natural solution is to grow true desert plants. In the Californian garden (top left) the rounded opuntias contrast agreeably with the soaring cereus. Many palms grow well in dry conditions and the Mexican blue fan palms will also tolerate a certain amount of frost. The photographs on left and right show native Californian poppies in contrasting settings, one carefully orchestrated, the other naturalized. The shady garden in Sydney, Australia (above), has an overhead trellis that supports grapevines to provide shade from the high subtropical sun.

PART IV

NATURAL GARDENING TECHNIQUES

Finding out about Your Garden

It's been said that "time spent in reconnaissance is seldom wasted". For our purposes, "seldom" really means "never". No two gardens are ever the same. Each has a singular personality, its own individual blend of nature and nurture, shaped by the winds that blow and the waters that flow, not just at present but in the past, too.

Because your aim is to work with nature, the basic elements must first be thoroughly understood. Earth, air, fire, and water (i.e. soil, winds, sun, and rainfall) can be observed subjectively, but this can take years. Neighbors can give useful information to start you off, but nobody else will have the same garden or the same objectives as you. Although it may seem slower at the outset, adopting a systematic approach will bring quicker results and maximize your chances of success. Creating a harmonious garden of living, growing things cannot be done without a great deal of informed reflection (see pp. 62–5).

The site survey should include every aspect, from soil to weather to wildlife. The more carefully this is done, the less likely you are to make expensive, time-consuming, and laborious mistakes, not to mention ecological blunders.

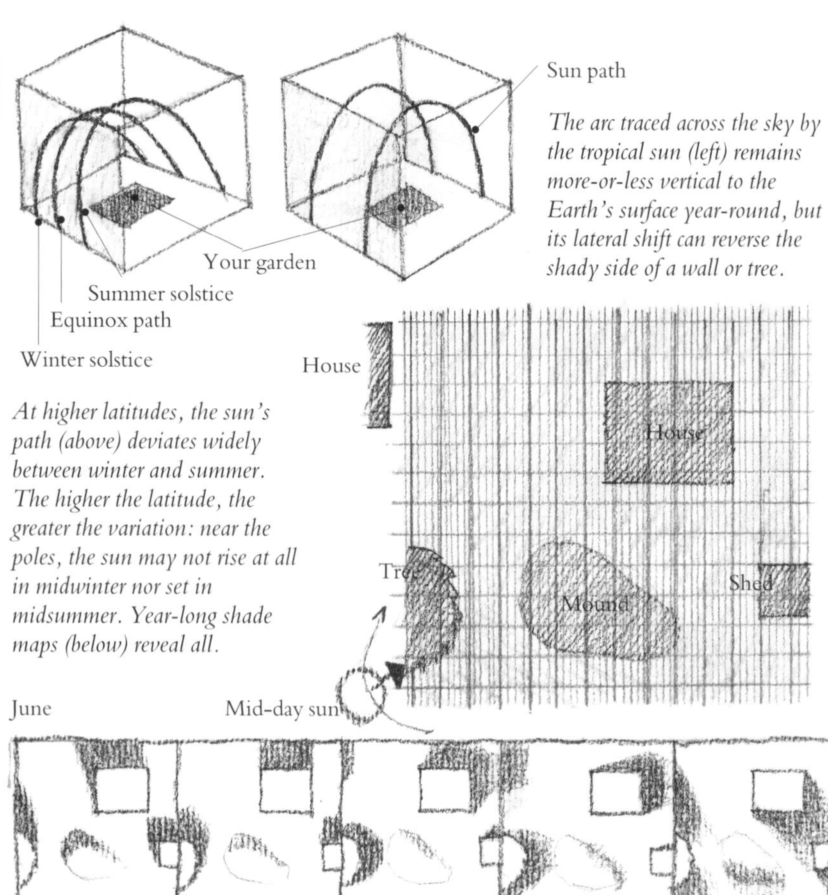

The arc traced across the sky by the tropical sun (left) remains more-or-less vertical to the Earth's surface year-round, but its lateral shift can reverse the shady side of a wall or tree.

At higher latitudes, the sun's path (above) deviates widely between winter and summer. The higher the latitude, the greater the variation: near the poles, the sun may not rise at all in midwinter nor set in midsummer. Year-long shade maps (below) reveal all.

Year one

Before beginning to alter the shape of your garden, treat yourself to a year of observation and recording. Look upon this as an active period of discovery. This doesn't mean that you can't touch anything, but what it does mean is that, by the end of your first year, you'll have collected a great deal of solid information. Another thing to start collecting right away is compostable material. Once you begin cultivation, you'll need as much compost as you can get! By the time your second year begins, aim to have a pile of compost and a set of records to provide the combination of nature and wisdom that will give your natural garden the best possible start. Just as a carefully made compost pile gives quicker and surer results than a haphazard pile, so will carefully recorded data lead to a faster and surer understanding than random impressions.

Mapping light and shade

The first essential is to draw a map to show all the permanent features. To do this you need to measure everything from two fixed points (such as the corners of the house). When you come to draw your master plan, choose a sensible scale (say ¼in:1ft) and draw an arc with a pair of compasses from each fixed point to the feature in question. The point where the arc intersects will give you its exact location. Record all this on your master plan, and make several copies.

Use some of these copies to chart the changing light and shade patterns through the year. The nearer you are to the equator, the less this is likely to vary from season to season, but in higher latitudes the differences between summer and winter might be dramatic. Knowing how the shadows move will enable you to make major decisions, such as whether to fell or lop an existing tree, as well as helping you to decide what plants would do best in which positions, and sites for furniture.

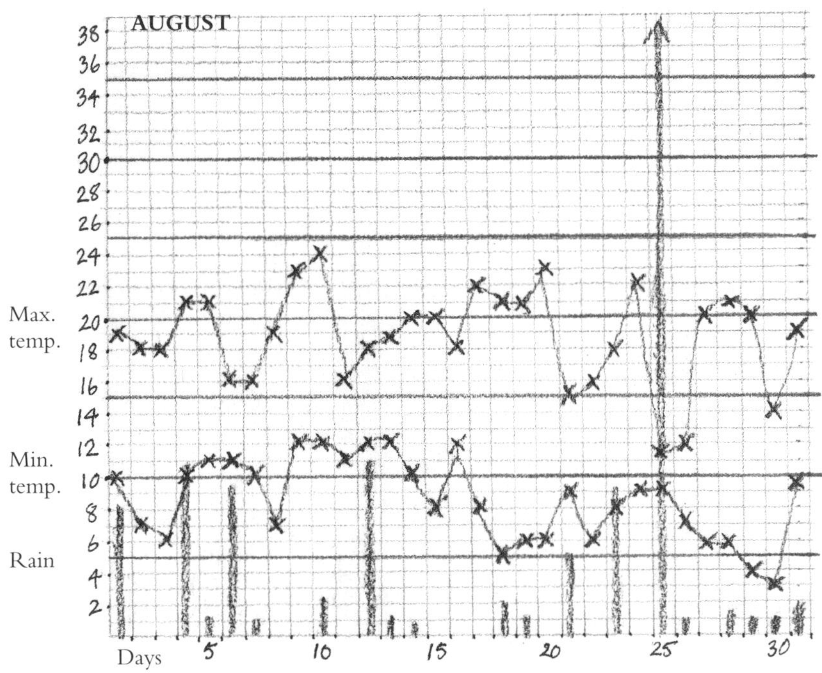

Recording temperature and rainfall
It takes just two minutes a day to record maximum and minimum temperatures. When it occurs, rainfall can neatly be incorporated with both temperature plots on a single graph.

Temperature

Light and shade patterns are easy to see, but temperatures may not tally with what you might expect, so be prepared to invest in a thermometer or two. A max-min thermometer can be left *in situ*, and will indicate the highest and lowest temperatures that occur at any particular spot within whatever time has elapsed since it was last read and re-set. Recording these two values on a year-long graph shows you the differences between day and night, summer and winter, and provides a guide as to the level of hardiness or heat resistance your plants will require. You can do this empirically, by placing just one thermometer on a shaded wall, or in greater detail by using a number of thermometers strategically scattered about the site.

Make your own rain gauge
Cut around the neck end of a flat-bottomed plastic bottle and reverse this section to create a funnel. Sink the bottle in the soil. Lift the funnel to measure the depth of the water with a ruler.

Soil temperature may differ from air temperature quite dramatically, even between one place and another. It's well worth making the effort to record soil temperatures, using a thermometer designed for this purpose.

Rainfall

You can obtain annual or monthly rainfall figures from your local meteorological office, but they only indicate the general state of affairs. Depending on local geography, your own garden may receive more or less than its share. It's easy to measure rainfall by means of a simple rain gauge (see diagram) sunk into the soil in an exposed position. This will give you the overall rainfall for your site; if you plant more rain gauges in a variety of places, such as under trees and next to walls or hedges, you will be able to see where (and whether) these features influence the amount of rain reaching the ground. Measure and record daily or weekly amounts.

Wind

It's not hard to see where the prevailing wind comes from, just by looking around. Any existing trees and shrubs will tend to lean away from the main airstream. It is, however, more difficult to be aware of local currents and eddies, and their relative strengths. Buildings and trees, and the contour of the land, may increase or decrease the power of air currents, and can change or even reverse the direction of flow. The simplest way of finding out which way the wind is blowing is the wet finger technique: you go to the place in question and hold up a wet finger; the side that feels cold first is the side the wind is blowing from. Additional information about relative wind speeds can be obtained from a few simple wind-speed gauges scattered around the site. These won't tell you the absolute wind speed, but if well placed they can give a good overall picture of where the wind is amplified or blocked. Combining each wind-speed gauge with a weather vane will give extra information about how the direction of air flow varies from place to place.

Water table

Somewhere under the ground there's generally a layer of dense soil or rock where the seepage of rainfall is blocked. Water collects on top of this layer, and the surface of this water is the water table. It may be just beneath the topsoil, or hundreds of feet down. It makes practical sense to explore this in easy stages. Do this at the wettest time of year, and begin by simply digging a hole and covering it over to prevent rain falling in. If water collects in the hole, that's your water table. If no water collects, even after more digging, then you will have to improvise a more technical approach. One method is to drive a narrow vertical shaft with a rigid rod and a mallet, withdraw the rod and replace it with a perforated pipe. If water collects in the pipe, you can use a plumb-line or dipstick, or devise a floating indicator, to measure its position.

The water table can be different in different places, so do this exercise in several locations. It may also change throughout the year, for reasons ranging from heavy seasonal rainfall to heavy water extraction by local farmers or water authorities. This information will be relevant when planning the different aspects of your garden, from digging ponds to planting trees.

For most practical purposes, there's not a great deal to be gained from going to the trouble of exploring deeper than 6 or 7 feet (2 metres), unless you plan to sink a well or are bent on establishing a naturally forming pond.

Land profile

Drawing a profile map is easier than it may seem. Imagine a horizontal plate balanced on the highest point, then measure down from this notional plate to ground level (1). Alternatively, you can mark out contour lines using a hose level (2). Both methods (see diagram, right) can be scaled up or down to meet your needs. Record the results as a series of "slices" through your garden. If you can make a model in clay based on these measurements, it will be very useful for predicting likely water flow and thus helping to form an irrigation or drainage plan.

The profile of your site, especially when coupled with careful temperature records, can also help to identify any frost pockets.

Frost pockets

Just as hot air rises, cold air sinks. It can flow down a slope to collect in a hollow at the bottom, and if it's cold enough, it creates a frost pocket. A true frost pocket (not a totally frozen garden) can be modified by simply erecting a barrier – a wall or hedge – to prevent the air running down, almost as if it were water. With a wall, it's advisable to provide some perforations to allow some leakage, thus preventing a new frost pocket forming above the wall, or a "flood" of cold air suddenly pouring over the top of it. Combining temperature measurements with profile details can be helpful in indicating where frost is likely to be a problem, and where this remedy is most likely to be successful.

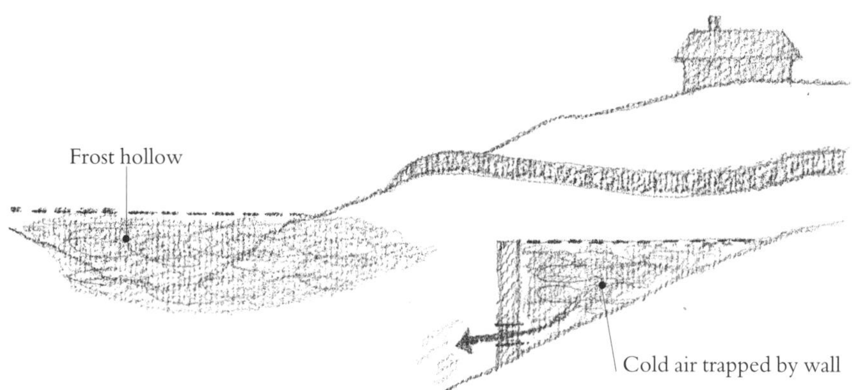

A frost-pocket can be "treated" by erecting a permeable barrier to control the downward flow of low-temperature air, thus reducing the frequency and severity of frosts in the pocket.

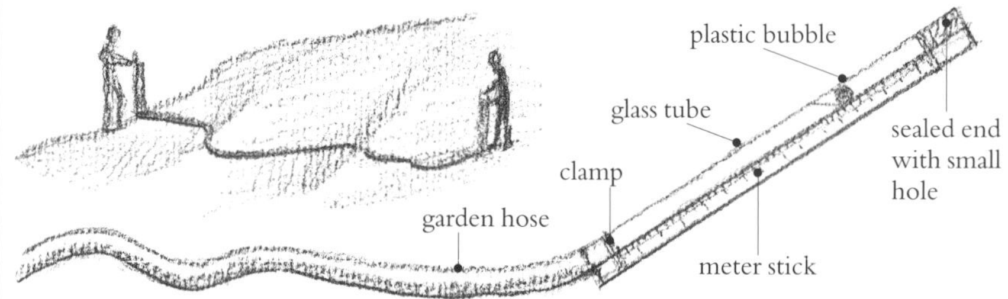

A hose level can be made with about 65ft (20m) of garden hose, plus a short length of clear tubing at each end attached to a rigid graduated stick. The hose is filled with water until the level can be seen in both clear tubes.

Keeping the water at the same level in both tubes, two people can mark contour lines around a slope. Create a differential to mark out a fall line for drainage or irrigation.

Soil texture

In general, soil particles range from the tiny ones which form clay to the large ones of gravel, with sand in between. Most soils consist of a mixture of different-sized particles, together with variable amounts of organic matter, or humus. A simple and accurate test for soil consistency is to shake a sample of soil in a jar of water and allow it to settle. Gravel and stones will instantly fall to the bottom, the smaller grades will settle out on top of them in order of size, and humus will tend to float on the surface.

Out in the garden, there is another simple spot test you can do. If you can squeeze a damp pinch of soil into a coherent lump, then you have a clay soil: the more it resembles modeling clay, the larger the proportion of clay. Sandy soil won't stick together at all; in between sand and clay, you will find a range of cohesiveness. Again, test the soil in different places and at different depths; the results are almost certain to vary. These investigations will tell you how good at holding water your soil is and help to indicate which plants will be most comfortable there.

Soils with a high proportion of clay hold water well, but they are apt to become waterlogged. When clay soil dries out it can become a hard, compacted pan with deep fissures that

A good general texture is based on equal quantities of silt or clay (particle size up to 0.06mm) and sand (particle size 0.06–2mm), plus organic matter.

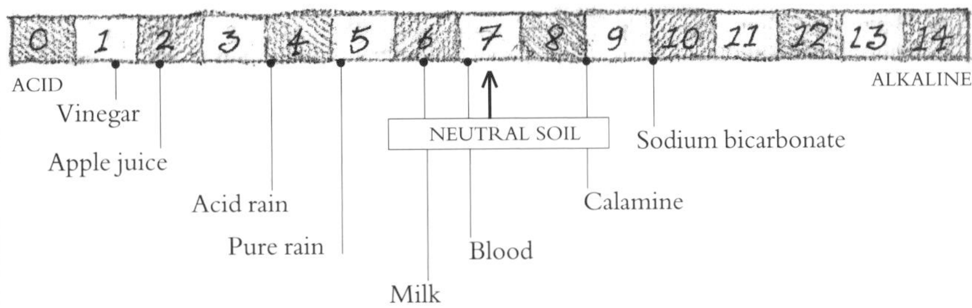

The pH scale is a logarithmic index of acidity. This means that the lower value in the preferred range of most plants, at 6, is ten times as acid as the upper value of 7.

drain away rain before it can penetrate properly. Clay can also be slow to warm up in spring, and contains less air than lighter soils. The air content is important, because roots need to respire just as all other parts of the plant do.

Very sandy soils, on the other hand, are well aerated, but can be so free-draining that they tend to be dry most of the time. They also do not hold roots securely, so that trees on sandy soil are more easily blown over.

Another important consideration is the crumb structure of the soil. Cohesive crumbs help air to penetrate; they are constructed by the activity of worms and other soil fauna, and help to perpetuate the life that created them. To discover whether your soil is well crumbed, first screen a sample, then sprinkle the crumbs into a jar of water and gently swirl around. If the crumbs don't dissolve, this is a good sign.

Both clay and sandy soils are improved by the addition of humus. In clay, humus opens up the structure and helps to improve drainage and aeration. In sand, humus improves water retention. By encouraging worms, adding organic material also improves crumb structure.

Acid-alkaline balance

The level of acidity of the soil is critical to plant growth. It is measured on a scale from 1 to 14, known as the pH scale. The lower the pH, the more acid the soil, with 7 indicating neutral. Cheap pH-testing kits for gardeners are widely available and easy to use. The best pH for the garden at large is just slightly acid, between 6 and 7. As soil becomes more acid, plant roots find it more difficult to extract nutrients, which is one reason why some plants of acidic boglands have resorted to feeding on insects to get the nitrogen and other nutrients they need. Many other plants are very particular as to pH, and some thrive on the comparatively extreme fringes. Heaths need acidic conditions, for example, while beech trees prefer quite alkaline soils.

Test your soil in as many different locations as you can and record the results on a map. Once the natural variations are known, you can plan around them, accommodating those plants which are suited to the prevailing conditions.

Color

Dark soil tends to be warmer than pale soil, chiefly because dark surfaces absorb more light energy than they reflect. Conversely, a light-colored surface reflects more light. Heat energy is absorbed and reflected in the same way, so we can use soil color as an indicator of its ability to absorb heat. Adding humus can darken the soil, and this is especially valuable in higher latitudes, where the speed of warm-up in the spring influences seed germination.

Color can also help to suggest the presence of certain minerals, but this subject is best approached with the aid of a local geology book or enthusiast, preferably both.

Acid rain

You could use the pH-test kit to find out whether the rainfall in your region is significantly acid. The best indicators of pollution, however, are the living, breathing inhabitants of the garden. Some plants and animals are remarkably tolerant of quite nasty air and water, whilst others curl up and die at the slightest whiff of one thing or another.

Lichens

These extraordinary alga-fungus organisms are among the best indicators of polluted air. A few types, such as the yellow or gray crusty ones, can tolerate relatively dirty air, but the larger, leafy shaped ones are much more sensitive. Find out about local varieties, and apply that knowledge in your own garden.

Wild flora

As you walk about your garden, it will become apparent that there are some dominant local weeds. Obviously, in a broad sense, cacti indicate a desert and reeds indicate a marsh, but you'll probably be well aware of such extreme conditions already! In in-between situations, however, some types of dominant weeds can give quite precise information, especially if you can record how they vary from place to place. The first job is to get a good book for identification of local species, and the next step would be to find out which species are fussy, and discover what their known preferences are. Their pollination and seed-dispersal patterns may give even more clues. A wind-pollinated or wind-dispersed plant will tend to spread downwind, for example. A burr-dispersed plant may indicate the presence of furry mammals, and berry bushes can show where birds perch or nest.

Wild fauna

The health of your garden plants is inseparable from the health of the creatures there – both large and small, but especially the small ones. No single creature is more crucial to the gardener than the earthworm.

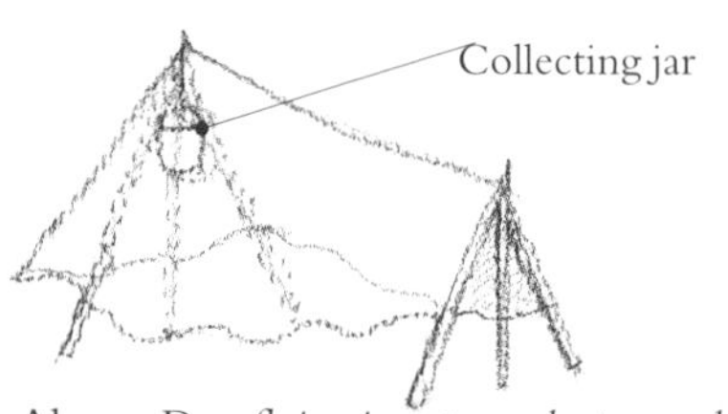

Above *Day-flying insects can be trapped in a muslin tent. The jar (containing rubbing alcohol) is optional, in case you wish to keep specimens as "hard" records.*

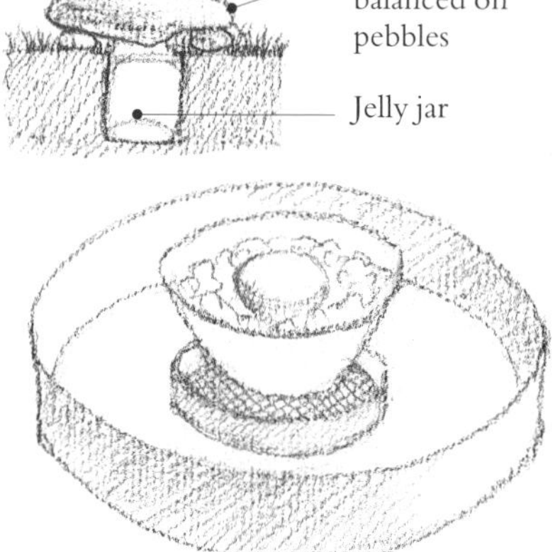

Light traps can be more or less elaborate than this. The essential elements are: a light; a settling place; and a variety of dark crevices for night-flying insects to crawl into and fall asleep.

Counting worms

Counting your earthworm population tells you more about the health of your soil than anything else you can do, and it's almost the easiest test of all. You could do it the hard way by digging up a cubic yard of soil and sifting through it by hand, but it's a lot simpler to sprinkle very slightly soapy water (1 part washing-up liquid in 200 parts water) on to a measured area and count the worms as they pop out. This process won't harm the worms, but if you feel bad about it you can rinse

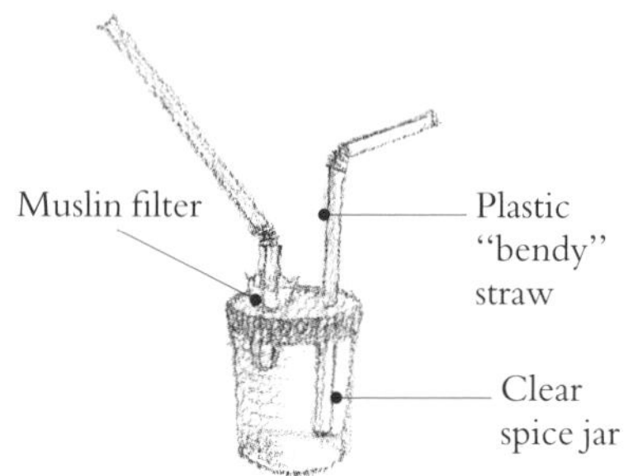

Above *A pooter can be used to suck in small, fast creatures. Take care to suck only the muslin-guarded straw!*

Left *Control the size of your target catch by varying the size of the pebbles that support the lid of a pitfall trap.*

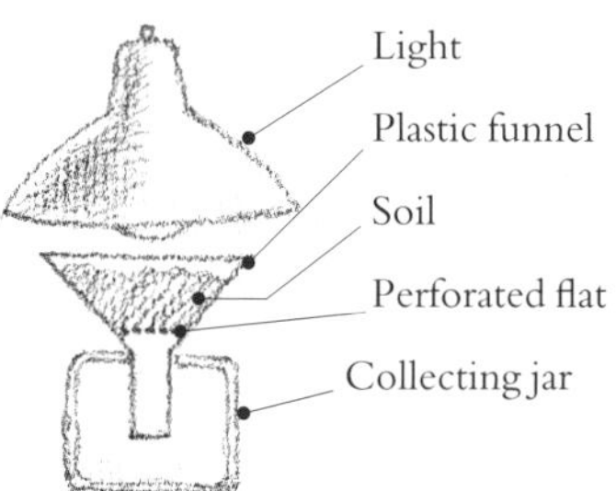

The light over the Tullgren funnel drives burrowers down to drop through the mesh. Fill the funnel and jar with water and dunk a muslin bag of soil to collect the tiniest nematodes.

them in clean water and sluice the soil well before releasing them again. Healthy soil can yield over 100 worms per square yard! If you find fewer than a dozen per square yard, there's either a serious shortage of organic material in your soil, or something very wrong with the pH, or it may be that you've inherited a garden which has been poisoned by toxic chemicals.

Other invertebrates

The variety of invertebrate life, both in the soil and in the air, can tell you a great deal more about your garden, as well as being interesting in itself. Air can be sampled by day, using a tent-shaped trap with a collecting-bottle strategically placed, as in the diagram. At night, a light bulb will lure insects into a similar collecting system.

Two other methods can be used on the ground and among vegetation. The pooter is a well tried and elegant method for picking up any creature too small and fast to be captured by hand. To discover nocturnal wanderers, the simple pitfall trap can be set for capturing large or small creatures. Even the smallest creatures can be lured out unharmed using a Tullgren funnel, which relies on the simple principle that these animals move away from bright light.

You will need a few good books to help you to identify your catch. Many such books use the key system, which is a step-by-step elimination process that's easy to follow as long as you're not tempted to take short-cuts.

Apart from learning a good deal about the wealth of life in your garden, your investigations can give valuable information about potential pests, such as the night-flying moths you'd otherwise be unaware of until they attack your fruit trees, or the soil weevils and wireworms lurking in wait for juicy roots to gnaw.

Experimental plots

If, despite having so much to observe and record, you're still keen to pitch into digging and planting something, there is a valuable exercise you can carry out in the first year. This is intended to give a rough idea of how well your garden will respond to different methods of cultivation. The value of the data you derive from it will be directly related to the care and effort you put into it, however, and it is going to demand a regular input of time and trouble for nearly a whole year.

First, select a suitable site where you can clear two narrow beds 4 feet wide and four times as long. They ought to be as uniform, to begin with, as possible. Cut the vegetation on both beds by mowing or slashing.

One plot is now single-tilled, and the other is not tilled at all. Half of each plot should then be top-dressed with identical quantities of identical compost or manure and watered well (unless they're already very wet).

Cover the no-till plot with a sheet mulch of cardboard (or weighted newspaper), carpet, or black plastic, and then divide each plot into four 4ft (1.2m) squares. Each square is to be planted up in identical fashion. Using a variety of vegetables will show up any difference between their preferences, thus giving a great deal more information (and a more varied diet) in return for a comparatively small extra effort. The mulched plots will have to be planted by cutting slits in the mulch. One possible arrangement is illustrated.

The no-till plot won't be weeded, but will be tested for watering needs. The dug plot will be tested for different weeding regimes, while being watered ad lib. Follow the weeding and watering patterns shown in the diagram, and record the results. As well as showing which sections received which treatment, your log should record:

1. How long digging, mulching, planting, watering, and weeding each section took.
2. How well the various plants in each section grew and/or cropped.
3. The state of the soil, and its worm population, in each section at the end of the growing season.
4. Any other factors (e.g. slug damage) that seem to vary.

Study the log during the off-season to see what conclusions might be drawn from your findings. For example: is digging worth the effort? Is weeding worth the effort? Did you need to water the mulched beds? Did the compost make a difference? Which plants responded best to which conditions? What was the soil like at the end of the season?

Finally, consider what further experiments might be necessary to either confirm your conclusions or extend your study.

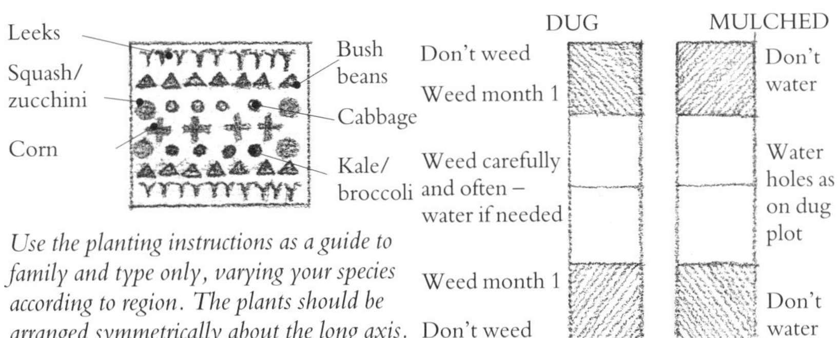

Use the planting instructions as a guide to family and type only, varying your species according to region. The plants should be arranged symmetrically about the long axis.

SHAPING THE LAND

The landscape painter's art lies in identifying and encapsulating the qualities of color, shape, and texture which are characteristic of the region portrayed, although not necessarily slavishly copying the scene. Artistic license gives a painter the freedom to exaggerate a slope or move a tree in order to enhance the composition.

When shaping your own garden, you are in the same position of power as the landscape artist. Working with the essential nature of the region, you can create beauty by subtly enhancing the composition, and this should be your aim.

In addition to beauty, however, you will wish to create amenity, and this presents an even greater challenge than that faced by a painter. You need to consider the best way to arrange things so as to put each component where it is most convenient, as well as keeping sight of the aesthetic composition of the whole, which is the problem that an architect faces. But unlike architecture, growing things are not static. They change shape, and they also impose their own will.

The success of natural gardening rests heavily on understanding and sympathy, setting things up with care, and going with the flow. Anything you import from outside the bioregion carries the risk of introducing a false note that will spoil the general harmony, either aesthetically or ecologically. Careful, sensitive planning is central to your approach.

First steps

By the end of your initiatory year, you will have given the garden a chance to "grow" on you. If there's a feature that jars, in an aesthetic or practical sense, you'll probably have found it by now, and be in no doubt about wanting to remove or change it. This is a good starting point. Begin by studying your profile plans, shade maps, temperature logs, and other first-year records, to predict what the effect of changing things might be. At the same time, you can also pick out other specific areas, such as wet or parched patches, frost pockets, and sun traps, and decide whether you want to make constructive use of them or not. Unless you feel positively antagonistic toward a particular feature, it's generally advisable to use it rather than obliterate it just for the sake of uniformity. Plans have a way of changing as you go along, and it's good to keep some variety to work with.

Trees

Always consider large trees carefully to see whether they could be lopped, pollarded, or even coppiced, rather than being felled. If a mature tree really must be destroyed, try to handle it in such a way as to make the most of the timber, and consider leaving a large enough bole to make a table or seat or other structure.

When deciding what to do with young trees, remember that self-sown saplings generally grow into stronger and more soundly rooted trees than transplanted ones do. On the other hand, you should guard against being too soft-hearted. It's a lot easier to remove an unwanted tree while it's small, and when your garden is still rough, than it will be when it has become a mature and dominant feature amongst well-organized beds and buildings.

When in doubt, leave the possible survivors until last. After everything else is cleared, it will be easier to see the effect of what's left sticking up.

Moving trees

Transplanting young trees is not difficult, as long as some basic principles are borne in mind. First of all, the younger the tree is, the better the chances of success are. Don't move a tree that's already stressed, especially by drought. If it's necessary to prune it beforehand, to make it easier to handle, do this well in advance and never at the same time as transplanting. Apart from these points, treat a transplanted tree as you would a "bare-rooted" one, which means moving it after leaf fall but, if possible, before the soil has become cold. If this can't be done, a winter move may be successful for deciduous trees but be sure to leave evergreens until early spring.

Prepare the planting hole beforehand, so that the roots aren't exposed for too long, and be prepared to dig a very deep and wide hole to get the tree out, especially if it's self-seeded. The anchor roots give stability but, if they have to be cut, you can at least provide some mechanical assistance to support the tree in its new position. The small, rubbery feeder roots supply the tree with water and nutrients. These are apt to spread widely, and are easily stripped off if the tree is pulled up rather than carefully dug out.

Once you have some idea of how widely the roots spread, prepare the planting hole accordingly. Proceed from here as outlined on p.000.

Mature trees

Moving a mature tree is a different matter, and only for the brave and resourceful. If the tree is so big that you'd need expert assistance to fell it, then it's definitely too big to be moved. A lesser tree might be worth a try, as long as you're prepared for possible failure. You'll need a combination of patience, common sense, and know-how, together with a lot of ingenuity and determination.

The job is best tackled in two stages, beginning in the early fall as soon as possible after leaf fall. First, prune the tree as hard as you dare. This is largely a matter of judgement: cutting away too much might kill the tree, but doing too little could reduce the chances of success as well as making the task heavier than it need be. Study the tree to see where (and whether) new growth might arise after trimming and where old growth could be usefully removed; think about the effect on the final shape. You could even consider pollarding the tree, which (depending on the species) might increase the chances of success. Next, because the existing root system will be extensive and you want to encourage new feeder roots at the periphery of a new root system, you need to prepare the tree's roots by careful root pruning. Mark out a ring around the trunk, roughly the same distance from the bole as the branches extend sideways (use your own judgement if you've pollarded it), and use this as the outer limit of a 2ft (60cm)-wide trench all around the tree.

From here, you can either dig out the entire trench in one go, or do it in two parts – one half this year and the other half next year. The object is to prune the main root structure while doing as little damage as possible to the fibrous feeder roots.

Begin your trench vertically, then undercut toward the central trunk. Check that each severed root is cleanly trimmed before backfilling the trench with loamy compost-rich soil. If you feel the tree might now be unstable, tether it firmly with guy ropes and leave until next leaf fall.

By this time, the severed roots should have grown new feeders into the soft compost. If you only did half last year, finish the trench now. If the entire trench has been in place for a year, now's the time to assemble whatever lifting gear you have, and as many willing hands and strong backs as you can muster.

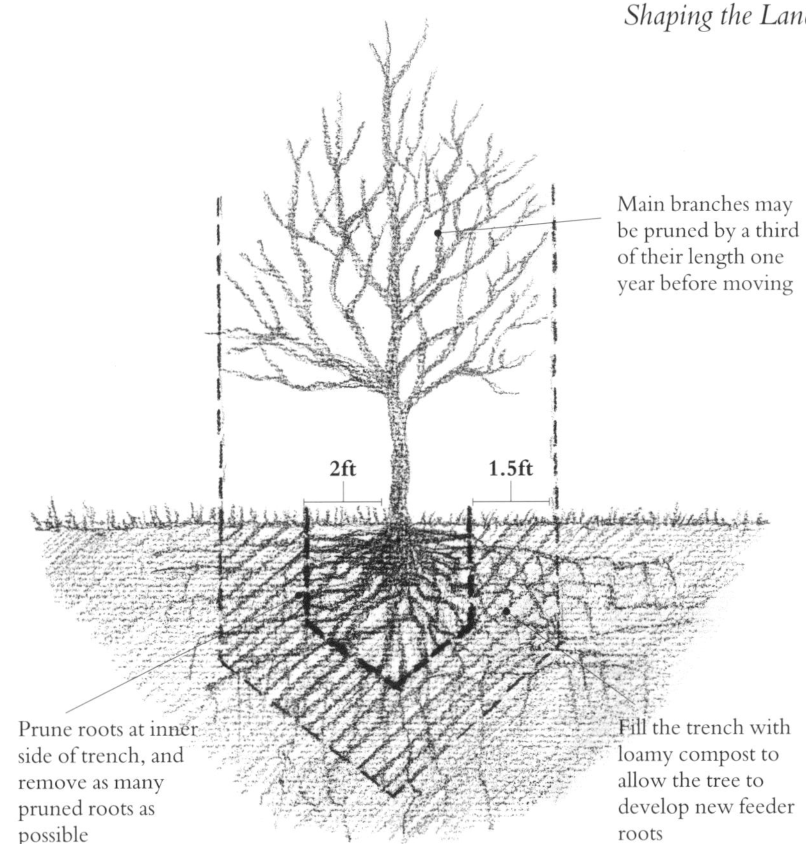
Main branches may be pruned by a third of their length one year before moving
2ft
1.5ft
Prune roots at inner side of trench, and remove as many pruned roots as possible
Fill the trench with loamy compost to allow the tree to develop new feeder roots

When the tree is settled in its new quarters it must be staked very firmly. The transplanted tree will carry a heavy leaf load and, with its already-rigid trunk, is vulnerable to rocking rather than bending in the wind. On clay soils, this can create an impermeable clay sleeve around the roots, which could kill the tree, a fate once known by orchard owners as "the death".

Before you start, mark a compass point on the trunk. When you relocate the tree, you should give it the same aspect that it grew up with. The best time to make the move is just before sundown, and a good way to spend removal day would be to water the trench-soil several times, while making final preparations to the new planting hole. Working gently around the tender new roots, loosen the tree from its bed of soft soil. If any large roots are still intact, sever them cleanly. Wrap the roots in burlap while moving it, to retain as much soil and moisture as possible and protect from physical damage.

Once you have your tree in its new hole and facing the right way, firmly backfilled and well watered, it must be anchored as securely as possible with guy ropes. The higher up the trunk they are attached, and the wider their ground span, the more stable your tree will be. Fit each guy with a long, stout stake. Mulch thickly and thoroughly over all the disturbed ground.

Clearing ground

When clearing or weeding any patch of ground, consider what use you might be able to make of the organic material you're removing. Unless it's diseased, nearly everything that grows has some virtue, and some common weeds are far too good to waste. If in doubt, treat greenery by wilting and then compost it or use for mulch; treat woody waste by drying, and then store.

Heavy machinery
If you're clearing a large area it may be necessary to bring in some machinery, especially when extensive underground roots are to be removed. Bear in mind that the heavier the equipment is, the more it will compact and crush the soil structure. Less damage is done when the soil is dry or deeply frozen. Try to get heavy clearing and earth-moving done in one operation (this will cut down on expense as well as damage), and restrict traffic to intended paths wherever you can.

Chainsaws and flame throwers
A tempting alternative to hard manual labor is the use of mechanical aids such as chainsaws and flame throwers. It may be cheap to rent or borrow such equipment but, as with all potentially dangerous machinery, unless you're familiar with its use, it makes good sense to call on expert help.

First flush
Removing scrub will stir the ground and let in light to stimulate a flush of annual weeds. To avoid this, mulch thickly as soon as the ground is clear. If the debris from clearance is suitable, you could leave it there to help suppress weeds until you're ready to work the soil. If you can rent a shredder or wood chipper, woody waste can be made into excellent long-lasting mulch.

Changing profiles
There are many reasons why you might want to alter the lie of the land, including:

- improving surface drainage;
- directing rainwater runoff;
- creating hollows, ponds, and banks;
- increasing the amount of level ground;
- improving a slope;
- altering microclimates;
- adding visual interest;
- removing visual barriers;
- creating sound barriers.

Bumps and hollows
Before grabbing a spade or calling in the bulldozer, remember that every bit of soil or rock you take away from one place has to go somewhere else. Match up additions and subtractions if you can, so that earth only has to be moved once. When digging a pond, there will be a great deal of spoil. Before you begin, consider whether to leave an island in place; some spoil can be deposited here, to raise the level of the island. If you want a really big pond, it may be possible to construct it partly by digging and partly by using the spoil to shape the banks. Bear in mind that

USING MATERIALS FROM CLEARED GROUND

MATERIAL	USE	TREATMENT
Bamboo stem	Plant support Drainage	Store (destroy root) Keep until needed
Bark	Mulch	Shred or smash
Briar	Magic mound	Store until needed
Broom	Compost	Store until needed
Brushy twigs	Pea supports	Store until needed
Grapevines	Basketry	Coil and store
Greenery	Compost	Store until needed
Nettle (young)	Compost; mulch	Wilt and use
Nettle (old)	Slow compost	Wilt first
Nettle root	Fiber Iron-rich	Ret as flax Pig feed
Osier	Basketry; drainage	Store
Sapling trunk	Post; prop; firewood	Season outdoors
Sawdust	Mulch; paths	Deposit where needed
Thorn twigs	Magic mound	Store until needed
Thorn branch	Kindling	Dry well
Twiggy wood	Magic mound	Store until needed
Willow withes	Basketry Green bank	Strip bark Plant immediately
Willow branch	Fencing; wattle; drainage	Split
Willow trunk	Posts; walk edges	Store dry
Wood	Dependent on shape, species	Store
Woody waste	Mulch	Shred or chip*
Wood ash	High-K fertilizer	Store dry or compost

**Machinery to do this can be rented*

topsoil is precious. Always keep topsoil and subsoil separate, so that you can use subsoil to build a new mound, and topsoil to clothe it or to line a new hollow.

Improving a slope
A slope of 45 degrees or less can usually be stabilized by the roots of well chosen vegetation, such as grasses. If the soil is sandy, or heavy rainfall causes erosion, or if the slope is greater than 45 degrees, you may need to amend the slope by stepping it. A series of low retainers can help to stabilize and reduce the steepness of the slope.

Swale and berm
Sloping ground can shed rain water too quickly, either wasting it or leading to erosion. Instead of retainers, you can use the bump-and-hollow technique to create a series of linear depressions which will hold water to give it time to seep in (see right).

This technique can also be used on level ground in order to guide rain water where you want it to go. Even where drainage isn't a serious priority, this approach could be used to create different conditions for planting into the dry berm and the moister swale, with a free-draining slope between. This might be useful when you want all your herbs in one spot, for example.

Terracing
A more drastic procedure, and one that can also be used to create level beds on a sloping site, is to turn the slope into horizontal terraces. If the steps aren't too big (i.e. less than 1.4m), you could tackle this job yourself. Taller steps might need expert help.

The standard method for terracing is known as "cut and fill". The first stage is to remove all the topsoil from the whole of the area you wish to alter, and to store it separately, which is easy to

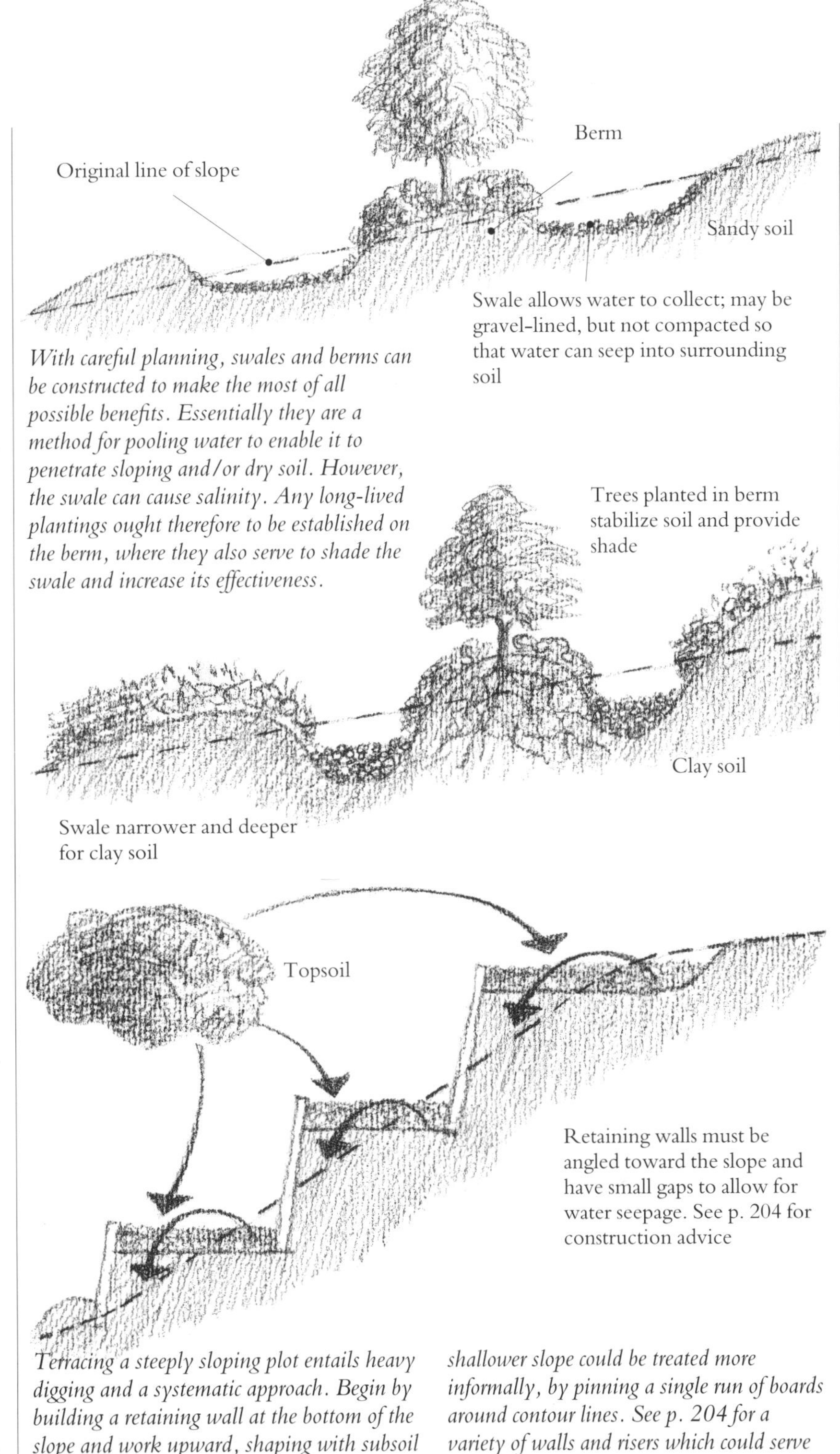
Berm
Original line of slope
Sandy soil
Swale allows water to collect; may be gravel-lined, but not compacted so that water can seep into surrounding soil
Trees planted in berm stabilize soil and provide shade
Clay soil
Swale narrower and deeper for clay soil
Topsoil
Retaining walls must be angled toward the slope and have small gaps to allow for water seepage. See p. 204 for construction advice

With careful planning, swales and berms can be constructed to make the most of all possible benefits. Essentially they are a method for pooling water to enable it to penetrate sloping and/or dry soil. However, the swale can cause salinity. Any long-lived plantings ought therefore to be established on the berm, where they also serve to shade the swale and increase its effectiveness.

Terracing a steeply sloping plot entails heavy digging and a systematic approach. Begin by building a retaining wall at the bottom of the slope and work upward, shaping with subsoil and topping off with reserved topsoil. A shallower slope could be treated more informally, by pinning a single run of boards around contour lines. See p. 204 for a variety of walls and risers which could serve for a variety of situations, slopes, and soils.

say but arduous to do (100 cu. ft weighs more than 1 ton!). Next, build a retaining wall (a little higher than the intended height of the terrace) at the base of the slope. Then, working with the subsoil, cut away a wedge at a time and turn it over to form the terrace below. Build the next retaining wall after the wedge is removed and before the next is deposited. Finally, cover each terrace with the reserved topsoil.

Retainers

Choose materials for building retaining structures with care and imagination. They remain exposed, and will therefore become an important visual feature. Always use natural materials if you can. Strictly speaking, this means either wood or stone, but well chosen bricks (especially old ones) can also look good. If you're forced to opt for reconstituted stone or concrete, this can be improved by painting it with an organic mixture such as cow dung to encourage the growth of moss.

If stone occurs naturally in your region, then this is often the best choice. It will fit into your landscape, it will be readily available, and it will last for ever. When building retainers of stone, backfill with soil layer by layer, as the wall is built up, and add some longer stones to tie into the soil behind.

Brick retainers can also be tied back in the same way. While building brick retainers, remember to leave some gaps for drainage; these can be used for planting through. Both stone and brick retainers become more stable if they lean backward, rather than standing vertically. Both brick and stone walls can be mortared, but take care to leave drainage holes, and avoid putting mortar where it will be conspicuous.

Wood is usually cheaper than stone or brick. It's relatively easy to handle, but it will eventually rot. When experimenting with steps in relation to walks and desire lines, wood is the obvious choice. Whatever wood you choose, however, make sure that your source is ethical. The heartwood of some trees lasts longer than that of others, and longer than any sapwood. Preservatives can slow down the decay process but, because these are either fungicides or pesticides (or both), you'll want to be certain that freshly treated wood is safe for your garden. Using wood, there's virtually no limit to the variety of different designs you could create for retaining walls.

Reserve large good stones for top

Angle wall toward bed

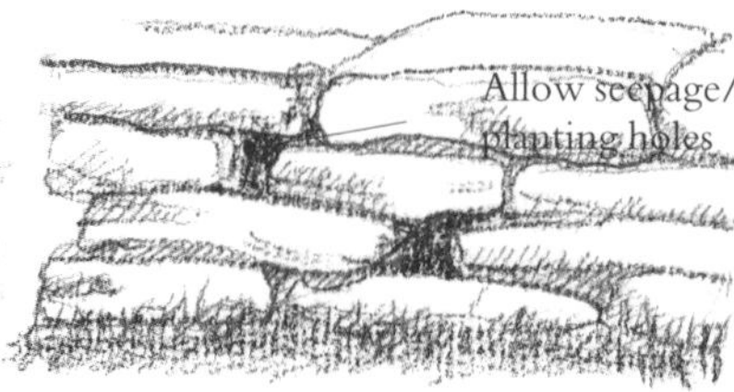

Stones projecting into bank will tie it in and stabilize it

Backfill as you build

Backfill as you go

Tie wall into bed

Angle wall toward bed

Above *Choose stone or brick which is commonly available in your region. A dry-stone wall can be built of flat, shaly, or slaty stones, pieced together like a 3-dimensional jigsaw puzzle. Avoid vertical seams, which will split apart, and key into the soil with backwardly projecting stones at regular intervals.* Left *Small brick walls can be built without mortar, but a dab of mortar between bricks will improve stability without necessarily being visible.*

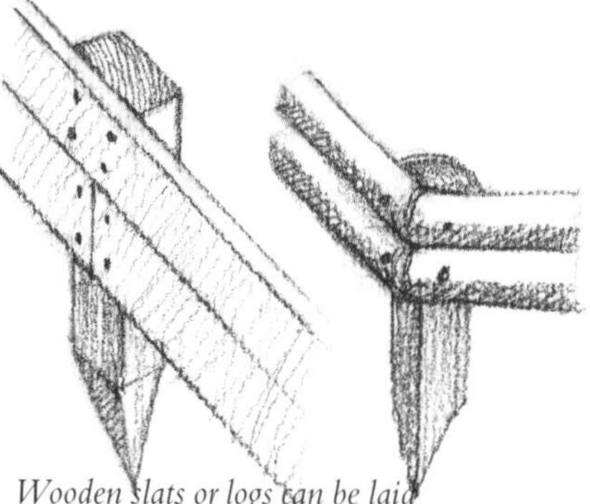

Wooden slats or logs can be laid horizontally, anchored securely by attachment to vertical pins.

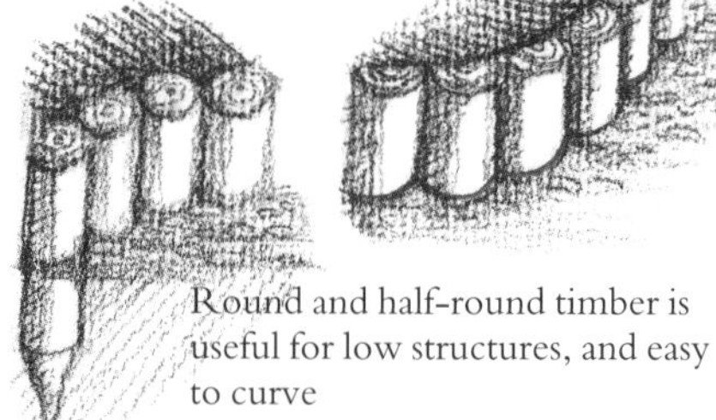

Round and half-round timber is useful for low structures, and easy to curve

Sharpened sections of sawed logs can be driven into the ground directly. This method is especially good for creating elegant curves, particularly on heavy soils, but is not suitable for high terraces. It uses a lot of lumber.

Locating walks

During your initiation year, you'll discover a number of natural routes which will indicate suitable directions for permanent walks. If the site is well drained, it might not be necessary to construct anything at all, especially if the ground is naturally stony. In this case, all you'll have to consider is whether to ease the line of the walk to make it a more attractive shape.

Such perfect conditions rarely exist, however, and it's usually necessary to create a firm, dry surface to carry regular traffic. Before commencing this rather laborious and not-easily-undone task, though, look carefully at the shape of the lines you intend to follow. When traveling from one place to another, people usually select the shortest route, which means a straight line. Permanent walks, however, become compelling sight lines, and straight lines crossing and intersecting your garden might be unattractive. Before you make the walks permanent, consider the general view and, if necessary, introduce some curves.

If you're planning to make major changes in the garden layout, some existing routes may become redundant and others might arise. It may therefore be necessary to lay some temporary walks as well as permanent ones.

Temporary walks

Temporary walks can be made of a wide variety of materials. Slow mulch material such as straw, old carpet (stair carpet comes in a convenient width), sawdust, or bark chips can be spread along the route – especially between vegetable beds – to suppress weeds and make a dry surface to walk on. These substances will eventually blend into the soil, or can be removed to the compost pile and replaced each year.

Ashes, gravel, fines, shale, or other loose, dry material can also be used to make quick temporary walks. These materials tend to be trodden in and are hard to get rid of later on, so they're more suitable for laying down along tracks that are meant to be made permanent eventually. They need no foundations, but should be given a retaining border to prevent the material from spreading sideways. The border can be made of logs, boards, bricks, or slabs, pinned or bedded into the ground to stop them straying.

Permanent walks

The aim is to construct a clean, dry, firm, and low-maintenance surface to walk on, at the same time as creating a permanent feature that is pleasing to the eye and to the walker, and leads somewhere.

The choice of materials depends largely on what's locally available. Walks are very conspicuous, so their surface appearance is very important. Other factors, such as durability, cost, and ease of laying, will also influence your choice but, whatever you decide to use, you will have to prepare the ground carefully beforehand and live with the result for many years afterward.

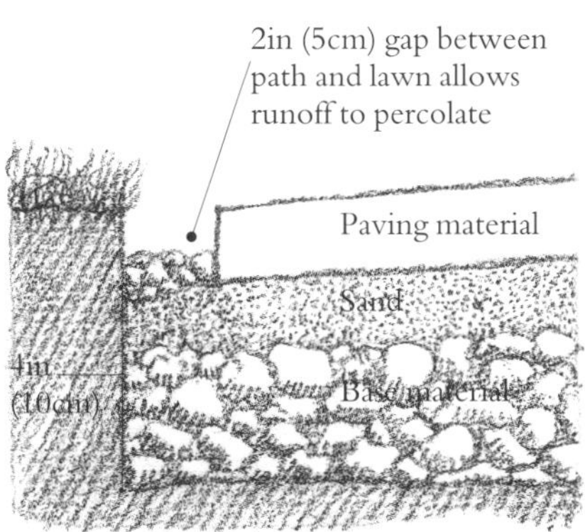

The basic requirements for a permanent walk: two-layer drainage; firm, sloped surface; gaps for drainage.

To ensure that the walk remains clean and dry, it must be given a free-draining foundation. Aim to remove about 10cm (4in) of topsoil (why waste it to walk on?), and replace at least half of this depth with rubble or crushed stone, or some other mixture of large and small sharp non-soluble material, rammed down hard and as even as you can make it. Top this off with sand to make a bed for the paving material itself. Precise depths will depend on the thickness of the paving material and whether you wish the walk to stand above or lie flush with the ground. A slightly raised walk tends to be drier, but a flush one doesn't interfere with the mower.

Drainage can be improved even more by using another two or three strategies: either incorporate a slight tilt in the walk's surface, so that water slides off sideways, or make the surface convex, so that it sheds water to both sides, or leave gaps for water to drain through. What you decide to do might well be dictated by the material you use (it's hard to create a convex surface with large stone slabs!), or you may be guided by the position of the walk itself. If your walk runs beside a hedge, for example, giving it a slope toward the hedge will help to supply rain water to the hedge roots.

It's not essential for the walk to be totally impervious – on the contrary, gaps and crevices will help it to blend in with the garden at the same time as assisting drainage. Several species of small plants can tolerate some trampling, and wild ones will often naturally move into gaps and crevices. Alternatively, selected species can be deliberately introduced. Using aromatic herbs, such as Corsican mint, dwarf thymes, or lawn chamomile, will make the walk even more delightful to use, as they will release their scent each time they're trodden on.

Paving materials
As with retaining walls, the best rule is to stick to local, natural materials. If stone occurs naturally in your area, it is the obvious choice.

Real stone, reconstituted stone, or concrete flags are easy to lay, but regular squares or rectangles can strike a discordant note unless they're used imaginatively. Allowing surrounding vegetation to fall over the walk's edges can help to obscure the rigidity of slabs and flags. The joints between flags tend to catch the eye, so the way they're arranged is critical. Experiment with loose-laid slabs before you even begin digging foundations.

In a region where houses tend to be brick-built, brick walks blend in well. Old bricks are especially attractive. They can be arranged in a variety of patterns, from square to herringbone, with or without mortared joints. One minor drawback of brick walks is that they tend to grow algae which can become treacherously slippery when wet, so pay special attention to drainage.

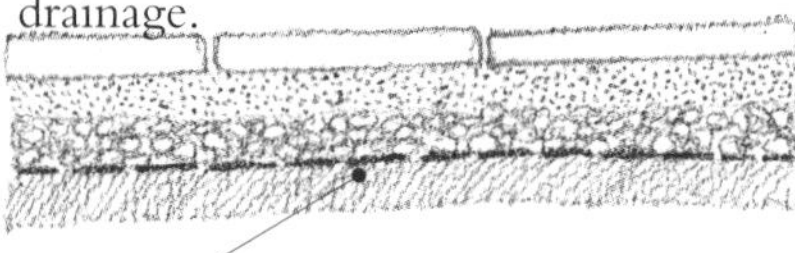

Synthetic materials such as geotextile can also be used to facilitate drainage. Coarse gravel laid on top of geotextile won't compact into the underlying soil.

As with most walks, loose-laid logs must be edged firmly with a retaining wall.

Other local materials may include cobblestones (rounded stones) or Belgian blocks (square stones with a domed top), and these, too, can make an attractive walk. They should be set into mortar to stabilize them.

Wood can also be used for paving, but is best reserved for dry or cold regions. Wet wood is very slippery, and wood tends to rot rapidly in warm, moist climates. As with bricks, a region where homes are built of wood is most likely to be a region where a wooden walk is both successful and harmonious. An attractive effect can be obtained by packing short (4–8in) logs vertically on a bed of sand, with a firm retaining edge. This uses up quite a lot of wood, and requires rot-resistant limber. Wooden cobblestones or hexagonal blocks can sometimes be obtained; these make a more durable walk because, at the same time as being trimmed to fit together more closely, they've had most of the fast-rotting sapwood removed.

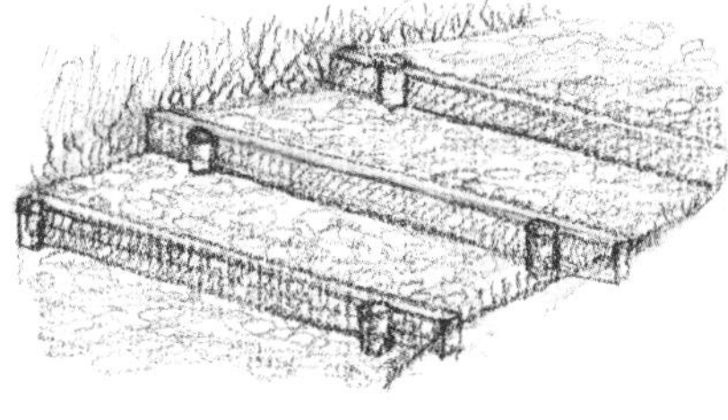

Use local materials imaginatively to create natural-looking walks and steps. Construct shallow steps with simple risers only, pinned firmly into place (above). Alternatively, paving slabs can make shallow steps with treads only (below). With steeper steps, remember to include a wheelbarrow ramp.

Steps
Where a walk climbs a slope, the best solution to all the practical problems this poses is to create steps. Apart from reducing wear on the slope and being easier to negotiate than a steep walk, steps can also add an attractive feature.

If steps are introduced into a terraced or otherwise-retained slope, they should be constructed of the same material as the retaining material. Apart from this general rule, your selection of material and style is a matter of personal taste, and local resources.

Building steps is not unlike building terraces, but with the priority on human use. The ratio of rise to tread should be at least 1:2, but 1:3 or even more is better. Because the rise is small, the retainer doesn't carry the same weight as a terrace retainer; on the other hand, it will have to resist wear from walking, and the forces generated by feet "pushing off". Simple wooden retainers of logs or boards, held in position by stakes, work very well. With this type of step, there's rarely any need to construct treads. On the other hand, if you have a supply of paving or stone slabs, they can be arranged as overlapping treads to make very stable steps up a shallow slope.

Ramps
Anywhere you build steps, you'll be making it more difficult to push a wheelbarrow. Where steps form part of an important supply route, running a ramp up the middle can avert much inconvenience and strain. If the steps are wooden, a board just 4in (100mm) wide is sufficient to take a wheelbarrow.

Another way to cope with a steep slope is to take the walk up hairpin-fashion, as roads are built up mountainsides. This is a good way to provide access for wheelchairs, as well as wheelbarrows.

Drainage

It's a good idea to think about drainage while you are still moving earth around. If your observations and records have shown up a wet spot you'd rather not have, or another reason for rerouting water flow, set in some drainage tiles now.

The traditional layout is the herringbone pattern. This directs water from a wide area into a central collecting channel, which can be led to a river, pond, or ditch. If the ground is flat, then the drains must start shallow and slope downward.

If there's no obvious outlet for your drainage system, and if you don't want to create a pond, you might be able to create a soakaway instead. This is basically a large underground sink, filled with rubble in the same way as a French drain (see below).

In order to be effective, though, a soakaway must cut right through the dense subsoil layer, or any hard pan, to reach into more open or porous strata beneath. This could mean digging a pit 1–4m (3–12ft) deep and 1–2m (3–6ft) across, which is no mean feat. If the problem of waterlogging is really bad, this might indicate that a soakaway isn't feasible, in which case you may need to consider other options (see pp.176–9).

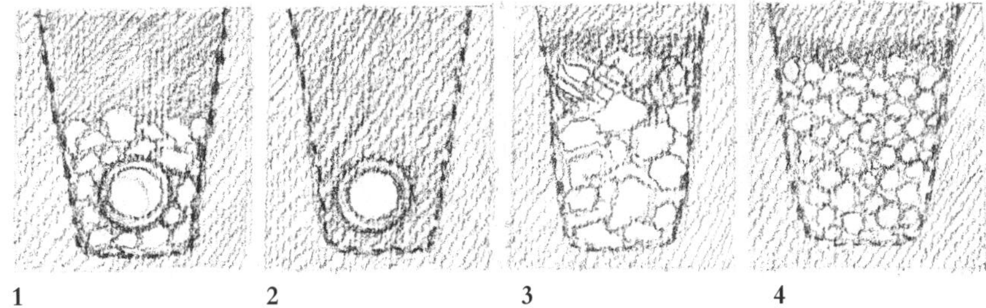

The usual cross-section for drainage systems is a truncated wedge, narrower at the bottom, refilled with a variety of materials. Clay drainage pipes can be laid with (1) or without (2) rubble. These drains last virtually for ever.

Quicker and cheaper, but shorter-lived results can be obtained by filling in with rubble (French drain, 3) or fagots (4; hazel lasts best). Make your own choice of the method which best fits your resources and needs.

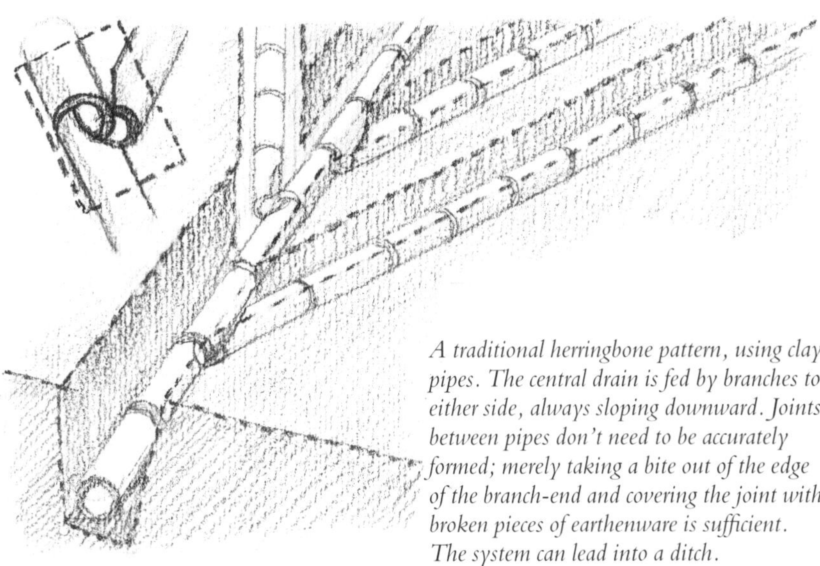

A traditional herringbone pattern, using clay pipes. The central drain is fed by branches to either side, always sloping downward. Joints between pipes don't need to be accurately formed; merely taking a bite out of the edge of the branch-end and covering the joint with broken pieces of earthenware is sufficient. The system can lead into a ditch.

French drain

The simplest drain is a trench filled with rubble. Once the trenches have been dug out and tested to see if the design works, they're half-filled with coarse, material which won't clog easily with finer soil particles. On top of the rubble, a thick layer of slow-rotting fibrous material will provide a base on which to replace sods or topsoil. It may even be possible to create your drainage system using only woody waste, if you have a plentiful supply (e.g. from initial ground clearance or hedge trimming). No compostable material lasts for ever, though, and there are modern materials (geotextiles) which, although expensive and not for the purist, do an excellent job virtually indefinitely.

Piped systems

There are a multitude of different kinds of drainpipes, but they all work on the principle of allowing water to enter through small holes or pores, under the pressure created by a volume of groundwater. These drainage pipes won't be visible, so the choice depends on your own circumstances, resources, needs, and/or feelings. Depending on the nature of the pipes you use and the type of ground you're draining, it may be necessary to create almost the same structure as the French drain, but with a pipe in the middle, so ready-made drainpipes don't always represent an easy option.

RECYCLING

Waste is no more than a word, a concept invented by humans to define a human problem. The proper sense of the word is expressed in the phrases: "What a waste!", or "Waste not, want not." There's nothing of this kind in nature. When we're faced with disposing of unwanted organic matter, all we need to know is how best to co-operate with nature in recycling it. Not to do this would truly be a waste.

Even the wastes from our own bodies, derived from the food we eat, really belong "out there". Although the process of recycling human feces is something you may not be in a position to do because of the dangers of disease (but see p. 217), urine carries negligible health risks and is a valuable source of nutrients that can greatly enrich the compost pile. In fact, the precious gallons of pure water we flush away, just to dispose "nicely" of a few fluid ounces of nutrient-rich urine, represent the real waste that most of us squander thoughtlessly several times every day.

Industrial wastes, on the other hand, can be totally unnatural materials, specifically manufactured for their quality of indestructibility. Plastics represent the pinnacle of human achievement in this respect, and the disposal of plastic garbage is a pressing world problem. Given that we're stuck with a lot of rot-proof lumber of this kind, it's good to find there are ways to reuse some of it.

Fortunately, much of our garbage falls somewhere in between the urine and the plastic, and there are many unwanted household materials that have a very good use in the garden.

Household Garbage

Organic

Material	Use/Danger	Method
Vegetable waste	Compost/animal feed	Fast pile/mash
Citrus peel	Slug trap	Halves for shelter
Tea/coffee	Compost/soil improver	Fast pile or scatter
Teabags	Compost/pot drainage pieces	1 in bottom of pot
Fat	Winter bird feed	Hang up or mix with crumbs
Meat scraps	Compost/animal feed	Slow pile/mash
Bones	Compost	Slow pile
Hair/wool	Compost (caution: parasites)	Slow pile
Coconut shells	Containers for bird feed	Fill with fat/crumb
Urine	Fertilizer/compost activator Scab and mildew control	Apply to compost. Dilute 1:3 with water
Pet litter	Compost (caution: parasites)	Slow pile
Vacuum dust	Compost	Fast pile
Soot	Warms soil, feeds trees	Top-dress around base
Wood ash	High-K fertilizer/high pH	Store dry or use immediately
Coal/coke ash	Improves drainage but low pH	Expose to rain until acid purged. Could help correct high pH
Waste oil	Recycle	Public system
Unidentified chemicals	Assume lethal	Dispose of safely

Household Garbage		
	Inorganic	
Material	Use/Danger	Method
Glass bottles	Recycle	Public system
Clear plastic bottles	Mini-cloche/slug collar or rain gauge	Cut as required
Yogurt and other pots	Flowerpot/slug collar plant label/earwig trap	Fashion as required
Squeezable bottles	Deter cats	Fill with cheap scent
Metal cans	Recycle	Public system
Plastic bags	Mini-cultivators	As required
Damaged trash-bags	Leaf compost	See p. 215
Car tire	Worm farm	See p. 216
	Semi-organic	
Paper and cardboard	Mulch	Various
Cardboard egg box	Potting	With or without base
Centers from rolls of toilet paper	Potting	Bottomless pots
Glossy magazines	Recycle	Public system
Natural carpet	Mulch	Lay and leave
Mixed carpet	Mulch	Lay and plant through
	Garden waste/materials	
Weeds	Compost	See compost chart
Sods	Seed/potting	Stack for use
Topsoil	Save at all cost	Clothing new bumps/lining new hollows
Worm-cast soil	Seed/potting	Use fresh
Spoil	Reshaping	Relocate
Rubble	Drainage/infill	Walks, drains, etc.
Builders' sand	Limited use	Not same as "sharp" sand. Leach well
Clean brushwood	Drainage/frost shelter/pea support/ magic mound	Do not burn
Clean prunings	Wildlife pile/kindling/ plant support/magic mound	Pile/trim/store
Clean logs	Construction/wildlife/fire	Season for use
Diseased green matter	Destroy	Burn
Diseased wood	Destroy	Burn
Leaves	Compost/mulch/potting/magic mound	As appropriate
Spent potting	Compost	Fast pile

Fire

Although our overriding concern must be – and is – the recycling of organic material, it would be hypocritical to forbid the natural gardener ever to light a bonfire. That same gardener may even virtuously possess a wood-burning stove in order to spare the Earth's fossil fuel resources.

Fire is a natural phenomenon; many plant species worldwide are adapted to grow only on burned ground, and such adaptations did not arise overnight! Fire also plays a part in maintaining environments such as heathland, where the natural vegetation cycle seems to invite an occasional flare-up.

Some gardening problems are best solved with fire. Diseases such as clubroot, potato blight, mosaic virus, die-back, and mildews and molds of various kinds are hard enough to control, without banning the bonfire. Old grease bands and sacking traps may have to be incinerated, and a gardener whose patch is too small to accommodate long-term compost has to destroy roots of perennial weeds.

There is no excuse for burning good wood or compostable material, nor for burning potentially toxic materials. However, faced with a pile of cankered trimmings and diseased stem and leaf material, the most effective solution is incineration.

Fire can, however, cause havoc, ranging from polluting your neighbor's garden to devastating an entire forest, so it must be done right.

Basic decisions

If you opt for a small purpose-built incinerator, then the equipment will come with instructions for use. The site for a "proper" bonfire must be chosen with care and located where it will be least likely to offend and where air movement is minimal and subject to least variation.

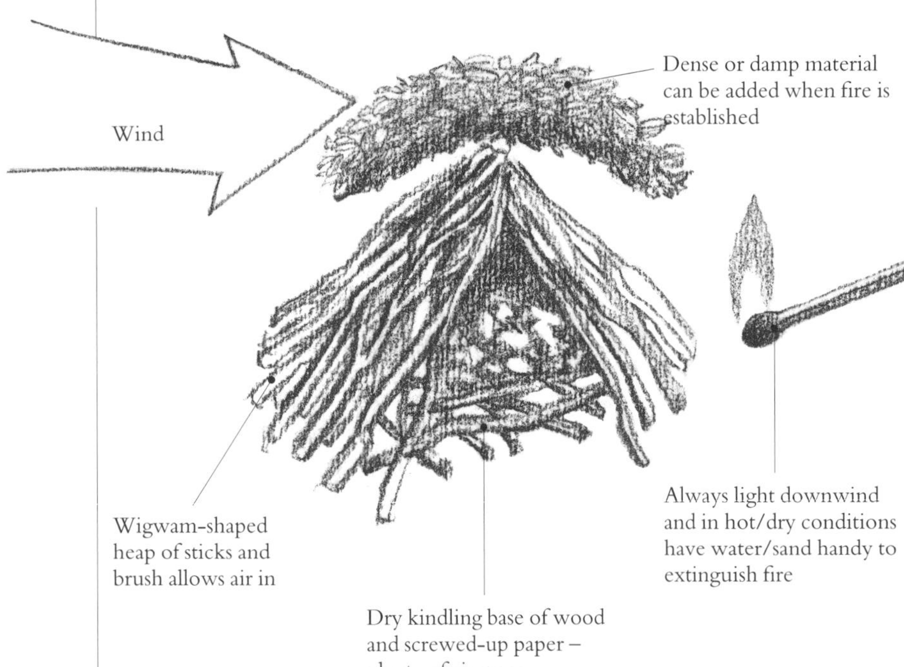
Dense or damp material can be added when fire is established
Wind
Always light downwind and in hot/dry conditions have water/sand handy to extinguish fire
Wigwam-shaped heap of sticks and brush allows air in
Dry kindling base of wood and screwed-up paper – plenty of air space

Preparing the site

A fire can either be laid on bare ground, which may necessitate lifting sods, or on a permanent paved base. It should be in a sheltered position, away from overhanging trees or other objects which may "catch" or scorch. It's going to generate a lot of heat, perhaps enough to kill and dry out nearby vegetation to ignition point, so clear a surrounding firebreak.

Laying the fire

A good arrangement is shown in the illustration. Use dry material and keep it open and wigwam-shaped, to allow air to enter underneath and create a draft that will take the flames and gases vertically upward.

Ignition

Don't light a fire on a windy day, when the risk of losing control is greatest. Have some emergency equipment to hand, such as a hose or pail of water. Always light the pile on the downwind side so the fire burns back into the wind and odd strong gusts can only push flames toward burned-out material.

Extinction

The heart of a burned-out bonfire can remain red hot for a long time. To make sure there's no risk of red-hot ashes blowing away to start a fire elsewhere, the ashes must be raked and turned over until no glowing fragments can be seen. Spreading the ashes will assist cooling.

Bonfire ash

Wood ash is rich in potash; "pot-ash" is in fact so called because the ashes from wood fires were once used to clean pots. Ash has a high pH and is very soluble and rapidly leached out by rain. So the cold ashes must either be stored somewhere dry or applied immediately where they are needed.

Magic mounds and carpets

The two great joys of the magic mound are that it thrives on slow-rotting material such as hedge clippings and woody brassica stems, and that its shape physically increases the surface area of usable ground. This combination makes it especially attractive for a small garden. Once built, the mound needs no more digging, making it an even more enchanting proposition.

The materials

You will need: slow-composting materials; sods; dead leaves; rough compost; and fine compost. With these components assembled, together with wheelbarrow, spade, rake, and watering can, you can assemble the mound.

Site preparation

As with most vegetable beds in high latitudes, the mound should run in a north-south direction. The first step is to dig a trench to a spade's depth and about 5ft (1.5m) wide, piling soil along both sides. In the center of this trench, dig a second one-spit trench 20in (50cm) wide, leaving a ledge at each end about the same width.

Filling and building

Into the central trench, pile roughly chopped tough plant material, heaping it up to ground level. Add a little of the dug-out soil. Next, pack a layer of sods, grass-side down, covering the rough material. Water this layer and mold and pat it into a smooth shape. The layer of leaves comes next, mixed with more dug-out soil and sprinkled with more water. Lay smaller leaves first and use big ones on top.

Use half-rotted material and green manure (see p. 222) here, adding more dug-out soil as you go. By now, the outer trench should be nearly filled.

The final layer is 3–8in (7–20cm) of rich finished compost.

Caution

If you import some of the components from neighbors or other sources, be alert to the risk of contamination with herbicides or pesticides. Take great care to ensure that nothing of this sort gets into your mound, because it will at best inhibit the vital microorganisms, and at worst could destroy the entire project.

Planting

The mound is obviously not suited for growing crops that need to be dug out, but otherwise can be treated as a normal vegetable plot.

Life cycle

As the components decompose, the mound will gradually sink until, after 4–5 years, it becomes almost flat. It can now form the basis for a conventional raised bed, or you may prefer to begin another mound elsewhere.

Carpet mulch

Another neat trick with a lump of large, hard-to-compost material is to put on a carpet mulch.

The principle of mulching to reclaim ground can be extended to using an old carpet, laid down on top of a patch of weedy ground. It will allow rain and air to pass through and provide warm, moist cover for earthworms, but smother the unwanted weeds.

A completely natural carpet will rot down completely in a year or two, leaving the sort of worm-rich soil that provides ideal growing conditions. Laying newspaper or cardboard under the carpet can provide longer-term cover and give even better results.

Semi-synthetic carpet is trickier, because it won't ever quite go away and may not be permeable enough, but it can be used for through-planting as black plastic or cardboard (see p.221).

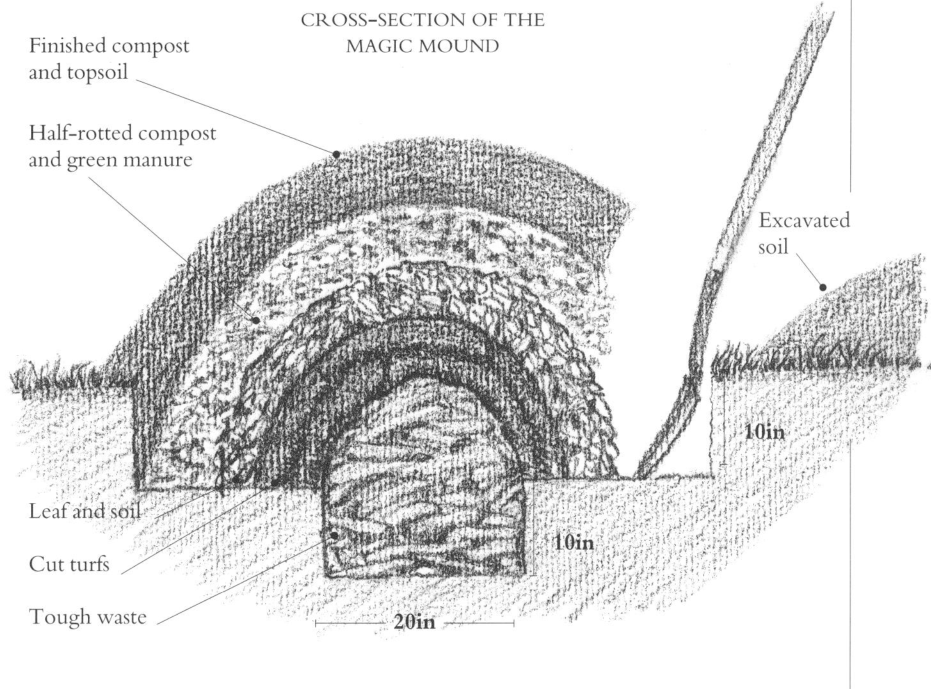

Making Compost

Nature is truly a matter of life and death, in that the continuity of life is inseparable from death and decay. Wherever there's life, a multitude of small, smaller, and smallest organisms feed on the dead bodies of plants and animals, and on each other, ceaselessly processing organic material for recycling. Apart from chopping woody wastes and crumbling shell and bone, they also reduce the complex molecules of leaf and meat to simpler substances which plants can feed on. Thus the cycle of life is perpetuated. And thus, one way or another, healthy soil will fertilize itself.

Anything organic, tossed on to the ground, will rot down sooner or later and get back into the system. The main difference between doing this and making proper compost is that when you build a compost pile you create a purpose-built structure to encourage and assist specific bacteria that work fast, instead of leaving it to chance.

Building organic material into a pile is a start. This will retain moisture and concentrate the decay organisms as they feed, breed, and multiply within the pile. First of all, air-breathing (aerobic) microorganisms attack the pile. They can soon exhaust the available oxygen, however, making life impossible for themselves while making it more suitable for non air-breathers – the anaerobic ones.

Anaerobic decay

The anaerobic way of life is more ancient than the aerobic way but, being primitive, it's also less efficient. Anaerobic decay is slower than aerobic decay; it uses less of the available energy, and can even cease altogether before it's complete. Coal is imperfectly composted wood that once sank into the airless, acidic mud of a prehistoric forest floor; when we burn it, we are in fact extracting the energy – genuine fossilized sunlight – that has been trapped inside ever since the leaves of those trees soaked it up, around 300 million years ago. Peat is formed by a similar process, though it's a great deal younger than coal. Peat bogs also reveal the acidity which is another cause of incomplete composting.

Air and acid

To encourage aerobic decay, then, the pile must be aerated. This can be done by tossing and turning it, by stabbing deep air holes with a garden fork, or by including layers of coarse, loosely packed materials such as straw or fibrous weeds. Acidity can be countered by any mildly alkaline material, such as powdered lime, crushed egg shells, calcified seaweed, wood ash, or ground dolomite.

Carbon: nitrogen ratio

The secret of commercially produced compost "activators" is, in a word, nitrogen. To turn your compost into nourishing plant food, rather than just a textured soil conditioner, the pile needs to be given enough nitrogen to balance out the high levels of carbon locked up in cellulose fiber. A handy source of nitrogen – and one that's free – is HLA (i.e. Household Liquid Activator), which is simply urine diluted 1:3 with water. Other activators are provided by fresh animal dung; fresh young stinging nettles; seaweed; dried blood; sewage sludge; and fishmeal.

Heat

An especially magical property of the aerobic compost pile is the heat it generates. This is a by-product of the hectic bacterial activity within, just a tiny fraction of the energy being exchanged. As well as helping to sustain the pace of life within the pile, the heat destroys weed seeds by cooking them. This can be enhanced by enclosing and covering the pile to prevent heat and moisture loss and also protect from rain. As decomposition passes its peak, the temperature falls. This means the aerobic phase is coming to an end, and the finishing touches are provided largely by anaerobic creatures or worms.

The four basics

Air, acidity, C:N ratio, and warmth are the cornerstones of successful composting. As long as they are understood and catered to, and as long as the moisture content is compatible with aerobic life, the selection and operation of your chosen system depends entirely on your own needs and resources. Carefully constituted and arranged, garden and kitchen waste can become compost in a couple of months, but even an *ad-hoc* pile will yield compost of some sort eventually, although it may take a full year.

TABLE OF C:N RATIOS FOR COMPOST MATERIALS

	C	N
Urine		★★★★
Dried blood		★★★★
Fishmeal		★★★
Poultry manure		★★★
Cow manure (neat)		★★★
Grass clippings		★★
Comfrey		★★
Pomace		★★
Hops		★★
Tomato stalks	★	★★
Pig manure		★★
Farmyard manure	★★	★★★
Seaweed	★	★★
Legume tops		★★
Pea and bean stalks		★★
Horse manure (with straw)	★	★★
Peat	★	★
Oat straw	★★	★
Garden weeds	★★	★
Newspaper	★★	
Wheat straw	★★★	
Woody stems	★★★	
Sawdust	★★★★	

(Materials are mixed in pile to give equal C:N ratios)

Heating Effect in an Aerobic Compost Heap

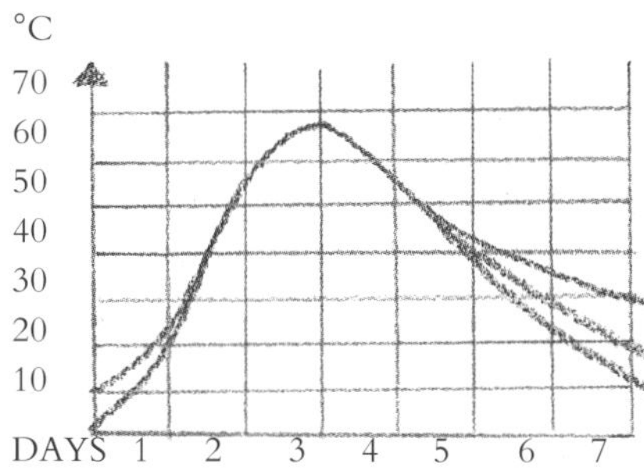
°C
70
60
50
40
30
20
10
DAYS 1 2 3 4 5 6 7

Given the correct balance of air, moisture, and solids, the aerobic pile rapidly heats up to over 140°F.

Site and general considerations

The compost pile should be sited in a shady place, out of direct sunlight. Remember to allow room for easy access, tossing, and turning. If you plan to construct a seriously scientific pile, such as Kitto's (see p. 214), the components will need to be assembled and stored separately until enough material of each type has accumulated, and this requires quite a lot of space.

The size of your garden and the state of your soil, together with the relative size of your vegetable plot, will probably influence your choice of system. A two-pile system is only really workable in a fairly large garden, and the more complex layered systems call for a wide variety of materials.

It's hard to imagine having too much compost but, even if production should outstrip demand, good compost can always find a home. If you need to store compost, take care to keep it covered so as to retain the soluble nutrients.

Using compost

Compost is your natural garden's staple diet. Like any good food, it can stand alone or be blended into any number of other dishes. You can simply use it as the rich, dark soil that it is, to cultivate exotic plants in flowerpots, to grow greedy vegetables in trenches or raised beds, or to raise anything else that requires good, nourishing earth. It can be a moisture-retaining and nutrient-rich mulch for permanent plantings or an annual top-dressing to replace nutrients harvested from the vegetable patch. Compost also improves the texture of virtually any soil.

Because good compost releases its nutrients most readily in the warm, moist conditions that also favor plant growth, once on the ground it can do nothing but good. Practically the only time you could "waste" your hard-won compost might be in a warm fall. On growing crops, its nutrients are used as they're released, and in winter it can be a duvet to keep your worms active while they dig it in for you.

Nil desperandum

Don't worry if your compost isn't textbook perfect. Incomplete compost is no less organic, and can still put goodness into the soil. If it isn't finished by the winter, you can either call it a slow pile and wait another year, or go ahead and spread it on to the vegetable plot anyway. The worms will enjoy the shelter and go on working underneath, dragging it, little by little, under the surface.

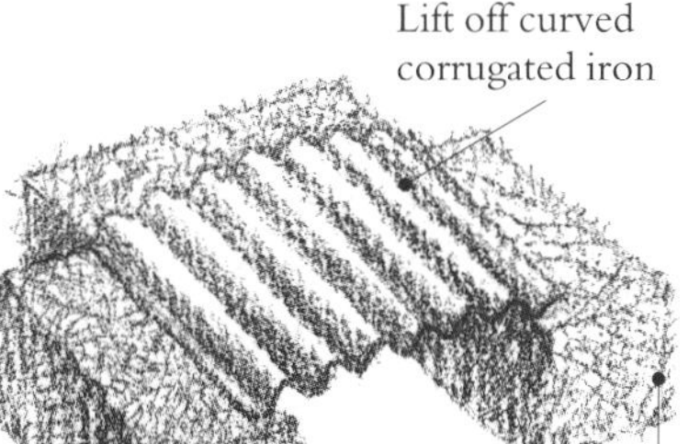
Lift off curved corrugated iron
Hay bales can be single or double stacked

The pile

A simple pile won't heat up properly unless it's big. It must be covered with straw, earth and/or tarpaulin to retain warmth, gases, and moisture and repel cold or excessive rain. If you're keen on lowest possible labor and can be philosophical about possible failure, this approach may suit you.

Home-made bins

A "passive" container might be built from pallets; an "active" one from straw or hay bales. Both allow ventilation and give moisture retention and insulation, but the bales will eventually become part of the compost while the pallet bin is emptied and reused.

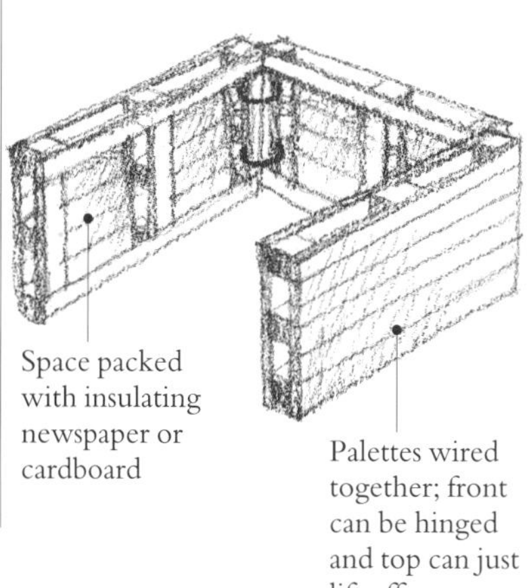
Space packed with insulating newspaper or cardboard
Palettes wired together; front can be hinged and top can just lift off

Above *Insulation is easily provided and helps the pile to retain warmth, assisting the decay organisms and sustaining seed-destroying temperatures.*

Left *A waterproof covering protects from cold rain and from waterlogging, which would chill the pile.*

Brandname bins
A bewildering variety of brandname compost bins exists, each claiming superiority. They may be better than home-made bins in deterring vermin, but they all use energy in their manufacture, and constitute yet another item that you may be able to avoid buying in. Bear in mind also that contact with the soil is believed to be biodynamically essential.

Conical bin
Turning the compost, at least once, works wonders. A lightweight container shaped like a giant flowerpot can help to make this easier.

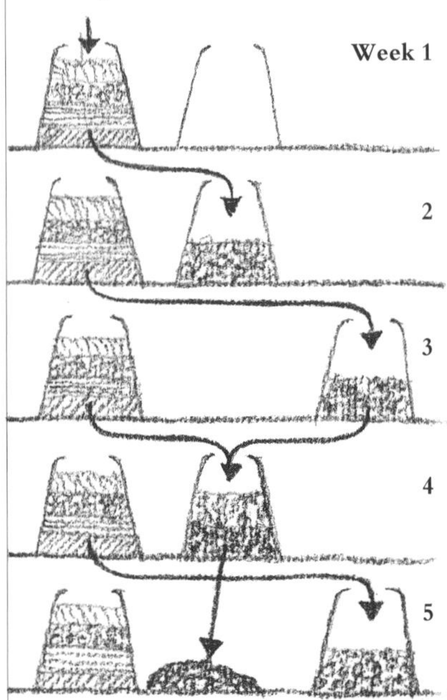

Using two bottomless plastic garbage bins and their lids, a pile of compost can be completed in a month. Bin 1 is filled with fresh waste each week. At the end of each week, bin 2 is lifted off and moved, and then refilled with the contents of bin 1 plus its own contents. In effect, this system tidily achieves weekly turning and topping up, while keeping the compost fully sheltered.

Continuous process
A bin with solid sides and open-mesh vertically sliding front can provide a continuous supply of compost. Raw material goes in at the top and compost comes out at the bottom. Replenishment and removal thus becomes an effective production line, so long as the in-and-out rates match reasonably well. This type of bin will need an annual clear-out.

Right *Making compost by the continuous process requires good ventilation. The wire-mesh allows air to enter the pile at all levels, while the sloping lid keeps out rain and helps to retain heat.*

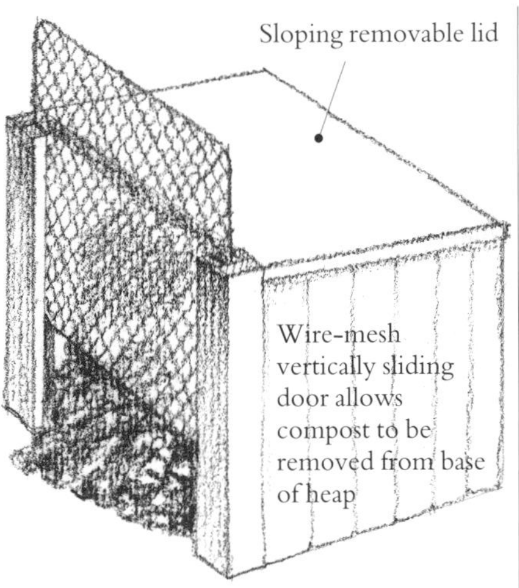

Kitto's method
The acme of composting systems is the three-bin method developed by Dick Kitto. Using this system, the compost materials are stored in the first bay, as and when they become available. When enough variety has accumulated it is arranged in layers in the central bay, like a large club sandwich, and watered well (with urine if available, or adding accelerator if not). After a couple of weeks, this pile is sliced vertically and the slices tossed lightly into the third bin, moistened again, and left to ripen to maturity.

Above *Fibrous material at the base lets air in. On top of this, pile alternate layers of high-C and high-N materials, with calcium to prevent acidity.*

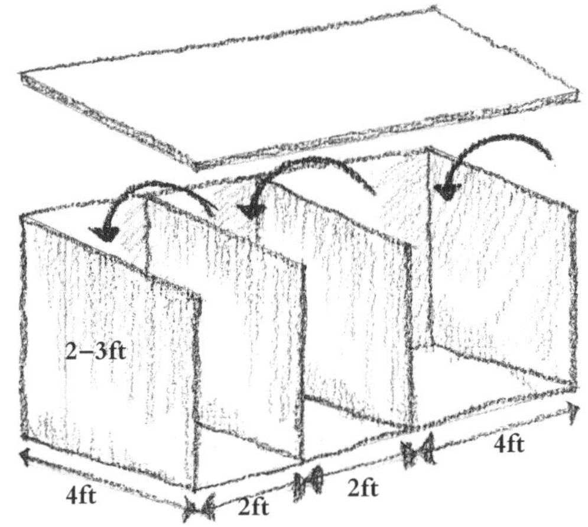

Left *In Kitto's method, you use the wide bay to store compostable materials separately, in bags or boxes as appropriate. When enough is collected to fill completely the central bay, arrange in layers as above, and moisten. After 2 weeks, chop into vertical slices and toss into left-hand bay, moisten again, and leave to ripen.*

Critical balance

All of nature is a complex balancing act, most of it still far beyond our understanding. It isn't surprising, then, that the most common reason for failure in an artificially constructed compost pile is a lack of balance. Carbon and nitrogen should balance out; so should wet and dry, animal and vegetable, coarse and fine, and so on. Oxygen supply must be adequate, and moisture for life must be set against chilling, suffocating damp.

Urine – liquid gold

The ideal compost activator is a fluid every gardener has a regular supply of. Fresh urine, watered on to the compost directly or via a watering can, balances the high-carbon material such as straw perfectly. In fact, a bale of hay or straw used as a urinal in the garden will transform itself into delicious, sweet-smelling compost in a few months.

The principle of the composting urinal is taken a stage further by the composting toilet, a system that was well known to our grandparents and still remains valid (see p. 217). In situations where this is possible, however, there is probably already a septic tank or a cess pit, which is halfway there.

Composting sewage

Septic tank sludge isn't compost, but it makes good fertilizer. The real "sludge" is dark and relatively odourless and settles out on the bottom after decomposition is almost complete. Check with local regulations to see whether sewage composting is permitted in your area.

In a one-tank system (cess pit) or the first tank of a two-tank system, the sludge lies deep beneath a floating crust of nearly raw sewage. If you're determined enough, and take sensible precautions, this crust can be combined with straw to make proper compost. First, lay a bed of straw (or dried bracken) in a deep, tall bin. Then, wearing rubber gloves, skim off the crust with improvised equipment and transfer it in a watertight wheelbarrow to the prepared bed. Add the crust-sludge in blobs and cover with 9in (20cm) more straw before blobbing more on top. Continue until no more crust-sludge remains and then top off with straw. Clean the wheelbarrow and all tools used, and leave them in the sun to complete cleansing.

After 3–6 months, turn the pile and add urine if it's too dry. In a year's time it will be suitable for composting non-edible crops.

> THE TWO-PILE SYSTEM
>
> In a large garden it is worth setting up two compost piles, one a fast system for making "safe" compost to feed edible vegetables, and the other for processing difficult things such as pet litter, woody waste, and other materials which break down very slowly and/or may be unsuitable for edible crops. The "slow" pile could be used to feed trees (including fruit trees) and non-edibles.

Leafmold

When they shed their leaves, deciduous trees first suck them dry so as to salvage as much goodness as they can. Fallen leaves therefore contain little in the way of nutrients, but they make good soil conditioner. Use them as they are in magic mounds, add to compost, or apply as mulch and let the worms dig them in for you.

Alternatively, store leaves in a plastic trash bag, stabbed here and there with a garden fork, or in a chicken-wire bin, and leave them to rot down into fibrous humus. This makes a good mulch or potting medium, but some rich, nourishing compost will have to be added to feed seedlings.

Generally speaking, evergreen leaves should be kept apart and rotted down separately, because they take longer to decompose and can contain aromatics that inhibit microorganisms.

Observe local trees and use your own observations to deduce the relative merits and rate of decomposition of their fallen leaves.

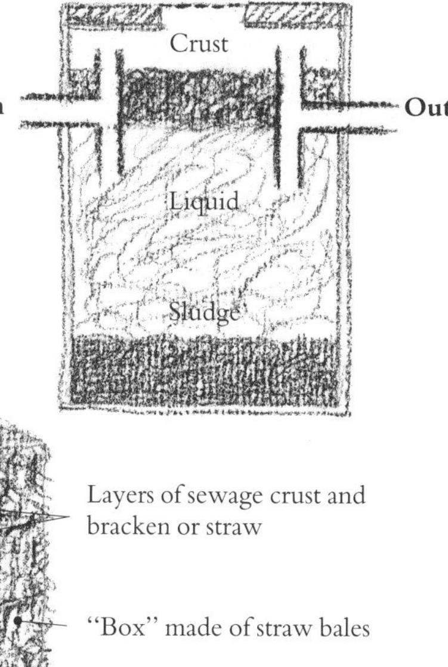

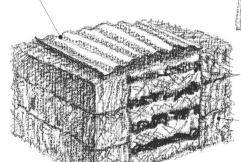

Cover with plastic sheet or corrugated iron weighted down

Layers of sewage crust and bracken or straw

"Box" made of straw bales

Wormpost

Every child learns that worms are the gardener's best friend, but the value of their labors is constantly being updated. Not only do they ventilate and fertilize the soil, but they seem to improve its water-retentive properties and even to protect growing seedlings from damping-off.

Worm compost is truly in a class of its own. It's an exotic yet utterly down-to-earth substance that anybody can get, in exchange for ordinary everyday kitchen garbage.

Garbage bin wormery

A simple way of setting worms to work for you is to make a few easy modifications to a plastic garbage bin. First use a heated skewer to make a band of small holes (for drainage) 3–6in (7–15cm) from the base of the bin, and another ring of holes (for ventilation) in the lid.

Inside the bin, lay a mixture of sand and gravel 6in (15cm) deep and place some wooden slats on top of this layer. Add water until it seeps from the drainage holes. On top of the boards, add a good layer of damp peat and follow this with your first load of chopped household waste, mixed with chopped paper, not more than 6in (15cm) deep. A sprinkling of calcified seaweed (or crushed dried egg shells) on the surface is all that's left to be done after the worms go in.

Introducing the worms

The worms to use are the red and manure worms that normally live in compost. Local names vary, however, whereas the Latin names, *Helodrilus foetidus* and *Lumbricus rubellus*, are universal, like the worms themselves. These small worms can cope with the richly nitrogenous waste that comes out of the kitchen. Place them on top of the peat, underneath the garbage.

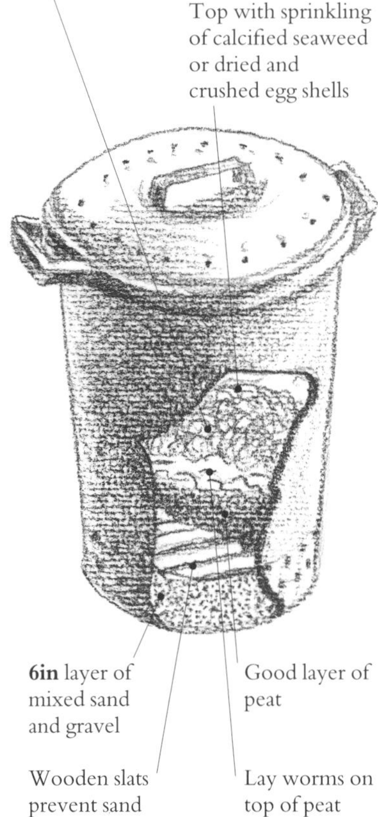
Chopped food waste mixed with shredded paper up to **15cm** deep
Top with sprinkling of calcified seaweed or dried and crushed egg shells
6in layer of mixed sand and gravel
Good layer of peat
Wooden slats prevent sand mixing in with other materials
Lay worms on top of peat

As they make themselves at home, dragging the garbage down into the peat to eat, you can add more scraps on top. Go easy at first, until the worms have begun to multiply, and remember to add more calcified seaweed (or egg shells) for each 6in (15cm) of garbage.

The end product

After about 6 months, the garbage bin should be full of dark, sweet compost, and heaving with worms! When emptying the bin, pick out as many worms as you need to start again. Use the compost as you would use concentrated well-rotted manure, lightly hoed into the vegetable plots and even mixed into potting mix.

St Christopher wormery

An outdoor wormery can be built of used car tires, stacked up on an earth base and with a wood or metal lid on top. Stuff the tires with crumpled newspaper, and fill up slowly with kitchen and garden waste (not forgetting the calcified seaweed or egg shells). More tires can be stacked up as required, and the beauty of this system is that when you remove the compost enough worms remain behind in the tires to begin the process again. Take care not to remove them! It also has the advantage of being warmer than the thin-walled garbage bin, especially if you insulate the lid.

Snug-fitting lid
Tire voids stuffed with shredded newspaper
Fill central hole with kitchen waste, weeds, etc. and add worms

Composting toilets

A dry composting toilet has the double advantage of operating without the need for flushing water, and providing you with a ready-made supply of compost. There are many designs available, ranging from the commercial "clivus multrum" used in Sweden, to the home-made twin-vault system, both of which are shown here. All work on the same principle, of encouraging the aerobic decomposition of organic food waste.

For the DIY enthusiast, the twin-vault system is probably the best one to tackle, because it involves virtually no handling of the product until it is ready. It consists of two chambers, each made of rendered concrete blocks, with removable plywood doors. A floor is made to sit on the top of these chambers with two holes, one of which is fitted with a toilet seat. One hole is used at a time, and after each use, sawdust is added to soak up moisture, absorb smells, and add carbon-rich material. When one side is full, a plate is placed over the hole, and the seat is moved to the other side. By the time this side is full, the contents of the other side should be ready to remove and use, being suitable for application near trees and fruit bushes.

THE CLIVUS MULTRUM WATERLESS TOILET

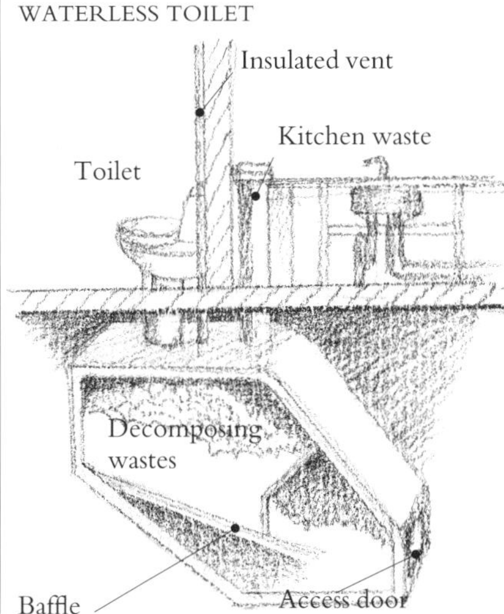

Recycling gray water

It makes sense to conserve water, especially in arid regions. Apart from being virtuous, if your water supplies are metered it makes good economic sense to use paid-for water twice over. The chief challenge in reusing household "gray" water comes from possible fats, salts, and other residues it contains, which produce a combination of minor physical and biological problems. You can either ignore the problem and use gray water only for irrigating permanent plantings, or make a greater effort and obtain water fit for the vegetable plot.

The simplest approach is to run gray water straight on to permanent plantings when needed. When planning to do this, though, it's important to allow for surges and to install several "switch" points. Surges can be dealt with by first running the water into a tank. The first and most important switch point comes before the water enters this tank. In case of in-house contamination of water, there must be a way to run the water straight into the normal sewage system. There must also (often, by law) be a valve to prevent gray water flowing back into the household supply.

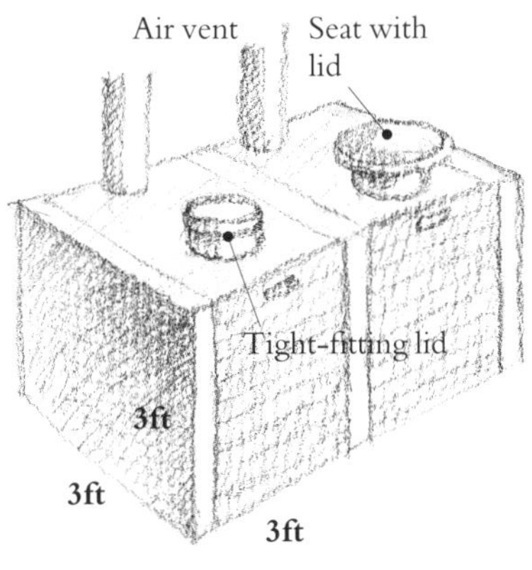

THE TWIN-VAULT SYSTEM
The walls and floor are of concrete, with removable wood doors at front.

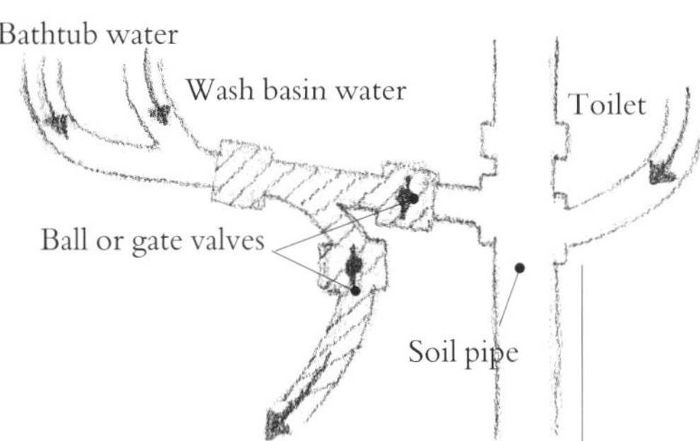

If kitchen gray water is excluded from the system then the worst problem, fat, virtually disappears. It is, however, possible to install a straw filter in the tank to remove food wastes (including fat). This must then be regularly replaced, and the old one dumped on to the compost pile.

The outflow pipe from the surge tank needs a gate valve for control. It may be necessary to introduce another switch point here, to run excess water into the main sewer.

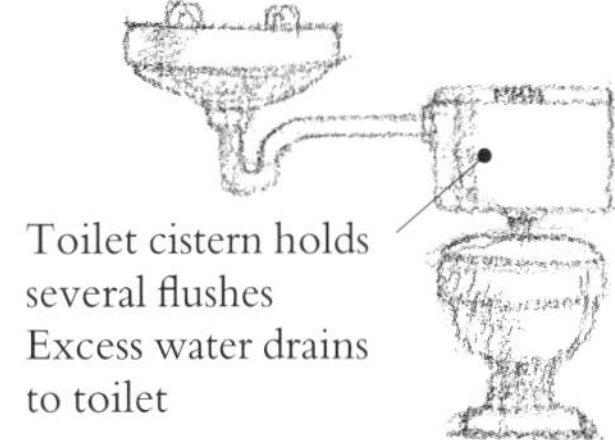

Gray water flush toilets

A neat way of reducing the amount of clean water used in toilet flushing is to collect the gray water released after handwashing in the toilet cistern. A simple plumbing modification (illustrated) is all that is needed.

Reedbed system
If you wish to conserve large amounts of gray water, it may be worth installing a simple reedbed system. In this case, instead of using a surge tank, the outflow pipe feeds into a much larger tank, containing gravel and planted with a local variety of *Phragmites* reed. Water from this processing tank will be "treated" by bacteria lurking in the reed root systems and can either pass into a soakaway or irrigation system, or be used for watering, or be designed to serve either purpose at will. This system doesn't work very well at low temperatures, so it may still be necessary to divert gray water from the house into the main sewer in winter.

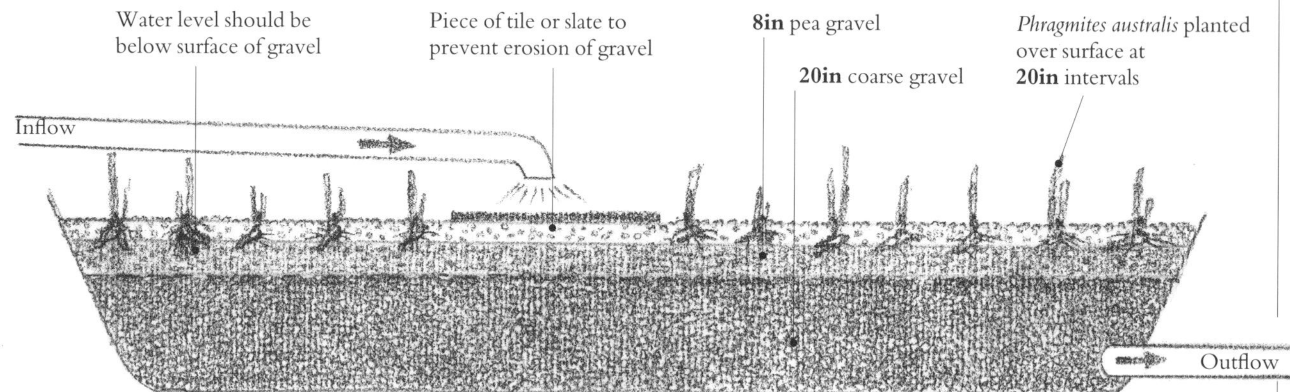

Using gray water
In times of drought, the vegetable plot generally receives its share of tender loving care via the watering can, but trees and other permanent plantings might be neglected. This is where gray water can serve very well. A simple permanent hand-irrigation system can be set up using lengths of perforated plastic pipe, bent upward and capped at both ends. It's simple to run in water from your holding tank or *Phragmites* bed to fill up the pipe, then disconnect after a day or so and leave the water to soak into the ground. If the water comes direct from the surge tank, rotating from pipe to pipe prevents the build-up of clogging residues and allows drying-out time, giving soil organisms a chance to break down raw organic matter before the next delivery. This system is especially useful for watering soft fruit bushes.

pH problems
The gray water will almost certainly be alkaline. On acid soils, this is beneficial up to a point. Test pH regularly, however, to make sure it does not rise above 7.

Hints on using gray water
• Use environment-friendly washing products • Allow a rest period between waterings • Apply to permanently planted areas, such as trees and soft fruit bushes.

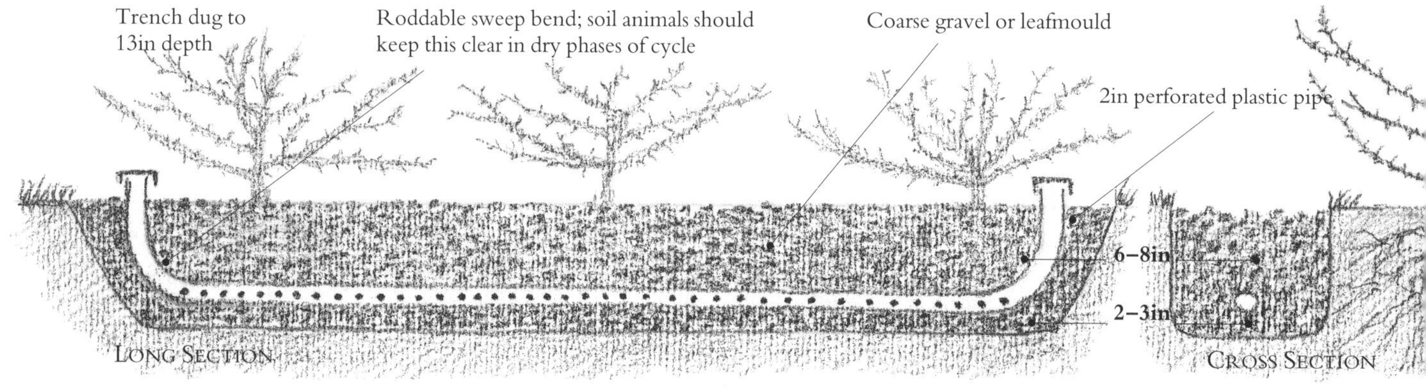

IMPROVING YOUR SOIL

Real soil is not inert stuff, with no function other than to provide a moist, fertile foothold for plants. Although this may unfortunately be true of much of the world's farmland, smothered and spoiled over the years by repeated application of unbalanced fertilizers and indiscriminate poisons, natural soil is a vastly complex ecological system.

Your investigations will have revealed many of your own soil's unique properties – its pH, texture, warmth- and moisture-retaining abilities, and the variety of living things that inhabit it (or depend on those that do). During the exploratory process, you'll inevitably develop a feeling for its intrinsic nature and begin to see how you can best work with it. At the same time, you may well have identified some features that you'd like to improve or correct – or even adapt more drastically to accommodate plants with special needs.

Even if the soil is healthy and well-balanced, the demands of cultivation will place a burden on it that a wild place doesn't suffer. You're going to ask more of your soil, in terms of variety, productivity, and traffic, than a garden-sized patch of the wild could ever provide. It makes sense, then, to prepare the ground carefully in anticipation of these demands, and to plan for continued sustenance.

Digging

The first reason for digging the ground is to remove unwanted growth from the area before introducing what you want to grow. This ensures that all available light, water, and nutrients go into your chosen plants, and that they aren't overwhelmed by other species which are already flourishing because they're very much at home.

Clearing and weeding are not the only aims, though. Digging introduces air, which helps roots and soil fauna to breathe; it breaks up the ground to allow roots to penetrate more deeply and widely; this also helps to encourage rain water or irrigation water to soak in and spread underground. And while you're digging, you add and incorporate a variety of substances to enhance and fertilize the soil.

Disadvantages of digging

Exposing new soil on the surface can accelerate drying-out and it can also bring deeply buried weed seeds to the surface where they'll be stimulated to germinate. Repeated digging can even do more harm than good to the soil structure as a whole. The basis of the "no-till" philosophy is that, once cultivation is under way, regular mulching and surface-hoeing are all that's necessary to keep the soil – and your back – in good condition.

Breaking new ground

Unless the soil is already in exceptional condition, even when you plan to adopt the no-till system, any "new" patch of ground must first of all be broken. Every single perennial weed should be removed now, taking care not to compact the already-dug soil by walking on it. At the same time, your soil analysis data will enable you to add whatever is necessary to remedy actual and potential problems by incorporating new material as you go along.

It pays to perform this ground-breaking ceremony thoroughly and carefully, to do it at the correct time of year, and in the best possible conditions. Generally speaking, heavy (clay) soil in temperate regions is best dug in the fall, leaving the clods to be broken up by frosts. With lighter (sandy) soils, and in warmer climates, early spring is a better time. Sandy soil is rarely difficult to dig; clay soil can be very heavy and sticky when wet or iron-hard when dry, so you need to catch the moment when it's moist enough to work but not so wet that it's impracticable. Whatever the soil type, you will be adding a forkful of compost, strawy manure, or other mixed organic material for each spade-square section of ground you dig, so don't even think about starting to dig until you have collected enough of this material. The reward for all this hard work is that, if it's done right, it may never have to be done again.

Single-dig

Begin by digging an exploratory hole two spits (spade's depths) deep. Look to see whether there's a compacted layer beneath the first spit. If the compaction is limited to the upper spit, and there aren't too many deep-rooted perennial weeds, it may be possible to get away with merely single-digging the bed. Follow the plan shown on p. 220, adding a fork-load of manure or compost to each hole before transferring the next weeded spit into it. Collect the extracted weeds as you go, to add to the slow compost pile. If you choose to take the risk, it is possible to cut down on hand-picking weeds by turning each spit of soil upside-down as you move it, thus burying the weeds. Don't expect this to be 100 percent successful, however.

Double-dig

Double-digging is more thorough, more laborious, and a little more complicated than single-digging. If the soil is deeply compacted, or if there's a hard pan below the top spit where rain water has deposited fine soil particles, however, the effort will be repaid in full by the resulting improvements to both topsoil and subsoil, both in the long and short term.

The important rule is that subsoil and topsoil must not be mixed or muddled up. A lazy way – which could be called one-and-a-half-dig – is to proceed as for single-till but, instead of just shoveling compost into the hole, first deeply pierce and loosen the subsoil with a fork and then stir the organic material in, before covering it with the next spit of topsoil.

Proper double-digging is begun by taking out a spit of topsoil from each of the first two squares, plus a spit of subsoil from the first only, and removing them to the diagonal corner. Now take the subsoil from the second square and drop it into the first hole, adding compost or manure at the same time. Cover this with topsoil from the third square, put subsoil from square three (plus organic material) into hole two, and so on.

Bastard trench

There are many more methods of digging, each with its champions and its critics. One that's worth mentioning is called bastard trenching. Here, the rule about not muddling topsoil and subsoil is reversed (see below), but there's still no getting away from the necessity of incorporating manure, compost, or organic refuse.

Bastard trenching breaks the rules. Topsoil becomes subsoil, subsoil becomes topsoil. Burying topsoil helps to smother weeds, saving hand-weeding; exposed subsoil will soon be improved by mulching. On the way, the base layer is broken, stirred, and compost-enriched.

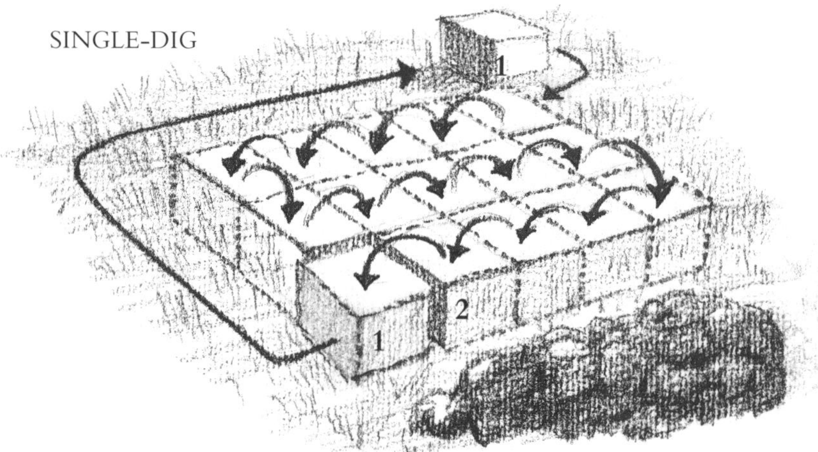

Whether single- or double-digging, it pays to be systematic. For single-dig, remove the first spit (spade's depth) of soil and take it to the opposite diagonal corner, where it will finally be used. All you need to do now is dig each spit in turn, weed it, add compost, and leave it in the hole that was vacated by the previous spit.

When double-digging, you first remove two top spits and one bottom spit, as shown. The bottom spit from square 2 is weeded, composted, and heaved into hole 1. Then the top spit from square 3 is weeded and used to fill up hole 1. The pattern has now moved one square sideways, and is repeated as follows: bottom spit from square 3 goes into bottom of hole 2; top spit from square 4 fills up hole 2.

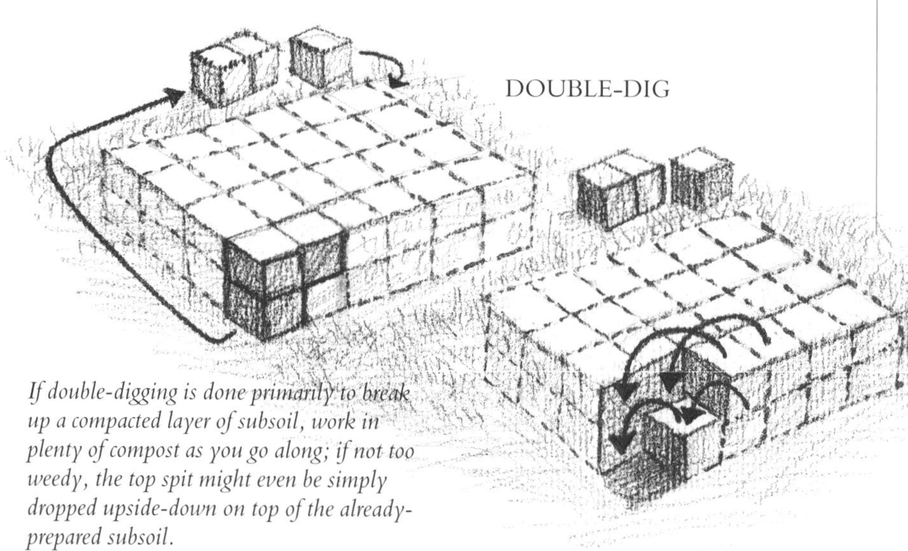

If double-digging is done primarily to break up a compacted layer of subsoil, work in plenty of compost as you go along; if not too weedy, the top spit might even be simply dropped upside-down on top of the already-prepared subsoil.

No-dig methods

Once the soil has been broken and mixed with compost, worms and other organisms will start to work and multiply in the improved conditions you have created for them. One of the benefits of abundant, healthy, busy soil fauna is that they will take over the digging for you. From now on, all that may be needed is a top-dressing of partly composted material, each fall, together with sheet mulch. By the time the sowing season comes around, most if not all of it will have been dragged under by earthworms. All you'll have to do is lightly hoe surface weeds (incorporating completed compost if you wish) before planting or sowing.

This is the basis of the classic no-dig method. A mulch helps to suppress weeds, thus removing one reason for digging; the organic material gradually disappears into the soil, thus removing another reason. If you're careful not to compact the ground by walking on it, the last reason for digging also disappears. Why it works and makes such good sense is that it's a perfectly natural system – there isn't a lot of double-digging going on in the natural world, after all!

But there are some natural diggers and stirrers of soil, such as moles and pigs, and therefore, nature being the economical system that it is, there are bound to be some plants that are adapted to grow on disturbed ground. Your vegetable plot, regularly disturbed by planting and removing crops, is the ideal habitat for these plants. You'll never do away with hoeing altogether, unless you can keep the entire surface of the plot blanketed with a light-proof barrier.

SOIL ADDITIVES AND THEIR USES

Name	Use	How	Additional
Blood (dried)	Fast N	2–4oz/sq yd	Activate compost
Bone (meal)	Slow P (Ca)	4oz/sq yd	
Bracken	K; P	1lb (ash)/sq yd	Cut green, compost or burn first
Calc. seaweed	50% Ca + K; P	4oz/sq yd	Also raises pH
Dolomite	Ca; Mg	4oz/sq yd	Corrects Mg deficiency
Fishmeal	N; P; K + traces	3oz/sq yd	Variable quality, expensive
Goat manure	N; P; K	Compost Liquid manure	Rot with straw. Hang bagful 1 week in water, dilute well
Gypsum	Clay conditioner	8oz/sq yd	Also adds S
Hair, fur, wool, feathers	Slow N	Compost	Dig into bed in winter
Hops	Soil improver	2–3lb/sq yd	Dig in, with N source
Horse manure	N; P; K	Strawy, rot well	Enclosed pile
Leafmold	Soil improver	5lb/sq yd	Mulch in spring
Mushroom compost	Alternative compost	Mulch	Beware insecticide
Pig manure	N; P; K	Compost with straw	Beware Cu
Poultry manure	P; K; N	Compost Powdered top-dressing, 8oz/sq yd	Good activator Leafy crops; can spoil clay soil
Rock potash	Very slow K	8oz/sq yd	Natural rock flour
Rock phosphate	Very slow P	8oz/sq yd	Natural rock flour
Seaweed	Many	Fresh, dry, spray	See p. 224
Soot	N; P	For trees	Darkens soil
Wood ash	Fast K (raises pH)	4oz/sq yd	Very soluble; store dry or use to activate compost

Sheet composting

The principle here is to keep the whole bed in darkness, except where your chosen crops are permitted to emerge into the light. Apply compost over the entire surface, and then cover it with a layer of newspaper, cardboard, or old carpet, or even heavyweight black plastic. Porous materials are best, however, since they allow rain water and air to penetrate, although, in high latitudes and especially with clay soils, clear plastic can help to speed up spring warming. Underneath, the worms will chew away happily, mixing the compost in, and you can simply cut slits in the sheet mulch to insert your seedlings. This way, you can encourage natural soil improvers at the same time as getting a crop.

Living compost

Green manures and cover crops do the same sort of job, but in two stages. While they're growing, they make dense ground cover that shades out seedlings already present and prevents new seeds from reaching the ground. Before they go to seed themselves, you can either cut the tops off, leaving their widespread roots to add organic matter, dig the whole crop in as "green manure", or pull them up and compost them separately. Some green manures, such as mustard, can be left in place to be killed by frost, but they'll naturally have set seed in the meantime. They are useful, however, when you want to keep a patch of ground "in hand" for more than a year, while steadily improving its condition.

Selecting green manures

When selecting green manures, it's important to choose horses for courses. The grass family tends to have widespread roots, and so is useful for penetration; Hungarian rye does a particularly good job in this respect. In temperate regions, winter hardiness is important because this allows a cover crop to stand through the winter, when the ground might otherwise be left idle.

Many of the best plants to use for green manures are those of the pea and bean family, called legumes.

Perennial legumes

The roots of leguminous plants – clovers, vetches, peas, beans, lupins, and many others – have the ability to grow lumps called nodules. These nodules shelter specific bacteria, which have the rare talent of being able to take nitrogen gas from the air itself and turn it into a chemical form that is readily available to plants. Although nitrogen gas makes up the greater proportion of air, plants cannot make use of this element unless it's fed to their roots in some chemical compound form, such as nitrates (which are breakdown products of proteins). Having nitrogen-fixing bacteria cuddled around their roots gives legumes a distinct advantage over other, plainly rooted plants. They can, in fact, flourish in places which are not normally fertile enough for many other plant species.

One benefit to the gardener is the fact that legumes can be grown in poor soil. An even greater potential benefit is

Green Manures

Name	Cover	Benefits	Drawbacks	Sow rate
Alfalfa	Perennial Sow 4/6	N, Ca, Mg, P, K, Mn, Zn. Deep root into subsoil	Hard to kill after 1 yr	⅛oz/sq yd
Beans (*field*)	10/11 – 3/4	Winter-cover legume	Hard frost can kill	6in apart
Buck-wheat	5 – 10/frost	Summer cover; deep roots good on poor soil	Can regrow	1oz/sq yd
Clover (*alsike*)	4/9 – 9/4	Very hardy legume	Hard to kill	⅛oz/sq yd
Clover (*crimson*)	5 – 10	Summer forage legume	Frost can kill	⅛oz/sq yd
Fenugreek	4/9 – 8/4	Fast-growing winter or summer cover	Frost can kill	⅛oz/sq yd
Lupin	4/5 – 9/10	Summer-cover legume good on acid soil	Woody stems if allowed to flower	2in apart
Mustard (*white*)	6 – 9/frost	Fast-growing summer cover, frost-killed	Is a crucifer, so rotate as brassica	⅛oz/sq yd
Phacelia (Calif. bluebell)	5 – 11	Fast-growing summer cover, heavy crop, bee attractant	Self-seeding, hoe before sets if not wanted	⅛oz/sq yd
Rape	7/8 – 9/10	Summer cover	As mustard	⅛oz/sq yd
Rye (*Hungarian/ winter*)	9/10 – 3/5	Winter cover, very fast-growing and hardy	Pigeons eat seeds	1 oz/sq yd
Winter tare	9 – 3	Winter cover legume	Slow growth	⅛oz/sq yd

Months numbered as northern hemisphere: 3–5 = spring; 5–8 = summer; 9–11 = autumn; 11–3 = winter.

that legumes can be grown to improve fertility. Whereas most plants, when they're dug into the soil they grew from, merely put back what they already took out, legumes put back more available nitrogen than was there to begin with. Leaving perennial legumes *in situ* for more than one season steadily enriches the soil, building up its nitrogen content without any extra input.

Legume inoculants

Legumes aren't always naturally well-endowed with nitrogen-fixing bacteria. If the soil is deficient in this respect, they won't grow nodules to house them. It's easy to see whether leguminous plants have root nodules by simply pulling one or two up and looking for obvious pinkish-white lumps. If your legumes have few nodules, or none at all, you can get things started by buying the bacteria, under the name *Rhizobium*, from a plant nursery or specialist supplier, and adding them to the soil. This only needs to be done once, and is very cheap. The easily obtained *Rhizobium* strains will cohabit happily with peas and beans but, if you're growing clover, make sure that the *Rhizobium* you buy is compatible with it.

Legume League Table

Legume	Nitrogen Power (lb/acre)	Other benefits
Alfalfa	*****	Fe; Ca; Mg; P; K; Mn; Zn
White clover	***	P. For honeybees
Red/alsike clover	***	P. Attract bees and other nectar- feeders
Soybeans	**	Edible crop
Hairy vetch	**	K; P; Cu; Co. Winter-hardy
Peanuts	*	Edible crop
Field beans	*	Animal feed/ compost

Soil inoculants

Other nitrogen-fixing bacteria also live independently in healthy soil. Among them are the type called *Azotobacter*. Adding *Azotobacter* at the same time as sowing seed has given increased yields of many different commercially grown crops. If you have inherited an impoverished or otherwise abused patch of land, it might benefit from inoculation with *Azotobacter*.

Dynamic accumulators

Legumes are very special because they add new nitrogen to the soil. Other plants can help to concentrate – or accumulate – other elements, by making extra demands on the soil for these elements in order to use them in building leaf and stem tissue. They are, in a sense, mineral prospectors. If they are allowed to grow in a particular spot, and then are pulled up, the minerals they've collected can be transferred from where they grew to a place where they're needed. There are two obvious advantages to be gained from using dynamic accumulators: to extract excess minerals and to add extra minerals.

In addition to this simple benefit, however, there is a further and more sophisticated advantage to be got from growing dynamic accumulators. Just as the legume bacteria "fix" raw atmospheric nitrogen into compounds

andling	Comments
eed until established	Keep grazing animals away
ther cut or dig in	Cheap if you save own seed
g in for winter	Attracts bees and hoverflies
eed until established	Better on low pH than other clovers
eed until established	Attracts bees
elf-seed unwanted, cut early	Cut tops, leave roots
g in young, cut older for compost	Goes with dug-in turf. Good for compost
g in	Densely sown can clear wireworm
ıt for compost or sheet, or dig in	Seed may be hard to find; once begun, grow your own
ıt and dig in (9); cut and compost (10)	Can cause hay fever
g in	Heavy cover, good on most soils
g in before flowering	Many other vetches have similar use

other raw elements to create mineral compounds that enable less-talented plants to make use of these elements – to pre-digest them, as it were.

Trace elements

Plants can make carbohydrates from air and water, using sunlight energy. In order to make protein, however, they need a supply of nitrogen (N), plus phosphorous (P), potassium (K), together with sulfur (S). This is why the N:P:K ratio is important in assessing fertility (sulfur is rarely deficient in soil).

The wide variety of enzymes and other proteins that plants need in order to develop properly, however, also requires a whole spectrum of other elements, though they're only needed in minute amounts. These are known as trace elements, and they include such substances as manganese, chromium, and copper, which may even be toxic in high concentrations but which, nevertheless, must be present as "traces" for healthy growth (and food value of crops). This is one sound reason for using natural rock flours (rather than synthetically manufactured NPK compounds), which contain a variety of trace elements in addition to N, P, and K. Dynamic accumulators are also useful for either removing or adding trace elements.

Seaweed

Among the wide range of possible additives, seaweed deserves a special mention. It is a dynamic accumulator, although not one that you'd actually grow in your garden. It contains less nitrogen and considerably more potassium than farmyard manure, and provides a very wide spread of trace elements and minerals. When you apply seaweed to your garden, you are in effect assisting the return of essential minerals from the oceans to the land.

A Selection Of Mainly Wild Dynamic Accumulators

Plant	Na	K	Mg	Ca	Mn	Fe	Co	Cu	B	Si	P	S	F	I
Arrowroot				★										
Borage		★								★				
Bracken		★			★	★	★	★			★			
Buckwheat											★			
Burdock						★								
Chickweed		★			★	★		★			★			
Chicory		★	★	★										
Cleavers	★	★		★										
Clover											★			
Coltsfoot		★	★	★		★		★				★		
Comfrey		★	★	★		★				★				
Dandelion	★	★	★	★		★		★		★	★			
Docks		★		★		★					★			
Garlic											★	★	★	
Horsetails			★	★		★	★			★				
Lamb's quarter		★		★		★					★	★		
Meadowsweet	★		★	★		★				★	★	★		
Nettles	★	★		★		★		★		★		★		
Parsley		★	★	★		★								
Plantains		★	★	★		★		★		★		★		
Purslane				★		★					★	★		
Sarsaparilla														★
Silverweed		★	★	★		★		★						
Sorrel	★			★							★			
Sow thistle		★	★					★						
Spurges									★					
Thistles		★				★								
Vetches		★					★	★			★			
Watercress	★	★	★	★		★					★	★	★	
Yarrow		★	★	★				★			★	★		

The richest source of iodine is various seaweeds, e.g. kelp, Iceland moss, dulse, bladderwrack.

Seaweeds contain a wide range of organic substances, including hormones and amino acids, which improve the growth of other plants. As well as promoting growth, they improve uptake and use of nutrients and even increase resistance to pests and diseases.

Fresh seaweed (if you can get it, and if it isn't contaminated with oil, radioactivity, sewage, or heavy metals) can be used as a mulch or added to the compost pile. Dried and powdered, it becomes a wonderfully balanced natural fertilizer. Although it's quite expensive, only 2oz is needed per square yard (70g/sq m). Powdered seaweed also makes good compost activator. Liquid manures based on seaweed are the ideal foliar feed, with all the properties listed above.

Calcified seaweed is a type which resembles coral, because it builds a limey skeleton. It's a marvelous way to add fertility and slow-release lime in one easy stage.

Adjusting pH

The optimum all-round pH is somewhere around 6, which is best for vegetables in general. This is slightly on the acid side, and ought to follow naturally from regular composting. If the soil is quite acid to begin with, however, or if lime-loving plants are to be encouraged, some alkaline substance can be added to correct this. The ideal slow source of lime, which will continue to maintain a constant pH for years after a single treatment, is calcified seaweed, although the ethics of seabed damage done while harvesting it are open to question. Similar results (but without the added organic benefits) can be got from dolomite or ground limestone, which can be added just before planting or sowing. Clay soils require more added alkali to raise pH than sandy ones. Lowering pH is more difficult than raising it, and must be done gradually, so check pH frequently to make sure you don't overcorrect. Although adding lime in a more drastic way (as quicklime or slaked lime) has in many regions been adopted as standard farming practice, it is also said to make farmers richer, but their heirs poorer. The fact is that lime and earthworms don't mix happily, and the worms succumb.

Limestone soils may have a pH that's ideal for growing clover, but is too high for general purposes. There are three truly natural ways of lowering pH, but they all take a little time. Improving drainage will help by taking away rain water, which leaches out alkaline. Paradoxically, drainage can help to correct acidic conditions, too, by allowing air in to tip the balance in favor of aerobic decomposers rather than anaerobic ones, which cause acidity. Adding compost will, in time, also balance out the soil pH. The third alternative is to grow a dynamic accumulator of calcium, and then remove it. All these processes can be combined, to speed things up. As a last resort, if the soil is seriously alkaline (pH above 8), you could gradually add sulfur in the form of "flowers of sulphur" [4oz/sq yd (140g/sq m) on sandy soil, twice as much on clay].

Mineral Deficiency Signs

Mineral	Signs	Use Accumulators or...
Nitrogen	Small, pale leaves, poor crop and poor overall growth	Compost; drainage; rotation
Phosphorous	As nitrogen, plus late development of flowers and fruit; leaves blue-green and fall early	Compost; raise soil pH; rock phosphate
Potassium	Stunted growth, scorched leaves, yellow between veins, spotting underneath	Seaweed; comfrey; rock potash
Calcium	Leaf tips scorch and die	Correct pH upward
Magnesium	Green-veined old leaves with yellow between veins	General compost, Epsom salt, dolomite limestone
Boron	As Ca, poor root growth, poor disease resistance	Seaweed. Avoid lime and nitrate. Borax
Copper	Young leaves blue-green	Cut out nitrate, seaweed foliar feed
Iron	Young leaves go yellow between veins	Compost to reduce pH
Manganese	Old leaves fade	Raise pH; improve drainage (do not compost)

Really difficult soils

Most of the strategies in this section are directed toward conditioning the soil for growing food plants. Ornamentals, after all, can be freely selected to fit your garden, whereas vegetables tend to be cosmopolitan species with specific requirements regardless of where they're planted. Three extremely difficult types of soil for vegetable growing are deep sands, limestone, and black vertisols. Sands allow water to run straight through, limestone is alkaline and physically difficult, and deep-crack clays can be impervious to water, except where open cracks allow it to run away uselessly. One way around such serious problems is to create a vegetable plot in the garden that is not of the garden.

On pure sand, it is possible to dig a pit and line it with plastic sheeting. This container can then be filled with potting mix (or any soil you like) as a growing medium. On limestone and difficult clays, probably the most sensible solution is to create raised beds (see p.239).

PERMANENT PLANTING

The permanent living features of a garden have greater power than mere appearances may reveal. While shaping the landscape and bearing fruit, they also influence air flow, affect soil water, and can make a significant difference to the temperature of your home. Some of your first-year observations will already have unmasked the effects of existing vegetation, and you can extrapolate from these records to predict the possible outcome of introducing new features.

Relative positions of permanent plantings can be critical. Where one tree alone might be perfectly happy, adding another one close by or even elsewhere, or creating a new hedge, could upset it. By the same token, a group of trees or shrubs could derive benefit from one another's company.

Trees and hedges take a long time to reach their full potential so it may take time to discover an error and then more time to correct it. Planning is therefore best begun on paper, with as many constructive calculations as your first-year mathematics can provide. No matter how laborious this might seem, it won't come anywhere near the inconvenience that could be caused by ill-considered planting.

Hedges

The outer limits of your garden are likely to be as immutable as the wind and the weather. The boundary is clearly defined, and the direction, strength, humidity, and temperature of the prevailing winds will largely dictate what you plant there. Given that this is the least flexible part of the plan, and that whatever goes within will be dependent on its influence, forming the boundary is probably the best place to begin your permanent planting.

The selection of species is guided by what will grow well, plus what you want it to do for your garden. If there's a constant drying wind from the outside, then your hedge must be resistant to desiccation. If your garden is sheltered from light breezes but is occasionally thrashed by a severe gale, then your hedge must do its most important duty during the rare bouts of serious weather. If it's livestock (or people!) rather than wind that you're keen to exclude, choose something thorny.

When planting a new hedge, bear in mind that it will occupy the ground for many years to come. If it's to be sheared, this means that good nutrients will be removed, year after year, to the compost pile. Careful preparation is therefore critical. This can be done well in advance, so that the new plants can be put in as soon as possible after they arrive. While double-digging and incorporating compost, add bone meal (even whole bones) or rock phosphate, and sand if the soil is heavy or extra humus if it's already sandy. If the plants do have to be kept waiting, either for suitable weather or for preparations to be made, they can be temporarily stored by "heeling in" their roots in a shallow trench, perhaps in the vegetable plot, for a week or two.

Beginning small

Starting with your hedging plants as tall as possible may seem to offer a flying start, but they may literally fly away or be knocked over by the first real wind. The smaller and younger your hedging trees are to begin with (and the slower-growing they are), the stronger the hedge will eventually become. If you need a fast windbreak, erect a screen of mesh or wattle to give temporary shelter to your plot at the same time as protecting the developing hedge.

Another way to combine fast shelter and long-term durability is to begin with a mixture of fast-growing and slow-growing species. By the time the fast ones are past their best, the slower, surer ones will be large enough to do the job. A possible problem that could arise from this approach is that the faster-growing elements might shade out or otherwise overpower the slower ones. To avoid shade effects, plant the slow species on the sunward side rather than behind or even between the fast ones; to prevent general overwhelming, it may be advisable to create a double hedge, with a row of slow-growers some distance from (and sheltered but not shaded by) the row of fast ones.

Aerodynamics and other effects

There are some things about windbreaks which are easily deduced, such as the fact that a permeable barrier is less likely to blow down than a solid one, and that a permeable barrier also causes less serious turbulence on the downwind side than a solid one does. But there are other effects, too, which you should be aware of before going all-out for a perfect windbreak.

For example, hedges may create a significant region of shade, and in high latitudes, this shade can extend a long way during the colder months. This might be just when you need sunlight the most, so think carefully about planting a high hedge if loss of sunlight is going to be a problem. Remember that a deciduous hedge, while not providing such a dense shelter as an evergreen hedge, can let light through during the winter.

Hedges also rob the soil of nutrients and moisture. Their roots can extend outward farther than twice their height, and this means that a hedge will compete with anything you plant beside it. If you require a sunny, sheltered site for growing things, it might be better to opt for a non-living fence or wall.

To make the best of these limitations, you could consider running a walk or driveway along the foot of the hedge. This way, you won't be squandering good ground by walking on it, and the walk can even help to restrict root growth on the garden side by compacting the soil.

Hedge management

How you choose to manage your hedge depends on the species it contains and on your own taste. Some factors to consider include:

- Wildlife. Don't shear the hedge while birds are nesting, or when winter berries are providing essential food.
- Specimen trees. You may wish to leave some individual components untrimmed to grow into mature trees.
- Shape. When trimming, aim to create an A-shaped or – even better, if you've space for a broad hedge or are faced with renovating an old, wide overgrown boundary – an M-shaped cross-section. This encourages basal growth, keeping the hedge thick and preventing it from becoming leggy. As well as providing wind-proof density, the thick base also shelters wildlife.

Traditional methods

If there's a local tradition of hedging in your region, why not adopt it or even revive it? The global spread of modern machinery tends to impose uniformity of hedge management, but you can be sure that a local tradition is based on of experience with local species and weather and it won't let you down. Ask around, search out old pictures, and discover how hedges in your region used to be managed in the past.

- Laying is a way of taking strong young shoots and bending them to give many new stems low down to thicken a mature hedge.
- Coppicing is a way of growing several new trunks from one.
- Pollarding is a way of turning the upward growth of a tree into breadth.

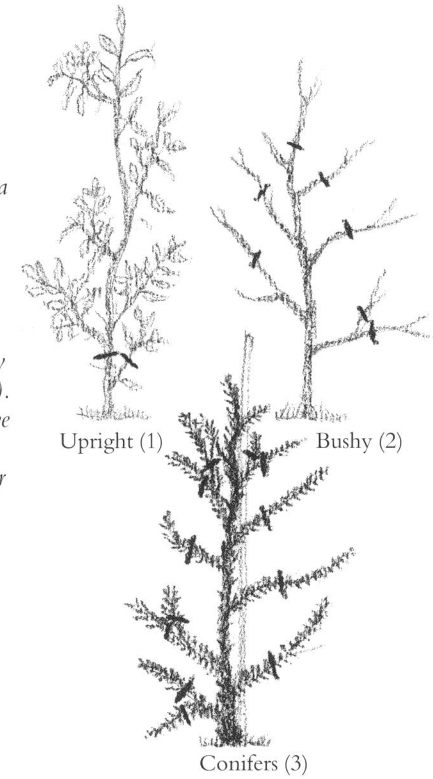

New hedges

Trees and shrubs intended for growing into a hedge have to be trained from the outset. Broad-leaved species should have their leading shoot removed immediately after planting; a tree with a naturally upright growth habit must be chopped off very low down (1), but one which won't immediately shoot upward can be pruned more gently (2). Conifers (3) retain the leader until they have attained their intended height. Side-shoots are also pruned back, to encourage buds near to the main stem(s) to break and produce a dense framework of branches, which will form the heart of the hedge. This ensures that, later on, the hedge is less likely to become hollow in the center. Slow, sound, solid growth is the aim, as opposed to fast and open.

1

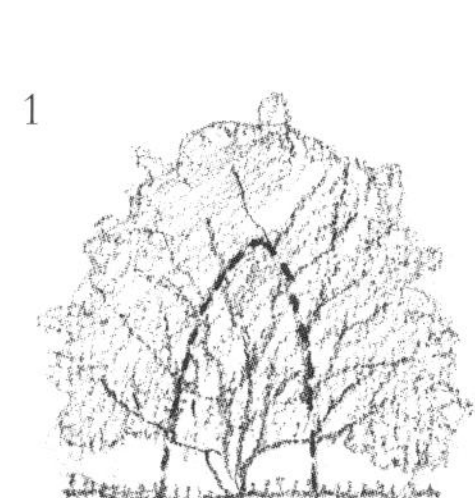

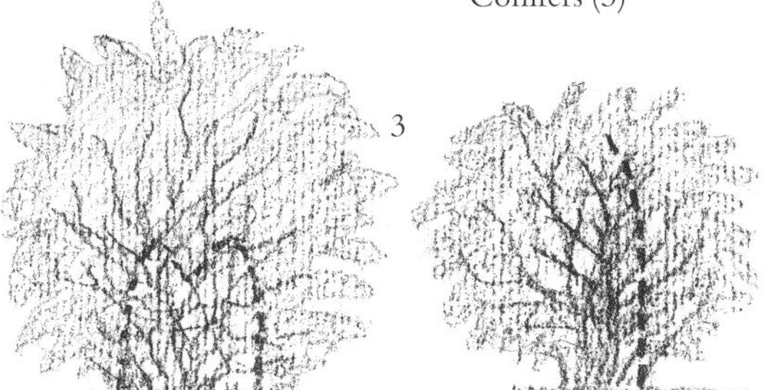

Pruning overgrown hedges

Most hedging trees and shrubs can be cut back hard, though they might take a few years to recover. Conifers generally resent this treatment and are best replaced. Tackle an overgrown hedge in winter or early spring, using clearly visible stakes to mark the new A-shaped profile, and cut off a foot more all round than you eventually want.

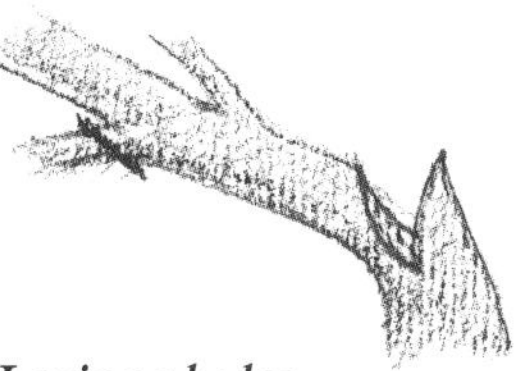

Laying a hedge

The principle of hedge laying is simple, although skill improves with practice. A young upright stem is cut up to two-thirds of the way through and bent over at an angle, thus stimulating buds to break and form a close-set row of new uprights. Bent stems can be anchored to the ground (above) or to other stems, and this can be developed by bending alternate stems in opposite directions.

Planting trees

Many of the same rules apply to trees as to hedges. Trees will occupy the ground for many years to come, and so their planting site needs to be prepared with care. It's advisable to begin with small, young trees which root better, grow on quicker, and will develop more strength than older specimens.

Prepare the ground by thorough double-digging, incorporating bone meal together with well-matured compost. If you removed a section of grassy sod to make the planting hole, this can be dropped into the hole, grass-side down, before setting the tree into place and backfilling. The roots of container-grown trees are usually disturbed when planting; so take this opportunity to unwind and cut overly long roots. Be sure to plant the tree at the right depth – neither too much trunk in the ground nor too much root near the surface. The best guide to use is the "earthmark" at the base of the tree. Grafted trees are always planted with the graft above ground.

Timing

Plant deciduous trees when they're resting. Between fall and early spring is best, but avoid frosty or waterlogged ground. Evergreens are best planted either in early fall (when the soil is still a little warm) or early spring (when it soon will be). Container-grown shrubs and trees can be planted but stick with the correct seasons if you can.

Support

To hold the new tree firmly until its own roots are established, you can choose from a variety of methods. A stout stake can be driven deeply into the planting hole before placing a bare-rooted tree. A diagonal stake driven in after the tree is planted is better for container-grown trees, as this won't damage the root-ball.

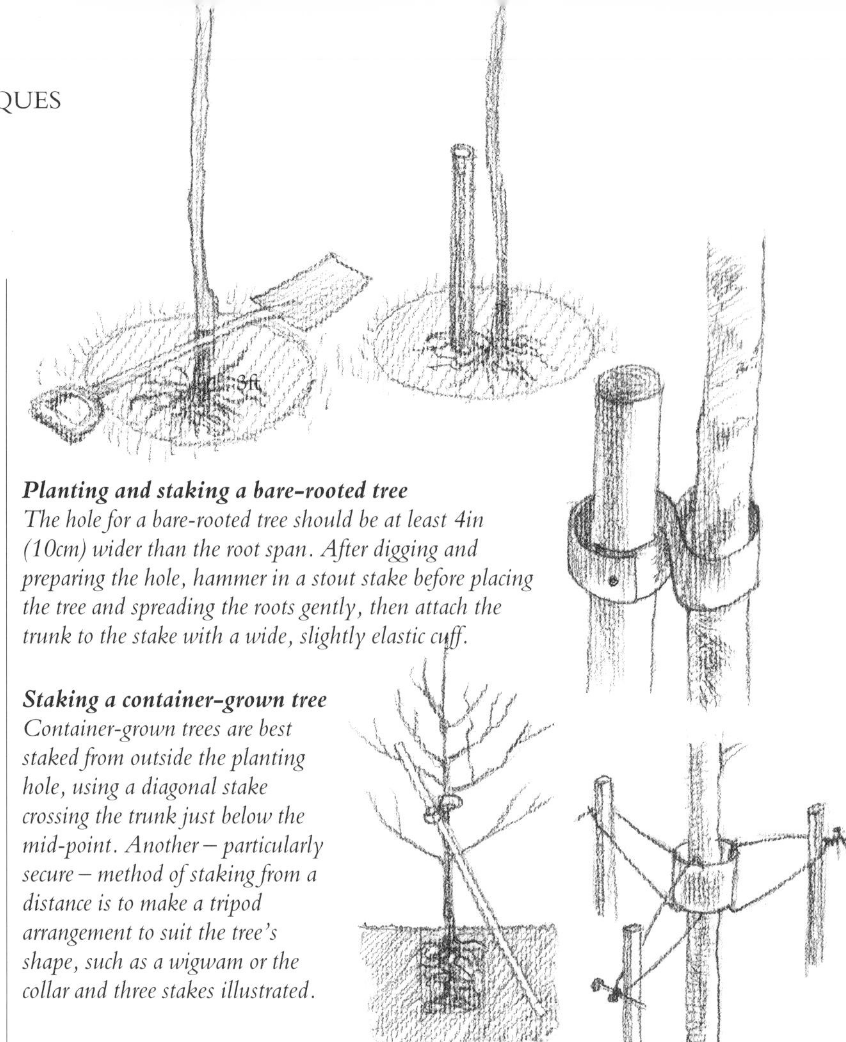

Planting and staking a bare-rooted tree
The hole for a bare-rooted tree should be at least 4in (10cm) wider than the root span. After digging and preparing the hole, hammer in a stout stake before placing the tree and spreading the roots gently, then attach the trunk to the stake with a wide, slightly elastic cuff.

Staking a container-grown tree
Container-grown trees are best staked from outside the planting hole, using a diagonal stake crossing the trunk just below the mid-point. Another – particularly secure – method of staking from a distance is to make a tripod arrangement to suit the tree's shape, such as a wigwam or the collar and three stakes illustrated.

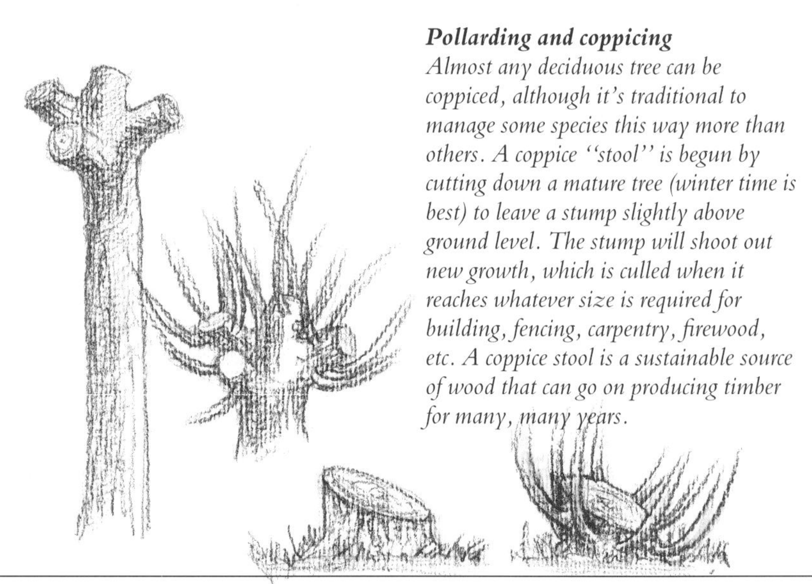

Pollarding and coppicing
Almost any deciduous tree can be coppiced, although it's traditional to manage some species this way more than others. A coppice "stool" is begun by cutting down a mature tree (winter time is best) to leave a stump slightly above ground level. The stump will shoot out new growth, which is culled when it reaches whatever size is required for building, fencing, carpentry, firewood, etc. A coppice stool is a sustainable source of wood that can go on producing timber for many, many years.

Take care not to bind the tree too tightly to the stake, because this can cause permanent damage as the trunk increases in girth. Using a naturally elastic material, such as a bicycle inner-tube, secures a tree firmly to its stake without the risk of chafing or strangling it. Alternatively, you might opt for a guy-rope arrangement or choose to construct a frame around the trunk. Soil type, species, and situation may well dictate the best method to use.

It's best to use a short stake (fixed to the tree's windward side) to support the trunk quite low down. Attaching the entire trunk to a long stake gives the young tree a false sense of security resulting in a weak trunk. Most stakes can, and should, be removed after a year or so.

Planting young trees in a tube to shelter them and get them off to a faster start also tends to produce a weak trunk, because a sapling naturally responds to the wind by strengthening its trunk and roots to suit the conditions. If the young tree must be protected from gnawing animals, a spirally constructed sleeve will do the job without interfering with natural flexion in the wind.

Finishing

In a dry garden, it's useful to create a shallow depression around a new tree so that, when you water it, the water doesn't run away. In a wet garden, it may be better to make a slight hump to improve drainage. Whatever the soil type, water the tree in thoroughly, adding more soil to make up for any settling, and then mulch around the base with a material chosen for water retention and weed suppression rather than nutrition, e.g. chipped bark, newspaper, or black plastic (according to your resources and/or aesthetic requirements). If planted in warm weather, a leafy tree will also benefit from a sprinkling of water on the foliage at night.

Willow bank

Willow can assist in making an invaluable natural earth bank, which gives shelter and makes an excellent sound barrier. If you can get a good supply of fresh willow cuttings, they can be inserted in the ground in a double trench, with the dug-out soil piled between them. As well as rooting at the base, they will send roots into the piled-up soil and anchor it. As they grow, more soil can be shovelled between the two rows; more roots will then form, and you will gradually build an earthen bank between a double row of willow trees.

Shading and cooling

As well as being used to block air movement, shrubs and trees can be arranged to direct and enhance air currents. This effect can be used to cool the air entering a house or greenhouse, or to create a favorable environment for heat-sensitive plants. At the same time as casting shade, tall overhanging vegetation also traps humidity, and this can be turned to useful effect in many ways.

One possibility is to establish a double row of trellised vines over an arbor to make a shady, humid tent or tunnel; this will permit sun to penetrate in winter when the vines are bare, but in summer the leaves will provide shade from strong sunlight as well as keeping the air beneath moist, either protecting delicate growth or making a pleasant, shady place to sit, or both. In this arrangement, the vines are planted with their roots well outside the arbor's uprights, to maximize the soil area available for underplanting. A walk, or even a small terrace, can run through the center, improving access and providing a firm base for seating.

Dealing with difficult ground

Nature abhors a vacuum, and practically every permutation of climate, soil, and weather has at least one tree or shrub species perfectly adapted to live there. The trick is to find the right species and make use of them. Sometimes, their extreme tastes may have made them unpopular, so you must exercise your own judgement.

Poplars and willows, for example, are very thirsty trees. Their roots extend far beyond their branch-span and can soak up an enormous quantity of available water. This can parch other plants growing nearby or damage the foundations of a building; the roots can even invade and block drainage and irrigation pipes. Although such trees are undesirable anywhere near a house, or in most modestly sized, modestly moist gardens, they can survive in seriously waterlogged ground, and can even help

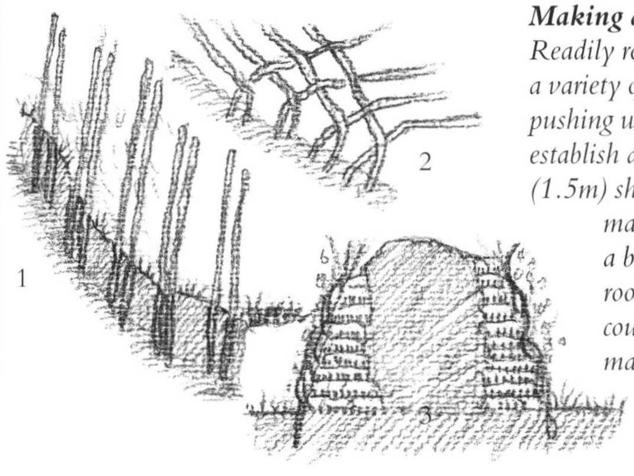

Making a willow bank

Readily rooting willow can be used to create a variety of "instant" barriers. Simply pushing willow shoots into the ground will establish a row of trees; a row of paired 5ft (1.5m) shoots (1) can be interlaced (2) to make a fast screen; a double row with a bank of turfs or soil between (3) will root into the soil and retain it, and could even carry a hedge on top, making an excellent sound barrier.

to "drain" it sufficiently to make it more tolerable for other species while gradually dying out themselves. This is a part of the natural process in many of the world's wetlands.

Lazy lawns

There are volumes written about the "perfect" lawn – uniformly verdant, weed-free, and bland in a way that entails a constant war with nature. The wildflower meadow has very little in common with a "traditional" lawn. It isn't uniform, it isn't bland, and it isn't hard work either!

Making and management

The secret of creating a wildflower meadow is to treat it like an old-fashioned hayfield. Mow the grass no more than twice a year (early and late), don't cut it too short, and always remove the clippings. Mowing early lets light in to stimulate growth of wildflowers (so pick your time carefully, before growth is well under way); mowing late enables them to set and scatter seed before they're chopped down (again, look at the state of the seeds to judge the right time); and removing the clippings steadily impoverishes the soil (on rich soil the grass grows so strongly that wildflowers are crowded out).

In fact, the wildflower meadow is a side-effect of traditional livestock-farming and isn't strictly natural at all. It is, however, much more attractive than the bland green lawn, and far easier to maintain. In return for doing less work you get wonderful hay for sale or barter, or feeding to your own livestock (from rabbits to cattle), plus a glorious home-grown picnic spot, and an ecosystem that's about as different from a conventional lawn as the Amazon jungle is from a pine plantation. The wildflower meadow is more tolerant of trampling than some perfect green swards, but if you prefer not to tread on the flowers you could keep some walks (or even picnic-places in the middle) more regularly mown. Fresh-cut meadow mowings make excellent mulch, too, especially for heaping around tree trunks.

Fertility

In almost any region where a wildflower lawn is climatically possible, the most likely problem is soil that's too fertile. High fertility creates a high risk that weeds and lush grasses will flourish, instead of the meadow flowers and hard grasses that coexist on poor, heavily grazed soil. If the good topsoil is so deep that it is physically impossible to cart away, making a wildflower meadow is probably not a feasible use of your land or labor.

The most promising site for a wildflower meadow is poor, alkaline or sandy soil with good drainage. With good but quite shallow topsoil, you could begin by removing most of it and just stirring the last inch or so into the subsoil. There might well be seeds lurking in wait for just these conditions, and it could be worth leaving the plot for a year to see what happens.

Starting from scratch

If nothing very interesting emerges, you can buy wildflower and grass seeds ready-mixed from a seed merchant and use them according to instructions supplied. Each locality will have its own native mix of suitable species, so resist the temptation to go for a "foreign" selection that looks more interesting. The basic mix can be supplemented with seeds gathered from wild plants growing by the wayside (but beware of contravening conservation laws) and scattering them on to your plot. Pot-grown wildflowers are sometimes to be had, and they can also be added to a quite mature meadow. As the variety of plants increases, so too will the visiting wildlife. Insects will increase seed yield by pollination, and small mammals and birds will accidentally contribute even more variety via seeds stuck to fur and feathers.

Tree fruit

When establishing fruit trees, all the usual tree-planting rules apply, plus one or two more. Once the trees begin to bear fruit you'll be taking it away to eat, so the fruit trees will need regular feeding to replace the lost nutrients. Easy access is therefore important, both for management and for harvesting. There is a bewildering variety of fruit trees to choose from, and making your selection requires some restraint and common sense.

An obvious starting point is to consider which fruits you most enjoy. It also makes sense to go for special varieties. There isn't much point in planting and tending a tree that rewards your hard work with apples you can get in any supermarket. Luckily, this isn't a great problem. Commercially grown fruits aren't selected so much for flavor as for "eye appeal" and uniformity of size. The best flavor is not necessarily associated with the prettiest (in marketing terms) fruit, so you have a wide selection to choose from. Having said this, though, there's a world of difference flavor-wise between an organically grown apple of any variety and its commercial counterpart.

Another important consideration is the size and shape of the tree. With fruit trees as with any other trees, appearances obviously affect the design of your garden. Apart from the "natural" shape of a fruit tree, however, many varieties can not only be trained into quite extraordinary shapes but positively thrive on manipulation, so they can also be used in a positive way to create special visual effects.

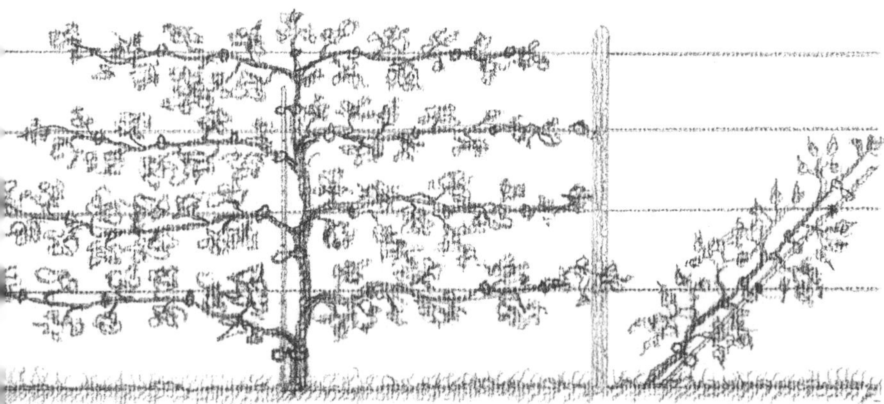

Fruit trees can be pruned and trained to give maximal crop in minimal space, either on stakes and wires in the open, or using the warmth and protection of a wall.

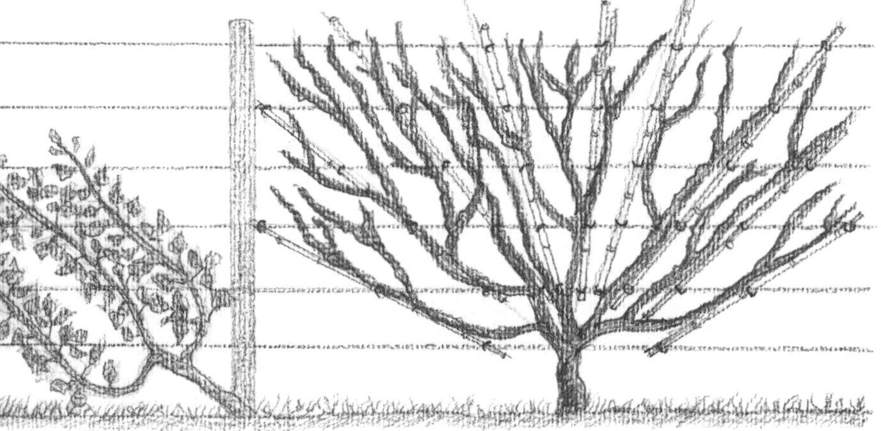

Four arrangements shown here are: espalier (top left); cordon (top right); multiple cordon (bottom left); and fan (bottom right).

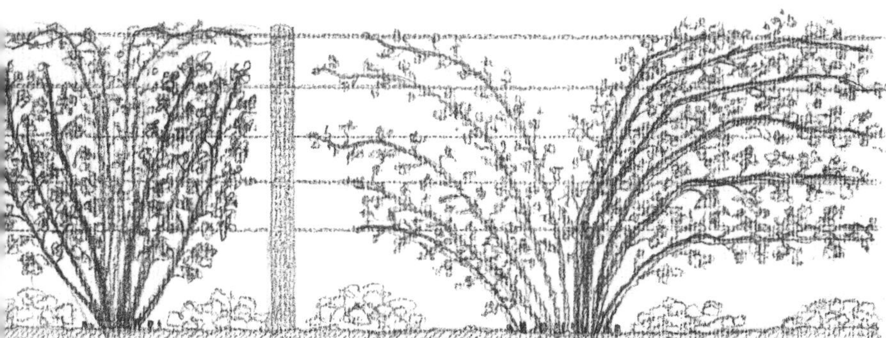

Wiring soft fruits is a useful way to support whippy growth and ensure that all the fruit has access to light, as well as letting light through to underplanted crops.

Orchard planning

The orchard is a place where the sensitivity and intelligence of the natural gardener can literally bear fruit. Establishing a naturally balanced system here helps many of the commercial fruit-grower's problems simply to disappear. Some key points to remember are:

- Bees are critical to the whole operation, and it's essential to make sure they come to pollinate the blossom. Siting bee hives in an orchard is an old trick but, because many fruit trees bloom early in the year before honey bees really get going, bumble bees may actually do most of the work. Early-flowering weeds and herbs can attract and sustain these early bees.
- Early flowering also makes fruit trees susceptible to cold weather, therefore avoid siting your orchard in a frost pocket. If frost does strike, the worst damage is done by a sudden thaw, so westerly exposure is better than easterly, which catches the early sun.
- A border of bramble, nuts, and berries can provide shelter, help to encourage bees, and provide distraction for pests, as well as sustaining the natural enemies of those pests.
- Sticky bands catch female moths as they crawl up the tree trunk to lay their eggs, without any risk to bees or other beneficial insects.
- Pheromones – insect "musk" – specific to particular pests can be obtained from some organic garden suppliers. These substances can be used to lure pests into traps, and don't interest other insects.
- Many birds will work through all the hours of daylight, feeding potential orchard pests to their babies. Put up bird houses to attract wild birds.
- Chickens will even turn wireworms into wholesome, golden-yolked eggs for you. Site the hennery in the orchard.

- Bats do the same job at night that birds do during the day, hunting moths on the wing or plucking insects from trees. Attach bat houses to your orchard trees.
- Nettles are said to help deter pests and diseases, and also to improve the "keeping" properties of fruit. Let them grow around the edge.
- Grass and some weeds can compete with trees, especially when they're young. Keep a ring (ideally, 3ft or 1m wide) around each tree weed-free, preferably by mulching (or by cutting the grass there very, very short). Alternatively, sow non-greedy annual ground-cover flowering plants such as nasturtiums around the trees.
- Geese keep the grass closely cropped.
- Healthy trees resist disease. Keep the trees well-fed and stress-free, and they'll bear enough fruit to spare to repay the birds for their help.

Soft fruit

Compared with tree fruits, soft fruits require a fair amount of ongoing effort. They need to be trained, pruned, fertilized and watered, and weeded. The cropping season tends to be very short and, if this coincides with a spell of unsuitable weather, you can lose the entire crop. Another problem is that, when the fruit ripens, early birds can strip your bushes before you've even got out of bed! On the other hand, these very problems tend to make soft fruits expensive to buy and thus worth some effort. When deciding which ones to grow, possibly the two most important considerations are how much you enjoy the fruit and how much use you can make of a glut.

Preparation and planting

Soft fruits need good, rich, loamy soil. Although their potassium requirements are particularly heavy, this is best supplied by digging in rock potash before planting rather than scattering wood ashes later on. As with any perennial planting, it's important to remove all perennial weeds before establishing fruit bushes. In order to ensure that the ground is totally clear, leave two months between preparation and planting in the fall.

Small plants are better to begin with than bigger ones, and they should be well spaced to take account of their eventual size. Most kinds need ruthless pruning after planting.

Weeding

Keep the ground weed-free with a thick layer of mulch. If weeding becomes necessary, do it by hand because hoeing can damage the shallow roots most fruit bushes possess.

Fertilizing

Soft fruit bushes produce a great deal of fruit which is taken away, as well as losing nutrients each time they're pruned, so they need to be well fertilized. Rich mulch (possibly underneath ground-cover mulch) helps to keep up the levels of nutrients in the soil. Feeding in spring with seaweed- or comfrey-based liquid ferlitizer also helps to improve disease resistance.

Coping with birds

The traditional method of protecting soft fruit from birds is to plant it in a cage. This is expensive but, if you're serious about bush fruits, it gives total security. A cage works both ways, however; although a bird's brain isn't very big, it is seriously dedicated to finding food and the bird has all day to ponder on the problem of how to get at a feast of berries which are literally asking to be eaten. If a bird does get in, it probably won't be able to get out again; this means that your fruit cage becomes a trap and/or the fruit gets eaten anyway. Another potential danger to birds is that their feet can get entangled in the netting, so if you do opt for a fruit cage it must be well designed, well made, well maintained, and absolutely bird-proof. At the same time, of course, it has to be easy for you to go in and out.

Cheaper ad-hoc strategies than building fancy fruit cages are:

- Planting your fruit bushes beside a wall, so that a net can simply be draped across during high-risk periods only. This also allows you to drape frost protection if necessary.
- Constructing a temporary cage around harvest time, using plastic netting draped over a framework of bean poles (attach yogurt pots to prevent the net from sliding down the vertical poles).
- Threading a random web of black thread among the bushes. This is only feasible for a very small fruit patch, carries a risk of trapping birds, and gives only partial protection. It works well with gooseberries, though. (There are a number of commercial versions of this, under various names.)
- Delaying pruning until the buds have begun to open. This will reduce the damage done by bud-peckers such as bullfinches, which will take the terminal buds you're going to prune off anyway.

Bear in mind that any netting you use must have large enough mesh to permit pollinating insects to come and go with ease, or you may not get a crop at all!

Vines

The chief difference between vines and other woody plants is that vines aren't self-supporting; they exploit other structures – in nature, these would chiefly be other trees – to climb up to reach the light. This habit makes them useful for covering ugly structures, or for adopting the shape of a structure built specifically with design or utility in mind. Some vines climb by twining, others have suckers or tendrils.

When planting vines, prepare the ground as for trees. Ornamental vines intended to cover unattractive features already in place should be planted far enough from their intended support to give them root space. This is because the soil at the base of walls and other support structures is often very dry and may be densely compacted.

Fruiting vines

Ornamental vines can be selected on the basis of suitability for the job, but fruiting vines are more likely to be chosen according to the desirability of their fruit. It may therefore be necessary for you to adjust the soil conditions of your plot to suit the variety of vine you wish to grow.

Grape, kiwi, and passion fruit are perennial species which can be both ornamental and fruitful. Where these fruits are grown commercially, they are in general ruthlessly pruned to increase crop density and ease of harvesting. However all three species can do double or triple duty in your natural garden, giving a worthwhile combination of shade, interest, and fruit.

Soil

Grapevines are a good choice if your soil is poor but well drained (stony rather than sandy). When preparing ground for grapes, try to create a mixture of stones and humus to start the grapevines off. On poor soil, add wood ash and some bone meal at planting time. If the soil at large is heavy, this might be an advantage in the long run, provided that really good drainage can be arranged while the grapevines become established. At this time, "mulch" with stones rather than compost; slate is ideal, as it later reflects heat on to the fruit.

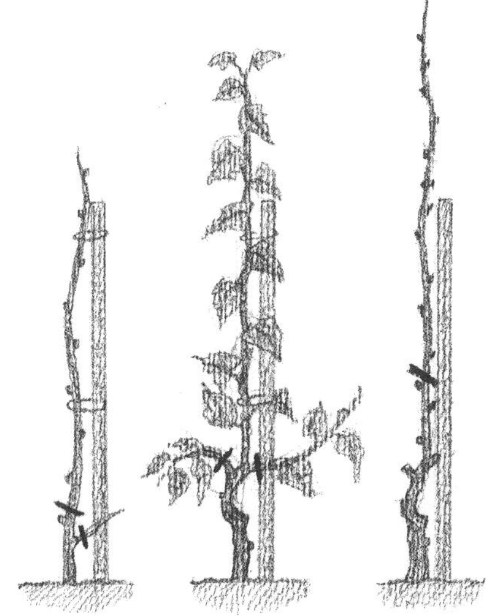

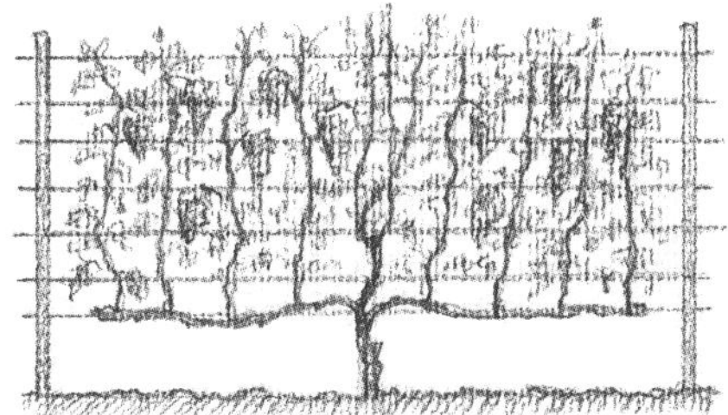

The stages in establishing a grape vine. Top row: first year. Bottom: final shape.

Sunlight

The amount of sugar that grapes produce depends on the amount of sunlight they receive, especially later in the summer, so that table grapes are only likely to succeed in very sunny situations. Wine grapes, however, ripen more easily. There is an enormous variety to choose from, and the best type to go for is one that is known to do well in your particular locality.

Planting and training

After planting in fall, cut each young grapevine back to just above the third bud. Next spring, if all three buds have survived two should be rubbed out to allow one good, strong stem to grow. This is the foundation of your grapevine, and its future management depends largely on what you want it to do for you. Any book on viticulture will give detailed, step-by-step directions for a range of varieties in a selection of styles. Basically, if you're growing for fruit the grapevine must be strictly disciplined and then have its developing berries thinned out to allow the optimum number to reach their full potential. If you're growing for shade, the grapevine grow unhindered and any grapes you get will be a bonus. Between these two extremes, you are free to adopt whatever pattern suits you.

A low cordon of fruit-priority grapevines can be trained on to three horizontal wires stretched between two posts. In this situation, the grapevine roots aren't impeded in any way. Grapevines grow wide-ranging roots so, if they are to be trained up a wall, they should be planted at least a foot (30cm) away.

Maintenance

Mulching mature grapevines with compost in the winter (widely, to feed those widespread roots) will encourage strong growth. Foliar seaweed-based spray during the summer will help to fertilize developing fruit and also to stimulate resistance against the multitude of pests, mildews, molds, and other ills which grapevines have acquired during centuries of cultivation. This problem should, in fact, be given serious consideration right at the start. While shopping around for suitable varieties, place hardiness and disease resistance at the very top of your list of priorities. If you choose to experiment with more vulnerable varieties, you should be prepared for a succession of battles and possible disappointment, although your natural garden may in fact be better equipped to ride out natural problems than a commercial vineyard can.

VEGETABLES AND HERBS

The atavistic attraction of "growing your own" must come from deep in our prehistory, when our ancestors stopped roaming around hunting and gathering and settled down to till the ground and control their own food supplies. Civilization is, in a sense, founded on this single step. It's not surprising, then, that growing vegetables is a deeply satisfying aspect of gardening.

It is also a very valuable way to use your natural garden. Here, in a clean, unpolluted environment, you can raise clean, unpolluted food. You know exactly where it's been, and you also have a fairly good idea of what it's made of because you even mixed the compost that nourished it. All this comes in addition to the pleasure and nutritional benefit of having the varieties you like best arriving on your plate in the freshest possible condition.

Which vegetables?

The first stage of vegetable-growing takes place on the drawing-board, planning what you're going to grow and how you're going to go about it. When deciding what to grow, it's wise to begin modestly, with types and varieties which aren't going to cause big problems. You may not have a large prepared plot yet, so aim to keep your first vegetable plot fully employed by working out a succession of good companions which are well suited to your soil and climatic conditions. Even with a small plot there will be the soil to attend to, seeds to sow and hoe, perhaps to germinate and grow before planting, and various stages of care for your growing plants. Two extremes to avoid are being spoiled for choice because everything ripens at once (and then there's nothing to eat for the rest of the year!), and having no choice at all because there's only one variety ready to eat each month. Running a vegetable plot sensibly and managing it well is an ambitious aim for your initiation year. When you're more experienced (and have accumulated a lot more compost!), you can become more adventurous.

Rotation

The traditional system of crop rotation applies above all to intensively managed vegetable plots, where the risks of disease and pest build-up are high and potentially devastating. Planting the same crop in the same place, two or more years running, invites colonization by pests and diseases that "go to ground" in the off-season, ready to attack in force the moment their food crop reappears. Some pests can attack whole families of plants. The clubroot fungus, for example, affects all the brassicas – edibles of the Crucifer family – which is why they're treated as one in a classic rotation system.

Another traditional basis for rotation is to enable high-nitrogen fertilizer to be applied and used first by crops with high nitrogen demand and tolerance; later, as nitrogen and other minerals are successively depleted, crops with successively smaller needs and tolerances can be planted in the plot. This principle is not nearly so important to the natural gardener as it is in more drastic regimes which use manure or other high-N fertilizer rather than ordinary compost.

Rotation cannot be said to be truly "natural", but then neither is interfering with natural growth on one plot of land in order to grow edibles. The natural way of things is a one-way succession of mingled species, culminating in a final, stable climax community, rather than going around in circles. Rotation resembles the early stages of succession, however, in that each crop makes the habitat less suitable for itself (by sequestering nutrients, altering soil structure, and attracting enemies) while at the same time tipping the balance in favor of another crop (which appreciates the new soil structure or balance and isn't susceptible to the first crop's enemies).

Rotation systems

Various detailed rotation systems are recommended by different authorities, according to different past experiences, prejudices, climates, and/or expectations. The natural gardener doesn't need to worry about the varying nutritional state of the soil, since regularly composted soil is consistently well balanced, without the extremes caused by a manure-binge at four- or five-year intervals. Disease is another matter, however. Rotation to thwart enemies makes especially good sense in the natural garden, where violent means of pest control are out of the question.

Where you have a permanent vegetable plot, a three-year (at least) rotation system should be followed.

A good three-year system can be based on three main enemies of staple crops: clubroot (brassicas); nematodes (potatoes); and white rot (onions). All brassicas occupy a single plot one year, potatoes can go into this plot the next year (brassicas now move over), and onions come the year after (potatoes move over). Then you can go around the system again.

Unless you have a vast cultivated area available to rotate other crops similarly, one at a time, these three main crops must be combined with others.

Two main food-plant families not catered for in the three-group system are the legumes and the carrot family, so they must be worked in. This is where more complex rotation plans begin to form, with the most detailed ones taking account of nutritional minutiae and even factors such as

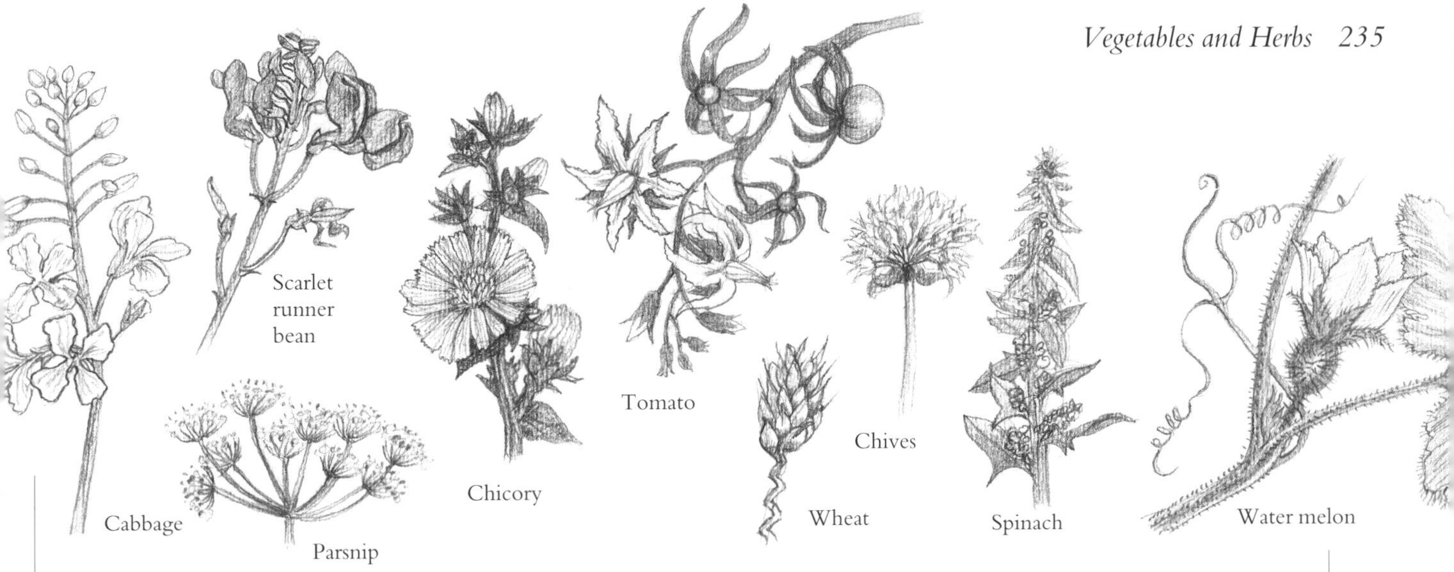

Scarlet runner bean

Tomato

Chives

Cabbage

Parsnip

Chicory

Wheat

Spinach

Water melon

VEGETABLE FAMILIES

AMARYLLIDACEAE: Chive (*A. schoenoprasum*); European/Welsh onion (*A. fistulosum*); Garlic (*A. sativum*); Leek (*A. ampeloprasum*); Onion, Shallot (*A. cepa*).

CHENOPODIACEAE (*goosefoot*): Beets, Chard, Spinach beet, Silver beet, Sugar beet (all *Beta vulgaris*); Good King Henry (*Chenopodium bonus-henricus*); Orach (*Atriplex hortensis*); Spinach (*Spinacea oleracea*).

COMPOSITAE (*composites*): Black salsify (*S. hispanica*); Cardoon (*Cynara cardunculus*); Chicory (*Cichorium intybus*); Dandelion (*Taraxacum officinale*); Endive (*Cichorium endivia*); Globe artichoke (*Cynara scolymus*); Jerusalem artichoke (*Helianthus tuberosa*); Lettuces (*Lactuca sativa*); Salsify (*Tragopogon porrifolius*); Shungiku (*Chrysanthemum coronarium*); Sunflower (*Helianthus annus*).

CRUCIFERAE (*brassicas*): Arugula (*Eruca sativa*); Bok-choi Chinese cabbage (*Brassica chinensis*); Broccoli, Brussels sprouts, Cabbages, Cauliflower, Collard, Kale, Kohlrabi (all varieties of *Brassica oleracea*); Cress (*Lepidum sativum*); Horseradish (*Armoracia rusticana*); Mustard (*Sinapis alba*); Pe-tsai, Wongbok, Chihli (all *Brassica pekinensis*); Radishes (*Raphanus spp*); Rutabagas, Salad rape (*B. napus*); Seakale (*Crambe maritima*); Watercress (*Nasturtium officinale*); Winter/Uplandcress (*Barbara verna*).

CUCURBITACEAE (*cucumbers*): Bitter gourd (*Momordica charantia*); Canteloupes (*Cucumis melo*); Chayote (*Sechium edule*); Cucumber (*Cucumis sativus*); Gherkin (*Cucumis anguria*); Pumpkin, Custard squash, Summer squash, Vegetable squash, Zucchini (all *Cucurbita pepo*); Watermelon (*Citrullus vulgaris*); Winter squash (*Cucurbita maxima*).

GRAMINAE (*grasses*): Barley (*Hordeum spp*), Maize (*Zea mays*); Millets (*Panicum spp* and others); Oats (*Avena sativa*); Rice (*Oryza sativa*); Rye (*Secale cereale*); Sorghum (*Sorghum bicolor*); Wheat (Triticum spp); Wild rice (*Zizania aquatica*).

LEGUMINOSEAE (*peas*): Asparagus pea (*Lotus tetragonolobus*); Black bean, Navy bean, Pea bean, Snap bean (all *Phaseolus vulgaris*); Black gram (*P. mungo*); Chickpea (*Cicer arietinum*); Fava bean (*Vicia faba*); Green gram (*Vigna radiata*); Jack bean (*Canavalia ensiformis*); Lentils (*Lens culinaris*); Licorice (*Glycorrhiza glabra*); Lima (*Phaseolus lunatus*); Peanut (*Arachis hypogea*); Peas (*Pisum sativum*); Pigeon pea (*Cajanus cajan*); Scarlet runner bean (*Phaseolus coccineus*); Soybean (*Glycine max*).

SOLANACEAE (*nightshades*): Cape gooseberry (*Physalis peruviana*); Peppers (*Capsicum annum*); Chili peppers (*C. frutescens*); Eggplant (*Solanum melongena*); Huckleberry (*S. intrusum*); Potato (*S. tuberosum*); Tomato (*Lycopersicon esculentum*); Tree tomato (*Cyphomandra betacea*).

UMBELLIFERAE (*carrots*): Carrot (*Daucus carota*); Celariac, Celery (*Apium graveolens*); Fennel (*Foeniculum vulgare*); Lovage (*Levisticum officinale*); Parsley (*Petroselinum crispum*); Parsnip (*Pastinaca sativa*); plus many herbs.

companionability, all without losing sight of the main objective of keeping the ground "clean". It's no wonder, then, that some rotation systems can end up looking very daunting indeed. It's up to you whether you choose to adopt a ready-made ultra-sophisticated system or simply stick with the three-year brassica/potato/onion basic pattern, inserting your own selection of other crops among them. As long as you avoid replanting any particular crop in the same place for at least three years, a rotation system will emerge.

Resistance

Another way to beat the potential enemy is to choose varieties that are naturally pest- and disease-resistant.

Plant breeders are constantly working to improve resistance, and their successes are well worth seeking out. Conversely, some very old varieties, which may have fallen out of favor due to lack of eye-appeal, short shelf-life, or some other commercial disadvantage, sometimes have good resistance. Using organic methods in itself reduces the stresses which lead to disease and, in addition, disease resistance of almost any plant can be improved by the use of seaweed-based foliar sprays.

Perennial vegetables

Rotation gives no place to perennials. The disease-prevention principle of rotation positively forbids having the same crop in the same place two years running, and with good reason. Being particularly vulnerable to pests, though, many perennials have evolved their own defences. Rhubarb leaves, for example, are famously lethal. One way to minimize the risks for species less well-equipped than rhubarb is to surround them with a variety of other species – which is the way most of them would grow in the wild. The best place to do this is in the garden at large, rather than in the ghetto of a vegetable plot. Another reason for growing these perennials is that they are expensive to manage on a commercial scale, for the very same reasons that make them ideal for the garden – being long-term inhabitants of a plot and needing a lot of care and attention.

Globe artichokes are generally supposed to require deep, rich soil, where they will certainly thrive. But since they are in fact native to the sandy shores of North Africa, it logically follows that they can be grown on light soil provided seaweed is incorporated and sprayed. They look wonderful in an ornamental bed, like gigantic thistles (which they are) but if the flowers aren't cut for eating before they open, the plants tend to weaken.

Jerusalem artichokes are related to sunflowers. Like sunflowers, they will grow almost anywhere; like sunflowers, they grow very, very tall and so make a useful wind break. Left in the ground, the tubers will throw up new stems year after year. Even when carefully dug, some tubers usually escape notice, so avoid planting Jerusalem artichokes anywhere you'd rather not see them again.

Asparagus is not only perennial but has to be in place for three or four years before a crop can be taken. It prefers well-drained soil, although it's not essential to make a traditional "mound" in order to succeed. The main problem with a standard asparagus bed is keeping it weed-free, since perennial weeds are almost impossible to remove from among the spidery asparagus roots. If you're prepared to accept the tender, delicious asparagus sprouts as a bonus rather than a crop, however, some crowns can go at the back of a permanent bed, mingled with ground cover to keep perennial weeds from invading; some sprouts could be cropped for food when in season, leaving later ones to grow into a ferny ornamental foil for other, even later,

Vegetables for Integration

Name	Situation	A,B,P	Management
Amaranth	Border	A	Tall pyramidal plants, red to green, used as spinach or for seed according to type. One species was once staple food of ancient South American civilization.
Artichoke, Jerusalem	Windbreak	P	Tall summer shelter, needs to be dug to harvest crop. Dies down in winter.
Artichoke, Globe	Fertile bed	P	Tall, heavy plants for well-composted permanent bed. Pick for eating before flowers open; permitting flowering will weaken plants. Feed annually.
Asparagus pea	Border	A	Deep maroon flowers, good ground cover, edible pods.
Asparagus	Fertile bed	P	Back of border, crop early, leave later shoots to mature into ferny foliage.
Basil	Sunny border	A	Choose red or ruffled-leaf varieties.
Beans, Scarlet runner	As vines	A	Climb up strings, poles or arbors, as in vegetable plot.
French	As vines	A	Climbing varieties either cropped green or left to ripen and cropped as navy. Some varieties have colored pods.
Beetroot	Border	A	Red-leaf edging for annual border, needs to be pulled or dug when ready. Not suitable if young tender beets required.
Cabbages	Winter bed	A/B	Choose ornamental varieties, crop while young, leave to mature for winter color.
Cardoon	Border	B	Tall gray-leaved thistle. Swaddle the whole plant in brown paper and banked soil in late summer, to give blanched leaf stalks 4–5 weeks later.
Carrot	Early leaf	A	Sow early variety among later-showing annuals or perennials. Pull young.
Cauliflower	Winter bed	A/B	Use exotic red or green varieties for winter interest and crop. "Perennial" type makes a large plant with many small green winter heads.
Chard	Border	P	Mix white- and red-stemmed Swiss chard for effect, cut leaf when required.
Chicory	Edging	A	Choose leafy red varieties, sow in front of border. Crop ad lib.

VEGETABLES FOR INTEGRATION

NAME	SITUATION	A,B,P	MANAGEMENT
Chili peppers	Sunny border	A	Neat bushes with vivid and useful peppers fruit.
Chives	Border	A	Neat and decorative as clumps or edging. Cut leaves with scissors as required, allow to flower for decoration.
Endive	Edging	A	Frilly rosette. Good for early and late planting. Do not allow to flower. Salads.
Herbs	Border	A/P	Nearly all herbs can be integrated, but avoid putting mints in mixed border.
Horseradish	Naturalize	P	Plant good roots in out-of-the-way corner, where natural invasiveness and difficulty of removal doesn't matter, otherwise keep to pot.
Kale	Winter bed	A	Green, textured foliage during winter, cut leaves as required. Edible sprouts in spring. Colored ornamental varieties available.
Lettuces	Edging	A	Choose different-colored varieties, sow at front of border. Crop ad lib.
Nasturtium	Border	A	Leaves give "bite" to salads, seeds can be pickled as capers, flowers added to salads.
Okra	Back of sunny border	A	Large plant. Choose red variety. Keep border fruit picked.
Orache	Border	A	Red-leafed goosefoot, leaves used as spinach.
Parsley	Edging	B	Ornamental leaf, pick as required. May self-seed or stand over winter in mild regions.
Radish	Catch	A	Useful winter crop.
Rhubarb	Fertile bed	P	Clump-forming perennial, pull as required in spring, then allow spectacular flower to form on 6ft stem.
Seakale	Sunny, open	P	Deep fertile soil gives good growth. Blanch in winter to cut stems 4in long, then leave to grow on and bloom.
Sorrel	Naturalize	P	Establish a clump, maintain by removing flower heads. Pick leaves for salad.
Squashes	Border	A	Compact varieties, yellow or white fruit, pick when young.
	Trellis	A	Climbing varieties, e.g. custard apple or cucumber "crystal apple".
Upland cress	Edging	A	Sow twice for summer and winter crop in moist bed, pick as needed. Flowers edible.

plants in front. Integrating asparagus helps slightly to protect it from asparagus beetles.

Rhubarb is an obvious candidate for any integrated garden. It's an almost indestructible perennial, with pink stems which can be eaten as fruit long before any real fruit is available, followed by magnificent, large leaves and extravagant, exotic flowers. Rhubarb takes care of itself and, even if you hate to eat it, it's worth growing for the sake of its naturally insecticidal leaves.

Other herbaceous perennial edibles include bunching and tree onions, seakale, Good King Henry, and strawberries – of which the wild species provides good ground cover and gourmet fruit.

Cut and come again

Most salads and leaf vegetables are harvested all at once, so you must carry out successional sowings to get a continuous supply. Others, such as kale and leaf beet (silver beet), are gathered leaf by leaf, and the plant makes good the loss. Even cabbages cut off at the stalk will yield again. There are also salad varieties with the same qualities, giving a long harvest without the need to resow: loosehead lettuces, sorrel, radicchio, endives, rocket, land cress, and most of the oriental salads such as mizuna and bok choy. There are also salad mixtures which are sown thickly and harvested en masse with scissors when they are a few inches high, then left to come again, and again.

Crops for storage

At the opposite end of the spectrum from dew-fresh salad is the deeply satisfying winter store of home-grown roots, tubers, rhizomes, and bulbs. This is another area where you can excel, since most commercially grown roots and tubers are intensively treated with chemicals. It is known that pesticides and other toxins applied to potatoes can become concentrated in the skin. Eating non-organically grown jacket potatoes is therefore risky, so even growing such a cheap-to-buy food is well worth while.

When raising your winter supplies, aim for vegetables with good keeping qualities and versatility in the kitchen. It doesn't matter if all your winter-store onions are ready at once – in fact, when you come to harvest them, it's helpful if they are. Any vegetables that stay in the ground until required, such as leeks, will more-or-less stand still until warmer weather stimulates flowering. Select your varieties with care, harvest are easier to stipulate than to create; use your first winter to test a variety of situations, with a batch of each crop in each place. Check them over regularly so you can pinpoint the best place for each crop. Good storage is priceless; if you find the ideal store, don't change a thing!

It isn't necessary to have a suitable building for storage, however. The reason why the roots we eat are full of food is to enable their biennial owner – the plant, that is – to overwinter before restarting the following spring with the object of flowering. If your root vegetables are hardy, they could theoretically keep in good condition in the ground. If you don't disturb them, however, they'll be preparing for growing on next year; if you do disturb them, it's possible that damage might start the rot process. Perfect storage therefore entails putting your undamaged but disengaged crop into conditions you'd expect to find under the ground in ideal weather – cool but frost-free darkness, moist but not wet. This is the basis of the traditional "clamp": first you dig out the crop and then you re-bury it in a sandy mound insulated with straw to keep out frost.

Bulbs store best with air circulating freely around them. Onions and garlic can be hung in net bags, but it's better to hang them by their dry leaves in bunches (1), or, better still, use the long leaves to make a kind of French plait (2).

Crops to freeze

As well as growing roots, rhizomes, tubers, and bulbs, which are designed by nature for overwintering, there are vegetables that lend themselves to other methods of preservation, such as freezing. Although the energy ethics of running a freezer are debatable, a full freezer uses no more energy (possibly even less) than a half-empty one, and a large freezer doesn't use twice as much energy as one half the size. Therefore, if your lifestyle does include using a freezer, keep it as full of home-grown produce as you can. Freezing freshly picked produce is also an excellent way of conserving its food value.

Growing for the freezer brings yet another dimension to your vegetable strategy. Instead of having to make intricate successional sowings, you can

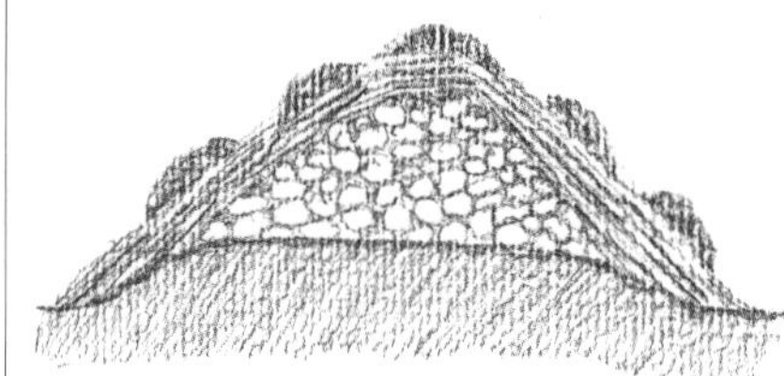

Potatoes are traditionally stored in an outdoor clamp, raised on a ridge of soil, covered with insulating yet ventilating straw held in place with more soil. The thickness of soil covering can be adjusted to keep the potatoes cool but frost-free.

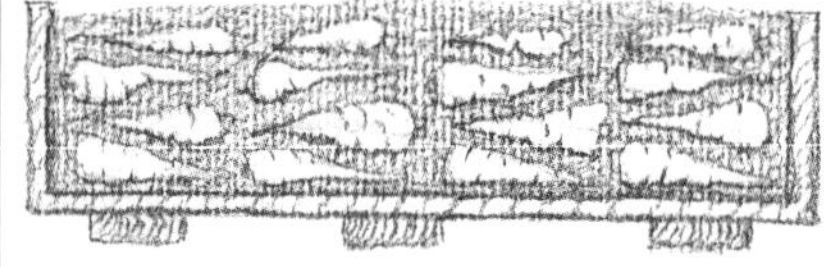

Root crops store well in a raised box of sand or peat, packed like sardines with a layer of filling between each layer of vegetables. Twist off the greenery first.

VEGETABLES TO STORE

VEGETABLE	METHOD	TIME
Artichoke, Jerusalem	in situ	
Asparagus	Freeze	6 month
Beans (green)	Freeze or salt	6–12 mc
Beans	Dry	6–12 mc
Beetroot	Clamp	3–4 mor
Brussels sprouts	in situ Freeze	2–3 mor 6–12 mc
Cabbage, green	Sauerkraut	12 mont
Cabbage, red	Pickle Freeze	4–5 mor 12 mont
Cabbage, savoy	in situ	2–3 mor
Cabbage, winter/ red	Hang cool, dry	2–3 mo
Calabrese	Freeze	3 month
Carrots	Clamp	
Garlic	Hang dry	4–6 mo
Herbs	Dried Freeze	4–6 mor 4–6 mo
Leeks	in situ	3–4 mo
Mushrooms	Ketchup Dry	
Onions	Hang dry	4–6 mor
Parsnips	Freeze young Clamp rest	6–12 mc
Peas	Freeze	12+ mor
Potatoes	Store dark	3–4 mor
Pumpkin/squash	Hang cool, dry	2–4 mor
Sunflower	Dry seed	6–9 mor
Swedes	Store dark	3 month
Sweetcorn	Freeze	6–12 mc
Turnips	Store dark Freeze	3–4 mor 9–12 mc

RIETY, CULTIVATION, SPECIAL EATMENT
t tubers, dig to eat after tops brown, leave some next year's crop.
l-drained perennial site, harvest very young, ch briefly.
nch, dwarf or runner. Pick young, blanch briefly lt.
ve pods on vine long as possible, then hang to plete drying. Store airtight.
st off leaves (don't cut), put large beets at bottom ore longer.
ter crop, freeze surplus when small and tight.
te Dutch or similar, ferment in traditional ner.
ter crop, pickle for variety. Freeze cooked for venience, long store.
ter crop, stands until cropped or spring, chever comes first.
g firm early-winter cabbages in dry nets, after oving outer leaves.
ch thick stems well, steaming tops.
ncrop/late varieties.
t cloves earlier than onion sets in dry, sunny .
early but dry, hang in shade or oven-dry, nble into jars when dry.
n freeze, crumble and wrap tightly in small packs.
g-term planting in deeply cultivated soil. Pull n required, to late winter.
-extracted "essence" for sauces. Slow-dry in n or sun. Store sealed.
en well, with roots loosened, before lifting. are neck rot.
p, well-cultivated soil not recently fertilized. Lift ng for freezing. er roots best frosted before use.
variety, blanch briefly after shelling. Mange- , unblanched but shorter storage.
ncrop or late. Best stored in paper sacks. Discard green tubers.
variety. Becomes dry during long storage.
ect ripe seed, store dry or roasted.
ncrop.
t solid square for good pollination. Blanch (and) well for good storage.
ncrop. ng tender roots, part-cooked.

now make good use of a glut of the sort of crops which normally have a very short season. Beans and peas freeze especially well, and so do asparagus, sweetcorn, and Brussels sprouts. Herbs, crumbled after being quick-frozen, can fill up corners.

Other preservation methods

As well as energy-consuming freezing, the time-honoured natural methods such as sun-drying, pickling, salting, and sugaring still work, although excess salt and sugar are not now considered to belong in a healthy diet. It's worth growing some crops especially for drying, and for making preserves, pickles and chutneys, to fill out the larder all the year round.

Which bed?

Traditional gardening used to entail a lot of digging – back-breaking labour, year after year. This is hardly likely to be necessary in your own garden, because the natural way is to let those experts, the earthworms, do the digging for you (see pp.219–21). You'll still need to decide whether you want raised beds or magic mounds, perennial plots or strictly rotated ones, even whether you want to set aside a formal vegetable plot at all or mingle vegetables with ornamentals (or grow as ornamentals) wherever there's a suitable niche.

Even if you do have frilly lettuces doing duty as ornamental edging and asparagus fern setting off the roses, you may still wish to establish some kind of vegetable plot. There are many different cultivation systems to choose from, and the choice depends on you, your soil, your climate, and what you want to grow.

Which direction?

When establishing a permanent bed, think first about the relationship between compass points and sunlight angle. Whether to run your beds in the conventional north-south direction or to align them west-east depends on combining several considerations. If you intend to plant rows of different-sized crops in the same bed, it may be sensible to run the bed west-east, so that the taller ones can be at the back, where they won't shade smaller ones, and can give shelter from a polar breeze. If the bed is to contain crops of a similar height, and more particularly if it's to be a convex raised bed, then it makes better sense to run it north-south, giving every single plant its fair share of sunlight. The farther away from the equator you are, the more important the effects of alignment become (see Orientation on p.240).

Raised beds

Raised beds can offer improved drainage; deep topsoil with no compaction; fast spring warm-up; and the potential to sustain much more closely planted crops (which also gives better moisture retention). All of this adds up to high productivity per unit area of ground.

Adding compost to your vegetable bed, year after year, will naturally raise it as time goes by, but if your garden is prone to waterlogging it may make sense to build a raised bed right at the start. A wall can be made to any height, depending on your needs, and from a variety of materials. Wood tends to rot in time, although old railway sleepers can last for many years.

A quick, functional wall can be made with planks pegged vertically into place, or corrugated plastic sheets driven well in, although these walls aren't especially attractive and cannot be leaned against or sat upon.

Brick or stone walls are more tricky to build, but can be both attractive and practical (see p.204). Seams and gaps can be planted with trailing herbs is to retain moisture rather than lose it, impermeable walls are preferable.

A raised bed is also easier to tend than one at ground level: it's easier to reach (even from a wheelchair) and less likely to be infiltrated by surrounding grasses and other wild plants. In a situation where the soil presents real difficulties, but where rainfall is adequate, a nutrient-enriched raised bed can provide an instant vegetable plot.

Constructing a raised bed can be done in one operation, or over several years, according to your needs and resources. When shifting topsoil from some other part of your garden (making a wildflower meadow, for example, or digging a pond), this could be mixed with compost to start a raised vegetable bed at the same time. Another way to approach the project is to regard it as a long-term plan, putting walls around a bed when it has risen naturally after regular addition of compost. A magic mound (see p. 211) can also be turned into a raised bed in time.

Construction

The bed should be narrow enough for you to reach the middle easily without walking on it (i.e. not more than about 4ft, or 1.2m, across). The height and length will depend on individual requirements, available space, and the nature of the wall materials. A high wall may have to support a considerable weight on one side only, and this must be taken into consideration, plus the fact that you might sit or lean on it while tending your patch. If you're using railroad ties, their size will dictate the height and length of the bed.

Raised beds don't always have to be contained. Where excess moisture is a problem it might be preferable to have a free-formed convex bed which presents a larger surface area both for planting and for evaporation. Flat-topped contained beds are best for retaining moisture, however, because their surface is smaller and the sides are sealed.

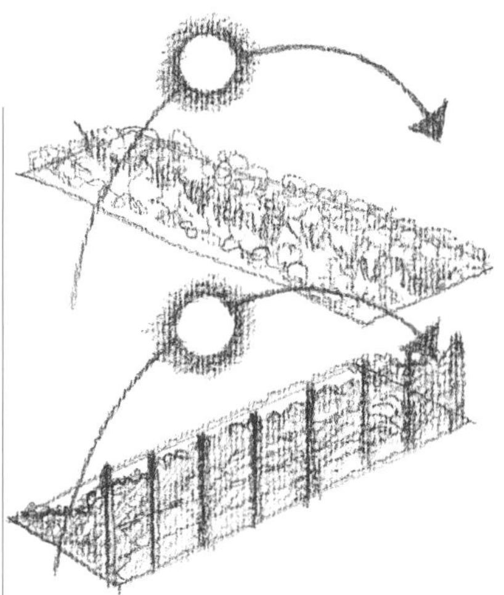

Orientation
Rows running north-south will receive morning light from one side and afternoon light from the opposite side, making it more suitable for low-growing plants. East-west alignment allows a row of very tall plants – even as tall as pole beans – at the "back", with other plants coming down in steps in front. It also lends itself to a cold site, with a wall or fence to the poleward side to cut out polar winds and reflect sunlight and heat on to the plants.

The walkways between raised beds can be firmed with temporary paving materials (see p.205), or even made into permanent walks.

Flat or deep beds

Where soil is dry and light, raised beds might need a great deal of compost and/or imported topsoil in order to succeed. Although a raised bed can retain moisture well if the crop is tightly packed to cover all the soil, a level bed is also appropriate on well-drained ground. If the ground is in fact too well-drained for your requirements, a level bed can be improved by converting it into a kind of sunken raised bed, or deep bed. Instead of building a deep bed above ground, the objective is to excavate a 4ft (1.2m)-wide strip and perhaps even line the walls with impervious material before filling in with enriched soil. On deep sandy soils, it may even be necessary to line the whole excavation with plastic sheet, like a pond, and to create a subsoil-topsoil system within this enclosure.

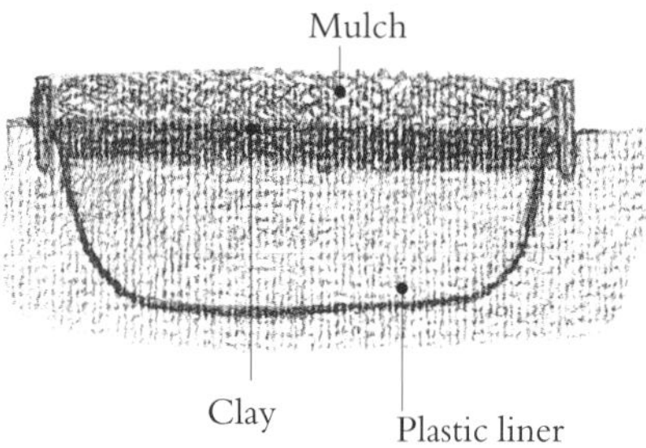

On very sandy soil, a sunken bed contained within a liner can provide a giant flowerpot to hold any kind of soil you like. Top it off with moisture-retentive clay and mulch thickly.

Hay bales

A hay bale can become a ready-made raised bed of developing compost. A layer of hay bales, watered with HLA (diluted urine) and/or smothered with fresh manure, then topped off with a 6in (15cm) crust of finished compost, becomes a mini-plot for a succession of crops. Once it's been built, the hay bale gateau needs to be kept moist for up to a month until the composting process gets under way, and then seedlings or seeds can be planted or sown into pockets or shallow drills of loamy soil ("potting mix") set into the surface layer. The best species to choose for this first year are green, leafy, nitrogen-greedy varieties.

This system is not for the dry garden, as it needs copious watering. In a wet and relatively difficult situation,

Hay-bale beds can be any size you like. Moisten thoroughly and then keep moist. Initial plantings are made into pockets of mild soil in the top layer. As time goes by, the high-N fertilizer acts on the hay to replenish nutrients removed from the soil layer by growing plants.

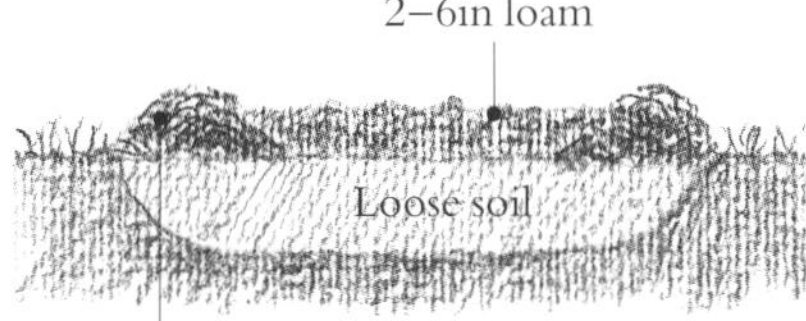

however, the hay bale could provide an instant vegetable plot. It's especially valuable on wet clay soil, which might take some time to form a decent tilth, and here the hay bale brings an extra bonus by stimulating worms to cultivate the soil beneath. As the bale shrinks away, so the worms incorporate some of it into the clay. Repeatedly placing hay bales in the same place will eventually create a deep raised bed of soft, rich humus, even on cold, wet clay. The warmth generated by the composting process also helps to encourage growth, rather like (but more mildly than) the traditional hotbed.

The hay can be old and moldy or fresh and green. Old and moldy has the advantage of being cheap or even free (but heavy to handle); fresh and green contains more nutrients but costs more to buy. If you have a wildflower meadow, you need look no farther for your hay – the only problem will be getting it baled tightly enough. Straw can be used instead, but it will need more nitrogen in the form of manure or urine to activate it.

No-bed

Although having a special bed for vegetables is an efficient horticultural strategy because it allows you to concentrate your resources and to achieve total control, you don't have to make a vegetable bed in your garden if you don't want to. Many vegetables can be grown almost as well among flowers, and some positively cry out to be used as ornamental or useful plants around the garden. Some of our vegetables, such as scarlet runner beans and tomatoes, were grown first as ornamentals and only later for food, and there are others which, in the course of being bred for appetizing appearance, have become very beautiful.

As well as the visual appeal of edibles in the flower bed or their usefulness as wind breaks, and the scope for originality this offers, there are sound ecological reasons for adopting the integrated approach. Firstly, it interferes with the problems caused by monoculture. Wherever a single crop is concentrated in one place, it becomes both a target and a paradise for a single species of "pest", and therefore invites a plague. Mingling vegetables with other plants and flowers reduces this element of risk.

Secondly, since integration is the basis of companion planting, it can bring some of the same benefits. Many vegetables, for instance, are gathered either before they flower or before their flowers open. The services of hoverflies and other flower-attracted insects which feed on aphids are therefore sacrificed. Mixing vegetables with flowers gives them the protection of these patrolling guards. In some cases, the surrounding plants can act as decoys, preventing pests from targeting your edibles. There are also pest-repellent talents of some non-edibles which can be exploited. Mixing edibles with ornamentals as an informal method of companion planting is more attractive than a rigidly formulated plan.

Wild edibles

If integrating your edibles is one aspect of gardening, another must be eating already-integrated plants.

Every single plant we eat is derived from something that once grew wild, which our ancestors would have picked and eaten when they stumbled across it growing somewhere. Along the line, some species became favorites because they were easy to cultivate and/or good for storing. Among all the edible plants in the world, though, only a tiny fraction is commonly cultivated, and the short-list of staples seems to have been quite arbitrarily formed. The vast majority of edible plants have either never been cultivated yet, or have somehow fallen out of fashion, but this doesn't mean you can't eat them, or that they aren't good – maybe even delicious – to eat.

Starting from seed

When raising seeds, there are several different strategies to choose from. The choice depends on the type of vegetable you're growing, the time of year, and the state of your soil.

For an early start, many seeds can be raised in pots or flats indoors or in a warm greenhouse. Later, when the soil is warm, it's possible to sow the seeds of fast-growing or biennial crops directly into the ground where they're going to grow on. In between, there's the cold frame for starting seeds that will be transplanted into their final bed later, or the cloche for protecting in-situ sowings until the weather is warm enough for them to be exposed.

Stratification

In higher latitudes, there is a winter season between the forming of seed and the coming of spring. It's important that seeds here don't sprout before the winter, when tender new plants could be killed. One way that plants insure themselves against this is to use frost as a trigger for germination; they won't germinate until after they have been subjected to low temperatures, so if you grow these plants you must allow for this either by sowing seeds in early winter and leaving them to be frosted naturally or by refrigerating them for several weeks.

Other plants have other special requirements, and some seeds can have sophisticated chemical devices to ensure germination at the "right" time. This makes them dependent on a brief exposure to light, arrival of water after a period of extreme drought, and so forth. Some seeds – especially those contained within berries – may stand a better chance of germinating after they have passed through a bird's gut. If your seeds have special needs like these, comply as best you can.

Pots and flats

When raising seeds, all kinds of containers and materials can be recycled.

- Plastic pots can be used instead of conventional plant pots. Drainage holes should be cut or pierced around the sides at the base rather than underneath, because a hole in a flat-bottomed pot won't drain freely if the pot is placed on a flat surface.
- Old rolls from toilet paper make long, bottomless pots.
- Make pots any size you want from cardboard or a double sheet of newspaper. Uncoated cardboard or newspaper pots break down completely when planted out with their contents.
- If you have some plastic trays of the type used by supermarkets for prepacking fruit and vegetables, you can help to make up for the waste they represent by piercing drainage holes and using them as seed flats.
- Recycle plastic bags by turning them inside out and using them as individual greenhouses for single pots or flats. Open the bags when the seeds sprout.

Growing medium

Seeds have their own food store and don't need rich soil to germinate in. Peat-based composts became popular because they're low in nutrients but high on texture, and generally "clean" of disease and viable seeds. Other more sustainable alternatives are now becoming available, and these should be used in preference to peat. These include mediums based on various by-products, such as coconut fiber, also called coir, and chopped bark. You can make your own seed starter mix from well-rotted leafmold, or by mixing coconut fiber with sand, and adding loam, perlite, leafmold, and/or well-matured garden compost. Sterilize the mix to prevent damping-off of seedlings. When the seeds have germinated, nourishment can either be tailored to their individual needs or supplied with a balanced organic feed such as a seaweed-derived product.

Seedlings

Once germinated, seedlings need light and air. They can be grown on until they're big enough to handle and/or thin out.

One of the greatest hazards to young seedlings is damping-off, a form of fungal stem rot which generally causes them suddenly to fall over sideways. The best defence is to keep everything clean and bring the seedlings on as fast as possible by keeping them warm. If the seedlings are covered with plastic bags or glass, take the covers off for a few hours during the day if it's warm enough to ensure good air circulation.

Worm compost is a powerful anti-damping-off agent which can be used by the natural gardener. For some reason, soil that has passed through a worm's gut gives both protection and stimulation to growing seedlings. If worm compost is blended into the growing medium, it reduces the risk of damping off as well as providing other benefits.

At the right time and stage of growth, pot-grown seedlings will be planted out in the vegetable plot, either by tapping them out of their plastic pot or by sinking the whole of a biodegradable pot into the soil.

Hardening off

If seedlings have been grown in a sheltered environment, such as in a greenhouse or cloche, or on a windowsill, they need time to become acclimatized to the outside world before being planted out for good. Begin by allowing them out during the day, in a sheltered position (or in situ with cloche opened), then increase the exposure – both degree and period – until they can clearly cope.

Herbs

Whether or not you consider herbs to be vegetables, they're bound to be on every natural gardener's list of essential plants. The first distinction to make is between annuals and perennials, which can depend to some extent on your situation. Many herbs are perennials from warm climates; some of these won't stand winter cold but can be grown as annuals in cooler regions. The warm-climate theme also influences the quality of culinary herbs, since most require plenty of sunshine to help them make the aromatic oils which give them flavor and scent.

It follows, then, that warm-climate herbs grown in temperate regions need to be situated in the sunniest possible spot. In the case of woody herbs, quality of soil is far less important than sunlight and warmth, because these herbs typically grow in light, rocky soils. Many other herbs prefer rich soil but still need the sun, while a few such as the mints will thrive with moist soil in half-shade.

Some herbs, such as thymes and mints, come in a large number of varieties. These offer scope for selecting the ideal type for your garden, for making a "collection", and for growing unusual varieties to create special visual and/or culinary effects. If you intend to use herbs for cooking, flavor is the most important characteristic, so it makes sense to select those species which are most at home in your particular region. On the other hand, even herbs whose aromatic content is too small for the kitchen can provide a decorative and fragrant dimension in the garden. The blossoms of flowering herbs attract bees and other pollinating insects, while the pungent scent of some herbs can also help to repel pests.

Wild Salads and Vegetables

Common Name	Latin name	Caution	How to Use
Arugula	*Eruca sativa*		Leaf in salad – tastes of roast pork.
Bittercress	*Cardamine pratensis*	Wash well	Identical in taste to watercress.
Chickweed	*Stellaria media*	Wash well	Salad leaf or cooked as spinach.
Cornsalad	*Valerianella locusta*		Winter salad. Very hardy, pest-resistant, self-seeding.
Dandelion	*Taraxacum officinale*	Wash well	Leaves for bitter salad, or cooked and eaten cold, dressed with oil and lemon. Roots roasted and ground as coffee substitute.
Dill	*Anethum graveolens*		Seeds for flavoring pickles. Leaf as digestive.
Dock	*Rumex* spp.	Try not to scatter. Hard to eradicate once established	Leaf as sorrel.
Fungi	Various	Only experts should gather fungi.	According to type, generally stewed or sauteed, often stored dried.
Garlic mustard	*Alliaria petiolala*		Leaves taste of delicate hedge bitter garlic – with no bad breath!
Good King Henry	*Chenopodium bonus-henricus*	Easy to distinguish from other goosefoots	Use fleshy, soft leaf as spinach.
Goutweed	*Aegopodium podagraria*		Young leaves edible raw or cooked like spinach. Thick mulch produces delicious shoots.
Horseradish	*Armoracia rusticana*		Pungent root used for sauce or pickle.
Juniper	*Juniperus communis*		Berries for tisane and flavoring, e.g. venison.
Lamb's quarters	*Chenopodium alba*		Spinach substitute.
Mullein	*Verbascum* spp.	Hay-fever sufferers avoid	Flowers added to salad.
Purslane, summer	*Portulaca oleracea*		Salad leaf.
Salad burnet	*Sanguisorba minor*		Leaf in salad – tastes of cucumber.
Salsify	*Tragopogon porrifolius*		Winter roots boiled, baked or soup. Young leaves for salad.
Samphire	*Crithmum maritimum*	Watch out for sea tides	Young plants only. Boil with vinegar, serve hot with butter. Cook and pickle. No need for salt.
Seakale	*Crambe maritima*		Best blanched, can happen naturally when sand or shingle blows over crown. Pick shoots 4–5in long.
Stinging nettle	*Urtica dioica*	Use gloves to pick	Pick young tips only to use as spinach, or for soup.
Watercress	*Nasturtium officinale*	Pollution/liver flukes	Leaf for salad.

Herbs

Common Name	Fam.*	Latin Name	A B P	Use	Grow	Harvest/Handle
Angelica	U	*A. archangelica*	B	Candied	Dry, sunny	Young stems sugared.
Anise	U	*Pimpinella anisum*	A	Flavor	Dry, sunny	Store dried seeds.
Balm, Lemon	L	*Melissa officinalis*	P	Tisane	Open, sunny	As required.
Basil	L	*Ocimum basilicum*	A	Flavor	Moist, sunny	Fresh, store dried or frozen.
Bee balm, Bergamot	L	*Monarda didyma*	P	Tisane	Fertile, sunny, moist moist	Leaves green or dried, added to tea or infuse alone.
Borage	Bor	*Borago officinalis*	A	Drinks	Dry, sunny	Leaf, add to fruit cup.
Caraway	U	*Carum carvi*	B	Seeds	Fertile, sunny	Gather and store ripe seed.
Catnip	L	*Nepeta cataria*	P	Insects	Light, sunny	Sprigs repel flies, attract cats
Chamomile	C	*Chamaemelum*	P	Tisane	Fertile, sunny	Infuse flower-heads.
Chervil	U	*Anthriscus cerefolium*	A	Flavor	Dry, sunny	Fresh leaf for salad; soups.
Coriander	U	*Coriandrum sativum*	A	Flavor	Fertile, sunny	Gather leaf before flowering; store ripe seed for spice.
Cumin	U	*Cuminum cyminum*	A	Spice	Full sun	Ripe seed. Best roasted.
Dill	U	*Anethum graveolens*	AB	Flavor	Fertile, sunny	Fresh leaf for sauces, ripe seed to store.
Fennel	U	*Foeniculum vulgare*	AP	Flavor	Fertile, sunny	Pick young leaves, use fresh.
Lovage	U	*Levisticum officinale*	P	Salty	Well-drained	Use fresh leaf to give salty savor.
Marjoram	L	*Origanum* spp.	PA	Flavor	Open, sunny	Fresh as required, or dry whole.
Mint, pepper	L	*Mentha piperita*	P	Flavor	Moist, fertile	Crush fresh or dried leaves.
Mint, spear	L	*M. spicata*	P	Tisane	Moist fertile	Fresh leaves best for tisane; dried or fresh to cook.
Oregano	L	*Origanum vulgare*, see Marjoram				
Parsley	U	*Petroselinum hortense*	B	Flavor	Fertile, sunny	Pick fresh sprigs for sauces, salads, and garnish.
Pennyroyal	L	*Mentha pulegium*	P	Insects	Sandy, moist	Companion, and dried leaves said to repel fleas. Plant late summer.
Rosemary	L	*Rosmarinus officinalis*	P	Flavor	Full sun	Dry leaves, airtight store
Rue	Rut	*Ruta graveolens*	P	Insects	Well-drained	Repels fleas, also cats. Can cause dermatitis.
Sage	L	*Salvia officinalis*	P	Flavor	Sunny, sheltered	Pick leaf as desired. Dry in sprigs, but use leaf only.
Savory, summer	L	*Satureja hortensis*	A	Flavor	Dry, sunny	Use fresh in summer for sauces.
Savory, winter	L	*Satureja montana*	P	Flavor	Open, sunny	Pick as required in winter, use as summer savory above.
Southern-wood	C	*Artemisia abrotanum*	P	Insects	Any, sunny	Hang sprigs in open window, closet, etc.
Sweet Cicely	U	*Myrrhis odorata*	P	Flavor	Dry, sunny	Eat whole plant raw or cooked, add cicely to sweet dishes to reduce use of sugar.
Tansy	C	*Tanacetum vulgare*	P	Med.	Fertile, sunny	Use a few leaves and young shoots in puddings, omelettes; candied root for gout; tisane as tonic in moderation.
Tarragon	C	*Artemisia dracunculus*	P	Flavor	Dry, warm, sunny	Fresh leaf in vinegar, mustard, tartare sauce. Aromatic oil destroyed if dried.
Thyme	L	*Thymus* spp.	P	Flavor	Dry, sunny	Gather as required.

Families: U = Umbelliferae; L = Labiatae; C = Compositae; Bor = Boraginaceae; Rut = Rutaceae.

FINE TUNING

Once your garden is laid out and growing, the nature of the challenge changes. It now becomes a new start, the beginning of the dynamic process of getting acquainted with what you've created and making subtle adjustments, season by season. The potential for fine tuning is virtually endless, limited only by your own interest and resources.

Plant-watching

It's said that talking to plants will encourage them to grow. There's no doubt that visiting your plants every day will help them to thrive whether you talk to them or not, if only because each time you see them you're bound to notice if they need water or some other assistance, and will supply the need. When you visit, be especially alert for the signs of stress.

- Check for limp foliage. This may be due to dry soil, but may also be caused by sapsucking insects, slugs, and snails, or cold and wind.
- Look out for yellowing and/or falling leaves, which may indicate nutritional deficiency, drought, or waterlogging.
- Watch closely for fungal disease, usually indicated by spots or other unusual marks. Fertilize the plant, and remove the damaged parts. If you recognize the infection as a deadly disease, take out the plant and burn it.
- Identify any small creatures you see wandering on your plants and learn to distinguish friend from foe. Don't be too hasty to take action.

Become familiar with the regular annual cycle of all your permanent plantings. Observe when new leaves appear; when flowers open and how they're pollinated; when and whether the fruit thins itself; when fruit ripens; when leaves fall, and what color changes they undergo first. Knowing all these things enables you to spot unusual developments as soon as they occur, so that you can take immediate action in an emergency. Above all, intimate acquaintance with your living plants develops empathy, a key ingredient of success and fulfilment in the garden.

Botanical basics

The basic life cycle of a flowering plant begins with a seed, which germinates to produce first a root and then a stem bearing leaves, and which later develops a flower so that it can reproduce sexually, finally forming seeds to begin the cycle again. In addition to sexual flowering, many plants can reproduce asexually (vegetatively) by means of suckers, bulbs, tubers, runners, or other devices. Asexual reproduction gives new plants that are genetically identical to the parent plant, but seeds introduce the element of chance.

The differences between plants come from the multitude of different strategies they adopt to do these things, depending on the niche they would normally occupy. The life cycle itself may take less than a year, or two years, or more. It may occur only once, or be repeated annually for more than a century.

Self-seeding

Plants invest a great deal of energy in producing seed, which is their chief goal in life. Dead-heading flowering plants removes potential seed-heads before they develop and deplete the plant, thus extending flowering time, increasing the absolute numbers of blooms, and/or prolonging the plant's life.

On the other hand, self-made seeds can be a free source of new stock. Depending on the genetic make-up of the original stocks, such seeds may grow into near-facsimiles of the parent plant or can give rise to new (perhaps quite exciting) variations on the theme. Generally speaking, wild-type plants such as native shrubs and herbs will breed true (although they can differ in habit quite a lot), while highly bred ornamentals are less likely to. Only 50 percent of seeds from any plants grown from bought seeds labeled F1 will germinate to resemble the parent plant, and the rest are often disappointing.

The simplest way to make use of self-made seeds is to let them fall where they will. This approach depends on a fine ability to distinguish between wanted seedlings and weed seedlings. Once identified, volunteers can either be left to grow where they began, or be dug up and transplanted elsewhere. A surer system is to target the plants you want seeds from and then watch them carefully until the seeds are ripe.

Collecting seed

To collect seeds successfully, you need to catch them when they're fully ripe but before they've been released. You may have to enclose a seed-head in a paper bag secured with a rubber band during the final ripening stage, to prevent the seeds scattering. Once collected, seeds can either be sown right away or stored somewhere dry and cool in labeled paper bags (plastic will suffocate them). Some seeds remain viable after years of storage, but others germinate best when sown immediately.

Saving vegetable seed

Reasons for saving vegetable seed obviously include economy, but the most important reason is the frequent difficulty of obtaining some old-fashioned varieties. Such varieties are especially good subjects for home-grown seed, because this is how they would originally have been handled.

When planning to raise vegetable seeds, you need at least two plants of exactly the same variety in bloom at the same time. Crossing different varieties will produce hybrids, which may (and probably will) be disastrous. Another problem is that many brassicas, e.g. broccoli, kale, cabbage, Brussels sprouts, kohl-rabi, are all derived from the same wild ancestor, and they are able to interbreed just as other "varieties" can. You'll also need to allow the very best of your crop plants to "run to seed", in order to get the best-bred seed next year. But set against that is the advantage of being able to select the best plants to breed from, and over many generations you will obtain a strain which is best adapted to your garden – a privilege surely worth striving for.

Propagation

A good way to get plenty of new plants identical to the parent is to make use of a plant's natural ability to reproduce itself vegetatively. The plant may have a well-developed system, such as regularly multiplying bulbs or creeping stems which make a bunch of roots at intervals, or many-eyed stalked tubers such as potatoes. Some plants can simply be divided in half, from the ground up – clump-forming plants can be teased apart, and rhizomes (e.g. iris) can be broken or cut into root-bearing sections. Taking advantage of existing rooted material is an easy way to increase your stock.

Even when plants don't give such obvious assistance, it's often possible to persuade a part of the plant – generally stem, occasionally leaf – to grow roots at some stage in the growth cycle. Different plants tend to respond best to particular treatments, and when you've acquired experience it's sometimes possible to use clues provided by the plant to help you guess which approach to adopt – all relatives of blackberries, for example, can be propagated by pushing a growing stem tip directly into the ground.

How to raise Vegetable Seeds

Type	A/B	Store	Pol	Method and problems
Leafy brassicas	B	8/9yrs	I	Permit only one variety to flower each year. Collect pods when yellow and unopened. Apart from broccoli, need 2 years to make seed – bad for rotation.
Alliums	B	2/3yrs	I	Ignore plants which bolt in first year. Lift onions, replant best bulbs late winter. Leave leeks *in situ*. Can be planted in border, where very dramatic and attractive to insects. Tall stems need staking.
Radish	A	9/10yrs	I	Radish is annual, other roots are biennials.
Carrot	B	5/6yrs	I	Ignore plants which seed first year. Select best of stored roots, replant in early spring (can go in border).
Parsnip	B	2/3yrs	I	As carrot.
Squash, etc.	A	5/6yrs	I	For squash and zucchini, limit vine to 1 fruit, ripen until hard, cut open (with saw) and extract seed.
Lettuce	A	2/3yrs	S	Many highly bred lettuces refuse to bolt. Use old-type variety, ignore early-bolting plants and choose best late-bolting specimens. Thistle-type seeds will fly, so check frequently to catch them in time.
Legumes	A	9/10yrs	S	Check selected plants by pinching out tip (bush) or upper side-shoots (stick), allow pods to ripen on vine, finish by laying vine flat.
Tomatoes	A	9/10yrs	I	Choose early-ripening plants, leave trusses 3 and 4 to ripen fully (ignore misshapen or miscolored fruits), rub seeds gently from split fruits, and spread to dry.
Maize	A	9/10yrs	W	One corn cob is enough. Ripen on stem until hard

Key to pollinators (Pol.): I = insect; S = self; W = wind.

The chart gives best methods for a variety of woody plants. If in doubt, it will do no harm to experiment for yourself. When a plant's branches naturally droop to touch the ground, it may be possible to play safe and try layering. If the branches don't droop you could try air-layering. Leaving the "cutting" attached to the plant in this way removes the need for precise timing. Compact plants can be approached with another method of layering, called stooling, which encourages them to grow roots at the base of near-ground-level branches.

If layering doesn't work, though, you may have to work through several seasons, perhaps even a whole year, trying different types of cutting, before you strike lucky. The main tips are:

- Herbaceous perennials tend to work best from softwood cuttings;
- Evergreens tend to do best from semi-hardwood cuttings;
- For deciduous trees and shrubs, try hardwood cuttings taken after leaf fall.
- Try taking cuttings in all of the three ways illustrated at the same time, and keep notes.

Cuttings from some plants "take" best when trimmed in specific ways. The main techniques are shown above. 1. A simple stem cutting. 2. Basal cutting, taken through a swollen leaf or stem base. 3. A heeled cutting, half cut and then pulled away with a "heel" of main stem attached. 4. Internodal, between nodes: 5. Nodal, cut through stem and just clipping beneath a pair of swollen bases.

Cuttings in open ground are literally heeled in place, i.e. inserted in the ground and firmed with the boot (right).

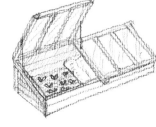

Methods for Propagating some Shrubs and Trees

Open Ground *Heel cuttings in firmly, leave until spring.*			
Buddleia	H	1 yr old	Early winter
Dogwood	H	Nodal/Basal	Winter
Forsythia	H	Basal	Early winter
Jasmine	H	Stem/Heeled	Early winter
Privet	H	Nodal	Early winter
Flowering currant	H	Nodal	Early winter
Willow	H	Stem	Winter
Spiraea	H	Nodal	Winter
Cold Frame or Pot and Plastic Bag *Cold frame traditionally for fall cuttings. Keep pot/bag in light but not direct sun.*			
Broom (*Cytisus*)	SH	Basal	Midsummer
Garrya	H	Basal/Nodal	Early winter
Ivy	SH	Nodal/Internodal	Midsummer/early winter
Lavender	SH	Heeled	Midsummer/early winter
Rosemary	SH	Basal	Fall

Key: H = hardwood; SH = semi-hardwood

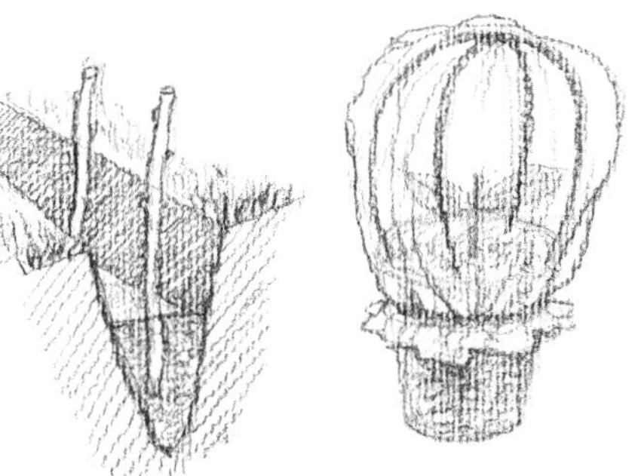

Two ways of delivering unheated shelter, pot-and-polyethylene (left) for indoor use, and a cold frame (above) for outside.

Air layering is done by wrapping damp moss around a wounded stem, enclosing it in plastic, and waiting until roots grow into the moss. It can take a long time, but involves no risk.

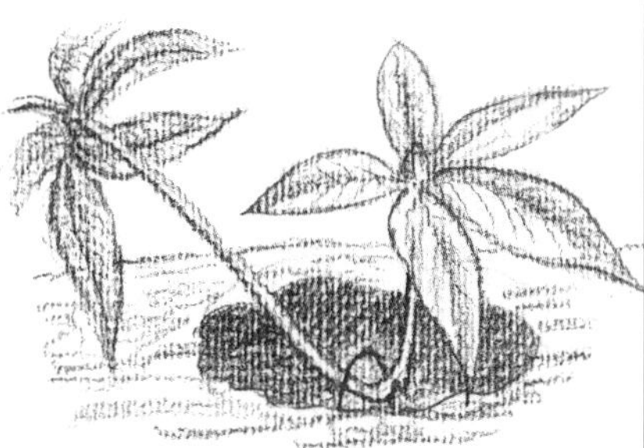

Tip layering (above) encourages rooting in brambles and bramble relatives, which would normally spread this way. Simple layering (right) is a good way to increase stocks of clump-forming plants. Soil piled around and into the clump stimulates the now-buried stem bases to root into it. When the roots are well formed, each stem can be cut cleanly away with a sharp knife and planted separately.

Pruning and training

Even if you select your woody plants carefully, taking account of their natural form and final size, it may still become necessary to influence their growth. If you've acquired somebody else's choice of trees and shrubs, it's even more likely that there will be some trimming to do, and if you're growing orchard, bush, or vine fruits it will probably be essential to prune and train at least young growth. The nature of the job is largely dictated by whether routine maintenance or major surgery is required, whether the subject is a pliable young sapling or a mature conifer, and so on.

Why prune?

In descending order of difficulty, the reasons for interfering with the growth of woody plants fall into a few main categories. First comes major tree surgery in case of urgent necessity due to disease, damage, or danger. You should consult an expert if the tree is large or the disease difficult to cure. Next comes renovation of old orchard trees, which is similar to but a little more demanding than removal of low-growing branches from other mature trees; and after that comes thinning-out and disease control of ornamental shrubs and orchard trees. Finally, there's the light pruning entailed in shaping fruit trees, bushes, and vines, and trimming hedges to keep them healthy and thick. Once the garden is in hand there should rarely be a need for anything beyond light pruning of fruits and hedges.

Big branches

Removing large portions of mature wood demands careful contemplation. A mature tree won't easily be able to hide its loss, so you need to make sure of creating a pleasing shape from the outset. Study the tree carefully before embarking on this irrevocable step, then do it in the winter.

Once you're sure of your aim, begin by cutting underneath the targeted limb at least 2ft (60cm) from the main trunk. When you've cut about a third of the way through, transfer your saw to the upper side and complete the cut from above. The undercut will prevent the heavy branch tearing loose toward the end and ripping a heel off the trunk. After the branch has been detached, you can trim the stump close to the trunk to leave a neat scar which the tree can heal over with callus.

When taking less than a complete branch away, avoid leaving an obviously chopped-off branch by removing the unwanted section at a fork, so that the new shape tapers off naturally.

A clean cut, made with clean tools, ought to heal cleanly, but you can make sure by sealing the cut with bitumen or some brandname antiseptic substance which will reduce moisture loss and help to keep out infection.

When removing heavy limbs from trees, avoid taking unnecessary risks:

- Branches too heavy to be supported with one hand are especially dangerous.
- Don't cut into a branch above your head, in case it breaks suddenly.
- Place your ladder carefully – out of the way of wood that may catch it when falling, and on the "tree" side of the saw.
- Always cut away a heavy or long limb in stages, working inward from the end.
- Be aware that the outer layer of wood can sometimes spring out suddenly with great force when cut.

Thinning

Where a tree has become cluttered with crowded, weak growth it can often be improved by reducing all smaller branches by half, and even taking away some larger branches. Begin by removing all branches that cross or touch one another, then take stock to see what more needs to be done. Aim for a largely unchanged silhouette, within which you have opened up the structure to let in light and air. This allows each remaining leaf to function properly, and at the same time reduces the burden on the roots caused by superfluous growth.

Diseased wood

When removing diseased wood, cut away all infected material, and disinfect pruning tools. Burn the trimmings, and paint the wounds left on the tree with an antiseptic substance.

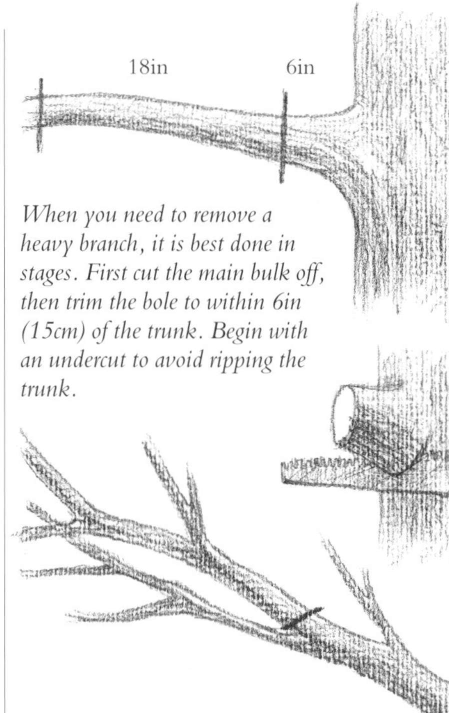

When you need to remove a heavy branch, it is best done in stages. First cut the main bulk off, then trim the bole to within 6in (15cm) of the trunk. Begin with an undercut to avoid ripping the trunk.

A half-cut-off branch is nearly always ugly. To shorten a branch without removing it altogether, select a suitable fork so that, after being trimmed, the main branch still appears to taper away naturally.

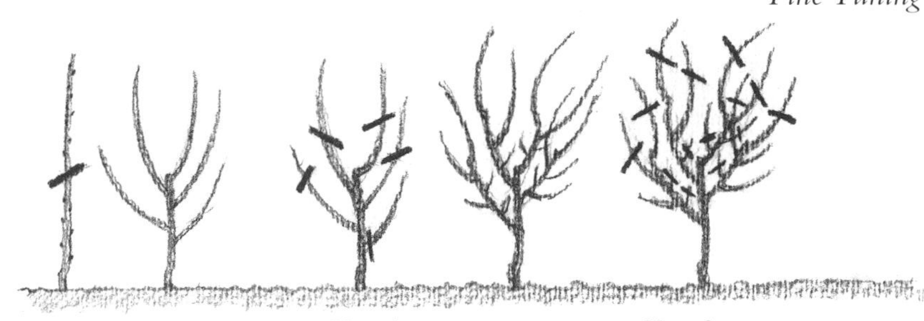

Year 1
As soon as a young fruit tree is planted, it should be pruned to half its height, to establish a low crown.

Year 2
Next year, remove any unwanted branches and reduce the rest by half again, to encourage laterals to form.

Year 3
In the third year, reduce vigorous leaders by half. Future management should aim toward keeping shape and encouraging fruit.

Routine pruning

The aim here is to channel growth into a desired direction rather than to shape the tree with shears and saw, there and then, as though it were a piece of furniture. Another aim, especially with fruit, is to direct the tree's energy away from growth and toward fruit formation. When planting a new tree, initial pruning establishes the future shape of the entire tree, allowing it to invest all its resources in useful growth, as well as curtailing the demands of the crown while the roots become established.

Established patterns of pruning are developed with the above aims in view. Naturally, different types of tree require different treatments, because they have different patterns and habits of growth. There are, however, some basic "rules" that apply to all types.

- Pruning is best done when trees are dormant (with important exceptions, such as apricots), to ensure that the spring flush of growth is channelled into forming new, strong wood.
- Always use a sharp, clean knife, shears, or saw.
- Make a cut above a bud, sloping the cut away from the bud so that it can eventually smoothly replace the cut portion.
- Select a bud that's already growing in the desired direction.
- The rule that "growth follows the knife" applies particularly to young trees. Overenthusiastic pruning of a young tree can result in a burst of side-shoots, whereas an older tree may have far fewer viable buds to work with.
- Learn to distinguish flowering shoots from woody ones, especially when pruning fruit or flowering shrubs.

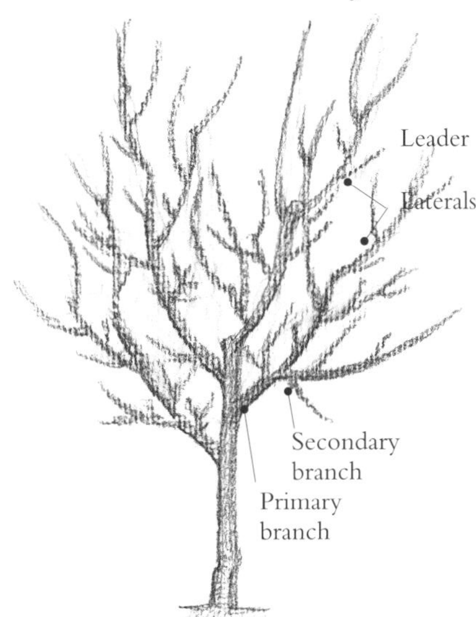

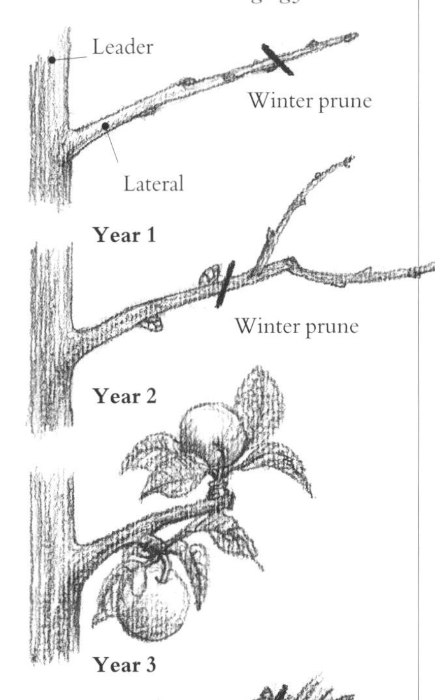

Creating and controlling fruit spurs
Most orchard trees bear blossom (and thus fruit) on ripened wood. As well as shaping, winter pruning (above right) concentrates the tree's energy into producing fruiting spurs. Cluttered spurs can also be thinned out (right) before the buds open, to give fewer and larger fruits. If a heavy crop of fruit sets, wait until the normal summer drop is ended before thinning out. Fruit also benefits from direct sunlight; if a warm, wet spring and summer encourage long shoots to grow, much of this new growth can be pruned back in the late summer.

Training

If you are seeking a stylized or extremely functional shape, you may need to combine pruning with training. Young and pliable stems respond best to this treatment, although if you are using wires or trellises, take care not to bind the stems too tightly (see p.000). Apart from creating pleasing or practical shapes, training can also help to turn a single stem into a series of stems, as in laying a hedge.

Hedge management

Whereas most pruning opens up the structure of a woody plant, hedges are required to grow densely from bottom to top. Hedge trimming depends on cutting off a growing tip to stimulate the buds behind it into growth. Doing this each year makes the bushes branch more finely, thickening the structure and creating a mesh of leafy twigs on the outside. But hedges tend to broaden with time, which eventually causes the inner structure to become spindly, or even die, due to lack of light. When this happens, radical cut back is called for.

A hedge whose "spine" consists of thick woody trunks can have the sides sheared off almost to the point where the branches join the trunks. This is best done in late fall for deciduous hedges; evergreens don't respond well to being drastically cut and, if they must be dealt with, are best left until late spring. The task can be spread over two years – one side at a time – to retain some useful shelter meanwhile. With a many-stemmed hedge (not conifers), it's best to cut the old stems almost down to the ground and use new growth to form the basis of a new hedge. Alternatively, every second or third stem could be retained to provide a framework for re-laying (see p.227). Aim to create an A-shaped profile, which will help to ensure that this operation need not be repeated.

Where the base of a hedge has become leggy, an obvious remedy is to taper the hedge above the bare region to allow light to penetrate. A bare base may, however, be normal for the species that make up the hedge, in which case try introducing some new low-growing species to fill the gap. On the other hand, the problem may have been caused by other plants competing for light, space, or nutrients. This raises the whole issue of compatibility, which

Good Companions

Main Crop	Good Companion	Keep Away From	Good Herbs
Apple			Nasturtium for woolly aphid; Chives for scab
Asparagus	Tomato	Basil, parsley	
Beans	Brassicas, carrot	Fennel, onion	Goosegrass deters leafhoppers
Beets	Bush beans, onion, lettuce, brassicas	Pole beans, mustard	
Brassicas	Pea, potato, garlic, cucumber, bush beans, tomato	Pole beans, strawberry	Nasturtium, dill, sage. Candytuft and shepherd's purse deter flea beetles; hyssop decoys butterflies and caterpillars
Carrot	Leek, lettuce, pea, onion, garlic, tomato, salsify	Dill	Chives deter rootfly; flax, sage
Celery	Brassicas, beans, leek, tomato		
Cucumber	Legumes, radish (sunflower and maize give support)	Potato, aromatic herbs (esp. sage)	Nasturtium, dill, sow-thistle
Fava bean	Brassicas, carrot, celery, potato, maize to climb	Onion, garlic	Summer savory *(Satureia hortensis)*
Lettuce	Carrot, radish, cucumber, strawberry		
Maize	Pole beans, potato, cucumber, amaranth	Tomato	
Onion	Lettuce, tomato, amaranth, leek	Legumes	Summer savory could deter onion root fly
Orchard			Stinging nettles improve keeping of fruit; Limnanthes and nasturtium attract hoverflies
Peas	Beans, carrot, cucumber, radish, potato, maize	Onion and garlic inhibit peas	
Potato	Legumes, brassicas, maize, amaranth	Cucumber, tomato, cherry, orach, sunflower	Horseradish; nightshade can attract and poison Colorado potato beetles
Radish	Cucumber, pea, lettuce	Hyssop	Chervil deters flea beetle
Strawberry	Beans, lettuce, spinach	Borage	
Sweet pepper	Eggplant	Brassicas	Basil decoys aphids
Tomato	Asparagus (deters nematodes), carrot, onion, garlic, radish	Potato, fennel, kohlrabi, maize	Basil decoys aphids; French marigold deters whitefly; sagebrush builds resistance; borage

you may also have to face elsewhere in the garden.

Companion planting
There is a natural logic to planting mixtures of different species. The whole ecosphere thrives and survives through interactions between species living cheek by jowl. Conversely, much of agriculture's problems stem from the artificial creation of monocultures, where a vast field of one crop makes single-minded demands on the soil while magnetically attracting its own particular pest species and providing an endless supply of food for them, their children, and their children's children. Mixed planting, on the other hand, ensures that each plant has different neighbors, attracting different predators, and using a different range of nutrients.

The principle of mixed planting goes even further than this, as it has been observed that some plants may benefit more specifically from being near to particular neighbors. The deliberate exploitation of these effects is called companion planting. The possible benefits include protection from pests and diseases, improved soil fertility, mechanical support, shelter from sun and wind, and attraction of pollinators. Sagebrush, for example, is known to stimulate tomatoes to produce high levels of a chemical that deters pests. Some species confer broad benefits on a variety of neighbors: stinging nettles appear to deter fungal diseases, stimulate essential oil production in herbs, and both speed up ripening and improve keeping qualities of fruit.

These benefits depend very much on particular circumstances, and are difficult to verify under controlled conditions. The most reliable effects seem to be indirect, to do with the attraction of pest predators. The chart on page 250 shows some of the groupings that have been reported. If you want to experiment, it is important to remember to set up a control without the companion plants, so that you may draw your own conclusions!

When is a plant a weed?
It has to be admitted that there are some plants which, given an inch, will take a mile. Whether these highly successful species are regarded as weeds or not depends largely on how difficult it is to control them if required.

One dividing line between tolerable and intolerable wild plants can be drawn between annuals and perennials. Annual weeds can usefully clothe temporarily vacant ground; many of them are dynamic accumulators; and they can also provide food, shelter, or distraction for a variety of insects and other animals. Annuals are usually fairly easy to control by mulching and/or hoeing.

Biennials, and plants on the annual-biennial borderline (e.g. thistles), however, can build fleshy and persistent roots which, if prevented from flowering, may go on trying for several seasons. These and the true perennials can be a great problem. Their deep and/or widespread roots compete with other species, and they may grow larger or spread farther afield each year.

Weeding
The first line of attack or defence against all weeds is mulch. Even perennial weeds will eventually succumb to being denied light, although it may take several years to eradicate them. A second strategy is repeated cutting or pulling, by hoe or hand. This is labor-intensive, but no plant can survive indefinitely when its green growth is continually cropped. The best time to attack is when the shoots first appear, giving the plants no time to replenish used-up food stores. The third and most laborious method is to root out the entire organism. Do this when making a new bed. Always remove perennial weeds as soon as they appear, before they can make deep, extensive roots.

Whatever your strategy, the golden rule is to tackle the weeds before they set seed, thus converting a necessity into virtuous green manure or compost. When using greenstuff directly on the garden, however, make sure it's well wilted – some tenacious weeds are quite capable of re-rooting, or even flowering and setting seed, while lying in heaps.

Pest management
Among all the creatures in your area, only a very few are potential pests, and even these are only likely to become a problem under monoculture conditions. If you maintain a diverse and well-balanced ecosystem where no one species is given the chance to dominate, pest control can become an entertainment rather than a desperate battle.

The "natural" approach to pests is mostly just allowing, or sometimes encouraging, natural controls to do their work. You can help by:

- banishing pesticides;
- growing only small stands of any single crop;
- providing a variety of habitat types: pond, bushes, trees, grass, stones;
- tolerating a wide variety of native plants;
- growing plenty of flowering plants for nectar-feeding predators;
- keeping your crops healthy by balanced fertilizing and watering.

Occasionally a pest species builds up in sufficient numbers to come to your notice. A well-balanced garden usually deals with this automatically, and you can relax and watch the predator-prey battles. Often the damage is slight.

Sometimes, however, specific actions are called for, but you should always aim to interfere as little as possible. Any specific action requires that you identify a pest and know something of its lifestyle. Often judicious timing of sowing or planting out can avoid a crucial phase in a pest's life cycle. Sometimes a simple barrier is sufficient. Covering a crop with horticultural fleece during a sensitive period is very effective against flying pests.

Some pests are easily trapped. A band of sticky paper around a tree trunk catches crawling pests that live partly in the ground. Strips of slabwood, or roof tiles, placed between crop rows can trap slugs and millipedes, and also act as a haven for predatory beetles. Such non-lethal traps must be inspected regularly and the pests removed.

Only if things become intolerable should you resort to sprays, and then only on a strictly local basis (see p.109).

Diseases

Most plant diseases are caused by fungi and are difficult to treat. The natural gardener's strategy is almost entirely preventive, and consists of keeping the plants as healthy as possible, with balanced nutrition and healthy soil: rotating annual crops; using varieties resistant to local diseases; and maintaining good hygiene.

Once a disease has appeared, try to identify it and the organism that causes it. Usually it is specific to a type of plant, and you can let it develop without risk to the rest of the garden.

Generally, "curing" a disease consists simply of cutting out affected parts, or removing the whole plant and burning it. Don't let diseased parts lie about. Often application of rich compost or urine, or a foliar seaweed spray, will help a plant fight back. Biodynamic gardeners set great store by spraying with a tea made from horsetail.

Weed Management

Species	ABP	Weed Rating	Uses	Specific Use	How to Control
Bindweed	P	*****			Heavy mulch; then dig
Bracken	P	***	DA	K/P/Mn/Cu/Co	Raise pH
Brambles	P	***	E	Berries	Cut repeatedly
Catchweed	A	**	CP	See p. 250	Pull before seeds
Celandine	P	*****			Dig/mulch/dig
Chickweed	A	*	E/GC/ DA	E: young leaves GC: green manure DA: K/P/Mn	Mulch
Coltsfoot	P	***	DA	S/Mg/Ca/K/Fe/Cu	Raise pH. Cut repeatedly
Dandelion	P	***	E/I/ DA	Salad; as spinach DA: Na/Si/Mg/Ca/ K/P/ Fe/Cu	Pull or dig
Deadnettle	P	**	I		Mulch, pull, fork
Docks	P	***	DA	Ca/K/P/Fe	Dig deep
Goutweed	P	*****			Heavy mulch, then dig (repeatedly)
Hedge garlic	A	*	E/I	E: young leaves	Pull late if at all
Horsetail	P	*****	AFA/ DA	Powdered leaf tea spray for mildew; DA: Si/ Mg/Ca/Fe/	Very hard if established. Improve drainage/raise pH
Mosses	P	***			Improve drainage/ sharp sand/rake out
Quackgrass	P	****			Fork, cut, mulch
Salad burnet	A	*	E/DA	Young leaf in salad. DA: Fe	
Shepherd's purse	A	*	CP DA	See p. 250 Na/S/Ca	Pull before seeds/ mulch
Speedwell	A	**			Mulch
Stinging nettle	P	***	E/CP/ DA/GC	E: young leaves as spinach. DA: Na/S/N/ Ca/K/Fe/Cu	Cut, dig, mulch/dig
Thistle, most	A/B	**	I/DA	Fe	Fork before flowers
creeping	P	****	DA	a/K/Fe	Dig/mulch/dig
Yarrow	P	*	CP/DA	CP: increases pest resistance in neighbors. DA: S/Ca/K/Cu	Fork/cut/pull

Weed rating refers to difficulty of control. Uses: AFA = anti-fungal agent; CP = companion plant; DA = dynamic accumulator; E = edible; GC = garden compost; I = attracts insects;

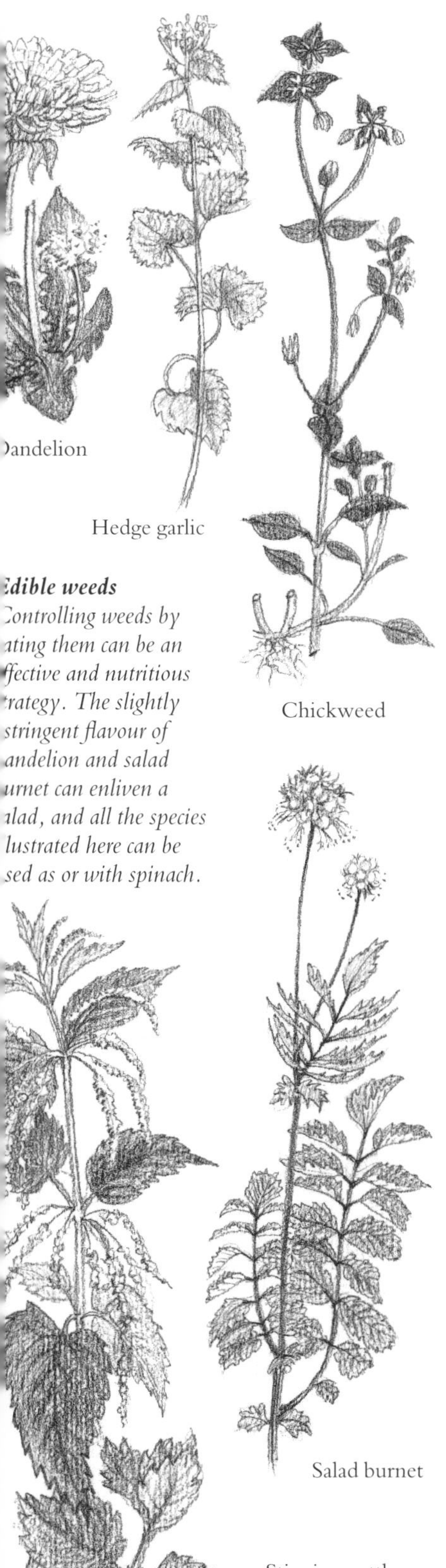

)andelion

Hedge garlic

Chickweed

Salad burnet

Stinging nettle

:dible weeds

:ontrolling weeds by ating them can be an ffective and nutritious rategy. The slightly stringent flavour of andelion and salad urnet can enliven a alad, and all the species lustrated here can be sed as or with spinach.

Organic Pest Control Strategies

Strategy	Recipe/Method	Caution	Controls
Hygiene	Clear dead/diseased fruit/material	Burn if diseased	Overwintering larvae, pupae, spores, etc.
Hand picking	Affected leaves		Leaf miners
Barriers	Collars around brassicas Fleece over entire stand Chicken wire under raised bed		Cabbage root fly Flying pests; birds, rabbits Burrowing animals: moles, gophers
Decoys	Comfrey leaves around crops		Distracts slugs
Traps	Yogurt pots on canes. Unwashed bottomless cardboard cartons as collars around seedlings. Wrap sacking around tree trunk in summer. Slabwood (or roof tiles) between rows	Check often Burn early fall	Trap earwigs Distract slugs while plants grow away Traps apple blossom weevil Traps slugs, millipedes
Sticky band	Use around trunks		Capsids, gypsy moth, etc.
Insecticidal soap	Safer's™ insecticidal soap		Aphids, scales, whitefly, mealy bugs, spider mites
Urine	Spray neat on tight winter buds, and on fallen leaf. Dilute 1:3 in water, on leaves just before leaf fall		Apple and pear scab, gooseberry and blackcurrant mildew.
"Bt" *Bacillus thuringiensis*	Make up suspension in water		Insect larvae, esp. caterpillars
Quassia in insecticidal soap	Boil 1oz chips for 1 hour in 2 pt water, strain and add 1oz insecticidal soap/2oz flakes. Dilute 1:5 water Dilute 1:3 water	Fairly weak remedy	 Aphids Sawfly, caterpillars, mites
Elder spray	1lb fresh leaves boiled 1 hour with 6pt water. Strain, use cold	Kills hoverfly	Fungus including mildews and black spot, small caterpillars, aphids
Borax	Mix 1:1 with icing sugar, sprinkle under cover along runs	POISONOUS Use only if essential	Ants
Rotenone	Dust as bought is a non-persistent plant alkaloid	Kills fish, amphibians,	Caterpillars, aphids, weevils, flea beetle, asparagus beetle

Biodynamic gardening

The practice of biodynamic gardening began formally in 1924 with a series of lectures by the Austrian philosopher and educationalist, Rudolf Steiner. The eight lectures build on traditional practices of organic land management, such as crop rotations and the use of legumes and other soil-building plants, by adding a wider understanding of the terrestrial and cosmic forces which can be consciously developed to maximize productivity – hence "biodynamic".

Terrestrial forces relate to the soil and are influenced by the near planets (moon, Mercury, Venus) through what Steiner characterized as the "limestone element". This element provides moisture and fertility to plants, making them sturdy and nutritious, with lush growth. The cosmic forces, by contrast, proceed from the sun and the distant planets (Saturn, Jupiter, Mars), expressing themselves in light and warmth, through the silica element in the earth. We can see the effects of silica in, for example, the growth of Mediterranean herbs. They grow best at high altitudes in poor calcareous soils. They produce less bulk, are smaller and sturdier, but with stronger flavor and increased essential oils. These forces are necessary to any fruit cultivated for its taste and odor; they help to deepen the color of flowers, and strengthen the growth of vegetable plants.

At the heart of the biodynamic approach are "preparations" which are used to enhance and optimize growing conditions. These preparations are specially fermented substances used in tiny quantities on the soil and in the compost pile. They do not add nutrients but act to regulate soil conditions and stimulate plant life.

There are eight main preparations made in a specific manner to "dynamize" them, so they can be used in very small quantities with a far-reaching effect. For no apparent reason they have been allocated numbers from 500 to 507. The first two, 500 and 501, are used as sprays on the soil, and the remaining six are placed in the compost pile at the time it is constructed.

The soil sprays

The two field sprays are the horn manure (500) preparation designed to enhance the forces of the Earth, supporting the limestone or terrestrial principle, and the horn silica (501) preparation, which radiates the forces of light and warmth, supporting the silica or cosmic principle.

Preparation 500, by working with the forces that come from the Earth, increases soil fertility with particular effect on root growth and primary shoot development.

Preparation 500 is made from cow manure which has been packed into a cow horn and stored underground over winter, the time when cosmic forces of light and warmth are at their weakest and the Earth forces are most active. It is generally sprayed on bare soil immediately before the last cultivation prior to sowing or planting. It can also be sprayed on grassland in spring or after it has been cut.

Preparation 501 is a silica spray made from finely ground quartz crystal or a silicate such as feldspar. This too is packed tightly into a cow horn and stored underground, but this time over a summer period, in a sunny spot, when the forces of light and warmth are strongest. Silica is found all over the world, as well as in the bodies of animals and plants. According to Steiner, its function is to mediate cosmic activities relating to light and heat. Its influence is on all the upward growing tendencies of the plant, especially the formation of flowers and fruit.

The use of the 501 spray affects whatever part of the plant is growing at the time, so it should be used when the part of the plant you wish to harvest is forming. For example, on root crops, when the tops are a few inches high and the root (the "fruiting" part) is starting to thicken; on cabbages when the inside leaves begin to turn; and on fruiting crops, including beans and peas, when the plant is at the bud stage before the flowers open.

Use of the sprays

Only very small amounts of the material are needed: a portion of 500 for one acre will weigh about 2oz (57g) and a portion of 501 for the same area of land about 0.05oz (1.5g). Each preparation then needs to be stirred in 4 gallons (18 liters) of clean, lukewarm water, preferably rain water. The stirring is a vital part of the process: it should be done vigorously for one hour, creating a vortex in one direction almost down to the bottom of the barrel, and then immediately breaking it to create a vortex in the opposite direction. In this way the water and the preparation are fully mixed and the dynamic influence is able to reach into every particle of water. The spray should then be used within three hours, otherwise it will have to be stirred again. Preparation 501 should only be used when 500 has already been sprayed.

Just as the rhythm of the year is followed in the making of the preparations, so best results are obtained by spraying at the right time of day. Therefore, in general, evening is best for preparation 500, when the Earth inhales. Preparation 501 is best sprayed in the early morning when the Earth is exhaling and its forces rise to meet the light and warmth of the sun. Spray 500 in large droplets and 501 using as fine a mist as possible.

Biodynamic Compost Preparations

Preparation	Composition	Action
502 Yarrow (*Achillea millefolium*)	Flowers placed in stag's bladder, hung in sun during summer and buried over winter	Regulates potassium and aids sulfur processes
503 Chamomile (*Chamomila recutita, Matricaria chamomilla*)	Blossoms placed in small intestine of cow, buried in good humus over winter	Regulates calcium, mediates health- giving powers to the soil, stabilizes nitrogen
504 Stinging nettle (*Urtica dioica*)	Nettle buried for a year, in bark or peat moss	Aids humus formation, carries potassium and calcium forces. Makes soil "intelligent"
505 English oak (*Quercus robur*)	Scrapings from outer bark placed in skull of domestic animal, buried under leaking drainpipe over winter	Draws calcium, strengthens against plant diseases
506 Dandelion (*Taraxacum officinale*)	Blossoms gathered and dried in spring, folded into mesentery of cow and buried over winter	Regulates silica in in relation to potassium
507 Valerian (*Valeriana officinalis*)	Juice from squeezed flowers is diluted in rain water, stirred for 10 minutes, and sprayed over compost	Aids phosphorous processes, surrounds pile with warmth

The compost preparations

The six compost preparations (502–507) are used together in the pile, and inserted when the pile has been completed. Their action is more specific than the two field preparations, and work more directly with the chemical elements active in plant growth and fertility (see chart). Again, the individual amounts are very small, a pinch of each is enough for several tons of compost.

For preparations 502 to 506, make a hole for each, using a stick or crowbar, about 12–18in (30–45cm) deep into the pile, evenly spaced out around the pile. Then make each preparation into a small ball with a little soil and drop it into the hole, which should then be filled up with some old compost or fine soil, making sure that the ball is in direct contact with the surrounding compost material. Preparation 507 is used as liquid, at the rate of one pinch to a gallon (4.5 liters) of water, stirred vigorously for 10 minutes and then sprayed over the pile.

In the first year of conversion to biodynamic production, it is a good idea to add half a set of compost preparations to each 4 gallons (18 liters) of rain water when making up your solution of preparation 500.

Lunar planting

In the age of electric light, it's hard to imagine the important place the moon occupied until relatively recently in the history of the human race. The moon was the brightest nightlight we – and all other life-forms – had. As well as shedding light to see by, it was also the picture-calendar used by people all over the world. This calendar helped people to decide when it was time to sow seed and harvest crops.

Planting by the moon is more than just a matter of checking your dates, though. Other aspects of the moon have also been observed to influence the speed of germination and the chances of success when transplanting, weeding, and harvesting crops. The varying amount of light shed by the moon in its various phases affects growth rates, and so does the moon's gravitational field, which is the same powerful force that controls ocean tides.

Many people have found that the two weeks of increasing moonlight (from new to full moon) stimulate leaf growth. Conversely, root growth is favored during the (alternating) weeks when lunar gravity is lowest, presumably because Earth's gravity has greater sway at this time. Putting these two effects together, the lunar cycle can be divided into four parts, beginning at the new moon:

- Week 1, lunar gravity decreasing, light increasing;
- Week 2, lunar gravity increasing, light increasing;
- Week 3, lunar gravity decreasing, light decreasing;
- Week 4, lunar gravity increasing, light decreasing.

Thus, week 1 is good for general balanced growth; week 2 favors foliage; week 3 favors root growth; and the combined effect of increased lunar gravity and dwindling moonlight in week 4 provides a period of rest or comparative dormancy.

Lunar gravity appears to act on germinating seeds by helping them to burst out of the seed-coat, so that rapidly germinating seeds are best sown a couple of days before the high lunar tide – to give them time to take in water in advance. Slow-germinating seeds are best sown around full moon, to allow a longer soaking time.

In addition to the weekly phases, and in keeping with biodynamic theory, there are said to be subtle effects related to the zodiacal house which the moon occupies. According to this theory, it is advisable to plant root crops when the moon is an Earth sign, leaf crops when in a Water sign. Air signs favor flowering, while Fire signs favor fruit and seed development.

WATER CONSERVATION

For many people, drought is a relative term, meaning "less rain than we expected". For others it's a regular event, even a way of life. Any water shortage, expected or unexpected, can be a disaster in the garden, though. It might never happen but, if it does, it pays to be prepared.

Many plants are adapted to survive in dry places. A naturally dry region will have its own spectrum of native species which can form the backbone of the non-edible permanent layout. A few drought-adapted species, such as prickly pears, also have edible fruits or other parts, but the vast majority of our edibles tend to be either fruits or fast-growing vegetables which are difficult to grow without adequate water, meaning the equivalent of about an inch (2.5cm) a week.

Our main concern, when choosing strategies for coping with minimal rainfall, is how to make the most of the water which is available to us.

Planning for water economy
General economy measures are applicable to managing all plants, both ornamental and edible. The main aim is to ensure that as much of the available water as possible is put to good use by the plants it's intended to sustain. When planning and preparing beds:

- Make use of your initiation year to pinpoint the most water-retentive areas. Use a moisture meter or auger to compare the moisture content in different places and make a series of recordings to find the spots where moisture lingers longest.
- Locate beds on a level or dished site where rain or added water won't immediately run off. If necessary, build terraces (see p.203).
- Cultivate deeply – up to 18in (45cm) down, to encourage deep rooting. Surface soil may dry out, and deep-rooted plants survive drought better.
- Add as much organic matter as possible to the soil. Humus increases infiltration and water-retentiveness, preventing rain or added water from draining away quickly and helping plant roots to extract as much water as possible.
- Apply mulch thickly over every inch of visible soil. Mulched soil takes at least eight times longer than bare soil to evaporate one inch of water, as well as helping to take the shock when heavy rain does fall, thus preventing erosion and compaction. Mulching is also the most economical way to control water-wasting weeds.
- Use organic mulches in preference to plastic, which can cause overheating.
- Create shade. Allow a minimum of six hours of direct sunlight, but arrange things so that the plants get this in the morning rather than during the hotter afternoon hours. Bear in mind that hedges also use water, so the shade is best provided by non-living structures or useful crops.
- Create shelter. Moving air dries plants and soil as well as the laundry.
- Reduce the area under cultivation by intensive planting. This reduces the area that needs to be watered as well as maximizing ground cover, which also helps to retain soil moisture.

Using water economically
Water saving can begin before planting. Starting seedlings off in flats is economical. Growing on in pots is less efficient and not really feasible for vegetables, but the principle can be extended by planting on into a subterranean pocket created by a large plastic bag. Being buried, this won't heat up as pots do, but it will retain water far longer than open ground. The method can be extended still further by lining a trench with a huge plastic sheet when making a sunken bed (see p.240). On a smaller scale, pot plants also remain cooler and moister when their pot is buried.

With plants in open ground, there are several ways to make the most of added water:

- Give plants the opportunity to develop natural drought resistance. Don't rush to water every plant that looks a little droopy at the end of a long, hot day. This may happen even with a well-watered plant, so wait to see whether it is refreshed by morning.
- Water in the early morning. As well as being easier to see which plants really need water (see above), the soil is coolest now and less likely to "steam". (Night watering can create warm humidity ideal for fungal growth.)
- Think watering can rather than hosepipe, especially with ornamentals. But make sure you water enough, particularly during hot, dry periods.
- Deliver water directly to roots. Trickle a steady stream with the watering-can spout on the ground rather than splashing it about or sprinkling. A permanent funnel next to a large plant can be used to place the water even more deeply and accurately.
- Concentrate watering on critical times, such as periods of rapid growth, flowering periods, and when fruits and seeds are swelling.
- Select drought-resistant varieties wherever possible.

Suitable plants
Trying to grow species with especially high water requirements carries a high risk of failure. Even if successful, it will require disproportionate quantities of effort and precious water. A quick method for spotting drought resistance is based on four main ways in which plants conserve moisture: (1) some plants (e.g. stonecrops) store water in fat leaves; (2) reduced or absent leaves, together with fat stems (e.g. cacti), indicate even greater water-storage

talent. (3) Gray, hoary leaves (e.g. sage, artemisia) also conserve water; and (4) hard waxy leaves (e.g. holly and periwinkles) are relatively waterproof. Most herbs can get by with very little water, and many kinds of decorative grasses are naturally adapted to living in dry prairies.

Suitable vegetables

Some vegetables require regular watering, others are more tolerant of dry conditions (see p.268 for lists). When choosing which vegetables to grow, it is worth considering what return you are going to get from the water you give them. One way to evaluate this is to look at the proportion of the plant which is edible. Watering a vast leafy plant with a tiny edible fraction is obviously not a very efficient use of water. On this score maize does very badly indeed, a single plant taking more than 50 gallons (227 liters) of water to produce two ears of corn. Another point to consider is the total amount of water a plant needs to come from seed to the point at which it is eaten, which largely depends on how fast it grows. Lettuce does well here, although its daily requirement is clearly large. On the other hand, a slow-growing species (e.g. carrot) may end up with a high total despite being undemanding, day by day. It isn't easy to come to firm conclusions from all these conflicting messages, but the process of careful deliberation can help to point out some obvious runners or non-runners.

A different way to select your vegetables is to go for drought-resistant varieties, which often means the older varieties. These stalwarts were assessed according to reliability rather than novelty or decorative value, at a time when missing a season's harvest could mean serious hardship rather than the slight inconvenience of a few extra trips to the supermarket. Finding old-fashioned varieties that were once widely known in your own region can present a challenge, but is well worth the effort. Once found, they can provide seed for next season (see pp.245–6) – and provide a valuable service to the cause of conservation.

Arranging vegetables

At the same time as weighing up water demands, some other factors can be incorporated into the equation:

- Interplanting helps to conserve water by giving shade and shelter and cutting down soil exposure. Drought-adapted plants can shelter and humidify small delicate ones (e.g. salads).
- Soil is cooler where the surface of a bed slopes away from the sun (but take care not to increase drainage).
- Narrow east-west trenches will hold shade; they can be used for irrigation and their sides for growing shallow-rooting salads.
- Plants on the crests between trenches will intensify shade and humidity in the trenches, keeping their own roots cool, sheltering smaller salads and reducing water loss from the trench.
- Closely planted broad beds are more water-efficient than spaced rows. Create these by broadcasting seed on to a patch 1–2ft (30–60cm) across and shallowly covering with soil.
- If not deliberately interplanting, group together crops with the same watering requirements.
- Create deeper rooting systems by planting out more deeply than the plant grew in the pot. Most plants will at least tolerate having their stem more deeply buried and some, such a tomatoes, will co-operate by forming more roots from the buried stem.
- Give serious consideration to installing permanent irrigation. It can deliver water entirely below ground. Although installation might be hard work, once in place the system can supply water to a large area at the twist of a single valve, for years. Combined with a reservoir (see below), irrigation is a practical and economical method of distributing water.

Dramatic water savings can be made by creating troughs of shade (enhanced by tall deep-rooted crops) where water will evaporate more slowly. Succulent salads also thrive on the shady slopes.

Ingenuity

Rules are meant to be broken, and generalizations don't always apply to individual cases. Your own site or climate may suggest an original idea or offer a combination of events that represent a particular challenge.

In an area with a distinct rainy season, for example, it makes sense to plan for fast-growing crops then, to use the water bonus before the ground dries out. If the timing is feasible, start slow-growers at this time, too, saving stored water for the critical times. Where rain tends to fall unexpectedly, you can capitalize by keeping some ground ready to use when it happens.

On the other hand, an unexpected drought can also occur at any time or in any place. The best way to be prepared for this is to keep some water in reserve.

Saving water

Even a region where rainfall is normally moderate to high can suffer occasional periods of drought, and cans full of water are often needed to sustain new plantings, so keeping a quantity of water in reserve is a good practice and not only for desert dwellers.

Using the public supply is wasteful, as well as most likely to fail or be forbidden when the need is greatest, and neither is it the best water to give your plants. The most acceptable way to ensure that water is available when it's needed is to have a store of "real" water somewhere. There are two main sources: one is recycled household water, and the other is rain water collected when it does come down for use when it doesn't. Either or both of these methods can be used, according to necessity and resources, and the size and nature of the reservoir can be tailored to fit the situation. The main problem with rain water is collecting it, and the main problem with recycling water is cleaning it.

Rain water

Planning to collect rain water entails a number of possible strategies, including:

- Laying drains to collect groundwater and channel it to a reservoir.
- Arranging guttering and pipes to collect roof water (not forgetting greenhouse) and convey it to a reservoir.
- Locating hard surfaces, such as paths, where water runs off in sufficient volume to be gathered for storage.
- Providing a suitable container for the collected water.

Reservoirs

The range of possible reservoirs runs from the purely utilitarian underground cistern to the highly ornamental fish pond. To be effective a reservoir only needs to be able to hold water. Try to arrange as much shade as possible, because evaporation can cause significant losses from all types of reservoir. This means putting a lid on a water barrel (and a little oil on the surface to deter mosquitoes) or planting trees and water liles to shade a pond.

Where drought is a serious problem, and especially in a region where there is a seasonal inundation, it may be worth going to the considerable effort of digging a cistern. One way to tackle this is to proceed as for making a soakaway with a comprehensive drainage system to feed it (see p.207), but line the pit with concrete instead of filling it with rubble. If large enough, the cistern, or above-ground galvanized iron or concrete tank, can receive roof water. An underground storage tank for roof water can be created by simply sinking a pre-formed container in the ground. It won't gather groundwater, but will serve the double purpose of keeping water cool in summer and unfrozen in winter.

Underground systems will need a pump or some other means of extracting the water, but even a water barrel needs a faucet for getting water out. Pulling a heavy watering can out of the top or trying to fill one when the level is low can be slow and arduous.

Reservoirs

	For	Against
Pond natural	Economical, permanent, looks best	May disappear with lowered water table in dry season.
plastic	Moderately priced	Vulnerable to mechanical puncture and UV degradation.
concrete	Expensive	May eventually crack and leak.
Butt plastic	Cheap	Eventually (depends on type) photodegrades.
wood	Attractive	Can shrink and leak if not full.
Tank steel	Long life	Unattractive, acid corrodes.
ferro-cement	Long life, versatile shape, home-made	Requires some skill to make.
fiber-cement	Long life, fairly cheap	Example: cattle trough, not large
concrete	Long life, strong, good underground	Expensive, laborious if underground.

Recycling gray water

Even an economical household pours away gallons of water a day, much of which has been only slightly contaminated and can be made fit for irrigation fairly easily. The one-tank treatment system already described (see p.217) is best suited for sporadic use because the irrigation pipes need to be regularly dried out to prevent clogging due to incompletely processed water. When a continuous recycling system is required, especially if it supplies virtually the only water the garden might receive for months on end, it's advisable to expand the system to include a second stage of cleaning, before storing in a reservoir.

Instead of the exit pipe feeding the irrigation system, it carries water to a second tank, similar to the first except for its contents. Here, the bottom is filled with 0.4in (1cm) gravel to a depth of 20in (50cm), with 0.8in (2cm) of coarse sand on top. Almost any water plants can be planted in this tank (*Typha* and *Phragmites* are recommended). The water in the final reservoir will be high in nutrients, probably bringing a bonus in the shape of floating weeds (e.g. duckweed) that can be skimmed off for compost or mulch.

Irrigation

Irrigation systems are used all over the world – and have been for probably thousands of years – to make cultivation possible in arid regions. Systems vary in detail, depending on local resources and the exact nature of the crop and conditions, but the principles are simple and broadly similar.

- Unless pressurized, water flows downhill. Any irrigation system must be designed with this fact in mind, but not sloping so steeply that the water runs away before it has a chance to soak in.
- Water is best delivered beneath the surface of the soil. Pipes are the obvious conduit but other devices, e.g. flat stones roofing a channel, can also serve.
- Regular and moderate watering is more economical and more productive than infrequent flooding.
- Irrigation can lead to salt build-up. Plants should therefore be rooted beside irrigation paths rather than in them.

Whether to buy sophisticated equipment or create an *ad-hoc* irrigation system is a matter of choice, necessity, and resources.

Simple beginnings

Sinking an unglazed pot beside an individual plant is traditional in some arid regions. Water in the pot slowly percolates into the soil, while a lid on top prevents it from evaporating. This is a good method to use for a few large plants. Sprawling plants, such as melon and squash, can be planted on an island in a moat; the greenery will soon grow to shade the moat, while the base of the stem remains dry. Linking the moats together begins to form a crude irrigation channel, and extending and enlarging this network soon forms a system. As it grows, the irrigation network carries greater and greater evaporation penalties, until a piped system inevitably becomes the obvious next stage of evolution.

Water delivery

Individual pots must be topped up, one by one. Correctly sloped channels can distribute water from a single spill-point, cutting down considerably on time and labor. Making a cunning irrigation network can be a highly satisfying and creative task. It can be lined with perforated guttering for greater permanence. Any open system, however, loses water by evaporation, so it makes sense to develop the system farther by using perforated pipes, and burying the pipes is better still (see p.218). Narrow buried pipes are the basis of the trickle system, which can be as sophisticated as you like.

Trickle drip system

A series of perforated or porous pipes, buried in the ground (see p.218), will deliver water economically as long as the water flow can be regulated correctly. This can be done by hand, but there are automated alternatives. A different system uses non-porous "spaghetti" tubing. An individual, very narrow "feeder" pipe runs water to each plant, making it emerge at the same rate at which the plant transpires. In effect, the "pull" of transpiration from the leaves is transmitted via the roots to the soil, where it sucks water from a device called an emitter, which is fitted into the end of the feeder line. Emitters vary in their sophistication and responsiveness to demand. Given pressurized water, trickle systems can even travel uphill. Installing a sophisticated system can be expensive, so shop around before embarking on such a project.

Emergency measures

Although the pattern of weather can be remarkably consistent, it can also throw up surprises. Gardeners have to plan firmly for the predictable but be prepared to cope with the unexpected.

In sudden dry spells look for danger signs, such as:

- Wilting young leaves (yellowing in fruit trees).
- Dull-looking foliage.
- Premature flowering.

Identify the plants most at risk and give them special attention:

- Recent plantings can be cut back drastically to reduce transpiration and thus water demand. Even though this might set back a pleasing shape for a year or so, the alternative could be death. Newly planted conifers can be left intact, but will benefit from screening (and perhaps a waterproof antidessicant spray).
- Shallow-rooted shrubs can also be cut back. Large-leafed ones can be stripped of up to half the leaves, and given screening.
- Remove weed competition from around fruit trees.
- Prune soft fruits after picking.
- Suspend woven netting over rows of vegetables to shade them.
- Harvest leaf crops before they deteriorate. Lettuce might survive cutting to come again when conditions improve.
- Concentrate available water on critical crops, e.g. flowering or setting peas and beans.
- Resolve to add humus and use mulches next year.

CREATING MICROCLIMATES

Every natural ecosystem is an amalgam of many smaller systems, corners where conditions are different, each making its unique contribution to the whole. Such variety is in fact critical to the survival of a great many species. An insect may depend on one microhabitat as a larva, another as an adult, and perhaps even a third for overwintering. Whereas conventional gardening practice tends toward creating an optimum and thus largely uniform environment, there's room in a natural garden for a multitude of niches. Although it's important to develop the best possible soil for growing crops, there's rarely a need to treat the entire garden as a potential vegetable plot. Instead of draining a wet corner, for example, it may be more imaginative and ultimately more rewarding to give it a slight nudge the other way, and turn it into a pond.

Hot spots can also occur naturally. These, too, could be enhanced to create microclimates for special plants, especially food crops that might not otherwise survive or ripen in your region. One approach to this is to use plants and/or walls and banks to increase the effect (see pp.74, 240). Another way of making the most of the sun's heat is to build transparent enclosures to allow light in while keeping cold air out.

Warmth and light

During your initiation year, you'll have located some places which are naturally warm. Even a slight slope can make a difference, especially in high latitudes where there's scope for a tilt toward the sun. The sun-facing side of a wall can be used to grow slightly tender fruits, or to cultivate a half-hardy flowering vine. A badly insulated house wall may even generate a frost-free zone a few inches deep, all the way up. By enclosing this sun trap with glass, you might be able to ripen marginally hardy exotic fruits.

Bear in mind, though, that merely increasing warmth does not increase sun-hours. Although it may seem to produce a tropical shift, this is just the result of getting the plants off to an earlier start, then making the most of all the sun which comes, and finally eliminating the full-stop of frost. Many plants use day length as a guide to flowering and fruiting, and truly tropical species expect to get 12 hours of light a day, every day. The best results possible in your region will come from siting your greenhouse where it gets as many hours of sun as possible; putting it in a place which becomes very hot for a few hours but is shaded for the rest of the day is confusing for tropical plants and may be counterproductive.

Greenhouse

Once you've erected your greenhouse, it will be easy to see its shortcomings but awkward to change. To get it right first time, consider the following points:

- Site. Choose a sunny spot out of the wind. East-west alignment is generally best. Even a lean-to against a sunny wall can help to moderate swings in temperature.
- Size. Think about this carefully. Once erected, a greenhouse in a small garden can loom larger than predicted. On the other hand, once you have it, you may wish you'd chosen a bigger one.
- The law. Before you buy or erect a greenhouse, check local by-laws.
- Materials. Whether you opt for glass or plastic, wood or metal, find out the pros and cons for all types.
- Allow for the cost of proper foundations, and benches and shading.
- Ventilation is essential. The range runs from simple open/shut vents to fully automatic systems.
- Adjustable shading helps to prevent overheating.
- Rain water. If guttering is fitted, why not collect the runoff in a water barrel?
- Consider details, such as whether the door is wide enough to get a wheelbarrow through.

To heat or not to heat?

The usefulness of a greenhouse isn't doubled if you heat it. The beauty of a greenhouse comes from the fact that it collects its own energy from the sun. Pumping extra heat into a building not designed to retain it is a wasteful exercise, and not justifiable. On the other hand, you can enhance the warmth of the greenhouse by allowing waste-water pipes to run through it on their way down the wall, by installing a hotbed, or by other ingenious means. The most efficient form of artificial heating is with electric cables under the soil for early propagation. Heat can be retained with cloches or horticultural fleece.

Cold frame

If your needs or your garden are small, you may not want a full-size greenhouse. A cold frame does some of the same work on a smaller scale. It can be used to raise seedlings or strike cuttings, and as a container for a hotbed.

You can buy a cold frame, or make one very easily. The basic cold frame is an insulated box which keeps out wind while allowing light in. Four hay bales and a sheet of clear plastic will do the job, but a ventilated frame performs better. Transparent walls let in more light, but thick walls retain more heat. When planning a permanent cold frame, be sure to allow for easy access, bearing in mind that plants will be bigger when they come out than when they went in.

Even if you have a greenhouse, a

cold frame can be used to help harden plants off before they are fully exposed.

Cloche, fleece, tunnel, and bottle
Cloches are mobile while cold frames are not. The special advantage of a cloche is that it can be used to shelter plants in their own growing quarters for as long as they need it, and then removed to leave them growing on in the open. It can be put on or closed up at night, or whenever required. It can also be used to warm up soil in advance of sowing or bedding-out. A cloche won't retain heat as well as a cold frame so it isn't the best choice for raising seeds, though it's far better than no protection at all. A modern alternative is horticultural fleece, supported by hoops or canes, or by the plants themselves.

Cloches are usually made of plastic, either rigid sections joined together or long sheets spread over wire hoops. Rigid shapes often have a built-in ventilation system; a tunnel cloche is ventilated by opening the end. When choosing, consider how much use it will get, how often you will move it, and where you will store it when it's not in use.

Individual cloches can be tailored from plastic bottles, and this is an excellent way to protect individual plants from marauding slugs and cold weather at the same time. Cut off the bottom of the bottle, so that the neck becomes a ventilation hole.

Cloche management is a matter of common sense, but here are a few tips:
- Site cloches in an open, sunny spot.
- Anchor them down well.
- Ventilate regularly, but make sure the end doesn't face into the wind, thus turning your cloche into a wind tunnel.
- Use a cloche to warm the ground for two weeks before sowing seeds.
- Don't remove cloches suddenly. Allow plants to harden off by exposing them in stages.
- Rotate as if they were vegetables, to avoid the build-up of disease.
- Keep them clean, so they always transmit as much light as possible.

Hotbeds
The hotbed is a natural and free source of "bottom heat", which is often prescribed for propagation and which can also give a crop of salads ready to eat in early spring.

The hotbed relies on heat generated by aerobic decay, as in a compost pile. In theory, constructing a hotbed is like building a mini-compost pile, covering it with soil, and planting the chosen crop in the soil. In practice this requires some skill, and can be done with fresh horse manure, which stays hot long enough to grow a crop.

Begin in midwinter by piling strawy horse manure, fresh from the stable and well wetted with urine, under a plastic sheet for a week or until heating begins. Using the cold frame as a container, dig out about 1ft (30cm) of soil and fill the hole with manure, treading it firm, until level with the ground. Top it off with 4in (10cm) of soil and compost, about 1:1, and cover the frame for a few days until the bed heats up.

Sow seeds such as lettuce, radish, turnip, and cauliflower. Keep the frame

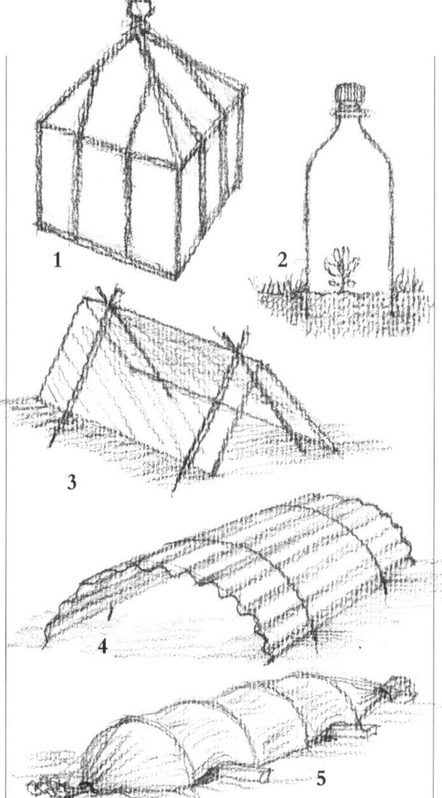

Different cloche styles and sizes: ***(1)*** *lantern,* ***(2)*** *PET bottle,* ***(3)*** *tent,* ***(4)*** *rigid tunnel,* ***(5)*** *miniature polytunnel.*

HARDENING OFF

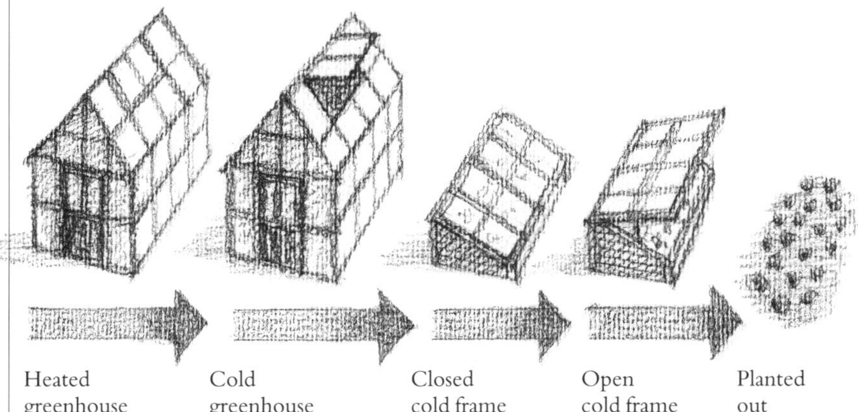

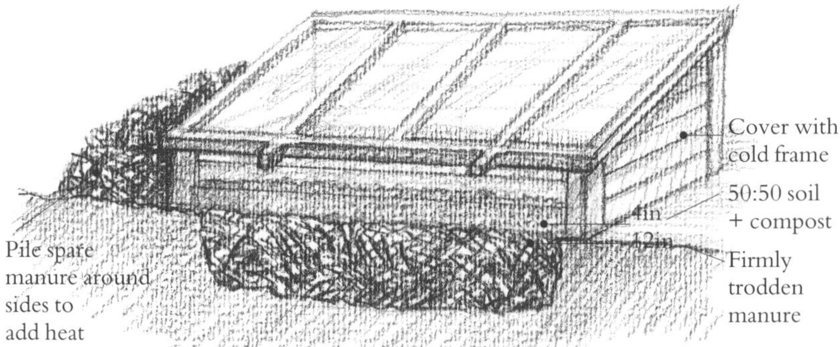

Converting a cold frame into a hotbed. Fresh horse manure provides under-soil heating. Fresh manure in a magic mound (see p. 211) can also create warmth.

closed until the seeds germinate, then ventilate daily when safe from cold. Left-over manure can be piled around the frame for added warmth and insulation. Radishes will be ready first, followed by lettuces. After the cauliflowers are harvested, the bed can be used for zucchini or squash.

Wild habitats

The hallmark of a natural garden is a healthy companion system, where pollinating insects thrive and pests and their predators live in balance. Not only do plants (including vegetables) flourish in this diverse environment, but people benefit too. A pond can be a focus of design and interest, as well as attracting birds, insects, and other creatures to drink or breed; a brushwood pile can keep hibernating animals warm in winter and then become part of a slow compost pile in the spring. Compost piles – especially slow ones – are another rich mini-habitat.

A small city garden could even be augmented with a rooftop lawn. Sods are already known as a roofing material in some cold regions, and they protect the roof from weathering. In a larger context, clothing rooftops with grass and other plants may also offer a method of replacing some of the vegetation lost to urban sprawl, bringing improvements in air quality as well as reducing city heat.

Even without going to such dramatic lengths though, any garden can be made into a richer environment simply by not being kept too tidy. Tidiness for its own sake is a human obsession, and can be antipathetic to nature.

Small but positive investments which pay large dividends are represented by sink-ponds, bird and bat houses, tiny corners of "waste" ground, and dead logs allowed to rot naturally.

Digging a pond

If you already have a boggy region or a shallow water-filled dip, all you may need to do to turn it into a pond is dig a deeper hole. Aim to make a gentle slope on one side, getting deeper nearer the center and, if you wish, carrying on deeply to the other side. The slope allows small creatures (and children) to climb out easily, and the deeper region (at least 2ft or 60cm, preferably more) gives a depth of water than doesn't easily freeze solid in the winter. An irregular outline is preferable to a tidy shape.

One possible practical problem is that digging the pond out could cut right through a natural crust of fine particles which serve to retain water, so the initial effect may be that your puddle appears to drain away. If this happens, you can either wait patiently until the particles re-pack themselves, or leap in and "puddle" the bottom yourself. Crudely, this means squelching around in the hole, compressing the bottom.

Lining the pond

A hole which doesn't hold water naturally will need a waterproof lining. The three main approaches to this are fiberglass, plastic, and cement.

Rigid fiberglass-reinforced resin shells are only suitable for small ponds. When using one of these, you must dig the hole to fit the shell so that all of it rests on firm ground. Sand can be used to mold the final fit.

Flexible strong plastic pond liners have the advantage of fitting almost any size and shape hole, and are quick and fairly easy to use. The disadvantages are that they can be punctured easily and may break down due to weathering. Careful attention to detail can minimize these problems. The hole ought to be smooth, without sharp stones, and free of bumps and hollows which might strain the plastic. Ideally you should protect the sheet on both sides by a geotextile mat.

The length of sheet you will need is arrived at by adding the length of the pond to twice the deepest depth. The width will be the sum of the pond width plus twice the average depth. Add 2ft (60cm) in all directions, to allow for anchorage.

Lay the sheet methodically, making sure no air bubbles are left underneath. It doesn't have to be absolutely smooth. After the water goes in, this sheet will become inaccessible unless you destroy the entire pond, so it's worth taking trouble at this stage. Ultra-violet light can perish the plastic, so make sure that all the sheeting which might emerge from the water is securely anchored with bricks bedded in sand and then covered up with sods, soil, stones, or gravel. If you use paving slabs they can overhang slightly, but leave escape-

Profile for a small pond. Ensure that all edging totally covers or always shades the liner, which may break down if exposed to sunlight.

gaps. The life expectancy of a plastic-sheet lining depends on how well it's laid, how well it's protected from UV light, and the quality of plastic. Standard-gauge polythylene, although initially cheap, only lasts for 2 or 3 years; nylon-reinforced PVC lasts twice as long; butyl and other proprietary membranes are much more expensive but last indefinitely, which makes them the best choice for a serious pond.

A concrete-lined pond is more expensive to create, and not feasible on a large scale. Once made, however, it's likely to last, although concrete can crack and leak, and be difficult to repair. Constructing a concrete pond is a straightforward mechanical job. It will need to be thoroughly weathered to ensure the chemicals in the cement are neutralized, before adding living things. Begin by filling the pond with water, leaving it for a few days, then emptying. Repeat this process a few times. After several months, fill with fresh rain water and add gravel, mud, and water from a natural pond. Some water weeds can be put in now, but don't introduce fish or other animals until a year has gone by. Smaller pond life will emerge from the added mud, and beetles, bugs, and other flying insects will probably arrive under their own steam.

Stocking the pond

A natural pond can be left to take care of itself. A plastic-lined pond can be kick-started with a good layer of muddy sand or fine gravel, brought quickly from a natural pond (without being allowed to dry out or be deprived of air on the way), which will bring plenty of life with it.

Plants

Water plants with submerged leaves provide essential oxygen. They need sunlight to do this, so some of the pond ought to be open to the sky; a shaded region (created by overhanging plants or floating leaves such as water lilies) will provide open water by inhibiting weed growth, as well as helping to prevent the entire pond from overheating in the sun. Various pond weeds can be obtained; choose a native species, but avoid introducing Canadian pondweed (*Elodea canadensis*), which grows too vigorously. If you do have too much weed, there's nothing you can do except clear out as much of it as possible in the fall. (Water weed makes good compost; leave piles of it to drain by the water's edge, so that small creatures can find their way back into the pond.) Regular maintenance can be done at the same time, before the animals settle for the winter. Fallen leaves ought to be removed (for composting) before they sink and decay, as this can deplete the oxygen content of the pond.

New ponds are apt to develop a spring flush of algae due to excess nutrients. This problem should clear up in a few years, and in the meantime you can rake off the weed for compost as soon as it floats to the surface.

Water-side plants provide a range of microhabitats for small creatures, and it's also essential to have some stems emerging from the water itself, to form a land bridge for aquatic insects such as dragonflies.

Animals

Many animals (and plants) will soon turn up. It may seem surprising that swimmers can do this, but pond creatures have evolved special techniques for getting around. Beetles and bugs take to the wing on warm days, and the tiniest one-celled creatures can turn themselves into a grain of dust to be blown on the wind. Unless you want to add a particular species, there's no pressing need to introduce any animals at all.

Aquatic creatures are very sensitive to chemicals, and also to pyrethrum and rotenone, so avoid applying these where they could find their way into the pond.

Making the most of existing microhabitats

Even a vast tract of apparently uniform prairie contains numerous microhabitats, from termite hills to little piles of dung dropped by grazing animals. Your garden is far richer than this, with trees and shrubs, hedges and walls, walks, and arbors. A single tree, for example, may offer permutations on north and south aspects, dry soil, summer shade, winter sun, winter shade, drip-zone, leaf litter, fallen fruit, exposure to wind, shelter from wind, and probably many more. Each individual spot could be the dream home for one or more very exacting species, or form part of the series of microhabitats necessary for an animal with a complex life cycle.

When introducing native plants, find out (by observation or from books) the microclimate they prefer and try to place them in a similar situation in your own garden. As well as making the best use of your space, this strategy is labor-saving, too, since plants that are thoroughly at home will thrive without much help.

Walls

Walls provide scope for introducing a montane community into any kind of garden, even one which is lush and wet. A raw wall can be made more inviting by painting or splashing with sour milk or diluted cow dung, to neutralize any alkalinity caused by lime mortar and provide nourishment for moss and lichens, which will in turn provide shelter and nourishment for other species. The shady side of a wall can be used to grow delicate ferns, while the hot, dry sunny side could support a completely different community. Many species of plants which naturally colonize walls tend to mature early in the year; they can provide welcome color in early spring.

Walks

Even walks need not be barren tracks, dedicated to human traffic alone. Instead of keeping walks meticulously tidy, you could allow plants to take their chances there. Apart from a few especially invasive weeds – and you'll soon learn to recognize them – it isn't usually difficult to remove anything that eventually gets in the way.

Many plants are adapted to colonize rocky cracks, and can even survive grazing by wild goats. A shaded, moist walk can be softened by clumps of violets, while a dry sunny one may support creeping thyme or chamomile.

Shade

Shady spots occur in many situations. The poleward side of a wall can be shady year-round, as it is underneath evergreen trees, and it's worth seeking out the specialized plants that will thrive there. The space beneath deciduous trees, on the other hand, tends to be shady during the summer and light in winter, which is an excellent place to cultivate wild woodland plants, whose life cycle is adapted to this pattern. They tend to be early-flowering species, getting through their year's work before the trees overhead blot out the sun, and they bring early bees to pollinate your plums and early apples.

Green roof

A roof with a slope of about 10° is ideal for greening, as it will drain freely but isn't steep enough to suffer from slippage. Flat roofs need positive drainage, and a steeper pitch (up to 30° is feasible) will need cross-struts to hold the growing medium. The strength of the roof must also be considered; a full load of sods needs a strong roof, for example, but a thin layer of sand planted with houseleeks could be supported by most reasonable roofs.

Before starting, the roof should be checked for cracks and leaks. A waterproof membrane with a geotextile layer on top will protect the roof from water and the plant roots themselves. Once the cover is in place, the roof will be protected from deterioration due to UV light. The growing medium goes on top of the drainage layer and then the plants themselves are added, with protective netting, if necessary, to keep them in place while the roots become established.

Rockery

A stony patch in your garden can be put to a variety of uses. Big stones can be used for edging beds and walks, where they can be interplanted with stonecrops or other hardy crack-rooters. Large chunks of stone – even broken concrete – can also be bedded around the banks of a pond, founding yet another microhabitat.

On the other hand, even a small pile of mixed stones can accommodate a variety of wildlife – hibernating newts in temperate regions or sunbathing lizards in tropical climes, for example. It will mellow slowly, accumulating soil and appropriate native plants and their followers. This is not to be confused with a conventional rockery, which is more difficult to make and less relevant to a non-rocky region (it's unlikely to be desired in a rocky one!).

Logs and log piles

Dead wood is a normal component of the natural world. A wealth of wildlife is adapted to make use of it, but it's in increasingly short supply in many places due to many human activities including obsessive tidiness. Any contribution you can make will therefore enrich the whole ecosystem as well as your own patch.

Leaving a pile to be recycled to destruction will naturally be of greater benefit than a temporary firewood pile. Top it up regularly, and it will become a valuable natural resource.

Bird houses

Nesting birds are among your greatest allies. Nearly all birds (except pigeons but including other seed-eaters) feed their babies on meat, so having a bird family in your garden ensures a dawn to dusk patrol picking off hundreds of caterpillars a day, and countless aphids. A titmouse's faster-than-vision beak action can peck up seven aphids a second, so it makes sense to tempt tits with customized nests. Situate bird houses facing west or poleward, about

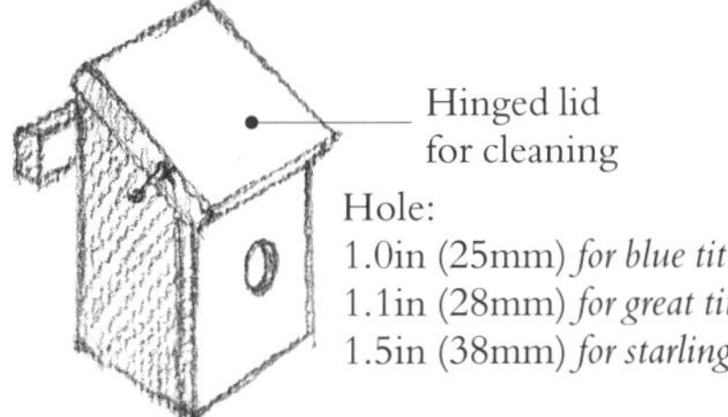

Hang birdhouses in half-shade, out of reach of cats. Leave them undisturbed while birds are nesting, but clean out in winter. Never use treated wood.

7ft (2.1m) high, ideally where cats can't climb. Adjust the hole to the smallest size the species you're targeting will use, or leave the front half-open for flycatchers.

Bat houses

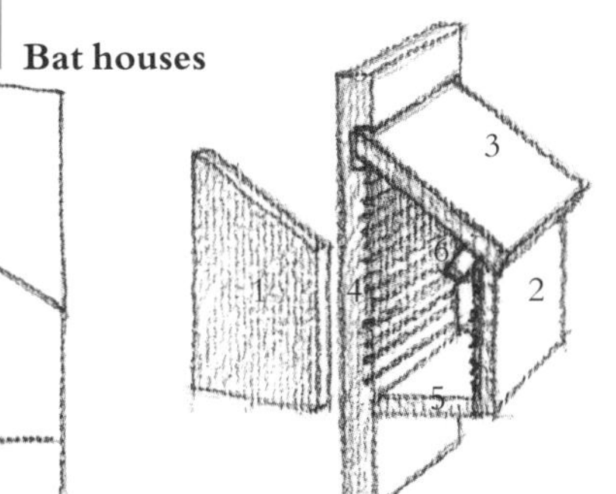

A rough plank, 6inx30in (15cm x75cm) becomes a batbox. Roughen it even more with saw cuts. Fix batboxes to tree trunks or walls in a polar direction for winter, sun-facing for spring/summer use, between 5ft (150cm) and 15ft (450cm) high (small and large bats). Never use treated wood.

A bat house is very similar to a birdbox, but with a slit and a crawl-board instead of a hole and a perch. The whole thing can be made from a single unplaned board of untreated lumber as shown. Hang bat houses on fruit trees, 6–9ft (2–3m) high, away from the sun. When the day shift of birds goes to bed, the night shift of bats will take over, picking off moths coming to lay eggs in the orchard. Bats regularly travel a long way between their roosts and their hunting grounds, so it won't be long before the houses are "discovered". They may be used for summer roosts or even for hibernation. In either case, try to avoid disturbing the bats while they're in residence.

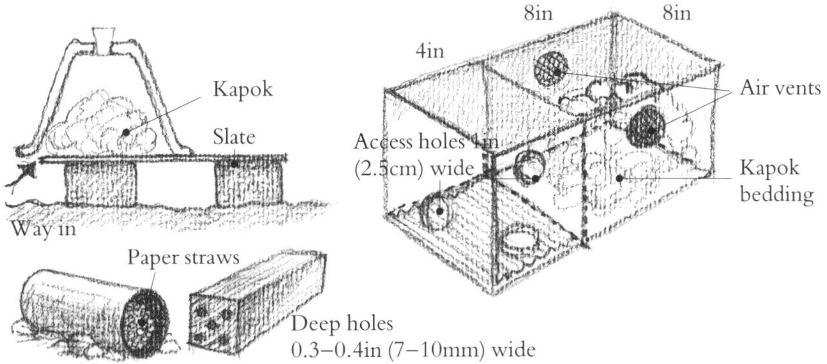

Bees nest in early spring but prefer a weathered nest. Tunnels attract small bees; the flowerpot in a shady spot suits big bumbles. With a lid of glass under felt, the two-room box (dimensions optional, kapok essential) becomes an observation hive.

Beeboxes

Honey bees are only one species among hundreds. Many of the wild bees coming to pollinate your blossoms are solitary types needing small nest sites rather than a single hive for a vast community. An original way to encourage them to stay is to provide them with places to nest. The simplest bee-quarters can be assembled from a can full of paper straws, 0.3in (7mm) in diameter. Paint the whole can with rustproof paint and lodge it in a crevice in a wall.

Tunnelling bees will be delighted to find ready-made tunnels 0.3–0.4in (7–10mm) wide in short 6in (15cm) lengths of softwood, slotted into the woodpile, attached to fenceposts, or suspended horizontally under eaves. Bumble bees can be tempted with a large clay flowerpot (drainage hole bunged with a cork) upside down on a suitable ledge. Add a filling of kapok (not cotton wool) a third deep.

Flexible options

Wherever possible, opt for permanence in your garden. Choosing a woody clematis instead of one which is cut back annually will clothe a trellis, wall, or dead tree stump winter and summer, providing shelter and food for wildlife.

Shun tidiness for its own sake. Bare soil serves no useful purpose; mulch is far better for maintaining fertility and moisture, and also shelters invertebrates and thus provides food for larger creatures. Cutting down dead stems in winter destroys the built-in protection from frost-heaving of many perennials, reduces ladybug shelter, and removes a potential source of winter food for birds.

Choose native trees and shrubs. Exotic ones don't fit into your ecosystem, which means they're not much use to the wildlife native to your region. An indigenous tree, on the other hand, may support hundreds of species and could even be a key component in the system.

Indigenous flowers and berries, too, will be more use to the wildlife than exotic ones. Bearing in mind that the flowers bloom for insects, by and large, and berries shine for birds, it seems only fair to allow both plants and animals to get the life-or-death benefits while we derive our merely voyeuristic pleasure.

APPENDIX

Tools and Garden Structures

It's amazing how dogmatic gardeners can get about tools. Once you have become used to a particular tool, and skilful at using it, you can't imagine gardening without it. Yet the range of tools used for the same sort of tasks can vary enormously. Here are some points to consider when choosing your tools:

- Never buy shoddy tools. Good tools are solidly made from the right materials, well finished, and nearly always expensive. Go for forged heads, straight-grained unpainted shafts, and well attached handles.
- Choose the right size of tool for your physique: this applies particularly to the bigger, heavier tools.
- If you can only afford a few tools, buy general-purpose ones or complementary sets. A spade, for example, will substitute for a fork and a shovel, but not the other way round.
- The tools which are available at your local store may not be the most suitable for you. Seek out specialist suppliers, who may be able to offer tools which you didn't realize existed (and may be more effective).

The basic necessities (and a few others)

Spade. Choose a spade that isn't too heavy or so big that it invites overloading. If you already have a weak back, there are spades with lever mechanisms to take the strain. A stainless steel blade costs more but lasts longer; it also stays cleaner in sticky soil. Footrests on the blade's shoulders let you step on it without damaging feet or footwear. The shaft should be as strong as possible without being too heavy, just long enough for you to stand upright while driving the blade fully home and levering it back to loosen the spit. If you expect your spade to double up as a shovel, choose one with a fluted head.

Tilling fork. The same considerations apply to cultivating forks as to spades, but with more emphasis on strength of shaft. Strength is more important than weight, since both tines and shaft are used for leverage but rarely for lifting. A long shaft gives more leverage but less strength; a short shaft is useful in tight spaces. The two-handed fork allows you to use both hands for leverage.

Hoes. There are so many different kinds of hoe that it's surprising they all share the same name. Most people think of hoes as light tools for making furrows, for shallow cultivation, and for slicing the tops off weeds, but in fact there is also a heavy or cultivating hoe which is used in place of the spade and fork in many parts of the world. This digging hoe is extremely versatile once you have mastered it.

Dibbles and diggers. Dibbles are for making planting holes, but their pointed ends give holes the wrong profile. An alternative dibble is a tool handle with a rounded end. You will also need a dandelion digger for removing deep-rooted weeds.

Trowels. Look for a sharp blade with a strong neck, securely and smoothly attached to a handle that fits snugly into your palm.

Rakes. These have two functions: leveling and creating a tilth; and gathering light, bulky materials. The standard garden rake is designed for the first but will also do the second under protest. The spring-tine rake will only do the second, but much better.

Pruners. A good pair of pruners is

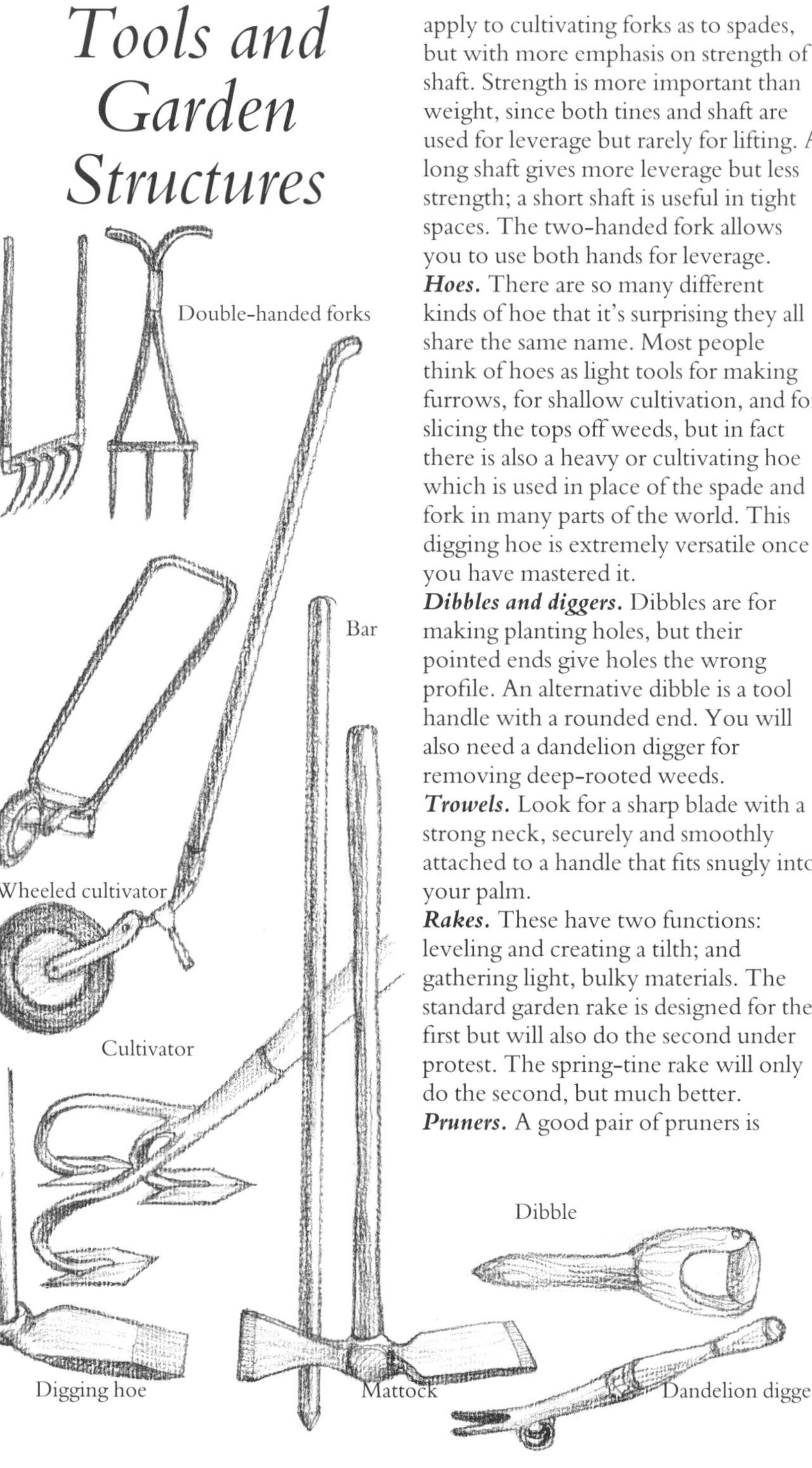

essential. For thicker woody stems add a curved-blade pruning saw with both cutting and raking teeth on the blade. If you have a lot of pruning to do, long-handled loppers will deal more quickly with intermediate thicknesses – and if you have the skill and strength, a billhook is even faster.

Cultivators. Use a long-handled three-hooked cultivator to break up surface soil and claw out shallow-rooted weeds. It's easier to replace broken hooks if they are attached individually. Use a similar short-handled tool to weed and cultivate at close quarters. You may find a wheeled cultivator a boon if you have a large area to cover.

Mattock and bar. Compacted heavy ground may resist even the fork, in which case you will need the services of a mattock and bar, or crowbar. The mattock will also cut and lever tree roots, while the bar can be used to break hard ground, lever rocks and tree stumps, and make post holes.

Sickles and scythes. Sickles or hooks are easier to use than scythes, and can be invaluable in clearing brambles and long grass. They must be kept sharp, however, so keep a sharpening stone in your pocket when using them. Tough and woody undergrowth is best tackled with pruning tools (see above).

Wheelbarrows. The single-wheeled wheelbarrow can travel along a narrow track, but sinks easily into soft soil. A double-wheeled cart is less manoeuvrable but holds more and is less likely to get bogged down. Avoid cheap, thin metal that will rust and break.

Care of tools

Owning good tools cuts down on maintenance, but the size of the investment makes caring for them more important. Before putting tools away each day, either clean with sand or wet-clean, dry thoroughly and oil. Sharpen hoes and other blades. At the end of the season, scour metal blades and oil thoroughly before storing them somewhere dry. Keep sharp-bladed tools out of reach of children at all times.

Garden Structures

As well as the living components of the garden, some non-living structures can enhance its appearance, utility, and productivity. It can be practical and satisfying to make at least some of these structures from natural or recycled materials, using rustic techniques appropriate to your region.

Wood

While clearing ground in the first year, take care to save any useful wood and store it for later use. In a large garden, you might even consider setting aside an area to plant with suitable trees for "coppicing", thus ensuring a continuing supply of wooden poles. Timber is best cut in fall or winter, when its sap content is lowest.

The trouble with wood, however, is that, being part of the food web, it tends to get eaten and degraded, so any structures you make (such as trellises, arches, arbors, seats, tables, fences) may fall apart after a few years. So you must either:

- accept that they will be temporary
- use naturally resistant lumber
- preserve the wood in some way
- use live cuttings to create a "living" structure.

Temporary structures. These can be made from wood or poles you have gathered from the garden: "coppice craft" structures include hurdles, rustic fences, and screens.

Naturally resistant wood. Every region has its own rot-resistant timber. In the north temperate zone, oak, hickory, and cedar spring to mind. Try your local lumberyard if you don't have a home-grown supply.

Preservation. This can be a difficult issue for the natural gardener. A structure that lasts for 50 years may have less impact in the end than a succession of 10 replacements each lasting 5. The point of fastest decay is where the structure meets the ground, so often it is enough to deal with this. Lumber which is driven into the ground can be inserted into a socketed metal spike, but in wet areas it may still deteriorate. Some lumber can be hardened by charring, although the correct degree of burning – enough to harden the wood, but not burn it up – has to be found by experimentation. If chemical treatment must be used, it should be confined to the portion of wood which will be enclosed in a socket. This is best done by standing poles, after shaping, in creosote (beware: extremely poisonous) until it soaks as high as required.

Above-ground parts can be hand-treated with preservative stains, the most environment-friendly of which are based on borax and natural oils. Another alternative is to have your wood commercially pressure-treated. This process seems to prevent the chemicals from leaching out.

Never use preservatives of any kind on wood intended for bird, bee, or batboxes, nor for compost bins.

"Living" structures. Many green sticks, stuck in the ground, will sprout roots and grow there and then. You can then weave, prune, and train your structure however you want it. This is the basis for the willow bank (see p.229) and the "fedge" (a cross between a fence and a hedge), but it can also be used for arbors, arches, and even gazebos.

Plant Lists

Plants for a Cold Garden

Evergreens

Aucuba japonica	spotted laurel
Berberis darwinii	barberry
Buxus sempervirens	common box
Ceanothus thyrsiflorus repens	prostrate ceanothus
Cotoneaster salicifolius	willow-leaf cotoneaster
Erica arborea alpina	heather
Hypericum calycinum	rose of Sharon
Ilex aquifolium	common holly
Lavandula angustifolia	lavender
Lonicera nitida	honeysuckle
Prunus laurocerasus	cherry laurel
Pyracantha spp.	firethorns
Sarcococca hookeriana	sweet box
Viburnum burkwoodii	viburnum
Vinca major	greater periwinkle

Extra-hardy deciduous trees & shrubs

Alnus incana	gray elder
Betula jacquemontii	Himalayan birch
Crataegis pedicellata	scarlet hawthorn
Hydrangea paniculata grandiflora	hydrangea
Philadelphus	mock orange
Ribes aureum	golden currant
Sorbus aucuparia	mountain ash

(see also Wind-tolerant Plants)

Plants for a Dry Garden

Trees & shrubs

Acer platanoides	Norway maple
Amelanchier lamarckii	snowy mespilus
Betula jacquemontii	Himalayan birch
Choisya ternata	Mexican orange blossom
Crataegus pedicellata	scarlet hawthorn
Myrtus communis	myrtle
Philadelphus spp.	mock orange
Potentilla spp.	cinquefoils
Prunus laurocerasus	cherry laurel
Ruscus aculeatus	butchers broom
Sorbus aucuparia	mountain ash
Spirea spp.	spiraeas
Symphoricarpus spp.	snowberry

Perennials

Alchemilla mollis	lady's mantle
Bergenia purpurascens	purple bugle
Chrysanthemum maximum	shasta daisy
Euphorbia spp.	spurges
Galega officinalis	goat's rue
Oenothera fruticosa	evening primrose
Papaver orientale	oriental poppy
Polygonatum multiflorum	solomon's seal
Pulmonaria saccharata	lungwort
Saponaria ocymoides	soapwort
Sedums	stonecrops
Verbascum spp.	mulleins

Plants for a Water Garden

Oxygenating

Callitriche verna	water starwort
Ceratophyllum demersum	hornwort
Fontinalis antipyretica	willow moss
Myriophyllum spicatum	water milfoil
Hottonia palustris	water violet

Floating

Azola caroliniana	fairy moss
Aponogeton distachyus	water hawthorn
Eichhornia crassipes	water hyacinth
Trapa natans	water chestnut

Marginals

Iris laevigata	Japanese iris
Pontederia cordata	pickerel weed
Scirpus zebrinus	zebra rush
Lysichiton americanus	skunk cabbage
Typha minima	miniature reedmace

Plants for a Fragrant Garden

Spring/summer

Convallaria majalis	lily of the valley
Hyacinthus spp.	hyacinth (bulb)
Lonicera spp.	honeysuckle (climber)
Myrtus communis	myrtle
Narcissus spp.	narcissus (bulb)
Philadelphus spp.	mock orange
Syringa spp.	lilac
Viburnum spp.	most types
Wisteria sinensis	wisteria (climber)

Summer/autumn

Cytisus battanderi	pineapple broom
Jasminum spp.	jasmine
Lilium regale	trumpet lily
Lilium auratum	golden-rayed lily
Nicotiana alata	(night scent, annual)
Nicotiana sylvestris	(perennial)
Matthiola bicornis	night-scented stocks
Stephanotis spp.	wax flower
Trachelospermum jasminoides	star jasmine (climber)

Winter/spring

Daphne mezereum	var. 'Alba'
Daphne odorata	
Hamamelis mollis	witch hazel
Sarcococca hookeriana	var. 'Digyna'
Viburnum x bodnantense	var. 'Dawn'

Plants for a Wet Garden *(see also Plants for Wet Places)*

Trees & shrubs: *Salix* spp. willows; *Alnus* spp. alders; *Cornus sanguinea* dogwood; *Taxodium distychum* swamp cypress

Perennials: *Aconitum* spp. aconites; *Anchusa* spp. alkanet; *Cimicifuga* sp. bugbanes; *Hemerocallis* spp. day lilies; *Iris laevigata* Japanese iris; *Iris sibirica* Siberian iris; *Iris kaempferi* Japanese flag; *Mimulus luteus* musk; *Peltiphyllum peltatum* umbrella plant; *Smilacina racemosa* false spikenard; *Trollius* spp. globe flowers

Plants fo

Aesculus hippocastanum
Althaea spp.
Antirrhinum spp.
Buddleia spp.
Calendula officinalis
Gypsophila paniculata
Hedera helix
Laurus nobilis
Ligustrum vulgare
Olearia haastii
Pelargonium spp.
Petunia spp.
Robinia pseudoacacia
Ruscus aculeatus
Saxifraga urbum
Symphoricarpus racemosus
Syringa spp.

Plants for a Mont

Trees & shrubs

Betula spp.
Buddleia variabilis
Carpinus betulus
Juniperus communis nana
Larix decidua
Pinus montana pumilio
Salix lapponum, lanata & arbu

Perennials *(see also Wild C*

Ajuga reptans
Alyssum saxatilis
Anemone pulsatilla
Anthyllis montana
Asperula odorata
Aubretia spp.
Dianthus deltoides
Euphorbia cyparisias
Galium olympicum
Gentiana spp.
Hypericum reptans
Myosotis alpestris
Potentilla spp.
Primula auricula vars
Primula farinosa
Saxifraga spp.
Scabiosa spp.
Sedum spp.
Soldanella alpina
Thymus spp.
Veronica fruticans
Vinca minor
Viola lutea

RBAN GARDEN

orse chestnut
ollyhocks
napdragons
utterfly bush
ot marigold
ypsophila
y
ay
rivet
learia
geraniums'
etunias
lse acacia
utcher's broom
ondon pride
nowberry
lacs

RDEN

rch
utterfly bush
ornbeam (H)
uniper
rch
warf mountain pine
owny, woolly &
ountain willows

reeping bugle
old dust
asque flower
ountain kidney-vetch
weet woodruff
ock cress
aiden pink
ypress spurge
ountain bedstraw
entians
reeping St John's wort
pine forget-me-not
nquefoils
uriculas
rdseye primrose
xifrages
abiouses
onecrops
pine snowbell
hymes
ock speedwell
eriwinkle
ountain pansy

Plants for a Coastal Garden

Achillea spp.	yarrow, milfoil
Arbutus unedo	strawberry tree
Centrabthus ruber	red valerian
Cistus spp.	rock rose
Dianthus gallicus	Jersey pink
Euonymus japonica	(good hedging plant)
Eryngium spp.	sea holly
Hippophae rhamnoides	sea buckthorn
Ilex aquifolium	common holly
Juniperus communis nana	juniper
Quercus ilex	holm oak
Santolina chaemocyparis	lavender cotton
Statice latifolia	sea lavender

(see also Salt-tolerant Plants)

Plants for a Wooded Garden

Shrubs

Cornus kousa	dogwood
Hebe pinguifolia	hebe
Hypericum calycinum	rose of Sharon
Ligustrum ovalifolium	privet
Lonicera pileata	honeysuckle
Pyracantha spp.	firethorn
Sambucus spp.	elder
Sarcococca spp.	sweet box
Viburnum opulus	guelder rose

Perennials

Ajuga reptans	bugle
Alchemilla mollis	lady's mantle
Avena candida	blue oat grass
Bergenia spp.	elephant ears
Convallaria major	lily of the valley
Geranium spp.	cranesbills
Helleborus spp.	Christmas rose
Lamium maculatum	deadnettle
Pulmonaria saccharata	lungwort
Saxifraga umbrosa	Pyrenean saxifrage

Bulbs

Anemone nemorosa	wood anemone
Solchicum speciosum	autumn crocus
Cyclamen hederifolium	autumn-flowering cyclamen
Cyclamen coum	winter-flowering cyclamen
Eranthis hyemalis	winter aconite
Erythronium denis-canis	dog's tooth violet
Galanthus nivalis	snowdrop
Hyacinthoides non-scriptus	bluebell
Trillium grandiflorum	wake robin

(see also Shade-tolerant Plants, Plants for Wet Places)

Plants for a Healing Garden

Special areas: Old-fashioned roses; Aromatic herbs
Trees: Aspen; Juniper; Lime
Shrubs: Buddleia; Daphne; Jasmine; Witch hazel
Perennials: Columbines; Chamomile; Creeping thyme; Feverfew; Holly; Hyssop; Lavender; Lupins; Marigolds; Pansies; Pinks; Primroses; Snowdrops; Sweet violets; Tansy; Teasel

Plants for a Wild Garden

Meadow

Achillea millefolium	yarrow
Bellis perennis	daisy
Cardamine pratensis	lady's smock
Centaurea nigra	knapweed
Fumaria spp.	fumitories
Galanthus nivalis	snowdrop
Malva moschata	musk mallow
Medicago spp.	medicks
Muscari racemosum	grape hyacinth
Narcissus pseudonarcissus	wild daffodil
Papaver rhoeas	field poppy
Primula veris	cowslip
Prunella vulgaris	self-heal
Viola sosoria	meadow violet

Woodland

Anemone quinquifolia	wood anemone
Arum maculatum	cuckoo pint
Berberis vulgare	wild barberry
Convallaria majalis	lily-of-the-valley
Cornus sanguinea	dogwood
Corylus avellana	hazel
Crataegus monogyna	hawthorn
Dryopteris filix-mas	male fern
Endymion non-scriptus	bluebell
Ilex aquifolium	holly
Malus coronaria	crab apple
Polygonum multiflorum	solomon's seal
Polypodium vulgare	polypody fern
Primula vulgaris	primrose
Viola riviniana	dog violet

Water and damp places

Anagallis tenella	bog pimpernel
Butomus umbellatus	flowering rush
Caltha palustris	marsh marigold
Filipendula ulmaria	meadowsweet
Geum rivale	water avens
Hydrocharis morsus-ranae	frogbit
Hypericum eloides	marsh St John's wort
Iris pseudacorus	yellow flag
Lythrum salicaria	purple loosestrife
Mentha aquatica	water mint
Menyanthes trifoliata	bogbean
Myosotis scorpioides	water forget-me-not
Nymphaea odorata	water lily
Potentilla palustris	marsh cinquefoil
Ranunculus aquatilis	water crowfoot
Sagittaria sagittifolia	arrowhead
Veronica beccabunga	brooklime

Rocky places

Armeria maritima	thrift
Cymbalaria muralis	ivy-leaved toadflax
Dianthus spp.	pinks
Dryas octopetala	mountain avens
Gentiana spp.	gentians
Helianthemum nummularium	rock rose
Potentilla rupestris	rock cinquefoil
Pyrola minor	wintergreen
Verbena officinalis	vervain

Shade-tolerant Plants

Bulbs

Anemone nemerosa	wood anemone
Colchicum speciosum	autumn crocus
Eranthus hyemalis	winter aconite
Galanthus nivalis	snowdrop
Hyacinthoides non-scripta	bluebell
Leucojum vernum	spring snowflake

Shrubs

Aucuba japonica	Japanese aucuba
Berberis thunbergi	Japanese barberry
Cornus alba	Tatarian dogwood
Hebe pinguifolia	hebe
Hypericum calycinum	Aaron's beard St Johns wort
Lonicera pileata	privet honeysuckle
Mahonia aquifolium	
rhododendrons & azaleas	
Vinca spp.	periwinkles

Herbaceous perennials

Ajuga spp.	bugle
Alchemilla mollis	lady's mantle
Euphorbia robbiae	euphorbia
Helleborus spp.	hellebores
Miscanthus sacchariflorus	silver grass
Pulmonaria saccharata	Bethlehem sage
Stipa arundinacea	pheasant's tail grass
Many ferns	

Plants for Wet Places

Trees: *Salix* spp. willows; *Alnus* spp. alders

Shrubs

Cornus spp.	dogwoods
Clethra alnifolia	sweet pepper bush
Spiraea billiardii	spiraea
Myrtica gale	bog myrtle

Herbaceous perennials

Gunnera manicata	gunnera
Osmunda regalis	royal fern
Many other ferns	
Cimicifuga spp.	bugbanes
Hemerocallis sp.	day lilies
Iris sibirica	Siberian iris
Trollius europaeus	globe flower
Caltha palustris	marsh marigold
Salvia uliginosa	bog sage

Wind-tolerant Plants

Aquilegia spp.	columbines
Aster novi-belgii	michaelmas daisy
Calluna spp.	heathers
Campanula spp.	bellflowers
Cotoneaster horizontalis	prostrate cotoneaster
Geum spp.	avens
Polygonum spp.	knotweeds
Potentilla spp.	potentillas
Pyracantha spp.	firethorns
Sedum spp.	stonecrops

Salt-tolerant Plants

Trees & shrubs

Cistus spp.	rock rose
Cytisus spp.	broom
Elaeagnus spp.	(good for hedging)
Euonymus japonica	Japanese spindle (hedging)
Genista spp.	broom
Hebe spp.	hebe
Olearia	daisy bush (hedging)
Pinus thunbergiana	black pine
Potentilla spp.	cinquefoils
shrubby senecios	
Sorbus aucuparia	mountain ash
Ulex spp.	gorse

Perennials

Ajuga spp.	*bugle*
Alchemilla spp.	*lady's mantle*
Artemisia spp.	*wormwood*
Asparagus officinalis	*asparagus*
Crambe maritima	*sea kale*
Foeniculum vulgare	*fennel*
Halimium spp.	*rock rose*
Lavandula spp.	*lavender*
Levisticum spp.	*lovage*
Malva spp.	*mallows*
Medicago spp.	*medicks*
Papaver spp.	*poppies*
Rosmarinus officinalis	*rosemary*
Salvia spp.	*sage*
Scilla spp.	*squill*

Pollution-tolerant Plants

Acer spp.	maples
Buddleia	butterfly bush
Cotoneaster spp.	cotoneasters
Crataegus pedicellata	scarlet hawthorn
Fagus spp.	beech
Laburnum spp.	laburnum
Ligustrum spp.	privet
Myosotis spp.	forget-me-not
Osmanthus delavayii	osmanthus
Pelargonium spp.	'geraniums'
Petunia spp.	petunia
Philadelphus	mock orange
Prunus laurocerasus	cherry laurel
Ruscus aculeatus	butcher's broom
Symphoricarpos	snowberry
Syringa spp.	lilacs
Tulipa spp.	tulips
Viburnum spp.	viburnum
Vinca spp.	periwinkles

Shade-tolerant Edibles

Fruit

Apple:
- 'Gravenstein Red'(C)
- 'Rhode Island Greening'(C)
- 'Wealthy'(E)

Cherry:
- 'Montmorency'

Gooseberry:
- 'Pixwell'(C)
- 'Poorman'(E)(C)
- 'Whinham's Industry' (E)*

Raspberry:
- 'Meeker'
- 'Latham'

Rhubarb*

Vegetables

Beans††
- broad Windsor 'Witkiem Major'
- bush 'Tender Crop'
- climber 'Kentucky Wonder'

Beet 'Kleine Bol'
Broccoli†
Cabbage 'Grenadier'
Celery††
Jerusalem artichokes*
Kale*
Kohlrabi*
Parsnip 'Hollow Crown'
Potato Early varieties†
Spinach*

Salads

Lettuce 'Little Gem'*
Radish*
Spr. onion 'White Lisbon'††

** = North shade; † = South shade; †† = light S shade; C = cooking; E = eating*

Water-loving Crops

Beans, climbing	Lettuce
	Pepper
Calabrese	Potato
Cauliflower	Radish
Cucumber	Scallion
Leek	Tomato

Drought-tolerant Edibles

Almond	Dandelion	Rutabaga
Apricot	Fig	Spinach
Artichoke,	Lemon	Squash
Jerusalem	Melon	Sweetcorn
Bean, bush	Olive	Sweet potato
Brassicas	Parsnip	Turnip
Carrot	Peas	

Dynamic Accumulators

Arrowroot *Maranta arundinacea*
Borage *Borago officinalis*
Bracken *Pteridium* sp.
Buckwheat *Fagopyrum esculentum*
Burdock *Arctium minus*
Chickweed *Stellaria media*
Chicory *Cichorium intybus*
Cleavers *Galium aparine*
Clover *Trifolium* spp.
Coltsfoot *Tussilago farfara*
Comfrey *Symphytum officinale*
Dandelion *Taraxacum vulgare*
Docks *Rumex* spp.
Fat hen *Atriplex hastata*
Garlic *Allium sativum*
Horsetails *Equisetum* spp.
Nettles *Urtica* spp.
Parsley *Petroselinum crispum*
Plantains *Plantago* spp.
Sorrel *Rumex* spp.
Sow thistle *Sonchus arvensis*
Spurges *Euphorbia* spp.
Thistles *various*
Vetches *Vicia* spp.
Watercress *Nasturtium officinale*
Yarrow *Achillea millefolium*

(see also Chart p.224)

Plants for Acid Soils

Acer rubrum	red maple
Azalea spp.	azaleas
Calluna spp.	heathers
Erica spp.	heathers
Gaultheria procumbens	wintergreen
Kalmia latifolia	mountain laurel
Ledum palustre	Labrador tea
Myrica gale	bog myrtle
Picea	spruce
Rhododendron spp.	rhododendrons
Trientalis europaea	chickweed wintergreen
Vaccinium myrtilus	bilberry
V. oxycoccos	cranberry
Celery, lettuce, parsnip	

Plants for Alkaline Soils

Deciduous trees	
Crataegus spp.	hawthorn
Fagus sylvatica	common beech
Malus spp.	apple family
Morus nigra	black mulberry
Tilia spp.	limes
Conifers	
Cedrus spp.	cedars
Cupressus spp.	cypresses
Juniperus spp.	junipers
Taxus baccatus	English yew
Shrubs	
Cistus spp.	rock roses
Philadelphus spp.	mock orange
Potentilla spp.	shrubby cinquefoils
Rosa rugosa	rugosa rose
Syringa spp.	lilacs
Wisteria sinensis	Chinese wisteria
Bulbs	
Colchicum spp.	autumn crocus
Crocus spp.	spring crocus
Narcissus spp.	daffodils
Muscari spp.	grape hyacinths
Scilla spp.	squills
Tulipa spp.	tulips

Crops: *Brassicas except calabrese*

Plants for Sandy Soils

Deciduous trees	
Betula pendula	weeping birch
Castanea sativa	Spanish chestnut
Quercus ilex	holm (or holly) oak
Conifers	
Juniperus spp.	junipers
Larix decidua	European larch
Shrubs & perennials	
Calluna vulgaris	heather
Cistus spp.	rock roses
Erica spp.	heathers
Genista tinctoria	dyer's greenweed
Lavandula spp.	lavenders
Rosmarinus officinalis	rosemary
Ulex europaeus	gorse
Foeniculum vulgare 'pupureum'	bronze fennel
Origanum vulgare 'aureum'	golden marjoram
Crocus spp.	spring crocuses
Muscari spp.	grape hyacinths
Scilla spp.	squills

Crops: *Carrot, parsnip, beetroot*

Plants for Clay Soils

Trees & shrubs	
Acer rubrum	red maple
Cornus spp.	dogwoods
Fraxinus spp.	ashes
Juglans nigra	black walnut
Populus spp.	poplars
Quercus robur	English oak
Salix caprea	goat willow
Sambucus spp.	elders
Other	
Butomus umbellatus	flowering rush
Caltha palustris	marsh marigold
Gunnera manicata	gunnera
Iris laevigata	Japanese iris
Osmunda regalis	royal fern
Rosa spp.	roses

Crops: *Brassicas, broad beans*

Plants for Poor Soils

Lavatera olbia	tree mallow
Leguminosae	legumes
Nepeta spp.	catmints
Papaver spp.	poppies
Potentilla spp.	shrubby cinquefoils
Saponaria officinalis	soapwort
Sedum spp.	stonecrops
Solidago spp.	golden rods
Stachys lanata	lambs' ears
Symphytum officinalis	comfrey
Verbascum spp.	mulleins

Crops: *Leafy crops*

Green Manures *(see also Chart pp.222–3)*

Alfalfa	*Medicago sativa*	*Perennial*
Beans (field)	*Pisum arvensis*	*Winter cover*
Buckwheat	*Fagopyrum esculentum*	*Winter cover*
Clover (alsike)	*Trifolium hybridum*	*Very hardy legume*
Clover (crimson)	*Trifolium pratense*	*Summer forage legume*
Fenugreek	*Trigonella foenum-graecum*	*Fast winter/summer cover*
Lupin	*Lupinus* spp.	*Summer-cover legume*
Mexican marigold	*Tragetes minuta*	*Summer cover*
Mustard (white)	*Brassica* sp.	*Fast-growing summer cover*
California bluebell	*Phacelia* sp.	*Fast-growing summer cover*
Rape	*Brassica napus*	*Summer cover*
Rye	*Elymus* spp.	*V. heavy winter cover*
Winter tare	Vicia *sp.*	*Winter cover legume*

Fruit Varieties	
Tree Fruit; a shortlist for flavour, season, tradition, and compatibility	
Apples: sweet, early:	Egremont Russet Iowa Beauty
sweet, late	Cox's Orange Pippin Blenheim Orange **NP**
sweet, mid	James Grieve Summer Pearmain
eat/cook (early)	Yellow Transparent Wellington
cook (early)	Early Harvest Freedom
(mid-late)	Bramley's Seedling **NP** Winesap
cider, sweet medium	Kingston Black St Edmund's Russet
Pears: early	Clapp's Favourite Rousselet de Reims
mid	Doyenne du Comice Beurre Bosc Seckel
late	Winter Nelis
NP = *trees no use for pollinating others, therefore must be planted as one of a trio.*	
Cherries: *Pollination of cherries is complex. It is thus essential to select compatible varieties from nursery lists. The few self-fertile varieties are:*	
bitter	Montmorency
sweet	Stella; Sunburst; Lapins
*(NB: sweet **SF** cherries are very modern.)*	
Apricots:	Chinese Moorpark
Nectarines:	Garden Delight Pineapple
Peaches:	Reliance J. H. Hale Rochester
Plums: early	Golden Nectar (**SF**) Opal (**SF**)
early-mid	Yakima (**SS**) Mount Royal (**SF**)
mid	Seneca (**SS**) Laxton's Delicious (**SS**)
late	President (**SS**) Sannois (**SS**)
SF = *self-fertile;* **SS** = *self-sterile.*	
Fig:	Brown Turkey
Medlar: large small	Breda Giant Nottingham
Quince: apple fruit pear fruit large fruit	Champion Meech's Prolific Bereczki

Soft Fruit selection	
Blackcurrant:	Boskoop Giant Laxton's Giant Wellington XXX Baldwin
Redcurrant:	Laxtons No. 1 Early, vigorous Red Lake Late, big bunches
Whitecurrant:	White Versailles Early White Dutch Mid
Gooseberry:	Careless (**D**) pale green Leveller (**D**) large golden Pixwell Whinham's Industry (**D**) red Whitesmith (**D**) pale green-yellow
Mulberry:	White (*M. alba*) for silkworms Black (*M. nigra*) for eating
Blackberry & hybrids	Oregon Thornless (blackberry) Boysenberry (black x rasp x logan) Loganberry (black x rasp) Sunberry (new black x rasp) Himalayaberry (early giant black) Tayberry (black x rasp) Japanese wineberry, orange fruits
Raspberry:	Glen Clova, reliable Glen Moy, thornless Leo, latest to ripen Malling Promise, standard variety
autumn	Heritage, dark red, hardy Zeva, large fruit September, oldest type, sweet flavour
Blueberry:	no varieties, need acid, sandy soil
Strawberry:	Royal Sovereign, century-old variety Cambridge Favourite, old and reliable* Bounty, new small mid-season Pantagruella, new small early
Grape: outdoor black	Cascade (**W**) Merlot/Baco Noir/Pinot Noir (**W**)
white	Madeleine Sylvaner (**D, W**) Carlos (**D, W**) Muller Thurgau (**D, W**)
*All but * could be hard to find* **D** = *Dessert* **W** = *Wine*	

Herbs for Tisanes

Melissa officinalis	lemon balm
Monarda didyma	bee balm (L)
Origanum majorana	marjoram (L)
Pelargonium graveolens	rose geranium (L)
Rosa spp.	rose (hips)
Angelica archangelica	angelica (L,S)
Anthemis nobilis	chamomile (F)
Borago officinalis	borage (L+F)
Galium odoratum	woodruff (L+F)
Mentha spicata	spearmint (L)
Sambucus nigra	elder (F/B/L)
Salvia officinalis	sage (L)
Sanguisorba minor	salad burnet (L)
Tilia spp.	linden (F)

B = *berry;* **F** = *flower;* **L** = *leaf;* **S** = *stem*

Herbs for Salads

Apium graveolens	celery (L)
Allium schoenophrasum	chives
Anethum graveolens	dill
Anthriscus cerefolium	chervil
Artemisia dracunculus	tarragon
Calendula officinalis	marigold (petals)
Coriandrum sativum	coriander
Foeniculum vulgare	fennel
Levisticum officinalis	lovage
Mentha spp.	mints
Ocimum basilicum	basil
Petroselinum crispum	parsley
Rumes acetosa	sorrel
Sanguisorba minor	salad burnet
Satureja hortensis	summer savory
Tropaeolum majus	nasturtium (L,F,S)

Culinary Herbs

Anethum graveolens	dill
Artemisia dracunculus	tarragon
Coriandrum sativum	coriander
Foeniculum vulgare	fennel
Laurus nobilis	bay
Levisticum officinale	lovage
Mentha spp.	mint
Ocimum basilicum	basil
Origanum majorana	marjoram
Origanum vulgare	oregano
Petroselinum crispum	parsley
Rosmarinus officinalis	rosemary
Salvia officinalis	sage
Thymus vulgaris	thyme

Plants with Fruits for Birds

Beech (S)	Holly (B)
Berberis spp. (B)	Ivy (B)
Bramble (B)	Mistletoe (B)
Buckthorns (B)	Oak (S)
Conifers (S)	Privet (B)
Cotoneaster spp. (B)	Prunus spp. (B)
Daphne spp. (B)	Thistles (S)
Dogwood (B)	Vaccinium spp. (B)
Elders (B)	Viburnum spp. (B)
Hawthorn (B)	Yew (B)

B = *berry;* **S** = *seeds*

Medicinal Herbs

Achillea millefolium	yarrow	tea, int. & ext.
Alchemilla vulgaris	lady's mantle	inf., ext.
Apium graveolens	celery/celeriac	leaf, tonic
Anthriscum cerefolium	chervil	a Lenten herb
Anethum graveolens	dill	leaf & seed, int.
Artemisia vulgaris	mugwort	tea, int.
Borago officinalis	borage	cheering
Calendula officinale	marigold	flower tea, int. & ext.
Carum petroselinum	parsley	general herb
Equisetum arvense	horsetail	vinegar inf., ext.
Foeniculum vulgare	fennel	tea, int. & ext.
Galium odoratum	woodruff	tea & aroma, relaxing
Hyssopus officinale	hyssop	cleansing
Juniperis communis	juniper	berries, 3-yr ripened
Laurus nobilis	bay	general herb
Levisticum officinale	lovage	int. & ext.
Mentha spp.	mints	digestive
Matricaria chamomilla	false chamomile	flower, healing
Monarda didyma	bee balm	leaf, tea
Myrrhis odorata	sweet cicely	sweetens without sugar
Ocimum basilicum	basil	general herb
Origanum majorana	marjoram	general herb
Prunella vulgaris	self-heal	healing, ext.
Rosa rubiginosa	sweet briar	fruit syrup
Rosmarinus officinalis	rosemary	general herb
Sambucus nigra	elder	flower & berry, wine & tea
Sanguisorba minor	salad burnet	tonic tea, int. & ext.
Taraxacum officinale	dandelion	leaf, tonic
Tilia europaea	linden	flower tea soothes
Tropaeolum spp.	nasturtiums	savory, tonic
Tussilago farfara	coltsfoot	tea, int. & ext.
Urtica dioica	stinging nettle	tonic

int. = *internal;* **ext.** = *external;* **inf.** = *infusion*

Wild Vegetables

Anethum graveolens	*dill*	*Rumex* spp.	dock
Armoracia rusticana	*horseradish*	*Rumex acetosa*	sorrel
Brassica kaber	*charlock*	*Salicornia europaea*	glasswort/samphire
Chenopodium album	*lamb's-quarters*	*Sanguisorba minor*	salad burnet
Chenopodium bonus-henricus	*Good King Henry*	*Stellaria media*	chickweed
Crambe maritima	*sea kale*	*Symphytum officinale*	comfrey
Eruca sativa	*rocket*	*Taraxacum officinale*	dandelion
Foeniculum vulgare	*fennel*	*Tragopogon porrifolius*	salsify
Nasturtium officinale	*watercress*	*Urtica* spp.	stinging nettle
Portulaca oleracea	*purslane*		

See also chart p.243

Climbers

Clematis spp.	clematis	S/S
Hedera helix	English ivy	S/S
Humulus lupulus	hop	Sun
Ipomoea hederacea	morning glory	Sun
Jasminum officinale	jasmine	Sun
Lonicera spp.	honeysuckles	S/S
Passiflora caerulea	passion flower	Sun
Parthenocissus spp.	Boston ivy *et al.*	S/S
Polygonum baldschuanicum	Russian vine	S/S
Tropaeolum speciosum	nasturtium	Sun
Vitis vinifera	grape vine	Sun
Wisteria sinensis	Chinese wisteria	Sun

Hedging

Acer campestre	field maple	D
Alnus incana	grey alder	D
Berberis spp.	barberries	D/E
Buxus sempervirens	box wood	E
Carpinus betulus	hornbeam	D
Corylus spp.	hazels	D
Cornus sanguinea	dogwood	D
Crataegus monogyna	hawthorn	D
Euonymous europaeus	spindle tree	D
Fagus sylvatica	European beech	D
Hippophae rhamnoides	sea buckthorn	D
Ilex spp.	hollies	E
Laurus nobilis	bay	E
Lavandula angustifolia	lavender	E
Ligustrum ovalifolia	privet	E
Lonicera nitida	honeysuckle	D/E
Prunus laurocerasus	laurel	E
Prunus spinosus	blackthorn	D
Pyracantha	firethorn	E
Rosa spp.	roses	D
Rosmarinus officinalis	rosemary	E
Rubus fruticosus	bramble	D
Santolina chaemaecyparis	cotton lavender	D
Taxus baccata	English yew	E
Ulex europaeus	gorse	E
Viburnum lantana	wayfaring tree	D

E = *evergreen;* **D** = *deciduious;* **S/S** = *sun or shade*

Windbreak plants

Hardy, for very exposed sites

Alnus incana	gray alder
Fraxinus excelsior	ash
Ilex aquifolium	English holly
Laurus nobilis	bay
Salix caprea	goat willow
Sorbus intermedia	Swedish whitebeam
Pinus nigra	Austrian pine

General use

Echinops bannaticus	globe thistle
Filipendula camtschatica	meadowsweet
Helianthus annuus	sunflower
H. Tuberosus	Jerusalem artichoke
Stipa gigantea	golden oats

(plus many climbers, if trained on trellis or wire)
(see also Hedging, above)

Trees, Sizes and Rates of Growth

Tree (Eng)	*Tree (Latin)*	*Rate*	*Height/Spread (m)*	*Use*
Alder	*Alnus cordata*	Medium	16 × 6	Wet soil
grey	*Alnus incana*	Medium	20 × 6	Cold wind
Ash	*Fraxinus excelsior*	Fast	22 × 12	★
Beech	*Fagus sylvatica*	Medium	15.5 × 15.5	**H/Orn★**
copper	*F. Syl. 'Purpurea'*	Slow	19 × 15	★
Birch	*Betula pendula*	Fast	12 × 5	**Orn**
	B. p. 'Dalecarlica'	Medium	26 × 8	**Orn**
Cedar	*Cedrus* spp.	Medium	30 × 15	★
Cherry, ornamental	*Prunus var.*	Medium	to 12 × 10	**Orn**
Chestnut, horse	*Aesculus hippocastanum*	Fast	25 × 15	★
Spanish	*Castanea sativa*	Fast	18 × 12	**Frt** ★
Crab apple	*Malus* spp.	Med/Fast	8 × 6	**Orn**
Cypress	*Cupressus* spp.	Fast	10 × var.	**Orn/H**
Elm	*Ulmus* spp.	Medium	35 × 15	★
Hawthorn	*Crataegus* spp.	Fast	6 × 6	**H/ Orn**
Hazel	*Corylus avellana*	Medium	6 × 6	**H/ Frt**
Holly, English	*Ilex aquifolium*	Slow	10 × 5	**H/ Orn**

H = *hedge;* **Frt** = *fruit;* **Orn** = *ornamental;* **WB** = *windbreak.* ★ = *wide roots, only suitable fo*

Threatened Plant Habitats

Ancient grassland

wild meadow could support cowslip; betony; orchids; great burnet; pignut; meadow saffron; poppies; cornflowers; fritillaries

Ancient woodland

coppice could support woodruff; wood anemone; lily-of-the-valley; primrose; bluebell

Wetlands

bog garden could support meadowsweet; marsh marigold; ragged robin; cuckoo flower; creeping jenny; reeds

Companion plants

Basil capsicum/tomato
Borage tomato/orchard
Candytuft brassicas
Chervil radish
Chives apple/carrot
Dill brassicas/cucumber
Flax carrot
French marigold tomato
Goose grass beans
Horseradish potato
Hyssop brassicas
Nasturtium apple/brassicas/cucumber
Sage carrot/brassicas
Shepherd's purse brassicas
Sow-thistle cucumber
Stinging nettle orchard
Summer savoury broad bean/onion

(see also chart, p.250)

Plants to Attract Beneficial Insects

Alliums
Buckwheat
Buddleia
Deadnettles
Flowering currant
Herbs
Honeysuckle
Limnanthes
Marigold
Thistles
Winter aconite

Trees, Sizes and Rates of Growth

Tree (Eng)	*Tree (Latin)*	*Rate*	*Height/Spread (m)*	*Use*
Hornbeam	*Carpinus betulus*	Medium	15 × 12	**H/** Poor soil
Laburnum	*Laburnum* spp.	Fast	7 × 5–12	**Orn**
Larch	*Larix europaea*	Fast	30 × 30	★
Linden	*Tilia* spp.	Medium	22 × 9	★
Maple	*Acer* spp.	Fast	to 20 × 16	Various
Mulberry	*Morus* spp.	Fast	10 × 10	**Frt**
Oak, English	*Quercus robur*	Slow	22 × 22	★
Oregon	*Q. garryana*	Slow	15 × 10	**Orn**
Plane	*Platanus occidentalis*	Medium	25 × 15	★
Poplar,				
white	*Populus alba*	Fast	20 × 10	★★
Lombardy	*P. nigra Italica*	Fast	30 × 2	**WB★★**
Ontario	*P. candicans*	Fast	15 × 6	★
Spruce, white	*Picea glauca*	Fast	30 × 12	**Orn**
Walnut	*Juglans regia*	Slow	22 × 15	**Frt★**
Willow,				
white	*Salix alba*	Fast	15 × 12	★★
weeping	*S. babylonica*	Fast	12 × 12★	★★
crack	*S. fragilis*	Fast	15 × 15	★★
goat	*S. caprea*	Fast	6 × 8	★★
Yew	*Taxus baccata*	Slow	10 × 15	★

. large garden; ★★ = invasive roots spread great distance from tree.

Trees for Coppicing

Tree (Latin)	*Tree (Eng)*	*Use*
Acer platanoides	Norway maple	wood for turning
Alnus glutinosa	common alder	for cold, wet soil
Carpinus betulus	hornbeam	general utility
Castanea sativa	Spanish chestnut	split poles for fencing
Corylus avellana	hazel	rot-resistant wood for drains; wands for hurdle-making
Fagus sylvatica	beech	fine wood for turned furniture
Fraxinus excelsior	ash	smokeless fire, burns green; poles for timber or turning
Ilex aquifolium	English holly	straight, strong poles
Quercus spp.	oaks	building, furniture, etc.
Tilia spp.	lindens	for dry soil

(also worth trying with most native deciduous trees)

Ground Cover Plants

Shrubs			
Calluna vulgaris	heather	E	Sun
Cotoneaster horizontalis	cotoneaster	D	Sun
Erica carnea	heather	E	Sun
Genista lydia	broom	E	Sun
Hedera colchica	Persian ivy	E	Shade
Hypericum calicynum	Aaron's beard	E	Sun
Lonicera pileata	honeysuckle	E	Sun
Salix repens	creeping willow	D	Sun
Vaccinium vitis-idaea	cowberry	E	Sun
Vinca major/minor	periwinkles	E	S/S

Perennials		
Ajuga reptans	bugle	S/S
Alchemilla mollis	lady's mantle	Shade
Armeria maritima	thrift	Sun
Dryas octopetala	mountain avens	Sun
Galium odoratum	woodruff	S/S
Geranium sanguineum	bloody cranesbill	Sun
Lysimachia punctata	loosestrife	Sun
Nepeta faassenii	catmint	Sun
Pulmonaria	lungwort	S/S
Rheum spp.	rhubarbs	S/S
Saxifraga urbum	London pride	Shade
Symphytum spp.	comfrey	S/S
Viola riviniana	dog violet	Shade

E = *evergreen;* **D** = *deciduous;* **S/S** = *sun or shade*

Invasive Plants

Bindweed	*Convolvulus arvensis*
Bent grass	*Agrostis* spp.
Bracken	*Pteridium aquilinum*
Buttercups	*Ranunculus* spp.
Carrot, wild	*Daucus carota*
Cleavers	*Galium aparine*
Couch (twitch)	*Alymus repens*
Cow parsley	*Anthriscus sylvestris*
Docks	*Rumex* spp.
Green alkanet	*Pentaglottis sempervirens*
Ground elder	*Aegopodium podagraria (R)*
Horsetails	*Equisetum* spp.
Japanese knotweed	*Polygonum japonica (R)*
Lemon balm	*Melissa officinalis*
Lesser celandine	*Ranunculus ficaria (B)*
Mints	*Mentha* spp.
Nettles	*Urtica* spp.
Nightshades	*Solanum* spp.
Plantains	*Plantago* spp.
Speedwells	*Veronica* spp.
Thistle, creeping	*Cirsium arvense*

SEEDS

Vegetables & Flowers

Bountiful Gardens
5798 Ridgewood Rd.
Willits, CA 95490
(707) 459–3390

Bluestone Perennials
7211 Middle Ridge Rd.
Madison, OH 44057
(216) 428–7535

W. Altee Burpee & Co.
300 Park Ave.
Warminster, PA 18974
(800) 674–4900

Comstock, Ferre & Co.
263 Main St.
Wethersfield, CT 06109
(203) 529–3319

William Dam Seeds Ltd.
P.O. Box 8400
Dundas, ONT
Canada L9H 6M1
(416) 628–6641

Down On The Farm Seed
P.O. Box 184
Hiram, OH 44234
(216) 274–8043

EcoGenesis Inc.
16 Jedburgh Rd.
Toronto, ONT
Canada M5M 3J6

Henry Field's Seed & Nursery Co.
415 N. Burnett
Shenandoah, IA 51602
(605) 665–4491

Garden Import Inc.
Box 760
Thornhill, ONT
Canada L3T 4A5
(416) 731–1950

Gurney Seed & Nursery
Page St.
Yankton, SD 57079
(605) 665–1671

Harris Seeds (Garden Trends, Inc.)
P.O. Box 22960
Rochester, NY 14692
(716) 442–0410

Johnny's Selected Seeds
305 Foss Hill Rd.
Albion, ME 04910
(207) 437–5357

J. W. Jung Seed Co.
335 S. High St.
Randolph, WI 53957
(414) 326–4100

Orol Ledden & Sons Inc.
P.O. Box 7
Sewell, NJ 08080
(609) 468–1000

Liberty Seed Co.
P.O. Box 806
New Philadelphia, OH 44663
(216) 364–1611

Lindenberg Seeds Ltd.
803 Princess Ave.
Brandon, MB
Canada R7A 0P5
(204) 727–0575

Mellinger's Inc.
2310 W. South Range Rd.
North Lima, OH 44452
(216) 549–9861

Ontario Seed Co. Ltd.
Box 144
Waterloo, ONT
Canada N2J 3Z9
(519) 886–0557

Pacific Northwest Seed Co.
Box 460
Vernon, BC
Canada V1T 6L8
(604) 542–5166

Park Seed Co.
Cokesbury Rd.
Greenwood, SC 29647
(803) 223–7333

Pony Creek Nursery
Tilleda, WI 54978
(715) 787–3889

Porter & Son, Seedsmen
P.O. Box 104
Stephenville, TX 76401
(817) 965–5600

Rawlinson Garden Seed
269 College Rd.
Truro, NS
Canada B2N 2P6
(902) 893–3051

The Seed Source
116 Tennessee Gap Rd.
Balsam Grove, NC 28708

Shepherd's Garden Seeds
6116 Hwy. 9
Felton, CA 95018
(408) 335–6910

R.H. Shumway's
P.O. Box 1
Graniteville, SC 29829
(803) 663–9771

Stokes Seeds, Inc.
Box 548
Buffalo, NY 14240
(416) 688–4300

T & T Seeds, Ltd.
Box 1710
Winnipeg, MB
Canada R3C 3P6
(204) 956–2777

Thompson & Morgan Inc.
Box 1308
Jackson, NJ 08527
(201) 363–2225

Tregunno Seeds
126 Catherine St.
Hamilton, ONT
Canada L8R 1J4
(416) 528–5983

Twilley Seed Co.
P.O. Box 65
Trevose, PA 19053
(215) 639–8800

Heirloom, Regional & Vegetable Specialty

Abundant Life Seed Foundation
P.O. Box 772
Port Townsend, WA 98368
(206) 385–5660

Butterbrooke Farm
78 Barry Rd.
Oxford, CT 06483
(203) 888–2000

The Cook's Garden
P.O. Box 65
Londonderry, VT 05148
(802) 824–3400

Cooper Seed & Feed
P.O. Box 798
Lawrenceville, GA 30246
(404) 963–2101

DiGiorgi Co., Inc.
4816 South 60th
Omaha, NE 68117
(402) 731–3901

Driskill's Siberia Seeds
6218 Quinpool Rd.
Halifax, NS
Canada B3L 1A3

Elixir Farm Botanicals
Elixir Farm
Brixey, MO 65638
(417) 261–2393

Evergreen Y.H. Enterprises
P.O. Box 17538
Anaheim, CA 92817

Fedco Seeds
52 Mayflower Hill Dr.
Waterville, ME 04901
(207) 873–7333

Filaree Farm
Rt. 1 Box 162
Okanogan, WA 98840
(509) 422–6940

Fisher's Garden Store
P.O. Box 236
Belgrade, MT 59714
(406) 388–6052

Garden City Seeds
P.O. Box 297
Victor, MT 59875
(406) 961–4837

Gleckler Seedsmen
Meadow Lane
Metamora, OH 43540
(419) 644–2211

Good Seed
Star Rt. Box 73-A
Oroville, WA 98844

H.G. Hastings & Co.
P.O. Box 115535
Atlanta, GA 30310
(404) 755–6580

Heirloom Gardens
P.O. Box 138
Guerneville, CA 95446
(707) 869–0967

Heirloom Seeds
P.O. Box 245
West Elizabeth, PA 15088

High Altitude Gardens
P.O. Box 4238
Ketchum, ID 83340
(800) 874–7333

Horticultural Enterprises
P.O. Box 810082
Dallas, TX 75381

Ed Hume Seeds
P.O. Box 1450
Kent, WA 98035
(206) 859–1110

KUSA Research Foundation
P.O. Box 761
Ojai, CA 93023

Le Jardin du Gourmet
Box 75-B
St. Johnsbury Center, VT 05863
(802) 748–1446

Mushroompeople
P.O. Box 220-G
Summertown, TN 38483
(615) 964–2200

Nichols Garden Nursery
1190 North Pacific Hwy.
Albany, OR 97321
(503) 928–9280

Ornamental Edibles
3622 Weedin Court
San Jose, CA 95132
(408) 928–7333

Peace Seeds
2385 S.E. Thompson St.
Corvallis, OR 97333

Pinetree Garden Seeds
Rt. 100
New Gloucester, ME
04260
(207) 926–3400

Prairie Grown Seeds
Box 118
Cochin, SK
Canada S0M 0L0
(306) 386–2737

Redwood City Seed Co.
P.O. Box 361
Redwood City, CA
94064
(415) 325–7333

Ronniger's Seed
Potatoes
Star Route
Moyie Springs, ID 83845
(208) 267–7938

Seeds Blum
Idaho City Stage
Boise, ID 83706

Seeds West Garden Seeds
P.O. Box 1739
Elprado, NM 87529
(505) 758–7268

Southern Exposure Seed
Exchange
P.O. Box 158
North Garden, VA
22959
(804) 973–4703

Talauaya Seeds
P.O. Box 707
Santa Cruz, NM 87507
(505) 753–5793

Territorial Seeds Ltd.
P.O. Box 46225
Vancouver, BC
Canada V6R 4G5
(604) 322–5266

Tomato Growers Supply
Co.
P.O. Box 2237
Fort Myers, FL 33902

Vesey's Seeds
Box 9000
Calais, ME 04619
(902) 368–7333

Westwind Seeds
2509 North Campbell
Ave.
Tuscon, AZ 85719

Willhite Seed Co.
P.O. Box 23
Poolville, TX 76487
(817) 599–8656

Wood Prairie Farm
RR 1 Box 164
Bridgewater, ME 04735
(800) 829–9765

Herb Plants

Companion Plants
7247 North Coolville
Ridge Rd.
Athens, OH 45701
(614) 592–4643

The Herb Farm
RR 4
Norton, NB
Canada E0G 2N0
(506) 839–2140

Hidden Springs Herb
Farm
Rt. 14 Box 159
Cookeville, TN 38501
(615) 268–9354

Lost Prairie Herb Farm
805 Kienas Rd.
Kalispell, MT 59901
(406) 756–7742

Marcella's Garden
P.O. Box 362
Colonial Heights, VA
23834
(804) 520–2263

McCrory's Sunny Hill
Herb Farm
33152 La Place Ct.
Eustis, FL 32726
(904) 357–9876

Mountain Valley
Growers
38325 Pepperweed Rd.
Squaw Valley, CA 93675
(209) 338–2775

Richter's
Box 26
Goodwood, ONT
Canada L0C 1A0
(416) 640–6677

Sandy Mush Herb
Nursery
Rt. 2, Surrett Cove Rd.
Leicester, NC 28748
(704) 683–2014

Sunnybrook Farms
P.O. Box 6
Chesterland, OH 44026
(216) 729–7232

Taylor's Herb Gardens
1535 Lone Oak Rd.
Vista, CA 92084
(619) 727–3485

Well-Swept Herb Farm
317 Mt. Bethel Rd.
Port Murray, NJ 07865
(908) 852–5390

Berries, Fruits, & Nuts

Allen Co.
P.O. Box 310
Fruitland, MD 21826
(301) 742–7122

Bear Creek Nursery
P.O. Box 411
Northport, WA 99157

Cumberland Valley
Nurseries
P.O. Box 471
McMinnville, TN 37110
(615) 668–4153

Edible Landscaping
P.O. Box 77
Afton, VA 22920
(804) 361–9134

Finch Blueberry Nursery
P.O. Box 699
Bailey, NC 27807
(919) 235–4664

Hartmann's Plantation
P.O. Box E
Grand Junction, MI
49056
(616) 253–4281

Ison's Nursery &
Vineyard
Rt. 1
Brooks, GA 30205
(800) 733–0324

Krohne Plant Farms
Rt. 6 Box 586
Dowagiac, MI 49047
(616) 424–3450

Lawson's Nursery
Rt. 1 Box 472
Ball Ground, GA 30107
(404) 893–2141

Living Tree Centre
P.O. Box 10082
Berkeley, CA 94709
(510) 420–1440

J.E. Miller Nurseries
5060 West Lake Rd.
Canandaigua, NY 14424
(800) 836–9630

Nolin River Nut Tree
Nursery
797 Port Wooden Rd.
Upton, KY 42784
(502) 369–8551

North Star Gardens
2124 University Ave.
St. Paul, MN 55114
(612) 659–2515

Northwoods Nursery
28696 South Cramer
Rd.
Molalla, OR 97038
(503) 651–3737

Oregon Exotics
1065 Messinger Rd.
Grants Pass, OR 97527
(503) 846–7578

Raintree Nursery
391 Butts Rd.
Morton, WA 98356
(206) 496–6400

Sonoma Antique Apple
Nursery
4395 Westside Rd.
Healdsburg, CA 95448
(707) 433–6420

Southmeadow Fruit
Gardens
15310 Red Arrow Hwy.
Lakeside, MI 49116
(616) 469–2865

St. Lawrence Nurseries
RD 5 Box 324
Potsdam, NY 13676
(315) 265–6739

Stark Bros. Nurseries
Box 10
Louisiana, MO 63353
(800) 325–4180

SEEDS, *continued*

Ornamentals & Specialties

The Banana Tree
715 Northampton St.
Easton, PA 18042
(215) 253–9589

Vernon Barnes & Son
P.O. Box 250
McMinnville, TN 37110
(615) 668–8576

Bluestone Perennials
7219 Middle Ridge Rd.
Madison, OH 44057
(800) 852–5243

Campberry Farm
RR 1
Niagara-on-the-Lake, ONT
Canada L0S 1J0

Carroll Gardens
444 East Main
Westminster, MD 21158
(401) 876–7336

Digging Dog Nursery
P.O. Box 471-C
Albion, CA 95410
(707) 937–1130

Far North Gardens
16785 Harrison, Dept. BH
Livonia, MI 48154
(313) 522–9040

Forestfarm
990 Tether Rd.
Williams, OR 97544
(503) 846–6963

Foxborough Nursery
3611 Miller Rd.
Street, MD 21154
(301) 836–7023

Glasshouse Works
P.O. Box 97
Stewart, OH 95778
(614) 662–2142

Greer Gardens
1280 Goodpasture Island Rd.
Eugene, OR 97401
(503) 686–8266

Heritage Gardens
1 Meadow Ridge Rd.
Shenandoah, IA 51601

Holbrook Farm & Nursery
115 Lance Rd.
Fletcher, NC 28732
(704) 891–7790

Hortico
RR 1, Robson Rd.
Waterdown, ONT
Canada L0R 2H1

J.L. Hudson, Seedsman
P.O. Box 1058
Redwood City, CA 94064

K & L Cactus & Succulent Nursery
12712 West Stockton Blvd.
Galt, CA 95632

Lilypons Water Gardens
6800 Lilypons Rd.
Buckeystown, MD 21717
(301) 874–5133

Logee's Greenhouses
141 North St.
Danielson, CT 06239]
(203) 774–8038

Manhattan Farms
Box 33972
Station D
Vancouver, B.C.
Canada V6J 4L7

Milaeger's Gardens
4838 Douglas Ave.
Racine, WI 53402
(800) 669–9956

Musser Forests
P.O. Box 340
Indiana, PA 15701
(412) 465–5685

Nature's Garden
40611 Hwy. 226
Scio, OR 97374
(503) 394–3217

Owen Farms
Rt. 3 Box 158-A
Ripley, TN 38063
(901) 635–1588

Pikes Peak Nurseries
RD 1, Box 75
Penn Run, PA 15765
(412) 463–7747

Pinky's Plants
422 G St.
Pawnee City, NE 68420
(800) 947–4659

Steve Ray's Bamboo Gardens
909 South 79th Place
Birmingham, AL 35206
(205) 833–3052

Savage Farms Nursery
P.O. Box 125
McMinnville, TN 37110
(615) 668–8902

Shady Oaks Nursery
700 19th Ave. N.E.
Waseca, MN 56093

Siskiyou
2825 Cummings Rd.
Medford, OR 97501
(503) 772–6846

Spring Hill Nurseries
6523 North Galena Rd.
Peoria, IL 61656
(309) 691–4616

Triple Brook Farm
37 Middle Rd.
Southampton, MA 01073
(413) 527–4626

Tropicals Unlimited
595 Uluhaku St.
Kailua, HI 96734
(808) 262–6040

Unusual Plants
10065 River Mist
Rancho Cordova, CA 95670
(916) 366–7835

Van Ness Water Gardens
2460 North Euclid Ave.
Upland, CA 91786
(714) 982–2425

Vesutor Inc.
P.O. Box 561663
Charlotte, NC 28215
(704) 597–7278

Wayside Gardens
1 Garden Lane
Hodges, SC 29695
(800) 845–1124

White Flower Farm
Rt. 63
Litchfield, CT 06759
(800) 678–5164

Wildflowers, Grasses & Native Varieties

Allgrove Farm
P.O. Box 459
Wilmington, MA 01887
(508) 658–4869

Boothe Hill Wildflowers
23 Boothe Hill
Chapel Hill, NC 27514

Frosty Hollow
P.O. Box 53
Langley, WA 98260
(206) 221–2332

Larner Seeds
P.O. Box 407
Bolinas, CA 94924
(415) 868–9407

Moon Mountain
P.O. Box 34
Morro Bay, CA 93443
(805) 772–2473

Native Gardens
5737 Fisher Lane
Greenback, TN 37742
(615) 856–3350

Niche Gardens
1111 Dawson Rd.
Chapel Hill, NC 27516
(919) 967–0078

Plants of the Southwest
Rt. 6, Box 11
Sante Fe, NM 87501
(505) 983–1548

Prairie Ridge Nursery
9738 Overland Rd.
Mt. Horeb, WI 53572
(608) 437–5245

Primrose Path
RD 2, Box 110
Scottdale, PA 15683
(412) 887–6756

Vermont Wildflower Farm
Rt. 7, Box 5
Charlotte, VT 05445
(802) 425–3500

Wild Seed Inc.
2073 East ASU Circle
Tempe, AZ 85284
(602) 345–0669

Woodlanders
1128 Colleton Ave.
Aiken, SC 29801
(803) 648–7522

SEED EXCHANGES

Alcyone Light Center
1965 Hilt Rd.
Hornbrook, CA 96044

American Conifer Society
P.O. Box 314
Perry Hall, MD 21128
(410) 256–5595

American Council for Plant Preservation
Rt. 5
Renick, WV 24966

Association for Living Historical Farms and Agricultural Museums
Rt. 14, Box 214
Santa Fe, NM 87505

Bio-Integral Resource Center
1307 Acton St.
Berkeley, CA 94706

Biological Urban Gardening Services
Box 76
Citrus Heights, CA 95611

Black Creek Village
1000 Murray Ross Parkway
Downsview, ONT
Canada M3J 2P3

British Columbia Provincial Museum
Victoria, BC
Canada

California Certified Organic Farmers
Box 8136
Santa Cruz, CA 95061

Center for Canadian Historical Horticulture Studies
Royal Botanical Gardens
Hamilton, ONT
Canada L8N 3H8
(416) 527–1158

Ecological Agriculture Projects
MacDonald College
Box 191
St. Anne-de-Bellevue, QUE
Canada H9X 1C0

GARDENING ORGANIZATIONS & HISTORICAL SITES

Ecology Action/
Common Ground
5798 Ridgewood Rd.
Willits, CA 95490

Educational Concerns for Hunger Organization
17430 Durrance Rd.
North Fort Myers, FL 33917
(813) 543–3246

Environment Canada
1600 Liverpool Ct.
Ottawa, ONT
Canada K1A 1G2

The Farm
Summertown, TN 38483

The Garden Club of Toronto
777 Lawrence Ave., East
Don Mills, ONT
Canada
(416) 447–5218

The Grist Mill
RR 1
Keremeos, BC
Canada V0X 1N0

Henry Doubleday Research Association
National Center for Organic Gardening
Ryton-On-Dunsmore, Coventry
England CV8 3LG

Heritage Park
1900 Heritage Dr. S.W.
Calgary, ALB
Canada T2V 2X3

Heritage Seed Program
RR3
Uxbridge, ONT
Canada L9P 1R3

ICOMOS Canada--
Historic Gardens and Landscapes Committee
Box 737
Station B
Ottawa, ONT
Canada K1P 5R4
(614) 749–0971

International Institute for Baubiologie and Ecology
P.O. Box 387
Clearwater, FL 34615

Kings Landing
Box 522
Fredrickton, NB
Canada E3B 5A6

Meadowcreek Project
Fox, AR 72051

Mystic Seaport Museum
Mystic, CT 06355
(203) 572–0711

Native Seed Foundation
Rt. W
Moyie Springs, ID 83845

Native Seeds/Search
2509 North Campbell Ave.
No. 325
Tuscon, AZ 85719
(602) 327–9123

Natural Organic Farmers Association
140 Chestnut St.
West Hatfield, MA 01088

New Alchemy Institute
237 Hatchville Rd.
East Falmouth, MA 02563
(617) 564–6301

North American Fruit Explorers
Rt. 1, Box 94
Chapin, IL 62628

North American Permaculture
Box 573
Colville, WA 99114

Nova Scotia Museum
Botany Department
1747 Summer St.
Halifax, NS
Canada

Old Fort William
Vickers Heights P.O.
Thunder Bay, ONT
Canada P0T 2Z0

Old Sturbridge Village
1 Old Sturbridge Rd.
Sturbridge, MA 01566
(508) 347–3362

Permaculture Institute of North America
6488 Maxwelton Rd.
Clinton, WA 98236

Regenerative Agriculture Association
222 Main St.
Emmaus, PA 18049

The Resources of International Permaculture
7781 Lenox Ave.
Jacksonville, FL 32221

Rocky Mountain Institute
1739 Snowmass Creek Rd.
Snowmass, CO 81654
(303) 927–3851

Rural Advancement Fund International
Box 188
Brandon, MNT
Canada R7A 5Y8
(204) 727–8995

The Scatterseed Project
Box 1167
Farmington, ME 04938

Seed Savers Exchange
RR 3, Box 239
Decorah, IA 52101
(319) 382–5990

Society of Ecological Restoration
University of Wisconsin Arboretum
1207 Seminole Hwy.
Madison, WI 53711

Upper Canada Village
Box 740
Morrisburg, ONT
Canada K0C 1X0

Van Dusen Botanical Garden
5251 Oak St.
Vancouver, BC
Canada V6M 4H1

GARDENING EQUIPMENT & SUPPLIES

A.C. Burke & Co.
2554 Lincoln Blvd.
Suite 1058-D
Marina Del Ray, CA 90291
(310) 574–2770

A.M. Leonard, Inc.
6665 Spiker Rd.
Piqua, OH 45356
(513) 773–2694

Beneficial Insect Co.
244 Forrest St.
Forest Mill, SC 29715
(803) 547–2301

Brookstone Tools
127 Vose Farm Rd.
Peterborough, NH 03458
(603) 924–9541

Cumberland General Store
Rt. 3, Box 81
Crossville, TN 38555

Denman & Co.
187 West Orangethorpe Ave.
Suite L
Placentia, CA 92670
(714) 524–0668

Dripworks
380 Maple St.
Willits, CA 95490
(707) 459–4710

Gardenville
6266 Hwy. 290 West
Austin, TX 78735
(512) 892–0006

Gardens Alive!
5100 Schenley Place
Lawrenceburg, IN 47025
(812) 537–8650

Gardener's Eden
Williams-Sonoma Co.
P.O. Box 7307
San Francisco, CA 94120
(415) 421–4242

Gardener's Supply Co.
128 Intervale Rd.
Burlington, VT 05401
(802) 863–1700

Harmony Farm Supply
P.O. Box 460
Graton, CA 95444
(707) 823–9125

Indoor Gardening Supplies
P.O. Box 40567
Detroit, MI 48240
(313) 427–6160

Jackson & Perkins
1 Rose Lane
Medford, OR 97501
(800) 292–4769

Kemp Co.
160 Koser Rd.
Lititz, PA 17543
(800) 441–5367

Lehman's
Box 41
Kidron, OH 44636

Mantis Manufacturing Co.
1458 County Line Rd.
Huntingdon Valley, PA 19006
(800) 366–6268

Mellinger's Inc.
2310 W. South Range Rd.
North Lima, OH 44452
(216) 549–9861

Morco Products
P.O. Box 160
Dundas, MN 55019

Natural Gardening Research Center
Box 149
Sunman, IN 47041
(812) 623–3800

Necessary Trading Co.
1 Nature's Way
New Castle, VA 24127
(703) 864–5103

Nitron Industries
P.O. Box 1447
Fayetteville, AR 72702
(800) 835–0123

Peaceful Valley Farm Supply
P.O. Box 2209
Grass Valley, CA 95945
(916) 272–4769

The Plow & Hearth
560 Main St.
Madison, VA 22727
(800) 527–5247

Ringer
9959 Valley View Rd.
Eden Prairie, MN 55344
(800) 654–1047

Rowlands
7404 Menaul Blvd. N.E.
Albuquerque, NM
87110
(505) 883–1951

Smith & Hawken
25 Corte Madera
Mill Valley, CA 94941
(415) 383–4050

Troy-Bilt
102nd St. & 9th Ave.
Troy, NY 12180
(800) 828–5500

Walt Nicke Co.
36 McLeod Lane
Topsfield, MA 01983
(508) 887–3388

Womanswork
P.O. Box 543
York, ME 03909
(800) 639–2709

BOOKS

General Reference

American Horticultural Society
North American Horticulture: A Reference Guide
Charles Scribner's Sons
New York, 1982

Bradley, F.M. and Ellis, B.W.
Rodale's All-New Encyclopedia of Organic Gardening
Rodale Press, Inc.
Emmaus, PA. 1993

Damrosch, Barbara
The Garden Primer
Workman Publishing
New York, 1988

Garden Way Publishing, ed.
The Big Book of Gardening Skills
Garden Way Publishing
Pownal, VT. 1993

Raymond, Dick
Garden Way's Joy of Gardening
Garden Way Publishing
Pownal, VT. 1986

Roth, Susan
The Four-Season Landscape
Rodale Press, Inc.
Emmaus, PA. 1993

Wyman, Donald
Wyman's Gardening Encyclopedia
Macmillan Publishing Co., Inc.
New York, 1987

Vegetables, Herbs, & Fruits

Creasy, Rosalind
The Complete Book of Edible Landscaping
Sierra Club Books
San Francisco, CA. 1982

Foster, Catherine O.
Building Healthy Gardens
Garden Way Publishing
Pownal, VT. 1992

Hill, Lewis
Fruits and Berries for the Home Garden
Garden Way Publishing
Pownal, VT. 1977

Jabs, Carolyn
The Heirloom Gardener
Sierra Club Books
San Francisco, CA. 1984

Jacobs, Betty E.M.
Growing & Using Herbs Successfully
Garden Way Publishing
Pownal, VT 1980

Kline, R.A., et al.
The Heirloom Vegetable Garden
Cornell Cooperative Extension
Ithica, NY. 1986

Kourik, Robert
Designing and Maintaining Your Edible Landscape Naturally
Metamorphic Press
Santa Rosa, CA. 1986

Michalak, Patricia
Rodale's Successful Organic Gardening: Herbs
Rodale Press, Inc.
Emmaus, PA. 1993

Michalak, Patricia and Peterson, Cass
Rodale's Successful Organic Gardening: Vegetables
Rodale Press, Inc.
Emmaus, PA. 1993

McClure, Susan
The Harvest Gardener
Garden Way Publishing
Pownal, VT. 1993

National Gardening Association
Gardening: The Complete Guide to Growing America's Favorite Fruits and Vegetables
Addison-Wesley Publishing Co.
Reading, MA. 1986

Riotte, Louise
Carrots Love Tomatoes
Garden Way Publishing
Pownal, VT. 1975

Riotte, Louise
Successful Small Food Gardens
Garden Way Publishing
Pownal, VT. 1993

Seymour, John
The Self-Sufficient Gardener: A Complete Guide to Growing and Preserving All Your Own Food
Doubleday & Co.
New York, 1979

Taylor, Norman, edited by G.P. DeWolf, Jr.
Taylor's Guide to Vegetables and Herbs
Houghton Mifflin Co.
New York, 1987

Trees, Shrubs & Vines

Appleton, B.L. and Scheider, A.F.
Rodale's Successful Organic Gardening: Trees, Shrubs and Vines
Rodale Press, Inc.
Emmaus, PA. 1993

Fell, Derek
Trees and Shrubs
HP Books
Tuscon, AZ. 1986

Hudak, Joseph
Shrubs in the Landscape
McGraw-Hill
New York, 1984

Wyman, Donald
Shrubs and Vines for American Gardens
Macmillan Publishing Co. Inc.
New York, 1969

Wildflowers & Grasses

Art, Henry W.
A Garden of Wildflowers: 101 Native Species and How To Grow Them
Garden Way Publishing
Pownal, VT. 1986

Dennis, J.V.
The Wildlife Gardener
Alfred A. Knopf, Inc.
New York, 1985

Greenlee, John
The Encyclopedia of Ornamental Grasses
Rodale Press, Inc.
Emmaus, PA. 1992

Phillips, H.R.
Growing and Propagating Wild Flowers
University of North Carolina Press
Chapel Hill, NC. 1985

Techniques & Specialty Interests

Ashworth, Suzanne
Seed to Seed
Seed Saver Publications
Decorah, IA. 1990

Baldwin, J. et al.
The Whole Earth Ecolog
Gate Five Publications
Sausalito, CA. 1990

Bardach, J.E., Ryther, J.H. and McLarney, W.O.
Aquaculture
John Wiley & Sons
New York, 1975

Barton, Barbara
Gardening By Mail
Tusker Press
San Francisco, CA. 1986

Bradshaw, A.D. and Chadwick, M.J.
The Restoration of Land
University of California Press
Berkeley, CA. 1980

Brand, Stewart, et al.
The Essential Whole Earth Catalog
Whole Earth Review
Sausalito, CA. 1986

Bubel, Nancy
The New Seed Starter's Handbook
Rodale Press, Inc.
Emmaus, PA. 1992

Cleveland, D. A. and Soleri, D.
Food From Dryland Gardens
Center For Food, People and the Environment
Tuscon, AZ. 1988

Coleman, Eliot
The New Organic Grower: A Master's Manual of Tools and Techniques for the Home and Market Gardener
Chelsea Green Publishers
Post Mills, VT. 1990

Ellis, B.W. and Bradley, F.M.
The Organic Gardener's Handbook of Natural Insect and Disease Control
Rodale Press, Inc.
Emmaus, PA. 1991

Gardner, Jo Ann
The Heirloom Garden
Garden Way Publishing
Pownal, VT. 1986

Gershuny, Grace and Martin, D.L.
The Rodale Book of Composting
Rodale Press, Inc.
Emmaus, PA. 1987

Hart, R.M.
Trellising
Garden Way Publishing
Pownal, VT. 1987

Henderson, Carol L.
Landscaping for Wildlife
Minnesota Dept. of Natural Resources
St. Paul, MN. 1987

Hill, Lewis
Pruning Simplified
Garden Way Publishing
Pownal, VT. 1986

Hill, Lewis
Secrets of Plant Propagation
Garden Way Publishing
Pownal, VT. 1985

Hobhouse, Penelope
Flower Gardens
Little, Brown & Co.
New York, 1991

Jeavons, John
How To Grow More Vegetables
Ecology Action
Willits, CA. 1978

Kourik, Robert
Gray Water Use in the Landscape
Metamorphic Press
Santa Rosa, CA. 1988

Margolin, Malcolm
The Earth Manual
Heyday Books
Berkeley, CA. 1985

Nabhan, G.P.
Enduring Seeds
North Point Press
1989

O'Keefe, John
Water-Conserving Gardens and Landscapes
Garden Way Publishing
Pownal, VT. 1993

Olkowski, W., Olkowski, H., and Soleri, D.
Common-Sense Pest Control
Taunton Press
Newtown, CT. 1991

Pain, J. and Pain, I.
Another Kind of Garden
Biothermal Energy Center
Portland, ME. 1986

Philbrick, J. & Philbrick, H.
The Bug Book
Garden Way Publishing
Pownal, VT. 1974

Proctor, Robert
Antique Flowers: Perennials
HarperCollins Publishers
New York, 1990

Rodale Press, ed.
Rodale's Illustrated Encyclopedia of Gardening and Landscaping Techniques
Rodale Press, Inc.
Emmaus, PA. 1990

Rogers, Marc
Saving Seeds
Garden Way Publishing
Pownal, VT. 1989

Soil Conservation Society of America, ed.
Sources of Native Seeds and Plants
SCSA
Ankeny, IA. 1979

Strange, Marty
Family Farming
University of Nebraska Press
Lincoln, NB. 1988

Wells, Malcolm
Classic Architectural Birdhouses and Feeders
Wells
Brewster, MA. 1989

Whealy, Kent
Garden Seed Inventory
Seed Saver Publications
Decorah, IA. 1984

PERIODICALS

American Fruit Grower
37733 Euclid Ave.
Willoughby, OH 44094
(monthly)

American Horticulturist
7931 East Blvd. Dr.
Alexandria, VA 22308
(bi-monthly)

The Avant Gardener
Horticultural Data Processors
P.O. Box 489
New York, NY 10028
(monthly)

BackHome Magazine
P.O. Box 70
Hendersonville, NC 28793
(quarterly)

Fine Gardening
P.O. Box 5506
Newtown, CT 06470
(bi-monthly)

Flower & Garden
4251 Pennsylvania Ave.
Kansas City, MO 64111
(bi-monthly)

Garbage
2 Main St.
Gloucester, MA 01930
(bi-monthly)

Harrowsmith Country Life
Ferry Rd.
Charlotte, VT 05445
(bi-monthly)

The Herb Companion
201 east 4th Ave.
Loveland, CO 80537
(bi-monthly)

The Herb Quarterly
Box 548
Boiling Springs, PA 17007
(quarterly)

Horticulture
P.O. Box 53880
Boulder, CO 80322
(monthly)

Hortideas
Rt. 1 Box 302
Gravel Switch, KY 40329
(quarterly)

The Journal of Wild Culture
Crawford St.
Toronto, ONT
Canada M6J 2V4

National Gardening
National Gardening Association
180 Flynn Ave.
Burlington, VT 05401
(bi-monthly)

Organic Gardening
33 East Minor St.
Emmaus, PA 18098
(nine times/yr.)

Permaculture Communications
P.O. Box 101
Davis, CA 75617
(bi-monthly)

Whole Earth Review/Co-Evolution Quarterly
27 Gate Five Rd.
Sausalito, CA 94966
(quarterly)

Sources of Books and Publications

Ag Access
603 4th St.
Davis, CA 95616
(916) 753–9633

American Botanist Bookseller
1103 West Truitt Ave.
Chilicothe, IL 61523

Capability's Books
Box 114
Deer Park, WI 54007

Hortulus
101 Scollard St.
Toronto, ONT
Canada M5R 1G4

OPUS Publications
669 Post Rd.
Guilford, CT 06437

Old Sturbridge Village Bookstore
1 Old Sturbridge Rd.
Sturbridge, MA 01566
(508) 347–3362

Index

bold figures indicate main text entries

A

acid-alkaline balance *see* pH
acidity 212, 224
acid rain 31, 198
acid soils 159, 197, 271
  plant list 271
activators: composting 70, 215
additives: soil 221
aeration 30, 197, 212
aerodynamics 226
agricultural development **44–50**
agrosystems 56
air-drying crops 76
air (element) 14
air pressure 34
air temperature 36, 153, 195
Alcazar, Spain 47
algae 13, 18, 30
alkaline soils
  plant list, 271
alpines 36
altitude 35, 36, 161
anaerobes 13, 212
anaerobic decay 212
anaerobic decomposers 224
analysis
  site 63–6, **194–9**
  light and shade 74–5
ancestry of plants 18–19
ancient grassland plants 274
ancient woodland plants 274
angiosperms 19, 20
animals 28, 32, 50, 104–7
  aquatic 176, 263
  cats/dogs,156
  corridors 112, 113, 116
  crop damage 107
  deterrents 169
  hibernation 262
  nocturnal 199
  in wildlife gardens 120
animal shelters 115
annuals 19, 59, 75, 251
  weeds 251
aquatic life 19, 176–8, 259, 263
  plant list 269
arbor 229
arid gardens **186–91**
arthropods 28
artificial fertilizers 55
atmosphere 35–7
autotrophs 12, 26

B

bacteria 12–13, 26, 30, 70
balance of nature 32–3
banks 160, 229
  see also earthworks
bastard trenching 220
bath herbs 132
bats 232
bat houses 115, 116, 265
bedrock 15, 28, 30
beds
  construction 85, 240
  design 81
  drainage 240
  orientation 75, 239, 240
  raised 75, 239, 240
  sunken 240
bees 171, 231
  boxes 265
  hives 173
beetles 26, 28, 33
berms 86, 89, 160, 183, 203
biennials 19
biodiversity 51
biodynamic gardening 56–9, 134, 252–4
BD preparations 56–8, 254–5
biogeographical realms 40
bio-intensive gardening 58
biological control 107–8
biomass 15, 16, 27, 32
biomes 36, 38, 40, **110–12**
bioregions, 40, 54, **110–12**, 119
  creation, 146
biosphere, 12, 14–18, 26, 110–12, 128
  human impact 45, **48–55**, 62
birds 127, 232
  boxes 231, 264–5
  feeding 114–15
  plants for food 273
  tables 116
black water 72–3
bog gardens 274
bonfires 71, 210
boreal forests 38, 40
botanical gardens 46
boundary areas 67, 142, 145, 156, 226
brassicas 271
buds 20–1
building materials 204–5
bulbs 25, 237, 246, 269, 271

C

C3/C4 leaves 22
cacti 186
Calvaria trees 25
cambium 21
carbohydrates 22, 224
carbon 22, 212, 214
carbon dioxide 22, 37, 51
carbon fixing 109
carbon-nitrogen ratios 70, 212
carnivores 32
carpet mulching 55, 109, 150, 211
carrot family 234
CAT (Centre for Alternative Technology), Wales 122, 156
catch crops 97, 100
cellular organization 13
cellulose 26, 28
Centre for Alternative Technology (CAT), Wales, 122, 156
Chadwick, Alan 58
chalky soils 224
Château Villandry, France, 47
chemical pesticides 32, 107
chickens 96, 231
chlorophyll 22
chloroplasts 13, 22
choices
  crops **96–101**
  planning **62–7**
chromosomes 13
city soils 148–9
clamping 236–7
clay soils 28–30, 197, 219, 224
  plant list 271
climates
  arid 186–91
  continental 75
  cool temperate 183–4
  Mediterranean 39, 40, 50
  oceanic 39, 161
  variations **34–39**
  zones 38–40
  see also microclimates
climax states 16, 108, 234
climbers 274
cloches 78–9, 86, 184, 261
coastal regions 39, 52
  gardens **164–7**
  plant list 269
  see also oceanic climates
coevolution 23
cold frames 78, 184, 247, 260
cold garden plants 268
  see also temperate gardens
colonization 16, 19, 31, 108, 234
comfrey 104, 105, 108, 232
commercial growers 59
communities (ecological) 16, 38, 42, 108, 234
community gardens 156
companion planting 235, 241, 251
  crops 250
  ornamentals 146
  plant list 275
  see also integrated gardening
composting 70–2, **211–18**
  activators 70, 215
  biodynamics **254–5**
  containers 69, 213–14
  Kitto's method 213–14
  toilets 72, 89, 215, 217
  two-heat system 215
conifers 20, 21, 31, 38, 227
  plant list 271
conservation 58–9, 73–4
construction
  beds 85, **239–242**
  compost heaps 70
  paths and retainers 202–5
  ponds 262–3
consumers 16, 32
container gardens 149
containers
  compost bins 69, 213–14
  plant pots 71
  rain barrels 90
  seed flats/pots 242
continental climates 75
control
  diseases 210, 248
  fruit spurs 249
  heat/light 75, 81
  negative 55, 117–18
  pests 107–8, 251–2
  weeds 96–7, 109
cool temperate gardens 78, 182–5
coppicing 82, 83, 227, 228
  plant list 275
corridors: wildlife 112, 114, 116
costs 17 *see also* time management
cover crops 104, 222
creation
  bioregions 146–7
  microclimates 260–5

creation *continued*
micro-habitats 115–16
ponds 202
wildlife gardens 117
cropping patterns, 75
crops **98–101**, **234–8**
choice 97
cut and come again 237
fuel 82
intercropping 75, 97, 100–1
nurturation 260–5
planning 100–1
protection 231–2
root 237–8
rotation 59, 100, 108, 234–6
salad 101, 237
shade-tolerant 169
spacing 101
storage 76, 237–9
succession 97, 100–1
vegetable 236–9
water-loving 270
cross-fertilization 20, 110
culinary herbs 101, 243, 273
cultivars 59, 97, 147
cultural methods 48–50, 54–9
currents, ocean 34–5
cut and come again crops 237
cuttings 246–7
cycles
gum arabic 48–9
nitrogen 30
rotation 104
see also natural cycles
cyclical organic food system 68
cyclical patterns 68, 74

D
damage 108
from birds 231–2
to crops 108, 231–2, 251
from pests 108, 231, 251
from root systems 229
dangers to wildlife
see threats
day-length 35
dead-heading 245
deciduous hedges 250
deciduous trees 21, 200, 228, 268, 271
decomposers 15–16, **26–33**, 42, 225
deficiency, mineral 225
deforestation 32, 50–1
desertification 50
desert regions 38, 40, 44
plants 191
desiccation 37
designing
beds 81, **239–40**

designing *continued*
gardens 67, 74–5, 163, 188
orchards 172
ponds 262–3
shade 74–5
water/energy efficient garden 92
see also sanctuaries
desire-lines 100, 205
destruction of ecosystems 50–1
see also environmental exploitation; threats
detritivores 28
dicots, 21, 22, 24
diets, 94, 138
difficult areas, 229
difficult soils, 224
digging 96, 199, **219–20**
double-dig 219–20
no-dig 55, 199, 219, 221
single-dig 119, 219–20
disease
control 107–8, 210, 245, 248, 252
prevention 236
resistance 235
ditches 160
diversity
creating 120
habitat 176
plant 18, 20, 117
of species 26
DNA 12–13, 18
double-digging 219–20
drainage 28–30, **84–9**, 104, 203, 225
beds 240
improvement 196–7, 205
recording 196
systems 207
drought 30, 258–9
drought-tolerant plants 187, 188, 256–7
plant list 268, 270
dry-well 84, 207
dynamic accumulators 104, 223, 224, 271
plant list 271

E
Earth 12, 34, 62
healing 124, 134
earth (element) 14
earthworks 89, 229
see also berms; ditches; swales
earthworms 30, 198, 224
ecology 66, 119–20, 252
ecosystems 26, 29, 51, 59, 260
woodland 32, 175

edibles 25, 94, 159, 241, 253
plant list 270, 272, 273
editing 121, 122, 147
efficiency
see energy-efficiency
elements (four) 14
elements (seasonal) 64–5
endosymbiosis 13
energies
consumption 69
cycles 15
harnessing 74–5
patterns 74
subtle 127–8
wind 81
energy-efficiency
gardens 64–5, **73–5**
systems 48–9
water/energy efficiency plan 92–3
environmental exploitation 50–1, 62, 68–9
epiphytes 42
equatorial zones 36
equipment 202, 267
ergonomics
see energy-efficiency
erosion 28, 42, 50, 51, 84
eukaryotes 13, 19
evaporation 23, 35–9, 81
evapotranspiration 37
evergreens 21, 39, 200, 268
hedging 250
propagation 246
watering 259
evolution 12–13, 32
gardens **44–7**
leaves 20–2
plants **18–24**
seeds 20–2
exotic plants 46
experimental plots 122, 199

F
feeding 25, 55, 104–5, 107
see also birds; foliar feeding
felling: trees 200, 201
feng-shui 54, 127–8
ferns 18
fertility improvement 29, 104–5, **212–225**
fertilization 24
fertilizers 55, 104
see also green manures
Fibonacci series 22
Findhorn, Scotland 137
fine tuning 245–55
fire (bonfires) 71, 210
flat beds 240
floating mulches 88, 108
flooding 42, 51

flowering plants 20, 23, 24
foliar feeding 55, 224, 232–5, 252
folklore 54, 55
food production 94–109
food systems 45
fossil fuels 69
fragrant flowers 126–8
plant list, 268
see also scented gardens
fragrant herbs 127
freezing produce 238
French drains 85, 207
fresh feeding 104–5
fresh water 37
freshwater regions 40
frost 86, 183, 196, 231
frost-hardy plants 183
frost-tender plants 183
fruit trees 95, 171, 230
pruning 231, 249
varieties 272
fuel crops 82
Fukuoka, Masanobu 55–6
functions of gardens 62–3
fungal diseases 107
fungal-feeding mites 33
fungi 13, 18, 25, 26, 28, 33
furniture (garden) 148–9

G
Gaia 12–13, 22, 26, 37, 44
Gaian gardening **142–7**
garbage bin wormery 216
gardens
botanical 46
climate 182–91
design 45–8, 67, 74–5
evolution 44–6
furniture 148–9
habitat 148–81
healing 124–39
in history 45–7
integrated 96, 142–7, 166, 170, 188, 241
mesic 94–7
planning **62–70**
productive 66, 97–105, 170, 183
purposes 124, 143, 146
resourceful 68–83
self-reflective 137
structures 143, 204, 266
useful 68–109
water-efficient 84–5, 92–3
water/energy efficiency plan 92–3
wildlife 58, 64–5, 110–23
germination 23, 25, 78, 78–9
giraffe/beaver analogy 45
grasses 21, 104, 119, 120, 188
grasslands 38, 40, 50, 119, 274

gravel 30
gray water
  recycling 89, 90, 215, 217, 258
  usage 218
grazing 21, 32
Great Plains, North America 50
greenhouses 46, 73, 78–9, 156, 184
  design 260
  heating 90, 185
green manures 85, 100, 104, 222–3, 251, 271
green roofs 264
ground breaking 219
ground clearance 118, 201, 202
ground cover plants 109, 232
  plant list 275
ground temperatures 195
growing mediums 15, 242
growth cycles 246
gum arabic cycle 48–9
gymnosperms 19, 20, 21

H

habitat gardens **148–81**
  coastal **164–7**
  mountain **158–63**
  urban **148–57**
  wetland 85, **176–81**
  woodland **168–75**
habitats 50, 112
  aquatic 19, 115
  creation 16, 112, 262
  diversity 40, 113, 114, 176
  plant list 274
  restoration 119
  woodland 174
hardening off 78, 242, 260, 261
Hart, Robert 171, 172
hay bales 240, 241, 260
healing 132, 137–8
healing gardens **124–39**
  plant list, 269
heat **78–81**
  in composting 212–13
  in greenhouses 79, 90, 260
hedges 226, 227, 250, 274
  plant list 274
herb gardening 101, 243
herbivores 16, 21, 23, 32, 50, 107
herbs
  bath 132
  culinary 101, 243, 273
  cultivation 243–3
  medicinal 132
  plant lists 244, 273
  scented 127

herbs *continued*
  wild 244
heterotrophs 12, 26
hibernation 262
history of gardens 44–7
Holmgren, David 56
horse manure 261
hotbeds 78, 216, 260, 261
hot spots 260
house/garden links 96
household waste
  composting 216
  recycling **69–72**, 118, 208–9
humans 32, 44
  and biosphere 45, 48
  and landscape
hunter-gatherers 44

I

incinerators 210
indigenous species
  animals 59, 119–20, 265
  plants 198–9, 263, 265
industrial waste 69–70, 208
initiation year
  analysis 62–5, 85
  experimental plot 122
  observations 107, 112, 194, 256
  planning 96–7
  projects 114
inoculants 222–3
insect-attracting plants 274
insects 120, 198, 231
  as decomposers 16, 28
  as pollinators 20, 110, 231
insect traps 198–9
integrated gardening 96, 142–7 166, 170, 188, 241
  planning, **142–8**, 171–2
  vegetable crops 236–7
  see also companion planting
intensive gardening 96, 100
interactions of species 32–3
intercropping 75, 97, 100–1
interplanting 101, 257
invasive plants 275
invertebrates 199
irrigation 89, 159, 188, 257, 259
  recording, 196

J

junk: recycling 118, 267

K

karesansui, 47
Kitto, Dick 213, 214
Kogi Indians 124

L

land profile 196
landscape influences 50–1
landscaping 46, 81, 202
language of gardening 142
latitude: variations 34, 36, 75, 194
lawns
  management 118, 119, 230
  mowing 73
  rooftop 262
  sunken 188, 189
layering 246, 247
laying: hedges 227
layouts *see* design
leaching 84, **85**, 104
leafmold 215
leaves: evolution 20–2
legumes 104, 109, 222–3, 234
leveling 202–3
lichens 18, 42, 198
light 14, 64–5, 74–5, 134
  mapping 194
light traps, 28
lignins 21, 28
lime-loving plants 224
lithosphere 28
liverworts 19
loams 28, 29
logs 264
lunar planting 255

M

machinery 202
macrofauna 27
macropores 30
magic mounds 211, 240, 262
management
  hedges 227, 250
  trees 169, 200
  weeds 252
manures 261–2
  see also green manures
mapping 63, 110, 112, 194–5
maximization: light 74
meadow plants 269
medicinal herbs, 102, 132, 273
Mediterranean climate 39, 40, 50
meristems 21, 25
mesic gardens 94–7
mesification 66, 96, 117
mesofauna 27
metabolic cost 17
microbes 30, 32
microbivores 26
micro-carnivores 26
microclimates **42–3**, 153
  creation **260–5**
microfauna/flora 16, 27
microhabitats 42, 263, 264
  creation 115
microorganisms 12–13, 26, 104
micropores 30
minerals 31, 224
  deficiency 225
minimalists 147, 159, 183, 187
minimum intervention 84
  arid soils 84, **187–91**
  bioregion creation 146–7
  experimental plot 121–2
  site improvement 117–19
  wetlands 84, **176–81**
mites 33
mitochondria 13
moisture 23, 35
Mollison, Bill 56
monocots 22, 24
monocultures 50, 52, 251
moon cycle 134, 255
moonlight 36–7
mosses 18–19, 42
mountain gardens **159–63**
  plant list 268
mountain regions 35–6, 40
mowing 21, 73, 118
Mughal gardens 46
mulches 72, 188, 233, 256
  acidity 31
  "floating" 88
  materials 90, 118, 211
multicellular plants 13
mycorrhizae 20, 25, 26, 31

N

N:P:K ratio 224
Nanzenji Temple, Japan 47
native plants 198–9, 263, 265
native animals 59, 119, 120, 265
natural cycles 34, 104, 246
natural gardening **55–9**
  see also Gaian gardening
natural selection 17
nature spaces 112, 114
negative organics 55, 104
Neolithic Revolution 44, 51
nest boxes 115
nitrogen 15, 30–1, 224
  cycle, 30
nitrogen-fixation 15, 31, 104
nitrogen-fixing bacteria 15, 30–1, 222–3
no-bed gardening 241

nocturnal observations 198–9
no-dig gardening 55, 199, 219, 221
nomads 44
non-flowering plants 39, 42
nurturation of crops **260–5**
nutrients 15, **25–31**, 104
nut trees 171

O

observations
- seasonal 134
- shade 81
- site 63
- wildlife 123, 198–9

ocean currents 36
oceanic climates 39, 161
- *see also* temperate gardens

omnivores 32
opportunist plants 16, 108
orangeries 46
orchards 172, 231
organelles 13
organic farming 32
organic gardening, 55, 235
organic matter 15, 104
- mulching 118
- in soil 30, 84, 104–5, 271
- water-retention 88

organic pest control 253
organic sprays 108–9, 252
organic waste: recycling 208–9
orientation 42, 159
- beds 75, 81, 239–40

ornamentals 146, 224, 233, 241
osmotic balance 43
overwintering 236–7
oxygen 12, 13, 15

P

partnership with nature **44–59**
paths 67, 174, 204, 240, 264
patios 92, 154
paving 205, 240
perennials 19, 25, 59, 251
- legumes 222
- vegetables 236–7
- plant lists 268–71

permaculture 50, 56, 59
permanent planting **226–233**
pesticides 32, 107, 117, 252
pests 32, 96, **106–9**
- control 107, 117, **251–3**
- damage 251

pH (acid-alkaline balance) 31, 104, 199, 218
- scale and testing 197–8

pheromones 231
phloem 21, 22
phosphates 31, 224
photosynthesis 12–13, 18–19, 21–3, 34
physic gardens 46
pinching out 21
planning **96–102**
- crops 100–1
- gardens 64–7, **142–7**, 194
- orchards 231
- master plan 194
- paths 67
- planting 226
- ponds 262–3
- production 96–7
- water conservation 256
- water/energy efficiency plan 92–3

planting 82, 115, 165, 233
- permanent **226–233**
- trees 174, 228, 229
- for water economy 256–7

plant kingdom 18, 23
plant lists **268–275**
plants
- aquatic 176–8, 263
- disease-resistant 235
- diseases 245, 252
- diversity 18, 20, 117, 122
- drought-tolerant 187, 188, 256–7, 268, 270
- evolution **18–25**
- flowering 20–4
- fragrant 268
- frost-hardy 183
- frost-tender 183
- non-flowering 18, 39, 42
- pollution-tolerant 270
- reproduction 20, 245
- salt-tolerant 165, 270
- self-seeding 245
- shade-tolerant 164–5, 169,270
- strategies 16–17, 24, 245
- stress signs 245
- woody 21, 28, 246, 248–9

polar regions 36, 38, 39
pollarding 83, 201, 228–9
pollination 20, 23, 24, 171
pollinators 171, 231
pollution 18, 68–9, 150, 153, 165
- indicators 198

pollution-tolerant plants 270
polycultures 48, 50, 251
polytunnels 184, 261
ponds 113, 115, 176, 178
- construction 202, 262–3

poor soils 149
- plant list 271

pooter pots 198, 199
population growth 44–5, 48, 50–1
porosity: soil 30
potassium 31, 224
pot-pourri 128
potting-on 100
prairie 50
precipitation 36–7
predators 32, 107, 108, 109
pregermination 78
preserving produce 239
problem soils 187
processors 26, 31
productive gardens 66, 97, 170, 183
profiles
- changing 202–5
- mapping 196
- planting 82

prokaryotes 12–13
propagation 242–7
protection
- frost 86
- sun and wind 188
- young plants 79

protozoa 13
pruning 200–1, 227, 248–9
pteridophytes 20
public water supplies 88–9, 258
purposes: in gardens **142–7**

R

rainfall 31, 34, 36, 89
- recording 195

rain forests 29, 38, 49
rainwater 87, 258
- containers, 90

raised beds 75, 85, 239–42
ramps 205
Rappaport, Roy 49
reclaimed materials 267
record keeping 195
recycling 14, 59, **208–19**
- garden waste 118
- gray water 89–90, 217, 258
- household waste 69–72, 118, 208, 267
- industrial waste 70, 208
- junk 118, 267
- mulches 72
- organic waste 68, 70–2, 208
- seeds 71

reedbed systems 87, 218, 258
relationship with nature 132–3
reproduction 19, 20, 23, 24, 245
reservoirs 258
resourceful gardens **68–76**
respiration 13, 18, 29
restoration 58, 119
retainers 160, 203, 204
retreats 153
rhizomes 20, 237, 246
rhizosphere 25, 43
rhythms 134
- *see also* cycles in nature

rockeries 264
rock flours 105
roof gardens 150
rooftop lawns 262
root crops 237, 238
rooting 78
root systems 25, 31, 88
- damaging effects 229
- trees 171, 201

rotation systems 59, 108, 234–6
run-off 89

S

salad crops 97, 100, 101, 237, 246
- herbs 273
- wild 243, 244

salt-tolerant plants 165, 270
sanctuaries 124, 137
- arid climate 189
- coastal 166, 167
- cool climate 184
- mountain 162
- wetland 178
- woodland 171

sandy soils 28–9, 30, 197, 219, 240
- plant list 271

sap 183
savanna 38, 40
scented gardens 126–8
- *see also* fragrant flowers; fragrant herbs

scrub clearance 202
seasonal cycles 34, 63, 134
seasonal variations 38, 75
seaweed 224, 252
seed banks 59, 108, 122
seedlings 78, 242
seeds 16–25, 59
- collection 245–6
  - *see also* seed banks
- containers 242
- germination 16
- propagation 242, 246
- recycling 71, 245–6
- sowing, 242
- vegetable, 246

self-seeding plants 245
self-sufficiency: economics 94–5
sense of place 54, 126
senses **126–131**
sewage composting 72, 215, 217

shade 264
  creation 73–6, 150, 176, 188, 229, 256
  mapping 194
shade-tolerant plants 164–5, 169, 270
shaping the land **200–7**
sheet mulches 109, 150, 199, 211, 221
shelters 115
shifting cultivations 48–9
shredders 71
shrubs 158–9, 268, 269, 271
  propagation 246–7
  pruning 248
  shade creation 229
  watering 259
  woodland gardens 174
side-shoots 21, 25
silica 254
siltation 51
silt soils 28–9
single-digging 199, 219, 220
site analysis **63–6**, 74–5, **194–9**
site improvement 202–3
slash-and-burn system 48–9
sloped-bed system 75
slopes 84, 85
  improvement 203
  orientation 159
  terracing 160
slugs 26, 120, 130, 199, 253
smell (sense) 126–7
snails 26, 120
soakaways 84, 207, 258
soft fruit 230–3, 272
soil
  color 197
  erosion 28, 42, 50–1, 84
  fauna 26, 27, 109, 197
  fertility 104–5, 219, 223–4
  formation 15, **26–31**, 109, 197
  improvement **219–225**
  profile 15
  sprays 233, 254–5
  sub 15, 30, 85
  temperature 78
  texture 30, 197
  top 15, 26, 30, 202–3, 240
soils
  acidic 159, 197, 271
  city 148–9
  clay 28–30, 197, 219, 224
  loams 28–9
  sandy 28–9, 30, 197
  silt 28–9
  temperate 29
  tropical 29
  waterlogged 84, 85, 176
solar energy 15
solar greenhouses 79
solar system 134
sound 54, 127–9
  barriers 127
sowing 78, 100, 246
spacing crops 101
spiritual gardening 137–8
spores 19, 33
staking: trees 228
St Christopher wormery 216
Steiner, Rudolf 56–8, 254
steps 205
stomata 22, 23
storage crops 76, 237–8
strategies
  pest control 117, 253
  planning 64, 66, 75, 81, 96
  plants 16–17, 24, 245
stratification 242
straw 70, 85
stress signs: plants 245
subsistence patterns 44–5
subtle energies 127–8
succession 16–17, 26, 107, 122–3, 234
succession crops 97, 100–1
sunken beds 240
sunken lawns 188, 189
sunlight 22–3, 34, 260
  control 75, 78
  protection from 188
  viniculture 233
sun path 65, 74, 81, 174, 194
sunrooms 46, 78, 92, 184
surveying 64–5
  fauna 198–9
  flora 198
  site 194–6
  soil 197
sustainable systems 50, 54, 104
swales 56, 87, 89
  construction 160, 203

T
taste (sense) 126
techniques 194–267
temperate gardens 78, **182–5**
temperate soils 29
temperature
  air 36, 153
  recording 196
  soil 78
termites 26
terracing 160, 162, 203
thinning: trees 248
threats
  to biosphere 50–1
  to habitats 274
  to wildlife 62
tidal influences 36–7
timber 32, 267
  diseased 248
  preservatives 204
time management 64
tisanes 97, 101, 273
toilets: composting 72, 215, 217
tools 266, 267
topography 35
topsoil 15, 26, 30, 202, 203, 240
touch (sense) 126
trace elements 224
traditional gardening 8–9, 62, 118, 142–7
  crops 96, 97, 234
  hedges 227
training: woody plants 248, 249
transition zones 120, 123
transpiration 23, 37, 78, 81, 88
transplanting 25, 123, 200
tree houses 171, 173
tree of life 51
trees 21, 134, 171
  management 123, 169, 200–1
  planting 123, 174, 228–9
  plant list 271, 274–5
  propagation 171, 246–8
  as windbreaks 81–3
trellis 75, 188, 229
trenching 220, 229
trickle drip irrigation 259
tropical rainforests 40
tropical soils 29
tropism 21
tubers 25, 237, 246
Tullgren funnels 198, 199
tundra 38, 40
two-heat systems: composting 215

U
ultra-organic gardening 55
ungulates 50
urban gardens **148–57**
  plant list 268
urine as activator 70, 215

V
vascular systems 22
vegetable families 235
vegetables 97, 100, 234, 238–9, 244
  families 235
  integration 236–7
  perennials 236–7
  propagation 246
  storage 238
  wild 243, 244
verandas 79, 184
vertical spaces 67, 149, 154
Villandry, France, 98
vines 75, 76, 79, 183, 229
viniculture 232–3
vision (sense) 127

W
walls 239, 264
warm temperate zones 39
waste
  see composting; recycling
water 14, 15, 159
  black 72–3
  collection
  conservation 256–7, 259
  fresh 37
  gray 89–90, 215–18, 258
  public supplies 88–9, 258
  rain 87, 258, 90
  retention 88, 104, 256
  sources 37, 84, 88, 258
water-efficient garden 84–5
  plan 92–3
waterfalls 127, 128
water garden plants 268
watering 25, 89, 199, 259
waterlogging 84, 85, 176
water-loving crops 270
water table 85, 196
weather 34, 63
  see also climate
weathering 28
  compost 71
weeding 199, 251
weeds 117, 251
  control 96, 97, 108, 109
  management 104, 252
wet garden plants 268
wetland gardens 85, **176–81**
  plant list 270
wetlands 176, 230, 274
wild accumulators 224
wild edibles 146, 241
wild fauna/flora 198
wildflower meadows 73, 230
wildflowers 117
wild habitats 262
wildlife corridors 112, 114, 116
wildlife gardens 58, 64–5, 110–23
  plant list 269
wild salads/vegetables 243–4, 273
willow banks 229
wind 35
  as energy 81
  protection from 188
  recording, 195
windbreaks 81–3, 88, 165, 167
  planning 73, 82, 183
  plant list 274
  temporary 188, 226

wind chill 35
wind instruments 127, 129
wind-tolerant plants 270
woodland 42–3, 43, 123, 274
  habitats 174–5
woodland gardens **168–75**
  plant list 269
woody plants 21, 28, 246
  training 248–9
worm counts 198, 199
wormeries 216
wormpost 216
worms 26, 70, 197
  see also earthworms

X

xeriscaping 187
xylem 21, 22

Y

year of initiation
  see initiation year
yeasts 26
Yekuana Indians 48

Z

zeroscaping 187
zones
  climatic 40
  transition 120, 123
  warm temperate 39

Author's Acknowledgements

Firstly, I would like to thank my collaborators *Jeremy Light* and *Chris Madsen* for their distinctive contributions to this book. Jeremy and I have been colleagues for many years, and the trajectory of our ideas is very much a double helix. The editorial team at Gaia Books, *Michele Staple* and *Pip Morgan*, kept us on the straight and narrow, and their vigorous editing will be apparent throughout. The designer, *Bridget Morley*, herself a gardener, was a fount of good sense.

The preparation of the book benefited greatly from discussions with many people, and I would like to express my special thanks to *Leigh Davison, Ianto Evans, David Holmgren, Max Lindegger, Kim Neubecker, Suki Pryce, Pete Raine, Chris Ryan, Lou Spratt, Chris Weedon* and – at a distance – *Robert Kourik* and *Eliot Coleman*. My brother, *Mick Harper*, was as always a source of lavish encouragement and colourful criticism. I am particularly grateful to my colleague and neighbour *Maritsa Kelly*, who always seemed to have the right book in her collection when I needed it. *Lesley Bradnam, Nigel Dudley, Suki Pryce, Andrew Sclater* and *Sue Stickland* read early versions of the MS and helped greatly with the weeding.

Many libraries were plundered, and I thank *David* and *Joss Pearson, Pete Raine, Lettie Rowan* and *Damian Randle* in particular for the extended loan of numerous books, not to mention the Bookshop and Mail-order service of the Centre for Alternative Technology, who tolerated my raids with wry insouciance.

All my colleagues at CAT deserve special thanks for turning a blind eye to my many derelictions of duty and sociability. In particular, my fellow gardeners, *Roger McLennan, Jane Mason, Eryl Davies* and *Steve Emerson*, did all the real work while I was laying out gardens in the air.

Above all, I must gratefully acknowledge the support and understanding of my partner *Janet Davies*, for whom this book has been "the other woman" for rather longer than either of us expected.

Publishers Acknowledgements

Gaia Books would like to thank the following individuals for their help in the production of this book:

Margaret Elphinstone, Bob Flowerdew, Gian Douglas-Home, Susan Mennell, and Jonathan Hilton (for early work on the project); Guy Dauncey and Carolyn Herriot (for early advice on the project); Gill Smith for her assistance with picture research; Rob Saunders and Joanna Chisolm for their editorial assistance; Suzy Boston for liaison.

Illustration Credits

Gaia Books would like to thank the following artists for their contributions to this book:

Bridget Morley: 64–65, 92–93, 122, all artwork in Part III and Part IV; *William Donohoe*: pp.40–41; *Ann Savage*: 14–15, 18–19, 27, 30–31, 34, 45, 54; *David Sumner*: 13, 16–17, 20–21, 22–23, 24–25, 28–29, 42–43, 48, 68, 74–75, 79, 81, 82, 112, 116.

(Key: b = bottom; t = top; c = centre; r = right; l = left)

Ancient Art & Architecture Collection pp. 46l; 51. Robert Ayres pp. 6/7; 37b; 60; 69t; 73b; 83t; 86/87; 91t; 113b; 129t; 130l; 146t; 172; 185. Elly Beintema pp. 80; 158. Bruce Coleman Ltd pp. 10 (John Shaw); 33t (Kim Taylor); 33b (Jane Burton); 36 (Kevin Rushby); 39 (Michael Freeman); 52 (Herbert Kranawetter); 53 (Anna Zuckerman); 86b, 157bl, 161b (Eric Crichton); 133br (Christer Fredriksson). Chrissie Cornish p. 129b. The Garden Picture Library p. 152tl; pp. 46r, 90, 133t (Marijke Heuff); 177 (Roger Hyam); 152bl (Gill Marais); 113t, 144, 164b, 179t, 181t, 181b, 186, 190t, 190b, 191tr, 191b (Jerry Pavia); 128b (Joanne Pavia); 164t (Philippe Perdereau); 145 (Hannah Peschar); 121 (Hans Reinhard); 76 (Gary Rogers); 150t (Gerry Rogers); 102, 155bl, 173l, 180t (Ron Sutherland); 95t, 99, 150b, 152tr, 152br, 192 (Brigitte Thomas). Peter Harper pp. 72t; 72b. Harpur Garden Library pp. 76/77, 139, 146b, 147, 168t, 191tl. Impact Photos pp. 47t (Alan Keohane); 135t (Michael Gover); 136b (Peter Menzel); 154 (Michael Mirecki); 156t (Juame Altadil, photographer; c Roca-Satre Agewa). Insight (London) Picture Library p. 95b (Jack Townsend). Robert Kourik pp. 56; 87; 157r. Andrew Lawson pp. 103t; 135b; 138. Marianne Majerus pp. 168b; 179b. S & O Mathews p. 47b. Tania Midgley p. 103b. Bridget Morley pp. 136t; 160. NHPA pp. 106 (N. A. Callow); 27 (Stephen Dalton); 49 (Fred Parker); 2 (John Shaw). OSF pp. 35 (Tony Bomford); 36 (Richard Packwood); 106b (Harry Taylor). Hugh Palmer pp. 69; 83t; 98; 125; 128t; 131t; 131b; 132; 133bl; 140; 155t; 155br; 173tr; 180b. Robert Perron pp. 148t; 148b; 151; 161t. Science Photo Library pp. 17, 130r (Dr Jeremy Burgess); 57t (Adam Hart Davis); 182, 185b (Simon Fraser); 111 (Claude Nuvidsanny and Marie Pevennon). Rudolf Steiner Library© Verlag am Goetheanum p. 57. Joe Wood p. 91b. David Woodfall pp. 143; 173br.